A DEFENSE OF RULE

A DEFENSE OF RULE

Origins of Political Thought in Greece and India

Stuart Gray

OXFORD
UNIVERSITY PRESS

OXFORD
UNIVERSITY PRESS

Oxford University Press is a department of the University of Oxford. It furthers the University's objective of excellence in research, scholarship, and education by publishing worldwide. Oxford is a registered trade mark of Oxford University Press in the UK and certain other countries.

Published in the United States of America by Oxford University Press
198 Madison Avenue, New York, NY 10016, United States of America.

CIP data is on file at the Library of Congress
ISBN 978–0–19–063631–9

9 8 7 6 5 4 3 2 1

Printed by Sheridan Books, Inc., United States of America

CONTENTS

Preface vii

Acknowledgments xxv

Introduction: Historical-Comparative Political Theory 1

1. Homer: Ruling as Distinction 21

2. Hesiod: Critique, Poetic Justice, and the Increasing Anthropocentrism of Greek Rule 64

3. Vedic Political Thought: Hierarchy, Connectedness, and Cosmology 105

4. Vedic Saṃhitās and Brāhmaṇas: Ruling as Stewardship 135

5. Comparative Considerations on the Meaning of Rule 175

Conclusion: Panocracy as a New Vision of Rule 193

Notes 223

References 243

Index 257

PREFACE

Rethinking the Question and Meaning of Rule

What does it mean to rule? At the core of politics are relations of rule, and thus at the heart of political theory is the question of what it means for human beings to rule over one another and share in a process of ruling. Interestingly, rule has also been one of the most criticized and even villainous of political concepts in the history of political thought, which reasonably leads us to ask the following question: if rule is so lamentable, then shouldn't we attempt to mitigate ruling relations as much as possible within political communities, or perhaps try to eradicate such relations altogether? A central aim of this book is to challenge this negative outlook and explain how rule need not be understood as anathema to political life. Not only has it been one of the most pervasive concepts in the global history of political thought, it is also a complex and potentially inspiring activity in which all people, I will argue, participate throughout their daily lives—and stand to do so in a more thoughtful fashion. To advance this claim is to suggest that we must be willing to alter, in a potentially destabilizing way, how we view the concept and reconsider its prospective meaning. I will embark on this project of rethinking the meaning of rule by undertaking two general tasks: first, to enhance the scope of our historical perspective in the Western tradition, and second, to broaden our cross-cultural understanding of rule.

In the chapters that follow, I thus retrieve, and comparatively re-examine, two ancient conceptions of rule that offer fascinatingly different ways of thinking about the concept and its attendant practices. In particular, I show how a comparative encounter between archaic Greek and Vedic Indian traditions provides critical distance from some of our most familiar intuitions about rule. This historical-comparative trek then helps expand our political imagination by supplying alternative ideas and outlooks that might serve as resources for rethinking the meaning of rule. Consequently, I aim not only to investigate the earliest works of political thought in the Western tradition but also to look for inspiration and provocation from outside political theory's more familiar haunts. Here I find the earliest Indian tradition of political thought to be particularly illuminating, as it throws into sharp relief some of the most significant, long-standing pitfalls in Western conceptions of rule. In short, this book undertakes the task of rethinking the question of what it means to rule and does so by considering what two incredibly influential traditions in the global history of political thought might have to teach us.[1]

Specifically, the Vedic notion of rule can help us better understand our relationship to nonhuman nature as non-instrumental, and a central aim of this book is to explain why human beings have a responsibility or duty to act as stewards for the interests of various nonhuman beings. Here ancient Indian political thought is invaluable because it shows us how the earliest discernable—and highly influential—tradition of Greek thought conceives a hierarchical and instrumental relationship between human and nonhuman nature. This instrumental position tends to predominate in the contemporary world and view the nonhuman as a mere resource for enhancing human desires and comforts, thus privileging human interests at the expense of nonhuman interests and well-being. Such instrumental understandings of the nonhuman world have gotten us into serious trouble in the modern and contemporary period. One could cite numerous examples, including deforestation, global warming, rising sea levels, species loss, and peak oil.

As is already evident in the early Greek understanding of rule, a serious problem then arises: nonhuman beings such as animals and plants, let alone entire ecosystems, cannot assert and defend their interests in *propria persona*. This makes it quite difficult if not impossible to understand how we could take account of nonhuman nature in our political decisions in a way that would be significantly different than our current instrumental approach. An alternative to this overly hierarchical and instrumental conception of rule would be to conceive nonhuman nature as having interests that human beings have a responsibility or duty to account for in both their personal and political decisions. As I will explain at greater length in this Preface and the Conclusion, we must view ourselves as stewards and not simply consumers of the nonhuman world. Importantly, our conceptual vocabulary has room for this conception of stewardship between a human political agent and less capable agents whose interests the full agent is obligated to consider when taking action that affects them all: the concept of rule. Thus reinvigorating the concept of rule seems like a uniquely available and promising way to reconceive of our relationship with nonhuman nature. Early Indian political thought helps us to better understand how the Western tradition has a narrow conception of rule that cannot solve the problem, as it continues to reassert the instrumental understanding. I will argue that Vedic texts pose a different conception that can help us reconceive the nature and meaning of rule in a non-instrumental fashion.[2] To explain how this is the case, it is helpful to begin by unpacking and theorizing what I take to be the various dimensions of rule.

The Multidimensionality of Rule and Ruling-in

To start, the concept of rule has a long line of critics offering numerous reasons to be skeptical of ruling relations in general. For example, most Western political theorists have understood rule to mean hierarchical domination of some people by others, often advancing a contrast between rule and politics, with the latter implying some degree of reciprocity of interests and participation. Thus, for those such as Aristotle, a society in which a king governs in his own interest is a corrupt form of rule while the term *polis*, and thus a truly "political" society, is reserved for a system wherein citizens experience rough equality and reciprocity by ruling and being ruled in turn. Although ruling entails some people telling others what to do and commanding obedience, Aristotle claims that rule can be turned into politics through an appropriate constitution.

Modern thinkers such as Hannah Arendt follow some of these basic distinctions by categorically parsing rule and politics, associating the more inspiring concepts of equality and freedom with politics, and more troubling concepts of hierarchy and domination with rule. Since Plato, Arendt argues that the Western tradition of political philosophy has attempted to escape the frailty and unpredictability of politics altogether, claiming: "The hallmark of all such escapes is the concept of rule, that is, the notion that men can lawfully and politically live together only when some are entitled to command and the others forced to obey" (1998, 222).[3] For Arendt, rule stands in stark contrast to action, which is the phenomenological and conceptual hinge for her political thought. Here I do not wish to dismiss entirely Arendt's laudable analysis of action, spontaneity, and natality in politics, nor the positions of scholars who have been heavily influenced by Arendt and her reading of Greek political thought.[4] However, I would like to comment on this position, since it aptly characterizes many modern and contemporary arguments against rule.

First, politics entails making impactful decisions and does not merely center on self-display in a condition of plurality. Ruling, understood as making authoritative decisions, enforcing these decisions, and considering their implications does not appear to be something that human beings can rid themselves of in any permanent way. Second, there is good reason to be skeptical of whether or not a non-hierarchical politics, and thus a firm distinction between rule and politics on Arendt's own account, is even possible in the first place. The act of distinguishing oneself from others—which I examine closely in chapters 1 and 2—may always begin with, depend upon, or result in sociopolitical hierarchies of some sort.[5] If we do not locate and pay special attention to these hierarchies, and consider the interests of those who find themselves subjected, this can easily lead to unjustified forms of domination. To take a Greek example, while Aristotle argues that free and equal male citizens of a *polis* should gather in a public space and act in a condition of plurality, a necessary condition of this phenomenological act is the existence of slaves and the hierarchical subordination of women. At least for Aristotle, such politically active (male) citizens cannot have a purely horizontal space that does not, in some constitutive sense, depend upon a vertical relationship between themselves and non-citizens. To rule and be ruled in turn, "*archein kai archestai*," is more complicated than it may initially appear. My first set of critiques of the Arendtian position, along with those who would idealize ruling with others, thus overlap with one another insofar as this idealization can lead to over-privileging the horizontal dimension of politics among equals by simultaneously underemphasizing how ruling with others rests upon ruling over others. Politics in any Arendtian sense relies on relations of rule, as the house of politics is built on the stilts of rule, and her overly abstracted conception of politics overlooks tremendously important, broader facets of governance.

My second critical point about the idealization of ruling with others concerns another category of "others" impacted by ruling over: the natural, nonhuman world. Again, Arendt's political thought provides a useful point of engagement. For her, the realm of the *oikos* represents the realm of necessity, which includes nonhuman nature, and part of the point of ruling over it was that it was both incapable of self-governance and a constant threat to the fragile achievement of the polis.[6] This suggests that rule is not merely inescapable in Arendt's theory but in fact central to it: ruling over others pervades politics, which includes ruling over the realm of necessity. Embedded in this theory of politics, therefore, lies a broader pre-political distinction between the human (ruler) and nonhuman (ruled), with the latter category including beings such as plants and animals. In sum, attempts to erase the hierarchical distinctions between human beings continue to rely upon and overlook an overly hierarchical understanding of human–nonhuman relations.

This is the key point that scholars tend to ignore and a central reason for my focus on what I will call the "connectedness of rule" (explained in greater detail later). While I contend that some degree of hierarchy is unavoidable, since ruling beliefs and practices will inevitably impact a broad community of nonhuman beings and entities, rule also entails the ability to consider, in a more nuanced and sensitive manner, the implications of human beings' ruling ideas and practices. This point suggests human beings view themselves as ruling-in and ruling-for the well-being of a broader community of beings, and not just ruling with other humans. While plurality, action, and politics always implicate people in hierarchical relations of some sort, albeit to varying degrees, I will argue that these relations can and should be critically reconceived. This "human/nonhuman" distinction in ruling relations is one of the central assumptions that I will examine and ultimately contest in order to enrich our contemporary understanding of rule. My aim here is to question some of our basic assumptions about the concept and its attendant practices, and hopefully, as Raymond Geuss articulates, "to inform our imagination for positive transformations of our own moral [and political] thinking" (2005, 231).

Skepticism about rule also fuels optimism in a particular normative conception of rule—namely, the rule of law. In general, those advocating the rule of law want to minimize arbitrary discretion and rely more heavily on impersonal or less discretionary offices, laws, rules, and procedures. In the Western tradition, this motivation extends all the way back to the Greeks. Political theorists such as Aristotle, whose ideal political order valued rational rules and correspondingly durable political constitutions, believed that virtuous, deliberating citizens could rely upon unwritten law (custom) to establish durable laws and constitutions. The resulting constitutional structures were intended to prevent impressionistic change and political instability that may result from privileging private interests and desires over the common good.[7] In a more modern manifestation, Max Weber (1973) explains in "Politics as a Vocation" how bureaucratic nation-states largely replace direct forms of human rule with less discretionary offices, rules, and procedures. In short, political theorists throughout the Western tradition have been suspicious of ruling practices and institutions that place tremendous amounts of discretionary, hierarchical political power in the hands of fallible human beings. Such suspicions have facilitated institutions and practices in contemporary democracies that aim to eliminate many deplorable aspects of discretionary rule.

The benefits of reducing such discretion, however, come with various costs. Modern rule of law and bureaucratic officialdom have contributed to contemporary democratic citizens forgetting or neglecting many of the responsibilities that stem from a basic human capacity to rule. Such neglect is exhibited in voter apathy and indifference to a variety of environmental issues, and thus democratic citizenship frequently falls short in addressing some of the most pressing problems of our age. As I have suggested, we can productively tackle these issues by expanding our historical and cultural perspectives on rule. Increasing our perspectivism allows me to revive the concept and explain how everyday citizens play an important, ongoing role in ruling relations, especially as it involves human relations to the natural, nonhuman world.

Returning briefly to the original objection and source of skepticism, ruling questions in the history of political thought have generally revolved around ideas of hierarchical domination, mastery, command, or obedience. These associations invoke the first and perhaps most obvious dimension of rule, that of "ruling-over." Hierarchical relations of ruling-over expose the important historical fact that Western conceptions of rule have been largely understood in a vertical manner. In Greece and many subsequent Western traditions, this has fostered an understandable amount of criticism and spurred a desire for greater sociopolitical equality and more horizontal forms of governance such as democracy. Such horizontal forms highlight a second dimension of rule, "ruling-with." In turn, identifying these two dimensions allows us to sketch out a rather familiar story in the West: equality and freedom are good, hierarchy is bad, and rule in human communities is necessary at best, inherently degrading at worst. Although rule inevitably entails a hierarchical dimension, Western theories of rule have failed to see how we might cultivate greater attentiveness to various dimensions of ruling and a more robust sense of horizontal interconnectedness that could make room for both political egalitarianism among citizens and a sound approach to human–nonhuman relations. Substantiating this claim requires that I first provide a basic definition of rule, including a few distinctions between basic subtypes.

Here one might begin by defining ruling as making and enforcing decisions for a perdurant group of people, which might involve various degrees of interpersonal participation. Such a definition of rule resembles at least two broader definitions of politics that are nicely summed up by Raymond Geuss. First, he explains how we can view politics as "any human activity of structuring or directing or coordinating the actions of a group" (2014, 147), and second, as centered on the question: Who does what to whom for whose benefit? (2008, 25–30).[8] At this level of abstraction or generality, politics and rule appear to be quite similar if not identical sorts of activities. In one sense, these general definitions provide a helpful starting point for cross-cultural inquiry due to their formulaic nature, as they could apply to a wide variety of human societies across both temporal context and geographic region—even if the specific content or substance of answers to various political/ruling questions might vary tremendously across time and space. In another sense, however, I want to suggest that if we remain at this level of generality then we lose something once we descend the ladder of abstraction to examine particular, concrete historical cases. In other words, if we collapse the definition of rule and politics across the board, then we will be prevented—or at least seriously hampered in our efforts—to identify a number of pressing issues associated with rule in particular cases. In subsequent chapters, I will thus locate and examine particular beliefs that come to light when we examine rule at a lower level of abstraction, investigating two specific traditions of rule within their respective conceptual contexts.

Broader definitions aside, I would like to explicate the underpinnings of more familiar ruling structures in Western political thought, which will clarify the theoretical criteria I use to evaluate ruling as distinction in Greece, stewardship in India, and an intercultural vision of world-making. When considering these differing conceptions of rule I suggest that we envision rule as possessing at least three distinct dimensions, and thereby parse three subtypes of ruling relations: "ruling-over" (vertical), "ruling-with" (horizontal), and "ruling-for" (depth and breadth of considered interests).[9] In turn, each dimension is characterized by a particular type of question. Ruling-over evokes the question, "Who rules *over* whom (or what)?," which could be one over many, few over many, humans over nonhuman, and so on. In contrast, ruling-with asks "*With* whom do rulers rule (if anyone)?," which could have answers ranging from nobody (monarchy) to many (democracy). Finally, ruling-for elicits the question, "*For* what or whose interests and well-being do rulers rule?," with answers that may include the maximization of private interests, corporate interests, animal interests, or protecting some common good. I will further argue that, taken together, these dimensions direct our attention to an additional dimension of "ruling-in." This fourth dimension evokes the fact that human beings rule not only within the context of human communities but also in a broader, more expansive context of human–nonhuman communities of interests. That is to say, various types of nonhuman beings also possess or express capacities and interests that should be considered in relations of rule.

As I explain in later chapters, recognizing relations of ruling-in is essential because it clarifies how human beings are inherently connected to and thus responsible for more than just human interests, that is, in the sense of being "response-able" for considering the interests of nonhuman beings and for keeping a watchful eye on the well-being of interconnected human–nonhuman communities. The ability to rule and ruling-in thus entails a particular conception of what I call "response-ability."[10] If something has an ability to affect something else in some way (which I believe is generally going to be the case with any being or entity whose existence is somehow felt or recognized by human or nonhuman beings) and has the capacity to recognize this ability, then this being would have a response-ability to respond in a way that ritualistically acknowledges, respects, and attends to that affect. This is not to say, of course, that human beings can ever fully comprehend or predict all the various implications, affects, and differences their ruling beliefs have upon or in the world but only that they have a rather unique ability to consider some of these implications. Accordingly, rule emerges as a political capacity that everyone possesses and carries with them daily. Therefore, I can further refine my definition in the following way: ruling is a power that human beings have to make decisions that always already, in both hierarchical and horizontal ways, implicate them to varying degrees in affective relations to broader communities of human and nonhuman beings whose interests are fundamentally intertwined.

Returning to the first two basic aspects of rule, ruling models that emphasize vertical relationships tend to privilege elements of ruling-over others and become associated with both domination and exclusion from ruling activities. For example, monarchy and aristocracy entail a single or small group of human beings exercising rule over others, often assuming that fewer have the necessary capabilities, rights, or authority to rule over others in a larger group. Therefore, in numerical terms this vertical dimension generally relies on greater exclusion of some individuals from political power, and in normative terms, this axis highlights how decision-making impacts—in both positive and negative ways—a larger community whose political identity and collective interests are affected by such decisions or commands. Alternatively, democratic forms of rule attempt to flatten such hierarchical relations by appealing to the horizontal dimension of ruling-with. Leveled types of rule are often associated with cooperation and inclusion, emphasizing shared decision-making or consideration of a common good or interests as we see, for example, in the Classical Athenian example of choosing juridical and legislative office by lot, Jean-Jacque Rousseau's notion of collectively interpreting the general will in *The Social Contract*, and civic republican traditions more generally (which emphasize a *res publica*, or "public thing"). Of course, these two dimensions of rule are not mutually exclusive, as the two are almost always bound up with one another. Take the United States, for example. In one sense, elected politicians and legal procedures (or laws) rule over common citizens, while in another sense democratic elections and propositions demonstrate how a broader array of common citizens engage in ruling-with one another. Modern and contemporary mixtures aside, in the history of Western political thought ruling-over has generally been the reviled opponent of both republican and democratic politics.

If we adopt a broader historical perspective, then the West's predominant understanding of rule as typified by ruling-over appears partly responsible for its bad reputation. Since the early modern period, Western nations have attempted to adopt more leveled forms of rule and emphasize the horizontal dimension of ruling-with. Political forms such as democracy and republicanism have thus become increasingly popular as normative models of rule. However, this attraction to forms of rule that emphasize its horizontal dimension and possibilities has led us to give ruling-over an excessively bad reputation, and ruling-with too easy a pass, partly because ruling-with emphasizes capacities shared by human beings alone. Ruling-with can lead, therefore, to an overly idealistic political position by distracting us from the ways in which horizontal forms of rule rely on institutionalized, vertical relations of power and ruling-over. This distraction comes with significant consequences, as the examples I provide display how ruling-with (and politics broadly defined) might always entail, and even require, some form of ruling-over in at least two respects. To make this point in a way that connects it to one of Geuss's definitions of politics: the question of "who does what to whom for whose benefit" always entails hierarchical power relations, and therefore commits people to some form of ruling-over other people as well as nonhuman beings.[11]

As I mentioned, transforming the way we think about rule requires us to think more carefully about the *connectedness of rule*. In theoretical terms, this refers to the implications and effects that follow from human beings' beliefs about what it means to rule. In adopting particular beliefs about the meaning of rule, human beings act, make collective decisions, and formulate practices that express and reinforce these beliefs over time. Within this idea of connectedness one can parse two distinct points of view. The first concerns the more humanistic viewpoint, particularly the idea that rule is a relationship between the person(s) who make and enforce the rules and those (human or otherwise) who are subject to them. Consequently, something like acquiescence but not full consent is required from the ruled for this relationship to be stable, which would include an appropriate level of concern for the interests and well-being of the nonhuman ruled—that is, if we expect those beings and the natural world to continue to exist in anything like their current state. Here the term "subject" is taken to mean someone or something, either individually or collectively, that is hierarchically impacted by and made subject to the thoughts or actions of another. This locution highlights a second point of view regarding the connectedness of rule, namely the idea that both human and nonhuman beings (or entities, phenomena) can be subjects of rule. That is, human beings are also "subjected" to both micro- and macro-level nonhuman forces, resulting in deep relations of interdependence between the human and nonhuman.[12] If we fail to take the connectedness of rule seriously and privilege human-centric conceptions of ruling-with, then we are led toward the following dilemma.

Forms of rule that emphasize ruling-with other people and ruling-for predominantly human interests often prioritize consent and active participation, which then makes it impossible for us to conceptualize, and thus problematize, the relationship between rule and the nonhuman precisely because nonhuman beings cannot consent or participate in ways we are accustomed to, say, in democratic societies. In this respect, ruling-with can and has facilitated particular sorts of delusions about the hierarchical implications of ruling-over. For example, we suppose that emphasizing the horizontal dimension of ruling-with somehow removes or diminishes the most deplorable aspects of ruling-over others in a hierarchical fashion, while more subtle yet equally consequential forms of ruling-over have not disappeared but merely (and one might say, surreptitiously) been shifted to the nonhuman. Put another way, the modern infatuation with democracy and republicanism tends to divert our attention from other, equally problematic forms of hierarchical rule that impact the health and future of our earthly estate. Therefore, focusing on ruling-over has some hidden benefits that we can revive to our advantage, insofar as re-emphasizing this dimension of rule can help us become more honest with ourselves and clear about the various hierarchical dimensions of human–nonhuman rule. As I will argue in the Conclusion, shifting our perspective in how we think about the meaning of rule and developing a new understanding of ruling in terms of stewardship and world-making can better account for the various dimensions of ruling-over, ruling-with, ruling-for, and ruling-in. However, to understand what ruling as world-making might entail, I want to clarify further the relationship between rule and cosmology.

Cosmological Aspects of Rule and Responsibility for Stewardship

While the connectedness of rule emphasizes an ongoing interconnectedness between human and nonhuman beings, the nature of such nonhuman beings admittedly changes over time and across cultures. In one time and place, people may believe that gods or a God play important roles in their collective lives, while in another period similar roles may be played by dark matter, neurons, major hurricanes, and increasingly complex technical devices. Regardless of time and place, human practices and beliefs have expressed a multitude of human–nonhuman cosmologies.

And while cosmology may seem like an odd category to invoke here, its connection to contemporary political thought and behavior is more pervasive than one might initially think. Broadly speaking, a cosmology entails an expansive and meaningful network of beings, entities, and phenomena that connect to and interact with one another in both predictable and unpredictable ways. Examples of various layers in modern cosmological thinking include: exotic subatomic particles that we try to understand using devices such as the Large Hadron Collider, and whose power we hope to harness for politically relevant purposes; neurons firing in our brains and genetic codes that are understood to impact human behavior and influence political beliefs; various bio- and nano-technologies that create new ways of relating to each other and the world around us, some of which increasingly blur lines between humans, nonhuman organisms, and machines; a complex and potentially threatening universe in which meteorites unsettle us and require that politicians and citizens in countries such as the United States decide how much funding NASA deserves; and environmental dangers that remind us of the interconnectedness of complex, delicate ecosystems involving nonhuman beings and entities, which raise important questions about how to construe more eco-friendly political practices. Each of these examples invokes questions, concerns, and human projects that involve collective decision-making and display how human–nonhuman connections are not archaic, apolitical artifacts. Whether we are conducting scientific research, hiking an outdoor trail, walking along a crowded city street, or voting on funding for public transportation, our modern lives require constant involvement in various layers and facets of political cosmology.

Whether or not human communities have made these cosmologies explicit is an important question because such connectedness often remains implicit in various political theories. From a philosophical and normative standpoint, there is an important difference between explicit and implicit theories of the connectedness of rule because implicit models can easily lead to a state of forgetfulness, and thus lack of awareness, of the extent to which human welfare relies on various connections to the nonhuman that are implied in the theory. Nevertheless, from an historical standpoint, both explicit and implicit theories highlight a more general point of convergence: the connectedness of rule does not appear to be something that human beings and polities can jettison altogether. The connectedness of rule seems to be a primordial feature of political relations across time and space, even if it is not thematized and brought to critical awareness. As part of my theory-building exercise, making such theories as explicit as possible helps us better understand the historically contingent nature of particular theories and traditions. Raising such critical awareness is important because it allows us to better evaluate and challenge particular assumptions within various traditions that may otherwise be overlooked or under-examined. In sum, clarifying historical and cultural contingency helps us locate and critically evaluate potentially problematic background assumptions.

At this point one might ask why human–nonhuman connectedness and interdependence necessarily create a responsibility or duty to preserve nonhuman nature. My normative position, to be clear, is primarily consequentialist. As I have begun to suggest, human-centric views of rule that only consider human interests and understand nonhuman nature instrumentally as a passive resource for human use and consumption are problematic for several reasons. First, anthropocentric positions are inaccurate and misleading, failing to capture the interconnected well-being of human beings and nonhuman nature. As I will explain in greater detail in the Conclusion, the porosity of our individual and communal identities means that our survival depends on our porous relations not only with other human beings but nonhuman beings as well. Failure to acknowledge this fact and act upon it by considering our potential responsibilities to those we rule over leads to an embarrassing performative contradiction. Second, anthropocentric views of rule are dangerous because they encourage the development of technologies and habits that threaten the survival of a nonhuman nature that sustains us (at least for the moment). If we do not reject destructive, human-centered assumptions, then human beings may assist in creating a world so fragile and unstable that we end up in an antagonistic contest for hierarchical specieist distinction, domination, and potential counter-dominance at the hands of nonhuman nature. Finally, current views about the nature of rule are limiting because they prevent us from getting clear about our contemporary predicament and how we might resolve it. Critically retrieving and modifying our predominant conceptions of rule that extend back to the Greeks can provide an invaluable way of addressing problems associated with anthropocentric political positions.

These claims lead to a consequentialist defense for responsible stewardship and world-making through our relations and practices of rule. In short, preserving nonhuman nature is overwhelmingly in our enlightened self-interest as human beings. Duties of stewardship and responsible world-making stem from our interests as a species and should be critically informed by reconceiving our understanding of rule along the various dimensions I have outlined. In fact, flipping the "connectedness of rule" around to identify what one might call the "rule of connectedness" could identify another consequentialist argument for normative duties.[13] This alternative locution helps demonstrate two important things: first, that connectedness is the ordinary and necessary condition of human life, and second, ruling will always impact our connectedness. Therefore, we have good reasons to understand rule as entailing a normative duty—or "rule" in the sense of a regulation or principle that governs our conduct within the sphere of politics—for stewardship. Because ruling will always involve and impact connectedness, human beings have a pragmatic need and responsibility to care for nonhuman nature and preserve it because it is in our best interest to do so based on the consequences.

In light of this normative position, I would like to make a few additional remarks as to why a comparative examination of ancient Greek and Indian conceptions of rule can be of particular value. To begin with, these traditions supply considerable historical distance and leverage for a critique of modern and contemporary ruling beliefs, particularly those that hinder our ability to recognize dilemmas concerning human–nonhuman relations. Modern traditions of political thought do not provide an adequate starting point for investigating these issues because they follow many of the human-exceptionalist conceptions of politics that already pervade Classical Greek, Roman, and Medieval Christian political thought. To put this point another way, Western political traditions and contemporary scholars generally celebrate human beings' "break" with some determinative natural or cosmic order—after all, this is often seen as a mark of our freedom and dignity as a species. Following such assumptions, Western traditions of political thought have largely ignored the implications of their ruling beliefs for human–nonhuman relations. In the process, we have failed to consider how re-tooling our ruling beliefs and practices might help humans interact less instrumentally, and more benevolently, toward a broader environment. While environmental political theorists have made laudable efforts to address these sorts of issues, they have not gathered all the potential historical and cultural leverage that would allow us to locate some of the most problematic presumptions we have inherited in the history of Western political thought.[14] A combination of premodern and non-Western perspectives help supply such critical distance.

On the Greek side, examining Homer and Hesiod explains how and why the Greeks began positing a political tension and rupture between the human and nonhuman. As this break is already assumed and articulated in the political philosophies of Plato and Aristotle, as well as the writings of early Classical historians and playwrights, Homeric and Hesiodic works offer the best starting point for critical inquiry. In their major works, we observe the earliest tensions concerning the connectedness of rule, including a particular ideational framework that emerges around these tensions. Having clarified the Greek vantage point and critical leverage it provides, a subsequent shift in perspective and engagement with early and middle Vedic political thought exposes how the Greek understanding of rule differs in a few startling ways. Instead of a cosmo-political rupture between the human and nonhuman, brahmins envision increased attachment between human and nonhuman beings. Importantly, Classical Hindu traditions—and even "heterodox" Buddhist and Jain traditions—are deeply influenced by early brahmanical thought and its conception of the connectedness of rule. This comparative study thus aims to step behind, chronologically speaking, both Classical Greek and Classical Indian political thought to better understand how and why such conceptual trajectories emerge in the first place.

Concerning the Greek case, I want to emphasize that Homer and Hesiod are helpful starting points for this project, but I do not want to suggest that they exhaust all potential philosophical viewpoints on the topic of human–nonhuman connectedness in ancient Greece, or in subsequent Western traditions for that matter. Various pre-Socratic philosophers such as Heraclitus and Democritus, as well as Classical philosophers such as Epicurus, may undoubtedly serve as positive resources for thinking about political cosmology and the connectedness of rule. Moreover, it is not unreasonable to assume that aspects of Homeric and Hesiodic cosmological ideas persist in various philosophies in the post-archaic period. Here I would simply like to make two points to clarify why I choose to focus solely on Homer and Hesiod.

First, in a historically situated sense, pre-Socratic philosophers do not tend to engage or take into account distinctly political questions such as the meaning of rule in the way that Homer and Hesiod do. Although various pre-Socratic and Classical philosophers may provide interesting arguments about the cosmological or atomistic ideas behind a potential politics and political theory, they do not generally provide explicit or convincing arguments for the normative connection between the two. For those Greek philosophers who might happen to draw more explicit connections between cosmology and politics, as Cynthia Farrar (1988, 192–264) argues Democritus had done, I maintain that such thinkers already tend to privilege a particular Greek approach to human–nonhuman political relations. For example, even Democritus's cosmologically informed position privileges individualistic self-reliance and human-centric aspects of politics, insofar as he focuses on personal well-being in the form of *euthumia* (contentment, lit. "temperate or good condition of the soul"). Because *euthumia* can be glossed as personal, corporeal moderation and atomic harmony of the body-soul compound, his position does not explicitly focus on implications that follow, for example, from the human–nonhuman connectedness of rule. In this regard, Democritus's political thought implicitly accepts some of the more fundamental conceptual distinctions that can already be found in Homer and Hesiod, particularly a political position that focuses on human interests and well-being as opposed to an interconnected and deeply context-based conception of human–nonhuman well-being.

While one might object that Democritus's atomistic materialism was cosmologically integrationist and holistic, as Farrar argues his political thinking leans in a direction that tends to conceive human well-being as the primary stakes of rule and political order. In addition, while Farrar (1988, 250) aptly points out that Democritus's conception of justice (*dikē*) includes the treatment of nonhuman creatures, whereby it is unjust to harm a creature that has done no harm to us nor intends any harm, the criterion for distinguishing between just and unjust behavior remains problematic due to a particularly narrow, and I would suggest, humanistic, standard for distinguishing just from unjust behavior. The idea of "harm" itself often implies the ability to discern intentionality on the part of the creature that purportedly harms us. However, it would be difficult in many cases to judge unjust behavior or "harm" by nonhuman beings on the basis of intentionality. How do I judge whether some animal "harms" me or not—is it understood purely in physical terms? Don't our assessments about hostility and security often require us to distinguish between intentional and unintentional harm, and if so, how do we extend our judgments of intentionality to such a wide variety of nonhuman beings and entities? For example, what if the physical harm an animal causes me is based on its instincts or sense of threat on its part, or perhaps its behavior toward me is based on mistakenly associating me (or even a part of me) with a potential source of food? Does this automatically justify me killing or harming it in every case, or perhaps only in some cases? What if I have very little or no interaction with animals on a day-to-day basis? How would this alter things? While preventing or drastically diminishing overt and systematic harm is important, appealing to positive interests centered on flourishing, self-determination, and interests is a more proactive approach and better addresses a number of difficult questions that Democritus's position presents.[15] Finally, from the standpoint of my own argument, Greek thinkers such as Democritus rely too heavily on a single, substantive conception of justice that does not make quite enough room for context, circumstance, and shifting relationality. This brings me to a second point.

My methodological motivation on the Western side of things is to locate, in a historically specified manner, some of the earliest concepts that explicitly or implicitly justify later political bifurcations between the human and nonhuman. While various post-Classical Western philosophers such as Spinoza might embrace some form of cosmological holism, they tend to be outliers in the Western tradition of political thought, and one of my central concerns is to ask why they are such marginal figures. What central distinctions are made in early Western political thought such that cosmologically oriented philosophers and political thinkers do not receive more attention? What is so attractive and influential about the human–nonhuman political distinction? And following from this, how can we locate and critique implicit yet problematic assumptions that may have been overlooked and might have justified the relative neglect of an Epicurus, Spinoza, and cosmologically holist political philosophies? Using a cross-cultural vantage point, and the Vedic tradition in particular, better highlights the contingency of various assumptions about rule in early Western political thought, and thus has greater potential to unsettle deep-seated cultural assumptions that pervade the Western tradition.

While Homer and Hesiod provide greater leverage for critiquing Classical, modern, and contemporary conceptions of rule in various Western traditions, the Vedas supply additional analytic leverage that allows us to better understand a wide range of Western beliefs about rule, starting with the Greeks. Using what I call a "historical-comparative" approach to political theory, I argue that the early Greek understanding of rule as *distinction*—whereby rulers aim to enhance their honor, glory, and reputation in an attempt to hierarchically distinguish and situate themselves above others—introduces particular problems for the connectedness of rule. While the conceptual developments in their political thought remain multifaceted and differ in certain respects, both Homer's and Hesiod's understanding of rule rely upon a strongly demarcated sense of individuality, agonistic competition, and relative disconnectedness between the human and nonhuman. In contrast, the brahmanical understanding of rule as *stewardship*, while emphasizing a much greater degree of connectedness and intertwined well-being between the human and nonhuman, introduces alternative problems that are associated with metaphysical holism, overly harmonious interconnectedness, and problematic human typology. After contrasting these conceptions of rule according to categories and concepts shared between each tradition in chapter 5, in the Conclusion I explain how a novel, cross-cultural vision of rule draws important insights from my comparative analysis and entails a "dual leveling" across both human and nonhuman registers. Here I formulate a unique intercultural perspective for thinking about the connectedness of rule. This intercultural conception better navigates the shoals of a more human-centric and overly agonistic individualism, on the one hand, and an overstretched conception of interconnected harmony and hierarchical inequality, on the other. In particular, this new understanding of rule pushes against the idea of rule being based on one or more of the following principles: human-centrism, disconnected individualism, impersonal institutionalism, proceduralism, static hierarchy, and human typology. Instead, ruling can be understood more along the lines of decentered interconnectedness, open and shifting identity, personal creativity, and leveled ruling capacities. Drawing on the Greek and Indian traditions, this alternative conception will place greater emphasis on the transformative power of bodily rituals, sacrifice, and cosmology, and my cross-cultural analysis will ultimately point toward a vision of rule grounded in everyday, leveled processes of world-making. Before arguing these points in subsequent chapters, in the next chapter I will outline and address the central challenges that this historical-comparative approach will confront.

ACKNOWLEDGMENTS

Many people contributed in making this book, and I owe a great deal to all those who have supported me as I developed the ideas that appear in the following pages. This book is based on my dissertation work in the Department of Political Science at the University of California, Santa Barbara. I want to extend my deepest gratitude to Paige Digeser, whose incredible support and insightful questions, comments, and suggestions helped me develop these ideas from their earliest stages. Special thanks go to Farah Godrej, Andrew Norris, Barbara Holdrege, and John Lee, each of whom provided invaluable feedback during the project's early stages and challenged me to think carefully about various parts of my argument. I would also like to express my sincere appreciation to Thomas M. Hughes, who patiently read and commented on multiple drafts of every chapter in the book, and without whom this book would undoubtedly be worse off. I am also incredibly lucky to have had a supporting family and friends over the years, who have provided the much-needed reassurance that I could in fact see this project through to the end. Most of all, I thank Sierra for her love, understanding, and unswerving support. She is so deeply a part of me that this book is just as much hers as it is mine—she can decide which parts she would like to take most credit for.

I would also like to thank the following people for their support and helpful comments on the ideas and arguments presented in the book (my sincere apologies to anyone I may leave out): Bentley Allan, Matthew Baxter, Jane Bennett, P. J. Brendese, Jon Carlson, Sam Chambers, William Connolly, Stefan Dolgert, John Fortuna, Greg Hillis, Jishnu Guha-Majumdar, Vicky Hsueh, Leigh Jenco, Anatoli Ignatov, Jacqui Ignatova, Jesse Knutson, Yu-chun Kuo, Quinn Lester, Brian Lovato, Timothy Lubin, Sophia Mihic, Matthew Moore, John Rapp, Vanita Seth, Chad Shomura, James Stoner, and Catherine Zuckert. It has been a tremendous pleasure to work with Angela Chnapko at Oxford University Press, whose support and professionalism have been invaluable in bringing this book to completion. Special thanks go to the incredibly careful reading and thoughtful feedback of the anonymous reviewers, whose critiques and suggestions pushed me to sharpen many of the ideas and arguments presented in the book. Their comments helped improve the manuscript tremendously.

Research for this book was carried out on campuses and libraries in California, Wisconsin, Maryland, and India, including the following: UC Santa Barbara; University of Wisconsin, Madison; Johns Hopkins University; Jawaharlal Nehru University, Delhi. I would like to thank the audiences who provided insightful questions and comments at Annual Meetings of numerous professional conferences, including the American, Midwest, Western, and Southern Political Science Associations. I presented earlier portions of this book and received valuable feedback at the Political Theory Workshop, South Asian Religion and Cultures Research Focus Group, and Borderlands Research Group at UC Santa Barbara, as well as the Political Science Colloquium at Johns Hopkins University. This research was supported by doctoral fellowships and grants at UC Santa Barbara, the Amy and Charles Scharf Postdoctoral Fellowship in the Department of Political Science at Johns Hopkins University, and financial support provided by Washington and Lee University.

Portions of chapter 4 have been published as "Cross-Cultural Intelligibility and the Use of History: From Democracy and Liberalism to Indian Rajanical Thought," *The Review of Politics* 78, no. 2 (2016): 251–83, for which I thank Cambridge University Press for permission to republish.

A DEFENSE OF RULE

INTRODUCTION

HISTORICAL-COMPARATIVE POLITICAL THEORY

In the Preface, I explained the importance of rethinking the meaning of rule and critically re-examining traditional approaches to the concept, which tend to express an oversimplified and narrow understanding of rule. I also argued that undertaking this project can best be achieved by placing some of the earliest and most influential Greek ideas found in Homeric and Hesiodic texts in comparative dialogue with a standpoint lying outside of the Western tradition entirely. In this chapter I outline why a "historical-comparative" approach provides a uniquely valuable analytic framework for achieving these aims. Broadly speaking, this approach to political theory entails examining two or more traditions, thinkers, texts, or concepts from different regions of the globe and potentially from very different time periods. Analytically, this approach employs external, cross-cultural vantage points that provide a greater degree of critical perspectivism by emphasizing historical and cultural difference. The increased conceptual range that this approach opens then supplies enhanced analytic leverage to notice novel conceptual change and continuity, as well as new avenues for concept formation, which we might not otherwise attain without shifting our cultural perspective quite dramatically. In so doing, this approach helps to reveal unforeseen background assumptions in our political ideas and practices as well as dismantle false universals.

Here, it is important to note how the study of political theory and the history of political thought have traditionally neglected non-Western thinkers, texts, and traditions.[1] This long-term trend has contributed to an overly narrow cultural focus and what has been called a pervasive Euro- or West-centrism in the field of political theory (e.g., see Black 2009a, b; Dallmayr 2004; Godrej 2011;

Jenco 2007, 2015). While the general neglect of non-Western traditions has been increasingly addressed in the past decade with the growing amount of research in the areas of non-Western and comparative political theory, much of this scholarship tends to focus on modern and contemporary thinkers, texts, and ideas, thus neglecting systematic examinations of important premodern traditions. This lacuna raises significant historical and cultural questions concerning the categories, concepts, and cultural frameworks necessary for a proper understanding of many modern and contemporary non-Western traditions of political thought. I thus argue that pulling the history of political ideas and comparative political theory into the same field of play clarifies how they can benefit one another. Not only can the history of political ideas bring a more critical, historical edge to comparative political theory, but the latter's cross-cultural orientation can help the former address its cultural narrowness. A historical-comparative approach to political theory seeks to accomplish this productive combination of studies and thus enhance the scope and analytic rigor of each area.

Analytic Challenges

Partly because a historical-comparative approach entails combining two different types of study that are generally undertaken separately, taking this approach will involve a few challenges. By formulating a response to the most pressing of these challenges I can explain how one can cogently examine the meaning of rule in two separate traditions. Such clarification is especially important because this approach relies on using (more or less) unconnected cross-cultural "vantage points" whose historical and analytic status remains underspecified at this point. Since these vantage points depend upon historical and cultural claims, one must provide warrants for how such claims can elude reductionist critiques. While particular methodological challenges confront a historical-comparative approach to ancient Greek and Indian works, some of them will also face historical-comparative studies in general.

The first challenge pertains to the types of historical sources available to a political theorist. Compared to most studies in political theory, one does not have ample access to a diversity of texts and authors, nor an abundance of historical evidence surrounding particular texts and authors, during the time period under study in this project. In my case, one can most reliably be said to have access to individual viewpoints and beliefs as found in particular works.[2] Lacking a variety of precisely datable texts and accurate historical accounts, there is a difficulty in placing works on a finely tuned chronological spectrum. This raises an associated problem regarding authorial intention. In the cases examined here, serious limitations exist when attempting to access authorial intention and employ intentionalist accounts of historical meaning that are tied to a particular author and the author's historical context. Without an uncontested author or context, one is constrained when arguing about the hermeneutic meaning of a work by way of the author's intentions in composing it. This limited access to occasionality problematizes an intentionalist theory of meaning because hermeneutic meaning is necessarily attached to authorial intentionality. This is important to my project because there is no precise access to the particular historical author(s) and occasionality of Homeric, Hesiodic, or Vedic works in the same way we have access, say, to Thomas Hobbes and the occasionality of the *Leviathan*.

Additional challenges arise concerning the comparative component of a historical-comparative approach. This set of challenges entails the danger of cultural reductionism and using a "Procrustean logistics." As I will explain, the comparative element of a historically grounded analytic framework relies on the possibility of identifying similar categories and/or concepts in two or more traditions.[3] Locating similarities and comparing ideas across cultures raises the question of whether the comparativist is "domesticating differences" by engaging in cultural reductionism, or unduly stretching concepts to fit some arbitrary normative standard (see Bloom 2002, 94; Gray 2010). A critic might claim that such cross-cultural comparisons require the comparativist to stretch concepts and their meaning to fit an arbitrary standard to the point that one loses adequate analytic precision, thereby doing damage to one or both traditions. Like the Greek figure Procrustes, if our guests do not fit the bed, do we either stretch or cut off their legs to make them the right size? If one uses historical beliefs from one cultural context as criteria to judge historical beliefs from a very different cultural context, then judgments may appear arbitrary and unjustified. In response to this objection, I argue that one can justifiably shift from talking about historical beliefs and comparisons to both pragmatic and theoretical considerations of implications particular ideas may have for our conception of rule.

I respond to these challenges by unpacking the basic framework of a historical-comparative approach. This approach to political theory is a qualitative one that focuses on the historical, textual, and philosophical analysis of concepts in different traditions.[4] Comparative analysis of Greek and Indian sources entails explicating historical beliefs about rule found in the available textual evidence, while paying special attention to the change and continuity of ideas within the texts. Attending to such nuance in these sources requires using an analytic framework composed of categories, concepts, and terminology that can be justifiably drawn from each tradition's own texts and language(s). Categories tend to be broader and more organizational in nature, helping establish a more inclusive analytic frame for cross-cultural comparative analysis. Hierarchy, for example, serves as a central analytic category for understanding the concept of rule in the Greek and Indian traditions. Following categories, concepts are more specific and denote abstract ideas that may or may not be shared across cultures. Ruling and kingly rule will be the central concepts for comparative analysis in this book. Finally, terminology refers to specific terms drawn from a particular language, genre, and historical-cultural context that one must use to explicate and make sense of various concepts.

Therefore, this analytic framework includes a combination of broad (intercultural) categories and concepts, as well as specific (intra-cultural) concepts and terminology, which provides a more responsive way of analyzing a given concept and its meaning across cultures. Using this framework, I focus on the intercultural categories of hierarchy, individuality, and the concept of rule, on the one hand, and more culturally specific categories, concepts, and terminology drawn separately from each tradition, on the other. Locating such categorical and conceptual similarities while maintaining the capacity to understand difference allows for the possibility of conducting a critical comparative analysis without doing any Procrustean damage to one's objects of study. This approach also entails a careful attempt to minimize the use of concepts and terminology that possess specific historical significance within later traditions of political thought. Such concepts and terminology tend to carry their own historical meanings and assumptions that often do not make sense within earlier historical contexts. When analyses of ancient Greek and Indian political ideas neglect this sort of textual responsiveness, the Procrustean logistics objection becomes a relevant one.

Moreover, this type of historical-comparative analysis should not be equated with any particular method, although I take it to be broadly compatible with a logic of the history of ideas and form of historical reasoning that has been defended by Mark Bevir (1999). The aspects of his logic that are most useful for historical-comparative studies are, first, his account of historical meaning as equivalent to individual viewpoints understood as expressed beliefs, and second, his position on synchronic and diachronic explanation.[5] While Bevir's logic helps clarify the historical rigor of historical-comparative theorizing, my approach builds upon his position in the following way. Bevir argues that the quality of a historical account is predicated on one's ability to argue against rival accounts according to criteria of accuracy, comprehensiveness, consistency, progressiveness, fruitfulness, and openness (1999, 78–126). One's ability to defend such historical accounts, I contend, is strengthened if one adds a cross-cultural, comparative component to one's analysis. A historical-comparative approach adds an extra interpretive dimension to historical studies by including dissimilar traditions to gain perspective and analytic leverage vis-à-vis a given tradition, thinker, or text. Employing a second, contrasting case that has something in common (e.g., conceptually or categorically) with the first case then increases one's ability to interpret meaning and undertake synchronic and diachronic explanation. As Michael Freeden and Andrew Vincent explain, we can sometimes identify "common, or at least adjacent, problematics [i.e., across cultural boundaries] that create the bases for comparison" (Freeden and Vincent 2013, 2).

In sum, cross-cultural contrast becomes part of the interpretive process and helps one examine aspects of particular cases that may not otherwise be recognizable, or perhaps only identifiable with tremendous difficulty. This type of move should be familiar to political theorists because comparisons within a broader Western tradition of political thought have played a central role in our understanding of this tradition. For example, our understanding of Machiavelli's political thought and its historical significance is partly shaped by our understanding of how he differs from Greek and medieval Christian thinkers. Contrast thus influences, and ultimately enhances, our conception of both ancient and modern political thought. A comparison between Greek and Indian understandings of rule similarly increases our knowledge of each tradition and helps expose new avenues for cross-cultural critique and concept formation.

I maintain, however, that this approach should not be equated with any particular method. Historical-comparativists should be skeptical about the interpretive rigidity that can be induced by strictly following a particular methodology or adopting a methods-centered position in general. Such single-method approaches generally imply that a particular methodology has the power to validate or invalidate the conclusions of any given study. Here I agree with Bevir insofar as I do not believe any specific methodology has the power to achieve this level of authority over its objects of study. In contrast, a multiple methods approach seems most appropriate for historical-comparative studies, especially given the cross-disciplinary nature and scope that such studies will often involve. For example, examining ancient Greek and Indian political thought requires engaging with scholarship and methodologies in multiple fields and disciplines. This cross-disciplinary, methodological pluralism helps strengthen my own analyses of Greek and Indian works, and I do not foresee how any particular method would be justified in claiming authority over all others. When undertaking a historical-comparative study one must simply remain as thoughtful and judicious as possible in choosing what one takes to be the most appropriate methods and literatures for a particular project. In these respects, the historical-comparative approach entails an open analytic approach that can incorporate methods and insights from multiple fields of study.

Comparative Political Theory and History: The Importance of Premodernity

As I mentioned earlier, this approach brings me into close proximity with positions in a somewhat nascent subfield of political theory, often called "comparative political theory." For example, my general emphasis on cross-cultural engagement overlaps with aspects of various positions in the field, including among them: Fred Dallmayr's (1996, 2002, 2004) hermeneutic-dialogic approach, which focuses on intercultural understanding through dialogue; Roxanne Euben's (2006) appeal to cross-cultural travel and contact between unfamiliar traditions; Andrew March's (2009, 2010) argument for the importance of "engaged" political theory, which involves genuine moral disagreement and normative contestation between various ideas and principles; Farah Godrej's (2009, 2011, chs. 4 and 5) cosmopolitan approach, which argues for combining context-sensitive engagement with interpretive and theoretical creativity, as well as viewing ancient texts such as the Vedas as potential resources of concept formation and theory building; finally, Michael Freeden and Andrew Vincent's call for more historically and culturally particularized, context-sensitive studies that "factor in more complex understandings of the nature of the political" (2013, 8).

The present study contributes to this literature in a number of significant ways. A historical-comparative approach establishes sturdier historical and linguistic foundations for Dallmayr's cross-cultural dialogue by engaging particular "historically grown cultural frameworks" in greater detail, which also dovetails with Freeden and Vincent's argument that comparativists should "re-particularize" their analyses. Such efforts entail addressing issues of translation and interpretation from the primary texts and languages—for example, both ancient Greek and Sanskrit (Dallmayr 2004, 249). In turn, this point highlights a glaring issue that has not garnered the attention it deserves: namely, the general lack in understanding of influential premodern traditions in various regions of the world, along with their potential connections to contemporary issues and dilemmas. This book, and the historical-comparative approach more broadly, shows how substantial progress can be made in addressing interpretive dangers such as conceptual distortion and ignorance of alternative epistemologies through more sustained engagement with premodern traditions outside "the West." In this regard, a historical-comparative approach heeds Godrej's argument by providing scholars with greater historical knowledge of non-Western traditions, especially premodern traditions of political thought, as recent investigations of non-Western political thinkers have tended to focus on modern or contemporary figures such as Gandhi (Godrej 2006; Klausen 2014; Mantena 2012; Parel 2006, 2008), Sayyid Qutb (Euben 1999, 49–92), and Zhang Shizhao (Jenco 2010). Engagements with premodern traditions can also help expand political theory's conceptual horizon and fulfill an important goal that Godrej identifies with cosmopolitan political theory, which entails taking "ideas, texts, and methods out of their original context, calling upon them and interpreting them in new ways and new contexts. . . . [hence] engaging in transgressive syntheses that bring about unforeseen excavations of existing resources" (2011, 16–17). As I explain in the Conclusion, such synthesis plays an important role in how I re-envision what it means to rule.

Finally, paying careful attention to the historical dimension of comparative political theory not only deepens our understanding of the reasons for fundamental normative contestation across cultural boundaries, which March aptly argues is an important project, but also clarifies how different vantage points may possess unseen potential for *intercultural* theory building on issues of shared concern that extend across cultural and geographic boundaries. Consequently, the current project has broader implications for a timely issue in political theory. Addressing debates surrounding the future of democracy under conditions of globalization, Melissa Williams and Mark Warren (2014, 26–57) have recently explained how comparative political theory can help enhance the social conditions for critical reflection and reasoning across cultural boundaries. In so doing, they clarify how contextual studies of non-Western traditions can help lay the groundwork for greater intelligibility and deliberation among "communities of shared fate" that exceed the boundaries of territorial states (Williams and Warren 2014, 31, citing Held et al. 1999, 81; see also Held 2006, 309). A central aim of comparative political theory, on this account, would be to identify and investigate historical pathways and conceptual frameworks extending from the ancient past to present in various political traditions around the globe. Following Williams and Warren, I agree that strengthening grounds for mutual intelligibility—especially across historical distance—can play a significant role in enhancing political theorists' capacity for critical reflexivity and practical reasoning.[6] The project outlined by Williams and Warren can be further advanced through sustained engagement with premodern traditions because such efforts create more space for historical and conceptual *co*-reflexivity within and across cultures. The historical-comparative approach thus opens new doors for innovative forms of questioning and problem solving that may flow critically in both directions, thereby expanding the categorical and conceptual scope of political theory as a field of study. In sum, my approach helps to achieve some of the most significant goals set out by previous approaches through combining cross-cultural and historical distance as a two-pronged analytic platform for engaging in comparative theory.

A significant contrast with existing approaches should also be emphasized—namely, the fact that I am primarily concerned with examining *historical meaning* in a cross-cultural setting. Currently, most studies in comparative political theory do not directly address the issue of historical meaning, and more specifically, the meaning of political ideas in the historical past. While some of the best existing studies in comparative political theory justifiably focus on the appropriate methods for cross-cultural interpretation, it is not clear that a history of ideas approach such as the one I employ cannot adequately engage in the cross-cultural interpretation of meaning as well. Leigh Jenco (2014) has recently made a similar point about historical interpretation, showing how particular Chinese thinkers help to show how cultural otherness need not be understood as qualitatively different than the historical otherness that is already found within our existing canons of thought. Because one need not posit a qualitative distinction between historical and cultural reconstruction (see also Jenco 2010, 11), there does not appear to be a good reason why scholars cannot simultaneously, and coherently, engage in both types of reconstruction in the course of a single study. In making a similar point within the field of comparative philosophy, Richard King draws upon Willhelm Halbfass's work to explain: "The so-called 'European tradition' is itself a mixture of diverse cultural sources, and there is no reason not to assume that the problem of understanding *between* cultures is qualitatively different from that of understanding *within* cultures, or between different time periods of the same culture" (King 1999, 13; Halbfass 1988, 165). This is an issue that Halbfass properly identifies in his comparative studies of Indian and European thought, drawing upon Hans-George Gadamer's philosophical hermeneutics to reiterate the point that "we have no reason to assume more than a difference in degree, which may, however, be very significant. Just as access to texts in foreign languages, the access to foreign traditions represents [citing Gadamer] 'simply an extreme case of hermeneutical difficulty'" (Halbfass 1988, 165; Gadamer 2004, 349).

Most pertinent for my own historical orientation, Bevir (1999, 159) similarly explains how a more limited concept of rationality as logical consistency within a given web of beliefs clarifies how the existence of a language entails that saying one thing necessarily rules out saying something else. This limited concept of rationality does not fall prey to the objection that has been raised in comparative political theory regarding the danger of imputing a Western concept of rationality upon a non-Western culture. For example, in her early work, Jenco (2007) argues that something like a methods-centered, cross-cultural "conversion" might be necessary to prevent Eurocentric interpretation. This position implies that one must be able to access a different rationality—or even something that falls completely outside a Western concept of rationality—to prevent Eurocentric interpretive tendencies and pose critical questions that emanate from within that particular non-Western tradition. However, as Bevir (1999, 189) explains, people might not share a substantive, objective concept of rationality but must nevertheless share a limited concept of rationality defined in terms of consistency, and such internal consistency provides the necessary leverage for understanding meaning within a very different set of beliefs. As Freeden and Vincent maintain, this requires careful attention to context during the interpretive process, and what they call a "re-particularizing of its analysis" instead of aiming, through dialogue, at "the convergence on a particular ethical singularity" (2013, 8). This is indeed an important insight, and my attention to the native and diverse categories, concepts, and terminology in the Greek and Indian cases attempts to provide the most contextually nuanced interpretations possible.

Environmental Political Theory: The Importance of Rule

In addition to questions and analytic approaches in comparative political theory, a central normative question driving this book is how we should modify our understanding of human beings' relationship to nonhuman nature. Once we come to understand rule as connected—that is, that human life and society are inescapably bound up with the survival of nonhuman nature—we must also recognize that we have a normative duty to act in ways that take the interests of nonhuman nature into account. The conceptual vocabulary of politics, as traditionally understood, is deeply problematic because politics assumes that the participants will be roughly equal agents acting in their own interests, which obviously presents a problem when humans try to account for the interests of nonhuman nature. The concept of rule is incredibly helpful for addressing this issue because it shows us how ruling relations between those in unequal standing can nonetheless serve everyone's interests. Importantly, theorizing rule along four distinct dimensions will allow me to connect and critically synthesize existing positions in environmental political theory, which includes liberal, civic republican, post-humanist, and critical theory approaches to ecological citizenship.

The concept of rule in particular allows me to reframe existing debates, many of which revolve around anthropocentric assumptions that start with demarcated identity and moral selfhood instead of constitutive, affective relations between human and nonhuman beings, or with institutional, policy, or technological fixes that ignore some of the deeper conceptual underpinnings driving current instrumentalist approaches to nonhuman nature. Clarifying a porous and dynamic cosmological framework for re-envisioning rule, without necessarily downplaying particular human capacities and responsibilities, provides a way of bridging diverse approaches within environmental political theory. For example, in the Conclusion I will clarify how the four dimensions of rule uncover potential lines of communication for scholars working from the more humanistic direction of the proverbial "mountain" with those working from animal- or object-oriented directions. At a general level I take many scholars in environmental political theory to be working toward the shared goal of developing a more thoughtful and effective political approach to nonhuman nature in an increasingly fragile earthly estate. While I will be working more from the humanistic direction due to my focus on the human capacity to rule, a central issue I address in the Conclusion concerns how to find productive hinges for conversing across particular theoretical or philosophical divides.

To elaborate on these points, the conceptions of identity (polycentrism) and temporality (poly-temporality) emerging from my comparative analysis explain why we do not need to adopt the individualism and instrumentalism connected to anthropocentric theories or ideas, such as those of classical liberalism. Traditionally, such theories view nonhuman nature as inert material for our consumption and comfortable self-preservation, to which we have no discernible political obligations. Polycentrism and poly-temporality, in contrast, gesture toward an expansive ecological and physio-temporal horizon for grounding the current generation's duties to future generations, as the latter depend on the former's willingness and capacity to consider future generations' interests. The present generation must consciously deliberate and participate in choosing the type of world it is in the process of building for both current and subsequent generations.[7] Here it is reasonable to assume that we would not consciously choose to build a world more fragile, unsustainable, and toxic than the one we have inherited—after all, wouldn't we wish previous generations had such consideration for how they built the world *we* now inhabit? In contrast to those focusing predominantly on the language of citizenship, I will argue that it is essential to begin the discussion about stewardship and world-building by employing the language of rule. One reason is that citizenship emphasizes a legal designation, grounded in nation-state boundaries and sovereignty, while the capacity to rule is pre-legal and operates at a more primordial level that supersedes and extends beyond nation-state sovereignty.

Accordingly, the four dimensions of rule are historically and culturally under-specified, which helps map a more inclusive terrain for developing specific, context-sensitive solutions to environmental predicaments facing a global community. The language of individual rulership also adds consequential weight to the ethical stakes involved with citizenship because it draws immediate attention to the pervasive yet inevitable hierarchies involved in relations of rule. Such relations can be easily overlooked when using the language of democratic citizenship because the latter implies a more egalitarian and human-centric, and thus less threatening, view of our contemporary condition. By initially de-emphasizing the language of citizenship, we can shift focus from individual nation-states as the political center of our duties and the matrix of citizen/state sovereignty as the predominant locus for solving environmental or ecological issues. Modern vocabularies of citizenship tend to be exclusionary because they are based upon the capacity for speech and discursive deliberation, making it difficult to conceive how members of nonhuman nature could be considered "citizens" in familiar senses of the term.

Nevertheless, there is much in existing environmental and ecological positions that accords with, complements, or otherwise can be incorporated into my position on "panocracy," stewardship, and world-building. First, akin to many liberal-democratic theories, I maintain the importance of *equality* by conceiving equal ability to rule. This equality would also support the value of *tolerance* in multicultural deliberation that involves alternative viewpoints on human–nonhuman relations, including the need for the free expression of contending ideas. Nevertheless, my interculturally hybrid position is post-liberal insofar as it rejects strong individualism and does not ground duties to nonhuman nature and future generations on natural right(s), negative liberty, or contractual reciprocity. While my theory of rule does not lead to a wholesale rejection of liberalism or democracy, I critically incorporate particular elements of both political traditions in order to construct a more adequate normative account of rule. For example, my position informs theories of ecological citizenship by explaining how the private sphere is a public space with far-reaching political significance, and how civic education and training in green virtues need not violate liberal neutrality. Virtues supporting the good of sustainability are compatible with such neutrality because sustainability, as Melissa Lane points out, "is a necessary ingredient of and condition on the realization of the good"—and this would include the pursuit of any particular or substantive interest or good (2012, 20).

Second, the theory of rule that I offer resonates with the following aspects of green republicanism: emphasis on *responsibility or duty* and common goods such as ecological sustainability and resilience to vulnerability due to our dependence on nonhuman nature;[8] an *active citizenry* and more decentralized decision-making; *civic virtues* such as justice, care, courage, and sacrifice. However, neither discursive-democratic nor civic republican traditions provide fully suitable conceptions of rule, as I will argue for what I call panocracy as a necessary foundation for successful democratic or civic republican political orders. In short, panocracy is a conception of rule holding that all human beings have the power and response-ability to rule as stewards, and that the ability to rule affects an incredibly broad array of human and nonhuman beings. Panocracy pushes us to think outside more familiar, inherited traditions of rule while simultaneously being able to diagnose problematic aspects of these traditions and incorporate the most useful facets of each. Along these lines, the rule of connectedness proves an invaluable resource for thinking about our political orientation toward nonhuman nature. Finally, my position intersects with various postmodern and critical theory positions in positing a porous human–nonhuman conception of identity, the role of nonhuman agency, and material flows that provide a basis for the integrity of intertwined human–nonhuman welfare.

At this point it may be helpful to clarify how my theorization and defense of rule cohere with the consequentialist argument I put forth in the Preface. First, I take it that the right choice in a given situation is one that delivers the best consequences for the intended goods under consideration, thus rejecting deontological positions that some actions are right or wrong in themselves, irrespective of the consequences. Applied environmentally, my theory of rule aims at the following goods: the cultivation of non-instrumental approaches to nonhuman nature and, correspondingly, more sustainable relations with myriad nonhuman beings and phenomena. Sustainability and resiliency are essential goods due to our connectedness and dependency on nonhuman nature, which highlight our inevitable vulnerability as a species. Therefore, I am most concerned about common goods of environmental sustainability and interconnected flourishing, arguing for a modified vision of rule that can support existing arguments for more sustainable political ideas and practices, particularly along the dimensions of ruling-over, ruling-with, ruling-for, and ruling-in. Along these lines, I broadly follow Seaton Patrick Tarrant and Leslie Paul Thiele's definition of sustainability as:

> an adaptive art, wedded to science, in service to an ethical vision. It entails satisfying current needs without sacrificing future wellbeing through the balanced pursuit of ecological health, economic welfare, social empowerment, and cultural creativity. Sustainability involves managing the rate and scale of change within a system, defined by its interdependencies, in a manner that conserves core values and relationships. (Tarrant and Thiele 2016, 117; Thiele 2013)

My theorization of rule provides strong reasons for pursuing these aims and the good of sustainability in general. As I explain in the Preface, human well-being will suffer if we continue to follow our current instrumental approach to nonhuman nature, and due to such consequences we should alter the way we think about ruling relations in contemporary life.

An additional good, related to the under-specification I mentioned earlier, concerns trans-historical and intercultural hybridity. My theorization of rule leaves considerable room for deliberation between a variety of Western and non-Western perspectives by expanding the historical and conceptual space for discussing our treatment of nonhuman nature. In chapter 5 and the Conclusion, I will show how scholars need not privilege one particular regional or cultural vocabulary over all others. On the one hand, existing debates in environmental political theory tend to pivot around modern Western categories and concepts, often drawing upon the frameworks of liberal democracy, civic republicanism, postmodernism, critical theory, or post-humanism. On the other hand, the relative minority who appeal to non-Western traditions often confront pitfalls of neo-colonialism or Orientalism by essentializing or fetishizing civilizational "Others." As Godrej explains, such non-Western traditions are often romantically depicted as "more gentle, less violent, and more holistic in their cosmologies" (2016, 42). I agree with

Godrej and do not wish to defend what she calls a "civilizational" position, partly because there is tremendous diversity within each geographic region and time period that cannot be captured under singular civilizational categories (e.g., such as "Hinduism" or "Confucianism").

In contrast, the conceptual framework that I defend not only allows us to identify regional diversity and specific practices for political critique but also provides fruitful grounds for thinking across both temporal distances to premodern traditions and to various non-Western traditions of political thought. Compared to many of the existing conceptual foci in environmental political theory, ideas about rule in particular remain temporally and geographically widespread and can therefore help us uncover new avenues for global deliberation about present dilemmas. Locating and examining a meaningful, shared political concept in multiple traditions provides a hinge for open discussion and globally creative practices for adaptation, even if reasonable disagreement or contestation may arise across geographic boundaries. For example, the four dimensional approach to rule does not initially commit interlocutors to a single, parochial vocabulary. One could start by examining a thinker's, text's, or tradition's stance along one or more dimensions of rule, explaining why the thinker/text/tradition stands wherever it happens to stand, and then explore the consequences and normative implications of its ideas. In this respect, my position provides a more culturally, historically, and linguistically inclusive framework than most current theories and approaches in environmental political theory, thus aiming to develop conditions for common vocabularies and practices for addressing shared environmental dilemmas.[9]

Greece and India, Poetry and Kingship

Thus far I have sought to clarify a particular theoretical framework for defining and thinking in a more nuanced fashion about the concept of rule, explaining what a historical-comparative approach has to offer as a new way of engaging in historical and comparative modes of political theory on issues of long-standing historical and intercultural concern. The aim of this final section is to explain in greater detail why comparing the ancient Greek and Indian traditions is a particularly worthwhile project, and to address a few conceptual and terminological issues that follow from this selection. Besides breathing new life into an important yet maligned concept, I will argue that there are good reasons to examine various ruling beliefs expressed in Homeric, Hesiodic, and Vedic texts.

M. L. West (2007) lucidly explains how early Greek and Indian thought share an Indo-European mythological and linguistic heritage, and thus exhibit a number of intriguing similarities.[10] To begin with, the Homeric, Hesiodic, and Vedic works that I will examine exemplify a particular style of poetry, which West explains is "a style which diverges from the ordinary by using elevated or archaic vocabulary, ornamental epithets, figures of speech, a contrived word order, or other artificial features" (2007, 61). In Greek and Indian society, the composers of this poetry were specialists that played numerous social functions such as priest, seer, and eulogist (27). In the Ṛg-Veda Saṃhitā, for example, figures called *ṛṣis* were seers who had the ability to cognize reality and things that had happened long ago, similar to the function that Homer and Hesiod play by channeling the Muses who "see and hear everything." Greek and Vedic poets not only possessed special abilities allowing them to understand and recall things that normal folks could not, they also created songs that were most pleasing to the gods. Because of this latter ability, rulers in both cultures often served as patrons for poets and their poetry, which rulers believed could help them achieve various personal and political purposes.[11] Moreover, in both Greece and India poetic composition, recitation, and debate among rulers often occurred in the same space, as ruler-warriors came together in assemblies to make various types of judicial decisions where poets also competed (72–73).

In both cultures, the poet-ruler relationship also evokes various cosmological beliefs about relations between gods and human beings, which further elucidate beliefs in the connectedness of rule. First, in both traditions one identifies ruling relations between kings or chieftains and the rest of their clan, and these relations are linked to the idea of gods, especially male divinities such as Zeus and Indra, ruling over human communities and their affairs. Second, a fundamental distinction exists between immortal gods and mortal humans, which played an important role in each tradition's conception of rule and made the issue of mortality—along with related concepts of remembrance and forgetfulness—a significant factor in the meaning of rule in both Greece and India. One issue the mortality/immortality distinction highlights is the central role of song, poetry, and sacrifice in Greek and Vedic thought, which were necessary means for preserving various degrees of cosmic order and harmony, as well as the glory and reputation of both divine and human rulers that might otherwise be forgotten over time.

Both Greek and Vedic poets made an additional cosmological distinction between male/sky (Gr., Ouranos and Zeus *patēr*; Vedic, Dyaus *pitṛ* and Indra) and female/earth figures (Gr., Gaia, Gē, *Xthōn*; Vedic, Pṛthivī, *kṣam-*) (West

2007, 166–93). Such bifurcations introduce a parallel and primordial hierarchical relation of ruling-over between the male and female genders. One might surmise that Greek rulers' attempts to distinguish themselves hierarchically over others indicates an urge to recreate, or perhaps mimic, what they took to be the broader yet gendered cosmological relationship between sky and earth. This hierarchical orientation then maps onto what Greek rulers would consider a pernicious gender relationship because it is a sign of weakness to be subjugated to someone or something else. This cosmo-spatial orientation also evokes a leveled and potentially gendered aspect of ruling-with insofar as the earth depicts a "flattened" space where some human beings rule with others. Consequently, ruling-with might have been associated with feminine qualities because this dimension of rule would mitigate the hierarchical positioning symbolized by a masculine Ouranos (Sky) and Zeus, as well as the desired goal of situating oneself over others to achieve greater honor and glory.

A cosmo-political gendering and privileging of what both traditions conceive as more "masculine" traits can also be identified in the warrior-gods Zeus and Indra, who both wield a thunderbolt as weapon in defeating and subjugating cosmic enemies and inducing awe on the part of human beings. Unsurprisingly, this warrior aspect of such male divinities will be an important characteristic of human rulers as well. Being a ruler in both cultures not only entails a warrior-like ability to defeat enemies and protect the community but also the strength to command others and enforce decisions. Here, there are some interesting etymological connections between Greek and Sanskrit terms for rulers. As West explains, "The relationship between the word for 'king' and the verb meaning 'make straight, direct' is a strong clue to the original nature of the kingship. There is a clear semantic connection between making things straight, drawing boundaries, guiding something in a straight line, and governing justly and efficiently" (2007, 413). In clarifying these points of overlap, my aim is to show how these two traditions share some of the same categorical and conceptual bedrock in their beliefs about rule. In turn, this also helps explain why these particular traditions provide such a fascinating case for comparative study and why their divergent developments in conceiving the meaning of rule are historically and theoretically intriguing.

As I argued in the Preface, the concept of rule has traditionally been characterized by hierarchical relationships between both human and nonhuman beings. On top of this, the fact that kingly rule (or monarchy) is the most pervasive ruling structure in early Greek and Indian political thought raises the concern that these traditions express inherently non-modern, and thus potentially irrelevant, understandings of what rule can mean in a contemporary context. While this is a pertinent concern, examining divergent developments in the meaning of kingly rule in ancient Greece and India will shed new light on each tradition, and in doing so, will supply insights that serve as a basis for critical engagements with contemporary thought and practice. However, dismissing kingly rule as worthy of political theorists' attention would also be a mistake because it is both massively influential in a historical sense and more theoretically intriguing than it may appear at first glance.

Since the Neolithic Revolution (ca. 8000–5000 BCE), kingship has been one of the most pervasive forms of rule adopted in human societies across the globe (see Oakley 2006, 4, 10). Kingship and monarchy (rule by a single person) are historically significant because they provide some of the earliest and most frequently occurring human responses to questions regarding communal organization and decision-making. Such frequent occurrence could be one reason why human beings have so readily associated rule with the dimension of ruling-over, including its simplicity and (often brutal) efficiency. As Francis Oakley points out, "For several millennia at least, it has been kingship and not more consensual governmental forms that has dominated the institutional landscape of what we today would call *political* life" (2006, 4). In other words, one must understand kingship to understand how many post-Neolithic human beings have tended to make collective decisions in organized communities. Oakley even claims, "In terms of its antiquity . . . its ubiquity, its wholly extraordinary staying power, the institution of kingship can lay strong claim to having been the most common form of government known, world-wide, to man" (4). Partly due to scholars' sustained interest in Western traditions of political thought, especially Classical Greece and democratic governance as a starting point for theoretical inquiry, they sometimes assume kingship is overly archaic and outside the purview of any worthwhile political theoretical inquiry. However, as Oakley suggests, a thorough historical understanding of political life must include a sustained examination of kingship.

Oakley also observes that inattention to kingship frequently follows from a focus on the secular aspects of politics. As both Oakley (2006, 5) and Antony Black (2009b, 15–19) point out, this focus tends to neglect the relationship between politics and sacrality, or politics and religion.[12] Not only is kingly rule historically and cross-culturally prevalent, but its existence also draws our attention to the fact that in many times and places human beings have not severed ruling beliefs from what scholars generally designate as religion, or claims about the sacred. When one takes a historical-comparative approach to political theoretical inquiry, examining kingly rule frequently requires attending to a variety of categories, concepts, and terminology that may not initially appear political but nonetheless give kingly rule its particular historical meaning within a given tradition. Such categories may include religion, scripture, cosmogony, and cosmology. Black and Oakley thus highlight why scholars should not neglect kingship or the importance human beings in many times and locales place upon the connection between politics and religion. One should also note that this connection between religion and politics is not merely an ancient or archaic one and continues to be relevant in the contemporary world.

From both a scholarly and political perspective, the persistent connections between religion and politics should disrupt overly simplistic associations between "political" and "secular" texts, on the one hand, and "religious" texts, on the other. For example, Michael Walzer's (2012) study of the politics in the Hebrew Bible helps explain why an examination of Vedic texts is a valuable exercise. Walzer shows how scholars can read a religious text (which might otherwise be read only by orthodox adherents) as a political theory text, or a text that contains interesting and influential political ideas within a given tradition. Following from this, the political theories exhibited in such religious texts can be compared *as political theories*, and in the case of my project, differing political theories about the meaning of rule. But examining the Vedas as political theory texts is not merely of scholarly value. In India the Vedas have been read as political works presenting ideas that are deeply relevant for modern and contemporary politics by various types of Hindu nationalists and neo-Hindu conservatives. For example, members of modern Hindu reformist and nationalist organizations such as the Arya Samaj have appealed to the Vedas as historical texts containing evidence for the superiority of Hinduism, further attempting to use these texts as a platform for both religious and political projects. One valuable outcome of my interpretation of Vedic political thought is that it helps prevent such exclusivist political groups—many of which promote dubious political projects—from monopolizing interpretations of these texts and early Indian political thought.

Shifting to specific terminological issues when comparing early Greek and Indian political thought, a critic might ask whether one is justified in using the terms "king" and "kingship" when translating Greek terms such as *basileus* and *anax*, and Sanskrit terms such as *rājan* and *kṣatriya*. This is an important question that should be addressed up front, and a few clarifications are in order. In the Greek case, scholars such as Robert Drews (1983, 25, 98–115) have argued against casually translating the term *basileus* as "king," contending that there were no kings in the *poleis* of Geometric Greece. Most generally agree that using the term "king" can be misleading when translating and discussing Greek terms such as *basileus* and *anax* (e.g., see Raaflaub 1993, 79).[13] I agree with Drews that "the Homeric *basileus* was not by definition exclusive" (1983, 102),[14] and in using the terms king and kingship, I do not mean to imply exclusivity. Neither a *basileus* nor an *anax* was necessarily a monarch in the sense of an exclusive leader or ruler. As I explain in chapters 1 and 2, many *basileis* are depicted in Homeric and Hesiodic works.[15] The main point I want to establish is that a *basileus*—whom one could alternatively gloss as a highborn political leader, chief, nobleman, or headman—was a ruler in Homeric and Hesiodic works. *Basileis* were rulers regardless of the particular word one uses to translate the Greek term, and almost any word one uses to translate these Greek terms can potentially invoke anachronisms and resonate with later historical institutions, figures, terms, and meanings. As long as one keeps these qualifications in mind, I believe using the terminology of king and kingly rule is relatively unproblematic. Any human kings referred to in the archaic period should be understood as medium- to small-scale communal chieftains, leaders, and rulers. Therefore, one should not get the mistaken idea that the term *basileus* necessarily refers to a single divine, hereditary, or firmly institutionalized figure ruling over a large-scale kingdom, as may be found in later Western traditions. While I generally use the proper Greek terms, I will frequently refer to both *basileus* and *anax* as a king or ruler.[16]

A similar clarification should be made in the Indian case. The terms *rājan*, *rājanya*, and *kṣatriya* have all been translated as "king" in the scholarly literature. While I parse finer distinctions in their meanings in chapters 3 and 4, here I will only make the most important general qualifications. *Rājan*s in the earliest Vedic texts should be understood more as communal protectors or guardians and not permanent rulers (see Scharfe 1989, 74, 93). In the earliest texts, a human ruler or communal chieftain is usually referred to as a *pati* (father, lord) of some sort, such as *viśpati* (lord of the people). Early Vedic rulership was sometimes hereditary, but not always so. Another important term, *rājanya*, refers to a king, ruler, or member of a royal family but does not appear until the later layer of the Ṛg-Veda Saṃhitā (ṚV 10.90.12). As Macdonell and Keith (1967, 2:216) explain, in later texts *rājanya* is generally replaced by the term *kṣatriya* as a designation for a member of the ruling class. Finally, the term *kṣatriya* refers to a king and warrior, the ruling social group, or a family to which a king or ruler belongs. To summarize, while the terms *rājan*, *rājanya*, and *kṣatriya* can all refer to a king or ruler in some capacity, one must remember that the earliest human rulers—referred to as *pati*s (lords, fathers) of various sorts—are transient tribal chiefs and guardians, and not permanent, institutionalized kings. Further clarification in Greek and Sanskrit terminology is the task of subsequent chapters.

To conclude, I have attempted to reopen and begin rethinking the meaning of rule by outlining what I take to be some of the most important theoretical, methodological, historical, and cultural stakes of a comparative engagement between ancient Greek and Indian political thought. The next step in this book's argument begins with a careful examination of Homeric political thought. Importantly, the *Iliad* and *Odyssey* supply the first sustained (oral, textual) accounts of the meaning of rule in ancient Greece. Moreover, because a broader tradition of Western political thought can locate some of its most significant conceptual foundations in both Homeric and Hesiodic ideas, their works deserve greater attention on the part of political theorists than they have hitherto obtained.

1 HOMER

RULING AS DISTINCTION

Political theorists have generally neglected Homeric political thought, at least partly due to ambivalence concerning the topic of rule and its hierarchical associations. Such aversions lead to significant oversights in our understanding of early Greek political thought, especially as it pertains to the connectedness of rule. This chapter focuses on two particular works, Homer's *Iliad* and *Odyssey*, and offers a critical reinterpretation of Homeric political thought.[1] The conceptual framework expressed in these works is not only significant for our understanding of Western political thought more broadly but also helps clarify ancient Greek *paideia* (teaching, training, education), including many of the ideas that Classical political thinkers would critique or develop in important ways (e.g., Raaflaub 2004, 30–36; Robb 1994, 159–82). The Homeric epics, in particular, provide a wealth of evidence depicting rulers' thoughts and actions as embedded within a broader, complex cosmology and metaphysics. While some of the most incisive work on Homeric and Hesiodic political thought has examined them independent of one another (e.g., Bartlett 2006; Hammer 2002a), I provide both synchronic and diachronic analyses of Homer and Hesiod in this and the following chapter. Here I should also reiterate that my analysis and argument concern the ideas expressed in the texts themselves. Because I focus on a philosophical and conceptual analysis of the concept of rule, I am not principally concerned with examining the particular historical circumstances and developments that influence the construction of various layers of Homeric works.[2] Since I am a political theorist as opposed to a historian or classicist, I am less interested in what lies "beneath the text" than I am with the ideas expressed in the texts themselves and clarifying what I take to be a rather coherent, unique expression of archaic political thought in Homeric works.

Although I focus on the concept of rule, it is essential to clarify the aesthetic and political stakes of the medium through which Homer speaks. First, Homeric poetry exhibits a musical idiom that reflects a form of divine, aesthetic inspiration in which the poet taps into what he takes to be a rich, multifaceted cosmos and storehouse of nonhuman beings and forces to express his political ideas. Homer is a *singer* of things past and present, human and divine. As subsequent Greek playwrights and philosophers consistently acknowledge, lyric poetry possesses a unique power to access, stir up, and alter human emotions in significant ways. These emotions both exhibit and influence the political dispositions of Greek individuals and communities, making epic poetry a potent form of political expression and *paideia*. Lyric poetry affects the hearts and minds of its audience partly because it can access the various nooks and crannies of a listener's personhood, drawing the listener forward to greater self-recognition as well as a heightened awareness of what lies outside oneself. As I will argue below, Homer conceives the self as a plural and complex entity that orients one toward the world in both predictable and unpredictable ways. Second, Homer's poetry expresses what the poet himself practices by showing these ideas in action—for example, how the various parts of someone like Achilles are affected through dynamic interaction with his fellow rulers and divine beings. This vivid form of aesthetic expression and speech displays some of the most basic beliefs, emotions, and impulses that underlie early Greek political thought. As we will see in figures such as Agamemnon and Achilles, Homer shows his audience what it is like to love deeply, rage against another, and be pushed or pulled in different directions by both human and nonhuman forces. Importantly, Homer not only shows his listeners (and readers) what it is like to be a mortal human being but also what it is like to be a ruler in an open and agonistic cosmos.

In the first part of the chapter, I provide an overview of the archaic cosmological landscape to contextualize my analysis of Homeric rule, clarifying conceptions of cosmic plurality and how this relates to issues of temporality such as fate, death, and memory/remembrance. Paralleling my treatment of Hesiodic and Vedic thought in subsequent chapters, I begin with broader analytic categories: cosmology (claims about the structure and nature of the cosmos), metaphysics (claims regarding the nature and structure of reality), ontology (claims about the nature of being and existence, especially human existence), and individuality (claims about personhood and the parameters of identity). After discussing the pertinence of these categories for conceptions of rule, in the following section I examine what I call "traditional-hierarchical" ruling beliefs to explain where the leveling of various hierarchical aspects of rule arises in Homeric thought. I then advance my central argument that the predominant meaning of rule is distinction in the *Iliad* and *Odyssey*.

Specifically, I argue that being a ruler means distinguishing oneself hierarchically from one's peers and social inferiors in an attempt to enhance one's honor (*timē*), glory (*kleos, kudos*), excellence or superiority (*aretē*), and reputation (see also Donlan 1980; Hammer 2002a, 58–62; Raaflaub and Wallace 2007, 25). Although distinction qualifies one for both ruling-over social inferiors (e.g., the *laoi* or common mass) and ruling-with other *basileis*, the activity of ruling itself is also a crucial means of achieving greater distinction. Relatedly, the ideals of honor, glory, excellence, and reputation are more important than communal harmony, protection, safety, or peace (see Donlan 1980, 8).[3] Concepts such as honor, glory, excellence, and reputation thus expose rulers' intense desire for maintaining and enhancing their status in the eyes of both present and future generations. As an ongoing *process* exhibiting that one is worthy to rule and give commands to others, distinction entails both recognition from and subordination of others. Commanding comes afterwards, and ruling should not be conflated with the mere giving of commands because a central aspect of rule follows from the distinction process itself (namely the garnering of honor, glory, and reputation), which peers and subordinates see as a sign that someone is worthy of their political obedience.

This pursuit of distinction also enhances a ruler's esteem to such an extent that he often loses sight of his connectedness to the broader community and its interests, often resulting in hubristic behavior and a strongly individualistic understanding of rule. This understanding can then lead to actions that are viewed as abusive by those whose interests are ignored or overtly rejected in the process. Therefore, in the final section of the chapter I track three basic clusters of concepts that help explain this behavior and the competitive nature of Homeric rule: rage or anger; contest and competition; honor, glory or fame, and reputation. These conceptual clusters expose primary characteristics of the distinction process, all of which highlight the relative disconnectedness between rulers and their impulse to rule over others. To support this argument I examine the most notable rulers in the epics and how they behave toward one another in speech and deed. My aim here is not only to explain how Homeric concepts support a broader interpretation of ruling as distinction but also to show how various *basileis* exhibit characteristics that foreground the dimensions of ruling-over, ruling-with, ruling-for, and ruling-in. Clarifying these distinct modalities of rule in Homer supports a larger aim of my comparative project by elucidating an analytic framework that makes possible a productive cross-cultural comparison with Vedic political thought.

Archaic Cosmology and Metaphysics

Homeric rulers find themselves within an open, agonistic cosmos characterized by intense levels of both beauty and brutality. Throughout the chapter, the term "agonism" will imply the idea of competition, and as Christa Davis Acampora explains, "agonistic engagement is organized around the test of specific qualities that particular competitors possess" (2013, 23). This locution highlights at least three distinctive aspects of agonism: what type of test, what sorts of qualities, and who are the competitors? The Homeric cosmos contains numerous levels of competitive engagement, and the three levels most pertinent for my analysis include: *cosmic* agonism, which operates at the macro-level and involves broader cosmological relations, for example, between gods and human beings; *public* agonism, which operates at the meso-level of intra-communal relations within both divine and human communities; *personal* agonism at the micro-level, which largely occurs within the self (divine or human) and requires navigating various impulses and forces. For example, Achilles not only struggles internally and experiences alternative, competitive drives between different parts within himself, but he also engages agonistically with other *basileis* and divine powers that conflict with his personal aims.

Greek ideas about the nature of reality and being (metaphysics, ontology) help further elaborate the complex dimensions of rulers' pursuits of distinction and exhibit efforts to quell anxieties associated with their mortality, the threat of being forgotten, and often unnerving sense of isolation in the cosmos. Inflected by tragic heroism, Homer's conception of ruling as the achievement of hierarchical distinction requires a certain amount of connectedness to others, yet also facilitates a ruler's strongly individuated existence within the broader cosmos. As I explain below, distinction often evokes efforts to confront and overcome the ruler's finitude by carving out an identity and imperishable glory (*aphthiton kleos*) that will survive, through lyric poetry, in the face of violence, death, and the potential oblivion of being utterly forgotten.

The Macro-Structure of Homeric Cosmology: Gods, Fate, and Temporality

The Homeric cosmos comprises a variety of beings such as gods (*theoi*), demigods, mortal human beings, and a wide array of earthly nonhuman beings. While this cosmos is incredibly pluralistic it also contains a significant amount of order. One should note at the outset that the Greek term *kosmos* generally refers to an arrangement, order, or organization of a plurality of potentially disconnected entities, although it can also refer in a more political sense to law and order, or to the social order. The internal dynamics of this order and the relations between various entities, however, display significant tensions and competitive flows of various forces. Although teeming with tensions and flows, this *kosmos* does not appear to need constant recreation or reconstruction, nor does it seem to be in danger of completely falling into some primeval chaos. Powerful figures such as gods, goddesses, and Fate (*moira*) help hold the cosmos together but also cause strife (*eris*: conflict, competition) and sorrow (*akhos, penthos*), thus leading to varying degrees of cosmic disharmony. Importantly, no unitary or unifying metaphysical principle dictates that it could operate otherwise.

Divine Olympus witnesses a similar amount of strife and joy as that of human communities because this divine realm contains a plurality of beings and interests that set an example for, and often facilitate, human conflicts. The gods' individual interests can manifest in destructive ways on earth and influence important human events—for example, the Achaean–Trojan conflict in the *Iliad* and Odysseus's torturous homecoming in the *Odyssey*. While the Olympian community reflects human communities in various ways, a significant distinction revolves around the category of temporality and the concepts of mortality (*thanatos, broteios*) and immortality (*athanatos, ambrotos*). The conceptual distinction between mortality and immortality plays a dominant role in the humanism of Homeric rule because human rulers, in grappling with mortality, find that one way to overcome their finitude is through distinction, especially by achieving *aphthiton kleos*, "imperishable glory." At a meta-level, the Homeric epics themselves are an essential vessel for this aim because they conserve an oral memory and type of immortalizing glory that can be achieved through the medium of song.

The Greek concept of fate (*aisa*) or the Fates (*moirai*) also plays an important role in understanding both cosmic pluralism and divine/human ontology. In particular, there are three distinct aspects or dimensions of fate, as the *Odyssey* refers to fate in the plural as goddesses. The first goddess is Klōthō (pl., Klōthes), "the Spinner," who spins the threads of one's life. Klōthō, in particular, evokes the constructive, ongoing image of weaving the present as it spins from the past and into the future. Odysseus is a good example of a ruler whose fate is constantly being spun so as to result in various twists and turns, which also highlights a general point about human ontology: human *being* is something spun with the seemingly uncontrollable, interconnected threads of the past, present, and future. In contrast, Lachesis is the "allotter" or disposer of lots, indicating how an essential aspect of one's fate is allotted to oneself and thus lies outside one's control. Mortals are the objects of fate just as much, and perhaps even more, than its subject. Lachesis elucidates the idea that human identity is not something that can be constructed *ex novo*, from the "ground up" as it were. Thus, Plato later elaborates on how Lachesis had charge of the past, in contrast to Klōthō's command over the present (*Republic* 617c). The third aspect of fate is Atropos, "unchangeable, inflexible, not to be turned." Atropos indicates that which cannot be changed, especially as it concerns the futural aspect of human being, including a mortal's inevitable death. One's death, and mortality more generally, is something that can be absolutely known in advance and is therefore "unchangeable."

Taken together, these aspects of fate (*moira*) help clarify various reasons for tensions in Homeric cosmology, divine–human relations, and internal relations within the self. Human existence is dogged by the lack of absolute control and mortality, thus exposing a degree of fragility that ruling as distinction and imperishable glory aim to ameliorate. Within this archaic Greek conceptual framework, distinction is one of the most reasonable ways to address some of the most predictable *and* unpredictable aspects of the human condition.

The Micro-Metaphysics of Immediate Experience and Individualist Ontology

While Homeric metaphysics and ontology operate within a cosmological "meta-structure" comprising a plurality of gods and fate, at the individual level Homer also shows mortals being pushed around or drawn forward to decisive, meaningful action by a complex array of both internal impulses and external forces. That is to say, an essential part of Homeric reality is understood as given over to humans in immediate (personal and interpersonal) lived experience, especially as experience unfolds in physical and visceral ways. Reality is not something that is merely abstract and distant but also has a vivid immediacy for Homeric characters. This immediate reality is literally experienced as something unmediated, confronted directly in all its brutality, beauty, and bewildering complexity.[4] Because mortal human beings, and even gods to some extent, are not in a position to alter some of the deeper structures of reality discussed in the previous section, this micro-reality of immediate experience is of tremendous importance to Homeric thought.

Human rulers do not participate in constructing the basic structure of the cosmos and reality—Zeus may be the only example of a ruler that can achieve this sort of thing—although they can adopt a more or less courageous stance toward it. This courage sometimes pays off for a ruler by allowing him to supplement this reality through achieving undying glory and a reputation that would last long after his death. As Gregory Nagy explains, Achilles's unfailing glory "refers to a poetic 'glory' that is 'imperishable' or even 'unfailing' in the sense that its vitality, which is imagined as something that flows, will never stop flowing" (2013, 104). This poetic and "acoustic" aspect of reality is essential because poetry and song serve as memory (*mnēmosunē*) in the sense of "poetic recall."[5] Lyric poetry thus furnishes long-lasting, acoustic memorials that prevent both divine and human achievements from being forgotten. In fact, memory is so significant that the Greek term *alētheia*, which literally means, "not forgetting," can also be translated as "truth." If something is forgotten, then it is as if it never happened, and poetry complements the experiential aspect of Homeric reality as something directly reported—that which is seen, heard, and reported by the Muses (and perhaps other gods) to human poets. In this sense, epics such as the *Iliad* and *Odyssey* are understood not only as credible reports about the past, but even more important, they capture specific parts of the past that are worthy of remembrance, such as the anger of Achilles and the dramatic homecoming (*nostos*) of Odysseus.

Consequently, Homer does not shy from depicting the brutality of battle and captures some of the most subtle bodily details and gestures of its combatants. For example, he speaks at length about the sights and sounds of razor-sharp spears entering and exiting specific parts of the human body, such as the skull, shoulder, or ribs, or slicing through jaws and severing tongues. As Richmond Lattimore (1961) eloquently translates in Book 5 of the *Iliad* (one of many such passages):

> But Menelaos the spear-famed, son of Atreus, stabbed him, as he fled away before him, in the back with a spear thrust between the shoulders and driven through to the chest beyond it. . . . Now the son of Phyleus, the spear-famed, closing upon him [Meges] struck him with the sharp spear behind the head at the tendon, and straight on through the teeth

> and under the tongue cut the bronze blade, and he dropped in the dust
> gripping in his teeth the cold bronze. (*Il.* 5.55–57, 72–75)

Accounts of battle and human death also exhibit the intensely agonistic nature of the Homeric cosmos. A harmonious metaphysics is largely foreign to Homeric political thought. Homer does not offer the solace of something like a Platonic form of the Good, or the possibility of climbing from a dark cave of shadows into a shimmering, peaceful light of the Forms (*eidē*), as later depicted in Plato's *Republic*. Consequently, Homer does not draw a definitive line between false or less real "appearance" and a reality lying *behind* such appearances. Even if one views the gods as superior beings, one should also note that these gods are passionate, deliberative, and violent just like human beings. Olympus is no less real than the killing fields of Troy. In fact, one often gets the sense in reading Homer that what is most real and meaningful is what is given directly over to various beings and experienced in the myriad desires and impulses that pervade both human and divine relations. Reality is personal and forceful.

In outlining a Homeric metaphysics, one must not only emphasize the centrality of lived, immediate experience but also what could be interpreted as a pluralistic "micro-politics" at the individual level of the self. Homer appreciates how personal desires, impulses, and pursuits may cohere or conflict both internally and externally to the desires and pursuits of others. One important ontological idea that underlies both personal and interpersonal conflict concerns a particular belief about individuality—what I will call *self-possessed individuality*. According to this idea, a given human being or god is understood to possess a self-contained, somewhat unified, yet morally neutral personhood that stands prior to and is more fundamental than its connections with anything outside itself.[6] This personhood possesses ontological boundaries that fundamentally demarcate and separate individuals at the most basic ontological and cosmological level from other entities such as plants and animals. Hence, there is no sustained discussion or explanation in Homer of a fundamental interconnectedness between animal, plant, and human interests or well-being. Human beings are connected to the gods, but the nature of this connection is more tenuous and antagonistic than the connections we will observe in the Indian case. Specific terms that help map out the internal geography of this complex, demarcated personhood include: *kradiē* or *kradia* (heart); *noos* (mind, heart); *phrēn* (midriff or area containing the heart and lungs; heart, lungs, and mind); *thumos* (soul, life-breath, life, enlivening vapor; seat of wrath and anger, sometimes anger itself);[7] *psuchē* (soul, spirit that persists after death).[8] Hence, the self is loosely unified but also internally plural in nature. These concepts display the idea that "what" is contained and possessed within the parameters of one's individuality serves as a basis for subsequent relationships with phenomena or beings outside oneself.

Due to such internal plurality a type of micro-politics also operates within the self, as particular parts of oneself—such as the *thumos*—can rule by deciding or urging a particular action. As Agamemnon angrily tells Achilles at the start of the *Iliad*, "By all means, flee if your *thumos* hastens you" (*Il.* 1.173).[9] Contra those who argue against a unitary and conscious conception of a "self" in Homer, Stephen Halliwell rightly asks, "How else, at the most elementary level, can (say) a man's *thumos* be called 'his' at all, unless it is conceived as constitutive of his [essential, non-fragmentary] conscious 'self'"? (1990, 38; see also 40–41). I agree with and seek to elaborate on positions such as Halliwell's by further examining the ontological grounds for this conscious self, including the nature of self-possession as it relates to archaic Greek political thought within a cosmological context. In both the *Iliad* and *Odyssey*, it is no coincidence that the types of beings discussed and of primary importance are gods and men. In fact, both Homer and Hesiod assume that gods and men are those truly distinct and unique types of beings that have self-possessed individuality (see also Griffin 1980, 81–102, 144–204). Accordingly, immortal gods and mortal humans are the primary characters through which both Homer and Hesiod interpret and discuss their surrounding world, and in particular, their ideas about rule.

While gods and human beings are born as individuals within their respective cosmological realms, due to their self-possessed individuality neither gods nor humans identify with a group or category that would provide a more fundamental basis (cosmological, metaphysical, or ontological) for understanding their identity. For example, Zeus clearly shares particular cosmological relations with his wife Hera, namely divinity and immortality, although a central aspect of Zeus's identity is not this divine relation but the fact that he exists as this particular (and quite distinguished) individual. Zeus's immortality is not unique since other Olympians share the same characteristic; rather, what seems to capture the most essential aspects of his identity and appear to be most important to him are particular attributes that he alone can trot out vis-à-vis his fellow Olympians—such as his unique strength and status as ruler on Olympus. My general claim here is that both gods' and human beings' broader cosmological identities, including their connection to other beings that share their cosmological status, are less important and fundamental than their self-possessed individuality. Nonetheless, gods and humans are not identical, since humans are aware of and consciously face their own death (see Griffin 1980). Death's radical individuation thus heightens and reinforces the stakes of self-possessed individuality for human beings. While this account only provides a basic sketch, this belief should become clearer as I examine both Homeric and Hesiodic political thought.

The major conceptual clusters that I outlined at the start of the chapter are connected to this conception of individuality in a variety of ways. Intense rage makes more sense in light of the belief that something important has been harmed or injured, and this "something" must, first, be possessed a priori and have distinct boundaries for it to be understood as unrightfully harmed, and second, stand as a minimally coherent self or subject that has enduring interests, such that the rage is based (first and foremost) on the subject rather than the object of loss. As I have suggested, this "something" that is possessed such that injury and rage have their particular Homeric (and Greek) force is self-possessed individuality. A deep sense of dishonor is partly predicated on this belief about individuality, which is clearly demarcated and fundamental to the way an individual relates to other beings and phenomena.

Homeric rage and anger possess a distinctly personal element, and part of what enhances interpersonal tensions is the internally plural nature of the self. For example, Homeric rulers are often pushed or pulled in different directions because of fluctuating impulses associated with the *thumos* or *noos*. Of course, impulses and decisive action do not always arise from an internal source but are sometimes drawn out of people by an external force such as a god or goddess. As Hubert Dreyfus and Sean Dorrance Kelly argue, such openness to the involvement of gods in human life also requires a significant amount of respect and gratitude, and pluralistic selfhood often overlaps with Homeric polytheism to highlight the multiplicity of roles that might coexist in the same person—Odysseus being a paradigmatic case (see Dreyfus and Kelly 2011, 58–87, 93). And while social roles can reign in fluctuations of the *thumos* or *noos* and play a part in determining an individual's expectations and reason-giving, contra Alasdair MacIntyre (1988, 14–22), I argue that Homeric and Hesiodic notions of individuality cannot merely be reduced to social roles and identities. Self-possessed individuality provides a unique lens for interpreting the world and relating to external phenomena, further supporting an understanding of kingly rule whereby gaining honor and glory are self-sufficient ideals. In turn, the existing honor and glory a ruler possesses as a result of past actions constitutes his reputation. Rage and the pursuit of honor and glory often manifest themselves in agonistic competition and contest, the results of which determine outcomes of honor, glory, and reputation.[10]

In summarizing these points, I want to reiterate that Homeric poetry itself reflects a steely-eyed engagement with human finitude and the challenges that it presents for political life. Epic poetry is a long-lasting vessel for Homer's own glory, as his *epos* or "word" is expressed in verse and continues to live on millennia after its composition. This epic glory helps highlight a more general point about transcending temporal boundaries as "Homer" stretches across time and space, thus throwing into great relief how easily human lives can be forgotten. As Adam Nicolson (2014) explains, glory and fame are found in not dying, and through this poetry Homer lives on. Following from this stance, we observe ideas about the human condition that extend naturally to individual rulers or *basileis* and help encapsulate their desire to transcend the inevitable destruction of their embodied personhood. Temporality is thus a crucial component of Homeric cosmology and metaphysics, and helps to clarify the broader conceptual context for my analysis of ruling as distinction.

Early Challenges to Hierarchical Rule

Having clarified the cosmological and metaphysical context for Homeric political thought, I would now like to focus more pointedly on the concept of rule, especially the underlying dimension of ruling-over in Homeric works and some of the central challenges it faces. While Homeric political thought ultimately provides a staunch, hierarchical conception of kingly rule as distinction, it also displays significant criticisms of this conception that point toward a more leveled conception of ruling-with other *basileis* and non-*basileis* such as Penelope, and ruling-for the interests of a broader community of *laoi* (the common mass). I thus begin this section by laying out what could be considered the more "traditional" aspects of hierarchical rule in Homer, and then examine the difficulties that rulers face in balancing such aspects with anti-hierarchical ideas about the importance of ruling-with others, as well as ruling-in a community and ruling-for interests other than the ruler's own. The Homeric understanding of rule thus exhibits a notable tension between the various dimensions of rule, further exposing a dilemma about the proper meaning of rule that remains unsettled in the *Iliad* and *Odyssey*, and receives greater elaboration in Hesiod.

In the *Iliad*, Agamemnon's kingship exemplifies a rather traditional form of kingly rule during the war in Troy. He commands the Achaean forces, and although other kings are present, he is undoubtedly the superior king, or *pherteros basileus*. Throughout the *Iliad* Agamemnon alone is referred to as the "lord (or ruler) of men [*anax andrōn*]." In the first book, Nestor says to Achilles: "Even if you are mighty and the mother who bore you is a goddess, nevertheless Agamemnon is superior [*pherteros*] since he rules more men" (*Il.* 1.280–81). When Agamemnon stands on the battlefield in front of Troy, Helen identifies him for Priam as "wide ruler (or ruling) Agamemnon, son of Atreus" (*Il.* 3.178)—the only *basileus* in the *Iliad* addressed as "wide ruling" (*euru kreiōn*)—and the breadth of this rule elucidates the scope of his presumable responsibility to those he commands. His "might" not only emanates from the numbers he commands but also from divine sanction, further evoking the cosmological dimension of Zeus's ruling-over. Zeus gave Agamemnon's family its kingly scepter, which serves as a divine anchor for the *basileus*'s ruling power and represents a distinct cosmological dimension of hierarchical kingly rule.[11] Consider, for example, the following statement:

> The *thumos* of Zeus-nurtured kings is great—their honor [*timē*] is from Zeus, and counselor Zeus loves him [i.e., the *basileus*] . . . Let there be one leader [*koiranos*], one king [*basileus*], to whom the child of crooked-counseled Kronos gave both the scepter and protection of rightful customs, so that he may advise them. (*Il.* 2.196–97, 204–6; see also 9.37–39)

This statement shows how *basileus*-rule is inextricably tied to Zeus and his concern for *basileis*, displaying a significant human–nonhuman connection and component of rule in archaic political thought. It also shows how there could only be a single commander (*koiranos* or *archos*), especially during wartime. Agamemnon eagerly reminds Achilles of this fact: "Going to your hut, I myself shall lead away the fair-cheeked Briseis, your own prize, so that you may know well how much better [i.e., in terms of bravery] I am than you" (*Il.* 1.184–87).[12] Therefore, Agamemnon sits at the top of a hierarchical ruling structure in which there are many *basileis*, but only a single overarching *basileus* that may stake a legitimate claim to ruling-over the rest.

The Trojan royal family provides another example of hierarchical kingly rule in the *Iliad*. Priam and Hector's Trojan palace hearkens the ancient Mycenaean palace system, including a sense of overarching responsibility for the king's people and native land. In book 6 the palace is described in the following way:

> But now he [i.e. Hector] arrived at the very fine palace of Priam, which had been furnished with polished corridors. But in it were fifty rooms

> made of polished stone, they being constructed near one another. And within them slept Priam's sons beside their wedded wives. And from the other side facing them from within the courtyard were the twelve rooms of polished stone of his daughters . . . (*Il.* 6.242–46)

The royal family lives in a large, luxurious setting—an image that likely portrays the poets' ideas of Mycenae (see Nilsson 1968; Snodgrass 1980, 27–29). While Priam is the king of Troy, Hector is its primary guardian and a king-by-extension as the eldest son and prince of Troy. With Hector one observes how a king's rule ideally entails a hierarchical responsibility to protect and rule for the well-being of his people. Shortly following the palace's description, Hector explains: "For now my *thumos* hastens me so that I may help the Trojans, for they miss me greatly when I am away" (*Il.* 6.361–62). Andromache, Hector's wife, provides the most powerful description of Hector as the city's guardian. After she loses her husband she acknowledges how "this city will be sacked from top to bottom. For indeed, you, its guardian, are lost, you who protected it" (*Il.* 24.728–30), as Hector's death implies the inevitable destruction of Troy. This represents a degree of hierarchical dependency (or at least an assumption thereof) upon a caring king and/or prince to provide protection from enemies and invaders. A strong sense of dependence on hierarchical kingly rule thus pervades the Trojan side, an idea that Nicolson captures nicely in explaining how Homer depicts Priam as the embodiment of Troy's virtues, including the city's walls and gates, and how "the city is goodness and connection, plain is horror and terror . . . city is the realm of the Trojan families, their women and children, while the plain belongs to Achilles alone" (Nicolson 2014, 202–5).[13]

Nevertheless, Zeus provides the best example of hierarchical kingly rule in the Homeric epics because he exhibits two distinct types of ruling-over. First, Zeus rules over the gods and controls various aspects of their decision-making, especially when a human battle occurs. Thetis, for example, must visit Zeus's "bronze-floored home" to gain his consent in attempting to help her son Achilles (*Il.* 1.426; see also *Il.* 1.503–10).[14] Even his brother, Poseidon, eventually backs down after the latter attempts to assert his power.[15] Zeus frequently threatens his own wife, Hera, reminding her of his superiority (*Il.* 1.517–27, 560–67), and due to this superiority all the gods fear his power and retribution. As Hera explains to the other gods: "Therefore, you must bear whatever evil he sends you—each of you" (*Il.* 15.109 [104–12]). During the Trojan War, Zeus makes the decision to turn the tide of battle and tells all the gods how to behave (*Il.* 8.381–431), which nicely captures the nature of his rule over the Olympian gods. The Olympians are not the only divine beings that fall under his rule, as he also rules divine beings that dwell on earth. In the *Odyssey*, for example, Zeus sends Hermes to give Calypso an order to release Odysseus: "Zeus commanded me to come here, though I did not wish to come; but certainly there is no way for another god to transgress or baffle the mind of aegis-bearing Zeus. . . . Now Zeus commanded that you send him off most quickly" (*Od.* 5.99–104, 112). Therefore, in both the *Iliad* and *Odyssey*, Zeus rules at the top of a divine hierarchy and all gods and divine beings know they must heed his commands.

While one observes a strong form of hierarchical rule in Zeus's rule over other gods, his rule over human beings is even more prominent. Zeus's power over human events is evident in the *Odyssey* whenever Odysseus appeals to him for help. For example, Odysseus acknowledges Zeus's power to decide whether he will have the opportunity to carry out his revenge against Penelope's suitors, repeating the phrase, "in the hope that Zeus ever fulfills our deeds of revenge" (*Il.* 17.51, 17.60).[16] Even though he is furious with the suitors' behavior, Odysseus's appeals show how he does not control the situation nor can he make a major move without Zeus granting it. Zeus also treats Agamemnon rather mercilessly, as the deceased king laments in Hades (*Od.* 11.435–39). Regardless of such treatment, throughout the *Iliad* and *Odyssey* phrases such as "kings' honor [*timē*] comes from Zeus" (*Il.* 2.196–97) and "Zeus rules over human wars" (*Il.* 19.223–25) frequently arise.[17]

As Menelaus explains, even Zeus's palace and possessions indicate how he is the mightiest ruler and role-model for earthly kings: "Dear boys, to be sure, no mortal man could rival Zeus; for his palace and wealth are immortal" (*Od.* 4.78–79). Such aspects of Zeus's rule expose agonistic tensions in the connectedness between human beings and gods. While rulers frequently seek gods' assistance (especially Zeus's), at key junctures the immortals show no innate or overriding concern for human well-being. As Hera suggests to Athena in book 8, they must let humans die rather indiscriminately, as Zeus so chooses (*Il.* 8.427–31). Ruling-for the interests and well-being of mortals does not appear to be of the utmost importance, and from this idea one might draw a further point about an example this sets for human rulers such as Agamemnon. Namely, the structure of archaic cosmology is such that those who possess greater power and rule over others may justifiably ignore the interests of those over whom they rule.

Zeus's cosmic rule runs even deeper than moment-to-moment decisions regarding who and who not to assist. According to multiple Homeric accounts, Zeus literally "makes" kings what they will be, deciding their fate(s) and attributes when they are born. In the *Odyssey*, Menelaus mentions to Telemachus how "easily recognizable the descent of a man to whom Zeus may spin good fortune in both marriage and birth" (*Od.* 4.207–8).[18] In this regard, Zeus possesses two jars from which he mixes gifts for men before they are born (*Il.* 24.527–33). In addition to making kings and deciding their fate, Zeus is the highest sacrificial outlet for kings. His divine rule is evident in the fact that kings frequently provide him with sacrifices and gifts, hoping to win his favor in a cosmic *quid pro quo* (*Od.* 4.472–74). Relatedly, Zeus is the defender of suppliants because he protects those who defend, and punishes those who violate, the ethic of hospitality (e.g., see *Od.* 7.163–66, 7.181, 9.268–71, 14.57–61). This power and divine rule facilitate hospitality because without individuals fearing his retribution and power to punish transgressions, hosts have less incentive to treat their guests (*xenoi*) with good hospitality. Zeus's absolute hierarchical rule over human beings is thus a precondition for hospitality as it exists in the *Odyssey*.

The Dilemma: Anti-Hierarchical Beliefs and the Disconnectedness of Rule

Throughout the epics one also observes significant critiques of hierarchical kingly rule, and while these critiques expose the development of more egalitarian ruling beliefs and a broadening sense of political self-worth, anti-hierarchical ideas are also accompanied by a disconnect and tension between individual human beings and general disregard for broader communal well-being. Although Homeric political thought predominantly displays a model of kingly rule as distinction, it is important to note relevant criticisms of this understanding as they appear in Homeric works. While kings have individual distinction as their utmost aim in ruling-over and ruling-with one another, they are also supposed to make decisions that will benefit a broader community. The unremitting pursuit of honor, glory, and reputation tend to impede just decision-making because these goals do not generally promote or demonstrate a deep concern for the interests of a broader community, whether human or nonhuman. In other words, the connectedness of rule is deeply attenuated by the force of, and underlying motives for, distinction.

Here one must keep in mind that Homeric works do not express a clearly defined conception of a "common good" and effective social structures to preserve such a good, although rulers and non-rulers alike note problems associated with distinction. While ruling as distinction pervades these works, each work also expresses the idea that rule should benefit more than a single ruler or small group of aristocratic rulers. The dilemma persists, however, because the idea of ruling-for others confronts a stronger impulse to rule with an eye toward one's own interests and the promise of immortality, which is quite reasonable within the broader agonistic context of archaic Greek cosmology. Rulers are deeply attuned to this cosmic context, and self-possessed individuality underpins this individualistic self-interest while simultaneously hindering any strong conception of interconnectedness, especially between the human and nonhuman. This tension between individual distinction and ambition, on the one hand, and communal obligation and well-being, on the other, is powerfully captured in a normative theme that Johannes Haubold (2000) examines at length—namely, the relationship between a ruler as "shepherd (*poimēn*) of the people (*laoi*)." While he explains multiple ways the Homeric narrator depicts *basileis* such as Agamemnon, Achilles, and Hector as necessary leaders responsible for the *laoi*'s well-being, Haubold also shows how these leaders are predominantly ineffective at fulfilling the task: "Instead of saving his people and fulfilling his task, the leader of early Greek epic traditionally destroys them" (2000, 46).

Numerous anti-hierarchical ruling claims pervade the Homeric epics, as one observes early in the *Iliad* when Agamemnon exhibits a combative relationship with other kings, especially Achilles. During the Trojan War a competitive, aristocratic form of hierarchical *basileus*-rule predominates among the Achaean forces. While Agamemnon's rule over other *basileis* is ultimately decisive, he is frequently challenged based on a belief in the relative equality between aristocratic kings (see also Morris 2000, 237; Raaflaub and Wallace 2007, 31). In the *Iliad*'s first book, Achilles makes the first and perhaps most significant criticism:

> However, we still accompanied you, great shameless one, so that you may be satisfied, to win honor for you and Menelaus from the Trojans, you dogface. You neither consider these things nor care about them . . . I, being dishonored here, do not intend to accumulate cattle and gold for you. (*Il.* 1.158–60, 170–71)

While Balot (2006, 18) has argued that this challenge represents an early argument for distributive justice, and distribution is indeed an issue in this scene, any systematic normative conception of justice is largely absent. The term *dikē* is not mentioned in book 1 of the *Iliad*, and first appears in book 16 (see 16. 388).[19] Rather, Achilles is infuriated with Agamemnon and chastises him in front of the other kings based primarily upon his sense of wounded honor and Agamemnon's arrogant pride (*hubris*). He critically questions Agamemnon's kingly rule, telling Agamemnon that he lacks courage and is a "king who devours his people [*dēmoboros*]" (*Il.* 1.231). While this verbal attack is relentless and Achilles only acquiesces because Zeus commands it, Odysseus also takes a stab at Agamemnon: "Son of Atreus, what sort of word is it that flees the barrier of your teeth? Ruinous one, if only you gave orders to another wretched army, and did not rule over us" (*Il.* 14.83–85). The concept of justice only seems to make a notable appearance as a normative model for rule within the context of the *Odyssey*, where we find a handful of references to Odysseus as a just ruler (*Od.* 2.230–40, 4.686–96, 5.7–12).

Although hierarchical *basileus*-rule remains the dominant paradigm in the *Iliad*, the frequent critiques of Agamemnon display an anti-hierarchical, counter-development in Greek rule and Agamemnon occasionally changes his mind because of such critiques. In this instance, after Odysseus finishes his tirade, Agamemnon admits: "O Odysseus, you have certainly touched me somewhere in my *thumos* with this harsh rebuke. . . . Now, if there shall be one who might relate a better plan than this, whether young or old (let him speak up); this shall be to my liking" (*Il.* 14.104–5, 107–8). This example exhibits a somewhat pliant, leveled relationship between *basileis* and the idea that rulers should view themselves as ruling-*with* one another, at least on occasion. One reason for such pliancy may relate to an essential connection between achieving distinction and ruling-with others. Namely, ruling-with indicates recognizing a connection that Davis Acampora identifies between agonism, gratitude, and shared responsibility: "One can claim responsibility on the basis of achievement, but this includes mindfulness that such achievements are possible . . . only because of others, only by virtue of dependence and *shared* responsibility. Each victor's achievement also rests on his ability to shelter the economy that makes his victory possible" (2013, 32). As she further argues, this entails an obligation to express gratitude to those who make one's achievements and hierarchical distinction over others possible in the first place. Thus, ruling-with and ruling-for a larger community and agon are preconditions for distinction, as ruling-for exhibits a sign of gratitude that helps stabilize and sustain an environment in which rulers can attain honor and glory.

Furthermore, as agonistic individuals whose strong sense of individualism critically extends to ruling practices, these kings do not assume that only one among them can make the best decision in every instance. This example also provides an alternative to hierarchically determined judgments imposed from above and blindly accepted from below insofar as it exhibits a leveled, participatory procedure wherein the best idea or most applauded one should hold sway. As Achilles likewise suggests when he criticizes Agamemnon, unrestrained hierarchical rule can be an impediment to effective decision-making. Therefore, even a common soldier such as Thersites criticizes Agamemnon: "Son of Atreus, with what, now, do you find fault or need? Your quarters are full of gold, and within them are many choice women. . . . We shall indeed return home with our ships, and leave him alone here in Troy to brood over his prizes" (*Il.* 2.225–27, 236–37). Both *basileis* and "the mass" (*laoi*) thus express critical, agonistic-individualist beliefs when questioning unmitigated hierarchical rule. In fact, Thersites's boasts display something of a "bottom-up" critique of ruling-over, including the idea that *basileis* should rule with an eye toward the *laoi*'s interests and well-being, and not forget they rule within a larger community of Achaeans. Put simply, the *laoi* play an important role in the war effort and have interests that should not be completely dismissed if their side is to be victorious.

As others have argued, particular passages in the *Iliad* exhibit the mass's central role in battle, which may be a reflection of common citizens' increasing importance in Greek society as a whole (e.g., see Raaflaub 1997; 2004, 35; Raaflaub and Wallace 2007; van Wees 1997). These passages are historically significant because they help show how the *laoi*'s enhanced role in war might indicate and lend support to their voices as equal citizens in early city-states. Common citizens' growing influence within the early *polis* gradually undermined, either directly or indirectly, the belief that hierarchical kingly rule was the only or proper ruling structure. As Raaflaub and Wallace contend, "the mass fighting in Homer reflects only the beginning of a development . . . which later produced the hoplite phalanx," and this development indicated a "transition, connected with the rise of the *polis*" (2007, 27). Heroes and kings dominate most of the dialogue and action in the *Iliad*, so it is difficult to gather lengthy, detailed accounts of the mass acting bravely and earning honor, let alone evidence for an early hoplite phalanx. Nevertheless, statements are scattered throughout the *Iliad* regarding the mass's role in winning battles. Raaflaub and Wallace highlight a passage in book 17: "Far fewer of the Argives went down, remembering always to fight in tight formation, friend defending friend from headlong slaughter" (*Il.* 17.364–65; Raaflaub and Wallace 2007, 27). This passage offers some of the best available textual evidence for the historical emergence and importance of close-knit fighting formations. Evidence can also be found in book 4, where Nestor instructs his troops: "Let no one, having been convinced as to his horsemanship or manliness, be eager to fight alone against the Trojans out in front of the other soldiers" (*Il.* 4.303–4, 307). This statement and Nestor's subsequent advice indicate that tight fighting formations were successful in past battles and did not require combatants to perform individualized heroic acts. Moreover, if tight fighting formations were successful and often led to victory, then both commanders and common soldiers would have good reasons to stay in formation—namely, they would share in the glory of winning the battle as well as the spoils that come from victory.

Although the passage must be carefully unpacked, Thersites's outburst provides further evidence for the mass's increasing social and political importance, as well as an independent mass/citizen mentality (see also Raaflaub 1997; Raaflaub and Wallace 2007, 26–46).[20] When Thersites criticizes Agamemnon, Odysseus rebukes Thersites and thrashes him with a scepter in front of his fellow men. This treatment suggests that the threat of poor morale among the mass was a serious one. While this example indicates the importance of the mass for fighting and winning battles, it also exposes some important beliefs on the part of the mass. This group's obedience and advice actually mattered to *basileis*, even if individual honor was each king's utmost concern. In one respect, Thersites's voice helps highlight an important point about rule that I made in the Introduction: the idealization of ruling-with among *basileis* (or any existing body of rulers) can lead to over-privileging the horizontal dimension of rule among (relative) equals by simultaneously underemphasizing, and thus obscuring, how ruling-with rests upon ruling-over others. Thersites's comments help expose this relationship and a lack of blind obedience, further displaying the reality that *basileis* must rely on rhetorical appeals precisely because the *laoi* would not automatically fall into line. At minimum, *basileis* such as Agamemnon had reasons to pay attention to the sentiments of the mass. This group believed it had some degree of independence and equal access to a sense of self-worth, and must consequently be convinced that its side would win the battle so that each individual would share its spoils.

If the *laoi* must be convinced, then disagreement is possible, and this indicates how common troops are able and willing to make up their own minds. The "Thersites episode" displays a sense of independence and perhaps even recognition on the mass's behalf that *basileis* need the *laoi* more than the *laoi*—as fighters, farmers, and heads of households—need the *basileis*. These common folk understand that they are partly fighting for their king's wealth and honor, and therefore they must be convinced to remain in Troy. Again, they can be convinced to stay if they think they will gain something from staying, and as Raaflaub (1997, 635–36) argues, these independent-minded *laoi* can earn their own honor (*timē*), glory (*kleos*), and display excellence (*aretē*). Leveling and a strong sense of demarcated individuality are thus clearly in effect. David Elmer (2013) provides an additional argument that supports this line of analysis. While Thersites resists, he must be silenced in order for genuine, open debate to take place. Rulers need the assembly and a silencing of chaotic (or chaos-inducing) speech because it is a precondition for legitimate discussion and the possibility of generating the mass's consent. Elmer thus argues: "Far from representing it as the suppression of a dissident voice, the poem constructs this exclusion as the application of a force that is necessary in order for a variety of voices (including, in principle, dissident ones) to be heard" (97). As Elmer adds, silencing Thersites allows Odysseus to address not only Agamemnon but all the Achaeans assembled (98). This clarifies how ruling-for and ruling-in a broader community may necessarily presume a degree of individual self-esteem on the part of common citizens and, in turn, their consent as a precondition for a ruler's distinction.

Interestingly, Odysseus's own kingly rule does not go unchallenged while he is away at war. In the *Odyssey*, Penelope's suitors devour Odysseus's wealth while he is absent, showing very little respect for hierarchical *basileus*-rule and its hereditary aspects. They also challenge Telemachus's potential claim to Ithaca's highest throne, as one of them states: "For I do not think that we will cease from our grievous courting, since there is no one we fear, especially not wordy Telemachus . . . again, his wealth will be harshly devoured, and there will never be any reparations, until the queen stops wasting the Achaeans' [our] time with respect to marriage" (*Od.* 2.199–200, 203–5).[21] Not only do the suitors openly mock and threaten Telemachus but they also disregard the prophecies foretelling Odysseus's return: "Old man [Halitherses], come now, go home and prophesy for your own children, lest they perhaps suffer some evil hereafter. I am much better than you at reading these prophecies. . . . But Odysseus perished in some far off place—if only you had perished with him" (*Od.* 2.178–80, 182–84). The suitors' threats are quite critical, as they respect neither the hereditary structure of *basileus*-rule already existing in Ithaca nor the gods' omens predicting their own demise.

This example not only shows how the suitors challenge established, hierarchical *basileus*-rule but also exhibits an apparent cosmological disconnect and waning fear of the gods. In fact, Eurymachus, himself a *basileus*, claims he can read omens better than the bird-interpreter Halitherses who, according to Homer, "in his age surpassed all others in his knowledge of bird signs and declaring fateful omens" (*Od.* 2.158–59). Eurymachus chastises the talented Halitherses and ignores the portent that signals Eurymachus's impending doom. These examples exhibit how the suitors view themselves first and foremost as individuals seeking honor and reputation based upon the possibility of gaining Odysseus's throne. Here a strong sense of individuality is assumed in critiquing hierarchical *basileus*-rule and its divine support system, for if a kingly suitor does not prefer a superior interpreter's reading of a particular omen, he challenges the reading and assumes he can better interpret the omen himself.[22] Odysseus's swineherd Eumaeus also depicts the suitors' lack of respect for the gods, including Zeus, before whom they show no apparent, reverential awe (*Od.* 14.81–83).

In the figure of Penelope and the art of weaving, the *Odyssey* displays yet another important example of a non-*basileus* who exposes how ruling-with other *basileis* relies on those excluded from this privileged group. As I mentioned in the Introduction, the Greeks understand poetry as a type of "weaving" that possesses political significance and can been understood as a method of statecraft (see also Silvermintz 2004). Through the art of weaving Penelope participates in ruling-over others in Odysseus's absence because the act of weaving and unweaving Laertes's burial shroud serves as a political act that denies them the throne and prevents succession. Consequently, she is able to maintain Odysseus's rule in Ithaca "by proxy," especially since Laertes had abdicated long ago and Telemachus is flagrantly dismissed by the suitors as a challenge to their potential ascension. Penelope's actions thus show how Odysseus's rule relies upon someone other than a male *basileus*, and we can explain the significance of this point by drawing attention to the connectedness of rule.[23]

This inherent connectedness includes a ruler's household and the realm of necessity—a realm that provides the often obscured foundation upon which ruling-over depends—and Penelope must rule over the suitors within this sphere so that Odysseus can retain his role as ruler once he returns to Ithaca. The parallel that I have drawn from the *Iliad* in the figure of Thersites shows how ruling as distinction requires a web of relations involving both commoners and women—precisely those who are supposed to be excluded from the political space and lack the capacity to rule. To highlight the particular importance of gender relations in this case, Odysseus's rule and ability to distinguish himself is also caught between, and made possible by, a set of both immortal and mortal female weavers: Fate(s) and Athena, on the one hand, and Penelope, on the other. In short, these female figures weave central aspects of Odysseus's fate. Such relations expose the significant role that gender plays in the Homeric conception of rule, which can be easily overlooked if one only focuses solely on a subset of male *basileis* or *anaktes*.

From a broader cosmological perspective, the process of distinction includes female figures such as Hera, Athena, and Fate, as observed in various challenges to hierarchical kingly rule on Olympus. While Zeus may appear to rule indiscriminately over the other gods, there are two major limitations to his kingly rule. First, other gods' opinions and interests often present a challenge to Zeus's will, forcing him to compromise or alter his original intentions. As Hera tells Zeus: "Do so [i.e., whatever he prefers to do]—but none among all the other gods will praise you" (*Il.* 4.29; see also *Il.* 16.443, 22.181). In book 4 of the *Iliad*, Zeus replies to Hera's threat, stating, "Fine, do as you wish" (*Il.* 4.37), and proceeds to bargain with her over future cities he might destroy. He also compromises with Athena when she levels the same threat later in the *Iliad* (*Il.* 22.183–85). Zeus thus values other gods' opinions and praise, which provides a perfect example of an honor-seeking ruler. On occasion, this search for honor and respect among the other gods limits or challenges Zeus's potentially indiscriminate hierarchical rule. Elmer's study of consent in Homeric political thought similarly defends the significance of *epainos* (praise, approval) and communal compliance for political decision-making. As Elmer (2013, 4, 146–73) explains, without the support of his fellow Olympians as a whole—indicated through the verb "*epainein*," collective praise and approval—no truly authoritative decision or policy of consequence to the community can be sustained.[24] Ruling-for the purpose of individual distinction thus requires ruling-with others who might approve or disapprove of particular, authoritative decisions for the broader community.

The second major limitation to Zeus's kingly rule is fate (*moira, aisa*), or the Fates (*moirai*). In the *Iliad* and *Odyssey*, it is difficult to clearly establish whether causation and cosmic decision-making ultimately fall upon Zeus or Fate, as Zeus seemingly shares this power with Fate. In the *Iliad*, Priam identifies Fate as the ultimate decision-maker for his son, Hector: "Thus powerful Fate (Moira) spun [Hector's destiny] for him with her thread when he was born" (*Il.* 24.209–10). This quote suggests that the Fates, including Klōthō, decide the course of each person's life.[25] This belief also appears in the *Odyssey* when King Alcinous states: "He will then suffer whatever Fate (Aisa) and the grievous Spinners [*klōthes*] spun for him with their thread when he was born" (*Od.* 7.196–98; see also 16.61–64). Relatedly, on the human plane the term *linon* (one's "thread of fate") can be interpreted as a particular lifeline. A ruler's past, present, and future—that is, his path toward death—could then be conceived in a linear fashion, leading down a singular path. As mentioned earlier, one of the Fates, *Atropos*, means, "not to be turned, unchangeable," which indicates a path or pathway with no fundamental ontological turns, and thus a life course and particular events that are prefigured. However, unseen or unpredictable events may also emerge while people are traversing their path, and this may provide space for a certain degree of divine or human agency.

While Fate's cosmic role raises questions about the extent of human rulers' agency, Fate's existence also raises important questions regarding Zeus's precise role in human life and events. Does Zeus play a role in deciding fate as well? If Zeus wanted, could he challenge or change what Fate had already spun? As far as the Homeric epics are concerned, there do not seem to be any consistent, final answers to these questions. One clue is found in book 22 of the *Iliad*, where Zeus "held out his golden scales, and placed upon them the two fates of death, which lays men low: one for Achilles, and one for horse-taming Hector . . ." (209–11; see also *Il.* 8.69). It seems that Fate may simply dictate to each person his or her certainty for death, denoted by the term *kēr*, both the goddess of death and abstract concept of doom (*Od.* 8.579–80). The details as to when, where, and how one dies could then be decided by a combination of human and divine agency, following the basic lifeline spun by Fate. In this passage (*Il.* 22.209–11), Zeus places the fates (i.e. the certain death) of two men on his golden scales to make a decision, yet this example also highlights the ambiguous relationship between Zeus and Fate.

Indeed, while Zeus makes the decision to choose to place the two fates on his scales, the scales—perhaps another manifestation of Fate and challenge to the principle of divine and human agency—make the final decision. This might indicate how Fate re-enters the decision-making process in the end. Complicating things further, Zeus possesses two jars from which he distributes the "good" and "bad" for each individual. Whether this distribution conflicts with, precedes, or follows Fate's decisions remains somewhat unclear. Nonetheless, Zeus clearly does not call all the shots. Something is left to this collective agent and principle, Fate/fate, which appears to indicate the limit of human agency as well as Zeus's cosmic rule: both human rulers and Zeus must rule within a broader, pluralistic environment of overlapping nonhuman forces and interests.

Returning to my earlier discussion of fate as a concept that invokes the broader category of temporality, the Greek conception of Fate intimates a deep recognition of the lack of *complete* control in efforts at distinction. In Zeus's case, this is because he does not possess absolute, indiscriminate control over the other Olympians, as we see in cases where communal deliberation and consent are necessary for making ruling decisions that affect a broader community of beings. In the case of human rulers, temporality and death cannot be jettisoned, and thus distinction by means of honor, glory, and reputation are hard-won achievements due to the fragile nature of human existence and their vulnerability to forces outside their control. In sum, while traditional-hierarchical ruling ideas pervade Homeric thought, we can also identify important limitations to ruling-over by a single *basileus* and themes of anti-hierarchical leveling that elucidate aspects of ruling-with, ruling-for, and ruling-in a broader community.

Kingly Distinction: The Role of Rage, Competition, and Glory

Leveling and agonistic individualism, however, are only part of the larger picture of Homeric rule. The idea that rulers should distinguish themselves from others in pursuit of honor, glory, and reputation exhibits the pinnacle of the Homeric meaning of rule. To advance this interpretation and argument, this section examines three basic clusters of associated concepts that best display and help explicate the meaning of ruling as distinction: first, rage or anger (e.g., *mēnis, menos, cholos*); second, contest and competition; third, honor (*timē*), glory or fame (e.g., *kleos, kudos*), and reputation. Examining these concepts brings to light a significant degree of disconnectedness on the individual level and shows how strong individualist beliefs solidify the conceptual groundwork for the leveling of rule in the human community. Focusing my analysis on the most important rulers in the Homeric epics allows me to pinpoint concrete examples of the Greek conception of rule that help further elucidate the overarching context for its meaning in archaic thought. Concluding with an examination of Homeric hospitality, I argue that examples drawn from the *Odyssey* show how rulers uphold this ethic during peacetime as another means of enhancing their distinction and honor. At a thematic level, one could also parse the two epics as offering alternative contexts for kingly distinction: the *Iliad* captures a land-based context that is solid and familiar, pitting a mobile and marauding camp (Achaeans) against a stationary, civilized camp (Trojans), while the *Odyssey* depicts a seafaring context full of unpredictability and unfamiliar creatures in the twisting journey of its central hero, Odysseus. As Nagy (2013, 12, 14–15) suggests, these contexts reflect the character of their main heroic figures—Achilles, who is stern, "monolithic and fiercely uncompromising," and Odysseus, the versatile hero whose "fluid" and flexible nature often reflects the sea upon which he sails.

The Powerful and Cunning Zeus: Divine Model for Distinction and Ruling-Over Others

As one might expect of the paradigmatic ruler, Zeus exhibits each of the characteristics associated with distinction. First, he frequently exhibits anger and an attendant belief in self-possessed individuality. He often becomes angry when dealing with his wife Hera, especially when decision-making and honor are at stake based upon whose son is victorious in war (see *Il.* 4.30–49).[26] Second, Zeus often finds himself in competition with other gods for decision-making prowess, especially during the Trojan War (e.g., *Il.* 1.565–67).[27] In fact, he actually enjoys conflict and competition among the gods: "And Zeus heard the chaos, throned on Olympus heights, and laughed deep in his own great heart, delighted to see the gods engage in all-out conflict" (*Il.* 21.388–90). He consistently displays this antagonistic streak as he enjoys seeing contestation between the gods as well as between human beings. In book 4 of the *Iliad*, he orders that the truce between the Achaeans and Trojans be broken, thus ending the temporary peace and any potentially peaceful outcome between the two sides (see *Il.* 4.70–72).[28] Zeus even uses human beings as pawns to compete against fellow gods such as his brother, Poseidon.[29] Competition for glory and honor among the gods reaches its climax in the *Iliad* in book 20, where all the gods choose a side—Achaean or Trojan—and fight on its behalf. Homer explains how Zeus commands the gods: "Now all you other gods, so that you arrive among the Trojans and Achaeans, supporting both sides, the way in which the mind of each of you determines" (*Il.* 20.23–25; see also 20.32, 55–57). Exhibiting Olympic plurality and disagreement, competition surrounds Zeus and he is frequently willing to incite it. He does so partly because he is the most powerful figure and receives the honor that results from winning each time a competition ensues.

This interpretive point raises an important question about the relationship between glory-seeking and honor-seeking. That is, one might contend that glory is something that mortals desire precisely because they die and want their name to live on, while the immortal gods would presumably not need their name to live on per honor and glory because they never perish. This objection raises a very important point of clarification regarding the nature of Zeus's rule, because Zeus also has a reputation to uphold when he acts and makes decisions. While he is immortal, there is still a futural mode connected to Zeus's identity and reputation insofar as human beings and communities pass away over time, and things can thus be forgotten. The gods cannot rest on their laurels and must remain active as well because human forgetfulness can gradually sap their reputations over long periods of time. Again, the concepts of mortality and forgetfulness are crucial to Homeric political thought. Human finitude means that seeking and earning glory must run both ways, as this finitude puts both gods and human beings in the precarious situation of having to distinguish themselves in an ongoing fashion in order to be remembered. Moreover, as a member of the community of immortal gods, Zeus faces a similar problem to the one that human *basileis* confront. Zeus's status as supreme ruler is always at stake and being challenged from a variety of directions, so he needs to bolster his reputation to retain his distinction as the supreme ruler among the gods. This reputation thus plays a similar role for Zeus that glory and fame play for human rulers: the issue of remembrance and fragility of a ruler's reputation require Zeus to distinguish himself in a manner that parallels human rulers' efforts to overcome their finitude by achieving imperishable glory.

As I have already argued, one of the few limits on his hierarchical kingly rule is his desire for honor among the gods, which forces him to compromise with Hera (see *Il.* 4.29, 16.439–57, and 22.181). He also relies on and flaunts his reputation among the gods, especially when allowing them to enter human contests: "All you gods and goddesses hear me, so that I may speak what the *thumos* in my chest urges; let no male or female goddess try to transgress my word . . . or, having snatched you up, I will hurl you down to gloomy Tartaros" (*Il.* 8.5–8, 13). Zeus brandishes his strength and reputation largely because he desires honor and its attendant glory. While this portrayal of Zeus does not appear nearly as often in the *Odyssey*, it still remains the norm. Contra the accounts of those such as Lloyd-Jones and Segal, who suggest that Homer's Zeus is a model of a just guardian of ethical norms or customs (*themis*) and enforcer of retributive justice (especially in the *Odyssey*), I argue that Zeus remains a model for kingly rule as distinction throughout both epics (Lloyd-Jones 1983, 6–8; Segal 1994, 219, 195–227).

For example, a scene at the beginning of the *Odyssey* shows Zeus acting as a ruler who seeks to distinguish himself and enhance his reputation, and it is important to note that the term *dikē* (justice) does not appear in either of Zeus's speeches (*Od.* 1.32–43, 1.64–79). Because Zeus competes with his brother Poseidon (see later), and Poseidon rages against Odysseus and stands as the only one among the gods who does not pity Odysseus (*Od.* 1.19–20), Poseidon becomes a clear target for Zeus's rebuke (*Od.* 1.67–71). It is not surprising that Zeus's defense of Odysseus arises in the context of an assembly of all the gods, minus Poseidon. One reason for this is that Poseidon's silence-through-absence, akin to what we see in the Thersites episode, makes it easier for a ruler to elicit consent from the other members of the assembly and thus make a legitimate decision. This situation also provides a perfect opportunity for Zeus to gain honor among his peers and maintain his reputation as leader in the assembly. When Athena appeals to Zeus on Odysseus's behalf, Zeus makes three notable moves in his response. First, he claims to respect Odysseus (*Od.* 1.65–67), which is a move that would endear him to the rest of the assembled gods. Second, he blames Poseidon for Odysseus's troubles (*Od.* 1.68–69), making his brother the clear villain.[30] Third, he starts a conversation about how to get Odysseus home safely (*Od.* 1.76–77). On this reading, this scene clearly displays Zeus's desire for honor among his peers. After all, if he was such a just guardian of ethical norms, then why did he not step in earlier to help Odysseus, especially if he cares for the weary traveller? He only appears to help Odysseus at this juncture because a situation arises to maintain, and perhaps enhance, his honor and reputation among his peers as well as contend with his brother's will.

The final point I would like to make about Zeus's distinction is its partial dependence upon a relative egalitarianism, which will parallel the disagreement between Agamemnon and Achilles and the tensions that result from ruling-with others. Distinction, honor, and glory are greater for Zeus if the possibility of another god challenging him possesses at least minimal credibility. Poseidon possesses this credibility because he is Zeus's brother and each rules over a different part of the cosmos—Zeus over the sky and Poseidon over the sea. As Gregory Vlastos explains, "Poseidon is Zeus's *homotimos* [like-honored, or held in equal honor] because he is his *isomoros* [having an equal lot or share]" (1947, 156). In book 15 of the *Iliad*, a competitive tension and possibility for distinction arises. When Zeus sends his order regarding the war, Poseidon expresses an agonistic-individualist response:

> Oh shame! Though you are brave you have spoken arrogantly, and you will hold me down by force, though I am unwilling and entitled to equal honor. For all three of us are sons of Kronos and have the same mother, those whom Rhea bore, Zeus and I, and the third, Hades, who rules the dead beneath the earth. The whole was divided into three parts, and each of us received his rightful share. Surely, when lots were shaken I was chosen to inhabit the gray sea forever, Hades drew the murky world below, and Zeus drew the wide sky in the ether and clouds. Yet earth is common to us all, as well as tall Olympus. Therefore, I will in no way toddle after the mind of Zeus; rather, though he is very powerful, let him abide satisfied with his third share [*moira*]. (*Il.* 15.185–95)

This statement is important for numerous reasons. To begin with, it helps clarify a tripartite cosmology in which each of three brothers rightly rules over one-third of the cosmos. While this overarching structure suggests that there is potential for these brothers to rule with one another within the broader cosmos, this is not how things will work out.[31] Poseidon becomes angry because he believes Zeus unjustifiably orders a divine and cosmic equal in a manner that incorrectly assumes absolute, hierarchical ruling-over. This cosmic equality allows Zeus's eventual victory over Poseidon to maintain as well as enhance his distinction within the cosmic community: "I claim that I am greatly superior to him in might, and born first. His heart does not trouble itself to prevent him from speaking as my equal, though the other gods fear me" (*Il.* 15.165–67). By defeating Poseidon in this war of wills, Zeus can maintain and perhaps increase his distinction by defeating another god who claims to be his equal and to rule *with* him. While Poseidon states that he is "equal in appointed lot" (*Il.* 15.209), he ultimately backs down: "Although I am indignant, I will yield" (*Il.* 15.211). This agonistic relationship between Zeus and Poseidon also arises in the *Odyssey*. After Zeus assures Odysseus's safe passage back to Ithaca, in book 13 Poseidon becomes angry and confronts Zeus. When Zeus tells Poseidon he is free to do what he wishes, Poseidon responds by saying that he would like to do so, but he "always has a fearful eye on your [Zeus's] *thumos* and avoids confronting it" (*Od.* 13.148). This interchange in the *Odyssey* thus exposes a competition between two supposedly equal *thumō* (du., *thumos*), although Poseidon again decides to back down. Here we see how Zeus rejects the idea of ruling-with his brother, thus serving not only as an agonistic model for human rulers but also a paradigm for rule that devalues ruling-for the interests of others for non-individualistic reasons.

Agamemnon and Mortal Ruling-Over: Descending the Cosmic Scale

One could view Homer's depiction of Agamemnon as a somewhat inferior human correlate to Zeus in the Achaean community, and like Zeus, Agamemnon consistently exhibits anger, competitiveness, and honor-seeking behavior. The first word of the *Iliad* is *mēnis* (rage, wrath), and Agamemnon is one of two kings (Achilles the other) exhibiting it from the start (*Il.* 1.105–20, 130–47, and 173–87). Agamemnon's rage exposes assumptions of wounded honor, competitive struggle, and a strong sense of individualism. In fact, the contest of words and deeds, along with the rage it incites between Agamemnon and Achilles, sets the *Iliad* on its tragic course. Agamemnon expresses a strong sense of individualism and desire for honor in his frequent self-referential statements: "Seer of evils! Never yet have you spoken a useful word *for me* . . . *I was not willing* to accept the shining ransom for the girl Chriseis . . . *I much prefer* to have her . . . *I prefer* her to my wedded wife . . . immediately prepare a gift of honor *for me* . . . (since) *my* gift of honor goes elsewhere" (*Il.* 1.106–20, emphasis added). Achilles, of course, detests this self-absorbed, arrogant pride (*hubris*). Consequently, Agamemnon greatly values prizes won in battle because receiving a greater share reinforces not only his personal wealth but also enhances his standing and reputation among other *basileis*: "But immediately prepare a gift of honor for me, lest I alone among the Argives go without such a gift, since that is not fitting" (*Il.* 1.118–19). Book 11 of the *Iliad* also portrays detailed battle scenes featuring Agamemnon's competitive urges and desire for glory (e.g., *Il.* 11.129–42, 238–47). In the end, these contests are necessary insofar as they provide opportunities for distinction by means of earning honor, glory, and honorific gifts.

Moreover, honor (*timē*) and glory (*kleos, kudos*) are closely attached to Agamemnon's reputation. After his fight with Achilles at the beginning of the *Iliad*, Achilles does not accept Agamemnon's material gifts as suitable forms of reparation. Achilles desires Agamemnon's recognition as a relative equal, just as Poseidon desires Zeus's, and wants Agamemnon to take responsibility for his *hubris*. Agamemnon, however, never does this and is not willing to do so because his honor is at stake, and this honor is based upon an assumption of self-possessed individuality and his reputation as a superior *basileus*: "[Agamemnon to Achilles] Going myself to your quarters, I will lead away the fair-cheeked Briseis, your own prize, so that you may know well how superior I am to you" (*Il.* 1.184–86). Agamemnon offers gifts and bribes as a superior and distinguished ruler, but he does not offer honor or reparation as an *equal*. As Walter Donlan (1993) argues, such recognition and dueling through gifts is an essential aspect of competitions over honor. Like Achilles, Agamemnon does not accept bribes or gifts when they are offered in place of honor earned through victory in competition.[32] The message is clear: material gifts cannot outweigh the potential honor available in contest, which is a fundamental precondition for distinguishing oneself while alive and earning fame or glory after death. As the clearly distinguished "*pherteros basileus*" among the Achaeans, Agamemnon resists, as much as possible, bowing to a weaker king's demands. Achilles nevertheless challenges him because Achilles's desire for distinction is just as strong if not stronger than Agamemnon's, and appeals to ruling-with and ruling-for the broader community of Achaeans provide additional justification for Achilles's criticism.

A ruler's reputation is also attached to how he manages debate and criticism in an assembly, partly because assemblies are places where rulers compete against one another in speech. As we see in book 9 of the *Iliad*, both Diomedes and Nestor call Agamemnon to account for his management of the Achaean forces when the battle turns in the Trojans' favor. Diomedes first challenges Agamemnon within the context of an assembly, calling attention to his lack of courage and riling up the assent of his fellow Achaeans (*Il.* 9. 29–49). Importantly, Nestor follows Diomedes's speech by encouraging Agamemnon to heed the best advice that emerges *within* the assembly and *for* the well-being of the Achaean camp more generally (*Il.* 9.74–78). This second public speech elicits the idea that Agamemnon's ruling-over should include ruling-with his fellow *basileis*, exhibited by his willingness to hear and heed their counsel. This idea aptly applies to the older and wiser Nestor, who encourages Agamemnon to listen as he "weaves" (*huphainein*) his wise counsel (*mētis*) for the broader good (*eis agathon*). After listening to Nestor, Agamemnon admits that he was blinded by a type of madness (*atē*) that is sent by the gods, thus acknowledging his hubristic behavior and some degree of accountability to a broader community. In sum, Agamemnon appears to follow the model of Zeus quite closely by privileging a more self-serving form of ruling-over and resisting not only the importance of ruling-with other *basileis* but also the need to rule for the interests of a broader community of Achaeans.

Raging Achilles: Distinction in the Context of Ruling-With and Ruling-For Others

After Agamemnon finishes his first rage-induced speech in book 1 of the *Iliad*, Achilles responds: "Alas, you are clothed in shamelessness, you crafty one: how shall any one of the Achaeans readily obey your words?" (*Il.* 1.149–50). Achilles's angry responses show that he assumes his status and honor are roughly equal to Agamemnon's, or at least that Agamemnon should give more consideration to ruling-with his fellow *basileis* on Troy's battlefield. After all, he believes the Achaean *basileis* traveled to Troy not only to defend Menalaus's wounded honor and perhaps Agamemnon's ambitions but also to earn their own honor and glory in battle and contests. Consequently, Achilles is offended because Agamemnon acts like his unmitigated superior and takes his duly earned prize, Briseis. Throughout book 1 of the *Iliad*, Achilles rages against Agamemnon and the hierarchical Achaean ruling structure, thus exhibiting a staunch agonistic-individualist stance.[33]

Homer eloquently captures this challenge to Agamemnon's ruling-over others in the embassy to Achilles by evoking a conversational image that involves a more "horizontal" gaze and receptiveness to criticism. Homer achieves this by explaining how Agamemnon might look straight into Achilles's eyes to speak and take counsel *with* him (*Il.* 9.374). The specific language that Homer uses in this scene is very informative because the verb *sum-phrazomai* means taking counsel with someone else and not considering things all on one's own. Supposedly, a good ruler would not act or decide without turning around (*Il.* 1.160, *meta-trepomai*) or looking side-to-side, which would show greater regard for the opinions and advice of others. Such consideration indicates an acknowledgement that a ruler is never alone but rather ruling among and within a broader community, and should therefore consider what is in the common good or interests of others. This episode also highlights the competitive speaking context of an assembly, within which one *basileus* can compete with another and distinguish himself in verbal combat as a superior speaker. For example, Richard Martin explains how a *muthos* (speech, often in the form of a command) can be understood in Homeric poetry as "a speech act indicating authority, performed at length, *usually in public*"; consequently, in a later quarrel between Agamemnon and Achilles (*Il.* 19.80) the latter outperforms the former, leading to a situation where the victor (Achilles) remains standing and the loser (Agamemnon) sits and bows out competitively (Martin 1989; Nagy 2013, 37).

Agamemnon's hierarchical rule also hampers Achilles's ability to earn fully his personal distinction in battle, displayed in his furious responses to Agamemnon: "For surely I would be called both cowardly and worthless, if I would yield to you regarding every deed, whatever you said—command these things to others, but do not command them to me" (*Il.* 1.293–96). This last quote not only exhibits Achilles's intense rage but also displays his competitive spirit, desire for glory, and strong sense of personal honor. After chastising Agamemnon's control over decision-making and gift distribution, Achilles challenges Agamemnon to take anything else besides Briseis from him and threatens to kill him if he does so: "Indeed, come and try, so that these men may know—at once your dark blood will flow around my spear" (*Il.* 1.302–3). Homer then comments, "Thus the two of them that had battled with hostile words stood up and dismissed the assembly . . ." (*Il.* 1.304–5). This sequence indicates the competitive spirit pitting Achaean *basileis* against each other as well as the Trojans, further highlighting the intense agonism among rulers. Here, words *are* deeds, and powerful ones at that.

However, honor and glory are not only earned through public speech and verbal debate but also through physical combat and contests (see also Hammer 2005, 115–16; Martin 1989; Schofield 1986, 14). Achilles's impatience in response to Agamemnon's banquet orders in book 19 exposes this fact:

> Most glorious son of Atreus, lord of men Agamemnon, you ought to labor at these things, rather, at some other time, when a stopping point in battle should arise and there is not such rage [*menos*] in my chest. At this moment our troops lie cut down on the battlefield, those whom Hector son of Priam laid low when Zeus gave him glory [*kudos*], and you hasten us to have a meal! But I, at any rate, would now advise that the sons of the Achaians fight . . . (*Il.* 19.199–206)

At this point, Achilles has just ended his self-imposed exile from fighting, which had denied him recent opportunities to win honor and glory. Not only does Achilles express his apparent jealousy over the spoils that Hector has earned by fighting, but he is so concerned with earning his due glory that he instructs his closest comrade, Patroclus, not to fight past a particular point because this would reduce Achilles's ability to maximize his own glory (*Il.* 16.86–92). Honor and glory must therefore be earned in competitive battles and are not simply a matter of public speaking and material wealth. In book 9, when Agamemnon orders an embassy to convince Achilles to enter the fighting, Achilles explains: "I have very many possessions, which I left behind when I came here . . . and other riches I have obtained here [in Troy] . . . except my prize of honor . . . which Agamemnon gave to me, then took back again *insultingly*" (*Il.* 9.364–69, my emphasis). While Achilles is referring to his female war-prize, Briseis, the underlying issue is not Briseis or any material wealth as such. Achilles is ultimately concerned with *how* Agamemnon treated him: Agamemnon took his prize, which was symbolic of his heroism in battle and exhibited his glory, in the way an unchecked superior takes what he wants from a paltry inferior. This violates both an assumption of relative equality between *basileis* and their rightful honor and glory earned through contest. No amount of material wealth can atone for Achilles's wounded honor, making him a paradigmatic hero. In fact, the idea of individual honor is so strong that something like forgiveness neither exists nor makes sense in this context. For example, Achilles reenters battle not out of forgiveness but rather because he realizes that his opportunity to win glory and honor among the Achaeans is slipping away.

Hence, in contrast to Peter Ahrensdorf's (2014) recent interpretation of Achilles as rationally detached from his community members and their esteem, I argue that Achilles's rage and pursuit of honor expose a deep, complex attachment to his fellow Achaeans through shame and reputation. Following Bernard Williams's (1993, ch. 4) observations about Homeric shame and Achilles's as a model: "People have at once a sense of their own honour and a respect for other peoples' honour; they can feel indignation or other forms of anger when honour is violated, in their own case or someone else's. These are shared sentiments with similar objects, and they serve to bind people together in a community of feeling" (80). The ethical and political binding power of honor, shame, and reputation apply to each *basileus* discussed in this section. On this point I also agree with Hammer (2002a), who elucidates Achilles's engagement with others during the funeral games for Patroclus and meeting with Priam. Hammer emphasizes the role of esteem, arguing that Achilles gradually moves from a more individualistic, self-sufficient ethos to "an esteem for himself as connected to, and bearing some responsibility for, the care and suffering of distinctive others" (182). Therefore, Achilles's own distinctive identity is intertwined with that of his fellow *basileis* and, to some extent, a broader community wherein ruling-with and ruling-for others is of deep concern in the face of hierarchical abuses associated with ruling-over.

Odysseus's Cunning, Polytropic Distinction: Ruling-in an Unruly Cosmos

Odysseus also exhibits a strong, honor-seeking individualism throughout both the *Iliad* and *Odyssey*, but does so in ways that diverge from Agamemnon and Achilles. While Achilles possesses paradigmatic physical force and warrior's strength that parallels some of Zeus's distinguishing characteristics among the Olympians, Odysseus epitomizes Zeus's mental cunning (*mētis*) and what I want to call his "polytropism." The term polytropic derives from Odysseus's epithet *polutropos*, which means versatile, wily, shifty, or more literally, "much-traveled or -wandering." Gregory Nagy provides a nuanced definition of the polytropic individual as "one who could change in many different ways who he was" (2013, 277). Odysseus's ability to hide things in his heart or mind (*phrēn*)—as Achilles's frustratingly notes (*Il.* 9. 312–13)—allows him to distinguish himself in novel ways, and correspondingly highlights the internally pluralistic yet demarcated personhood in Homeric thought.

In a notable example drawn from the *Iliad*, Odysseus exhibits a crafty, competitive spirit directed toward earning honor and reinforcing his reputation among the Achaean *basileis* as he marauds through the night and steals prizes such as horses from the Trojan camps. When he returns with beautiful horses, Nestor asks him, "Come and tell me, illustrious Odysseus, the great glory of the Achaeans, how did you get these horses?" (*Il.* 10.544–45). Here, Odysseus succeeds not by fighting in hand-to-hand combat in the light of day but rather by moving stealthily under the cover of darkness to acquire honorific prizes, and his success at hiding and thievery reinforces his reputation among the Achaean kings and soldiers. He is equally stealthy in the *Odyssey*, where he outwits the unruly Polyphemus,[34] the cave-dwelling Cyclops, by enticing him to get so drunk that he passes out (*Od.* 9.345–50). This drunken stupor allows Odysseus to blind Polyphemus and cleverly escape under the name "Nobody" (*outis; Od.* 9.364–436). Under the cover of this name, Polyphemus's appeal to his neighbors for help fails because he must proclaim that "Nobody has harmed him," which prevents them from potentially coming to Polyphemus's rescue and tracking down Odysseus. The wily one then devises an escape plan for he and his surviving comrades, as they hide in the Cyclops's own woolly sheep. Such cunning exploits and the attendant reputation that he earns helps to sustain his *kleos* (fame) among the Greeks.

More generally, Odysseus distinguishes himself from those such as Achilles and Agamemnon by surviving a prolongated, torturous return from Troy and successful arrival home. For example, in the *Odyssey* he deftly navigates two notable sets of obstacles—first the Sirens, then Scylla and Charybdis. In the first case, he has himself tied to his ship's mast-block so that he can listen to the Sirens' voices, while his comrades plug their ears with beeswax so as not to be enticed (*Od.* 12.28–54). In this way he is able to escape death yet not deprive himself of the pleasure of listening to the Sirens, showing how he is simultaneously able to enjoy the beautiful or pleasurable aspect of something without necessarily falling prey to its destructive characteristics. In the second case where he navigates between Scylla and Charybdis, he displays a similar restraint after Circe advises him to avoid Charybdis altogether and sacrifice six of his men to Scylla (*Od.* 12.73–126). Odysseus wants to try fighting Scylla off altogether, but ultimately chooses to shed his stubbornness and false belief that the route between a "rock and a hard place" can come without suffering or a sacrifice of some kind. Such powerful, dangerous forces draw and repel Odysseus in various ways, and his distinction here lies in his ability to discern how to navigate such treacherous forces. One lesson is that being a distinguished ruler often requires a tremendous amount of polytropic cleverness, sensitivity to powers outside one's control, and willingness to sacrifice those dear to one.

In another dramatic example, Odysseus is stranded at sea on a plank of wood and appears doomed. Nevertheless, he is suddenly inspired by Athena, who places it in his mind (*epi-phrēn*) to grab a particular reef while being carried on an ocean swell. In this sequence of events, Odysseus displays his receptivity to external forces and deftly submits, thus allowing him to survive a harrowing circumstance at sea. These examples help explain why Odysseus is such a distinguished ruler, and human being more generally. That is, he possesses the ability to successfully navigate destructive and potentially life-ending circumstances, on the one hand, and life-saving situations that garner glory, on the other. Odysseus is not headstrong like Achilles—he is fundamentally polytropic, a man of "many ways." In cosmological terms, this flexible character allows him to adapt to the unpredictability that he consistently faces due to the multifarious, divine incursions in his mortal life. Odysseus thus provides a paradigmatic example of ruling-in an unruly cosmos because, as I explained earlier in the chapter, human beings do not decide or control their fate from the ground up. Likewise, human rulers such as Odysseus are not in a position to rule over Fate or the gods, but they are nevertheless committed to ruling-in both their respective human communities and an often unpredictable, threatening cosmos.

As with other Greek *basileis*, Odysseus also understands quite well how material wealth provides means for distinguishing oneself by enhancing and maintaining one's honor. This is best exhibited in the *Odyssey* in relation to hospitality, where great material wealth allows kings to lavish gifts upon guests, which then adds to their honor as hosts and their reputation within a broader community of *basileis* from other lands. When Odysseus arrives in Ithaca after years at sea, he first worries about the safety of the wealth he received and brought with him from the Phaecians: " 'But come now, I shall inspect and count my possessions, lest they left with anything of mine on their hollow ship.' Thus he spoke and began counting his very beautiful tripods, cauldrons, gold, and finely woven garments" (*Od.* 13.215–16). This scene shows how it is not enough for a *basileus* to survive, as he must constantly obtain the means for earning more honor and glory. In this example, Odysseus's actions expose his understanding of how material wealth can provide these means. Rather than simply being satisfied that he survived such a horrendous series of death-defying events during his trip home, Odysseus is more concerned that he will have nothing to show for his time away and his success in the Trojan War. Rather than dropping to his knees, crying, and celebrating the fact that he had arrived home, the first thing he does is *turn around* to check to see if his booty is intact. Possessing great prizes and wealth would allow Odysseus to be a better host in the future, thereby enhancing his future prospects for earning greater honor and a shining reputation.

Daniel Silvermintz takes a slightly different tack and interprets kingly rule in the *Odyssey* as revolving around the reinstatement of just and equitable rule in Ithaca. On his reading, the theme of weaving plays as central role, as both Penelope and Odysseus work in tandem to repair Ithaca's unstable political situation and reinstate Odysseus's legitimacy as ruler. Silvermintz argues that Odysseus "integrates the competing factions of the city, and weaves the new regime as a mixed polity, like a cloak composed of threads of many colours, embroidered with flowers, and shining like the sun or the moon" (2004, 41; see *Od.* 24.48). While this interpretation complements my reading of Odysseus's polytropic cleverness as a ruler, it does not sit as easily with the agonistic, competitive, and glory-seeking aspects of my interpretation. For example, Silvermintz's Odysseus introduces "an equitable standard of justice [which] constitutes a radical transformation in political governance. Whereas other kings meted out justice according to their personal prejudices, Odysseus governed by treating each man with impartiality" (37).

While Silvermintz astutely locates evidence in these Homeric passages for justice and equanimity as normative standards for rule, I maintain that this standard remains overshadowed by an understanding of rule as distinction and would not want to overemphasize the role that justice plays here. Outside Penelope's statement that her husband was a fair ruler (*Od.* 4.686–96), evidence of Odysseus's benevolence as a ruler is somewhat thin. Besides the fact that Penelope's love for Odysseus would surely influence her understanding of the positive qualities of his rule, this situation shares structural similarities to the "Hector vs. Andromache" scenario (discussed later). Like Hector leaving Andromache and his family to fight Achilles, Odysseus leaves his family in Ithaca with similar intentions—namely, to gain honor, glory, enhanced reputation, and wealth in battle. This is a central reason he is so concerned about his Phaecian bounty. Rather than remaining in Ithaca out of concern for justly ruling his subjects and living peacefully with his wife, he sought something he cared about more deeply than his community's well-being. Odysseus restores order to his household (and thereby Ithaca) more out of anger and a desire to reacquire his distinguished position than from a desire to reestablish a just political order. Contra Silvermintz, the political art, which is also understood as the "weaver's art," is more so a skill used in service of distinction than out of natural benevolence. Rather tellingly, as Silvermintz cites in a key passage at the end of the *Odyssey* where the gods force Odysseus "to stay this quarrel in closing combat" (2004, 41; see *Od.* 24.539–48), we are reminded of a similar situation concerning Achilles in the *Iliad*: Odysseus is not prepared to check his destructive anger and only does so due to the intervention of more powerful, divine forces.

Hector's Distinction: Caught in the Bind of Ruling-for Oneself versus Others

Achaean kings are not the only *basileis* that seek distinction, as Hector's competitive drive for glory arises early in the *Iliad*. For example, he duels with Ajax in book 7 in front of all the soldiers, explaining: "And if I kill him, and Apollo grants me glory, having stripped him of his armor I will carry it to sacred Ilium" (*Il.* 7.81–82). Hector's desire for honor and glory are among the most striking of any *basileus* in the *Iliad* because one directly observes how he weighs them in relation to his family and native land. When Hector returns to Troy in book 6, his wife Andromache is reluctant to see him leave again and worried that he will not return. She blames this circumstance on his heroic courage, stating: "You piece of work, this rage of yours will destroy you, and you feel no compassion toward your young child nor toward me, ill-fated, who will soon be your widow" (*Il.* 6.407–9).[35] As Andromache points out, Hector forsakes time with his immediate family and perhaps an opportunity to protect them personally. And why? Before fighting Achilles, one observes how Hector's thinking is paradigmatically heroic, honor-based, and linked to his reputation:

> Woe is me: if I retreat behind the gates and walls, Poulydamas will be the first to lay shame upon me, who earlier bid me to lead the Trojans back to the city on that deadly night when brilliant Achilles was stirred to fight . . . but now I am ashamed before the Trojan men and women, lest at some point another man who is worse than me states: "Hector, unduly convinced by his own might, killed his troops." Thus they will speak. Now then, for me it would be more advantageous to stand against Achilles face to face, kill him, and come back alive, or die gloriously by his hands in front of the city. (*Il.* 22.99–102, 105–10; see also Donlan 1980, 23–24)

Hector is acutely aware of his reputation among the Trojan people and what they might think and say about him if he does not fight Achilles. In this passage, public disgrace holds more weight for him than his family's immediate safety and protection. It is also relevant that he explains how he must fight

Achilles in front of the city (*pro polēos*), indicating how Hector's identity and reputation are predicated upon others' expectations and how they view him. Consequently, he must be seen as a hero fighting or competing against a worthy opponent before the people's eyes if he wants to earn what he cares about most—namely, honor and glory.[36]

This tension between responsibility to one's own family and community, on the one hand, and one's personal glory and reputation, on the other, could be interpreted politically as a tension between ruling-for one's personal interests and the interests of others. In fact, one might say there are multiple tensions here. Hector cares greatly about his personal reputation, but part of his heroic reputation is enhanced by properly fulfilling his duty to protect the broader community of Trojans. What he gains from ruling-for his own interests thus overlaps, in one sense, with his responsibility to rule for the community's safety and well-being. However, this personal urge for distinction and communal duty separate him from his family, whose interests seem to stand at the crossroads between individual and public interests. That is, his family and its interests—so eloquently captured in Andromache's laments—place Hector as ruler/prince in a rather unique bind that we do not observe with various Achaean *basileis*: his close ties with family and sense of responsibility for others contrast with his efforts at individual distinction, thus displaying the tragic complexities of simultaneously ruling-for others and one's individual interests. Self-possessed individuality plays a significant role here because this strongly individualistic conception of identity makes it more difficult to understand why a ruler should sacrifice personal distinction for the sake of helping others. In taking his mortality seriously, Hector clearly understands that individual distinction is one of the only ways to overcome being forgotten and perhaps achieving some degree of immortality, and that helping others can get in the way of achieving this goal.

Hospitality: Distinction during Peacetime

The ethic of hospitality in the *Odyssey* offers yet another example of how Homeric rulers attempt to distinguish themselves in pursuit of honor, glory, and reputation, particularly when they are not immediately engaged in battle.[37] Generally speaking, hospitality is the idea that a stranger must be treated well as a guest in a host's home, and *basileis* throughout the *Odyssey* strive to uphold this ideal. I argue that kings provide hospitality partly because it provides opportunities to display their glory and wealth as well as distinguish themselves from prior hosts a guest may have had. *Basileis* strive to be the best possible hosts partly because it increases their honor and reputation as both self-possessed individuals and hosts among a broader community of *basileis*. Here it is important to note that the term *timē*, or honor, is a term applied broadly and in a variety of settings, not just during wartime or on the battlefield.[38]

Menelaus provides a good example of this point. In book 4, when he is told that strangers have arrived at his palace, he replies: "Surely, now, the two of us enjoyed many tokens of guest friendship from other men by the time we arrived here. . . . Moreover, un-harness our guests' horses, and lead them forward to be entertained" (*Od.* 4.33–46). In this scene Menelaus's attendant, Eteoneus, offends Menelaus when he suggests that Menelaus consider pushing the strangers along to another host. This clearly offends Menelaus because the king recalls the hospitality he received on his way home from Troy. In this instance, his honor and reputation as a host are at stake because if he denies these strangers, then he will have failed to live up to the standard of his previous hosts. Memory thus preserves a broader, imagined community within which *basileis* understand themselves as more or less distinguished members.

In addition, Menelaus's statements about hospitality exhibit an implicit competitive urge. If his hospitality does not match the hospitality he received from other hosts, then he may believe that his reputation as both *basileus* and host will be tarnished. As I argued earlier with Odysseus, material wealth is a means of earning honor and enhancing a king's reputation. In Menelaus's case, his material wealth gives him the ability to enhance his reputation, but only if the strangers have the opportunity to view his wealth directly and accept gifts as guests:

> Then the carver lifted up and placed before them platters full of all sorts of meats, and placed before them golden goblets. And welcoming the two guests, blond-haired Menelaus said to them: 'Take part in eating the food and be delighted' . . . then Telemachus uttered to Nestor's son, as he held his head near him . . . 'Observe, son of Nestor, the dazzling bronze throughout the echoing halls, and the amber gold and both silver and ivory. Doubtless, such a courtyard could be found in the palace of Olympian Zeus, how many unspeakable things as are here. Awe grips me as I look upon it.' (*Od.* 4.57–60, 69–75)

This statement displays a possible motive for Menelaus's hospitality—namely, a desire for hierarchical distinction and belief that competition is a necessary means of situating oneself over others. Menelaus likely understands that in failing to offer impressive hospitality he would also be forfeiting the opportunity to impress the guests with his material wealth. In this situation, attaining honor by enhancing one's reputation is possible only through the recognition granted by others. If one links this claim to Menelaus's statement about remembering the hospitality that he was shown and considers the wealth Menelaus possesses, then this example exposes a competitive aspect of hospitality. By choosing to provide hospitality to these strangers Menelaus can "put his wealth to work" to increase his reputation in his guests' eyes. Even if this is not Menelaus's primary motive, the fact remains that his guests are struck with wonder and would undoubtedly speak highly of Menelaus when they leave. Therefore, his intentions do not change the fact that his prestige will be enhanced regardless.[39] It is also significant that his guests, Telemachus and Pisistratus, are royal youths. Because they are from different lands, each can return home and spread word of Menelaus's greatness for years to come.

This example of hospitality thus exhibits a peacetime opportunity for *basileis* to distinguish themselves. Offering grandiose hospitality to other *basileis* and heroes during peacetime is an effective way for kings to enhance their reputation, because during peacetime they do not have a battlefield or wartime contests to display their fighting ability and earn glory among their peers. While the *Iliad* provides many examples of *basileus*-rule as distinction in wartime, the *Odyssey* alternatively supplies examples of this meaning during peacetime. Opportunities for offering hospitality display occasions for a more passive, long-distance competition whereby *basileis* can earn approbation through gift giving and exhibiting their material wealth when a stranger arrives. Throughout the *Odyssey*, hosts take tremendous pride in their hospitality, while the guests often show their appreciation by complementing such hospitality (e.g., see *Od.* 4.587–619, 8.412–15). *Basileis* and princes, therefore, take great honor in providing the proper hospitality in the form of gifts and conducting the proper rites. This ethic not only exhibits an occasion for contest but also a deep sense of individual honor and a desire to enhance this honor. To be clear, I am not arguing that competitiveness is the single or even predominant motive for hospitality. I only claim that hospitality possesses a competitive aspect insofar as it provides an opportunity for *basileis* to enhance their honor as rulers of various lands. As such, hospitality is instructive for understanding the meaning of *basileus*-rule in the *Odyssey*.

The final evidence for *basileus*-rule as distinction that I will draw from the ethic of hospitality is the rage exhibited when someone violates the honor associated with this ethic. In the *Odyssey*, Odysseus is primarily portrayed as a guest in numerous characters' homes, including demi-goddesses (Calypso,

Circe), a nonhuman figure (Polyphemus), and a human king (Alcinous). By the end of the *Odyssey*, Odysseus becomes hospitality's avenger and defends his own honor by slaughtering the suitors who had afflicted his home and wealth. In this example the suitors, as *basileis* who challenge Ithaca's established hierarchical rule as agonistic individuals, violate Odysseus's honor by violating the rules of hospitality (e.g., see *Od.* 2.196–204, 17.454–80, and 18.356–64). When Odysseus returns to Ithaca, Athena alters his appearance so that he returns home as a stranger. Because of his appearance as a beggar the suitors berate and physically accost Odysseus. While these transgressions take place Odysseus rages on the inside: "He shook his head in silence, brooding over ugly deeds" (*Od.* 20.184). His intense anger exhibits a belief in self-possessed individuality and the connected belief in a ruler's personal honor and glory. When someone violates a ruler's honor, this time through hospitality, rage is triggered. In this episode, Odysseus becomes angry when the suitors violate the ethic partly because it entails a valuable custom that *basileis* depend upon to distinguish themselves and sustain their honor during peacetime. Kingly rage is a special sort of rage because a special type of good—namely, distinction among fellow *basileis*—provides higher stakes for rulers that are not available to every type of host. Because the stakes are greater, the anger would likewise be more intense. In sum, anger is a justified response to hospitality's violation because this ethic provides opportunities for enhancing *basileis*' honor and glory, which are fundamental aims of *basileus*-rule as distinction.

Conclusion: Ruling Tensions and Transitions

Examining some of the central concepts and beliefs associated with rule helps elucidate how the predominant meaning of rule is distinction in Homeric political thought, further exhibiting the earliest coherent strain of political thought that can be gleaned from the Greek tradition. This tradition also exposes a particular trajectory for Greek conceptions of rule and how these conceptions are undergoing an important transition during the archaic period. As this reading of Homer has suggested, traditional-hierarchical beliefs uneasily co-exist with anti-hierarchical ideas. While this tension elucidates various ruling models and raises the question of whether *basileis* can refrain from hubristic abuses—for example, in balancing ruling-over with efforts to rule with fellow *basileis* or rule for the well-being of a broader community—in the *Iliad* and *Odyssey* we ultimately observe an understanding that distinction is the primary aim of rule. Of course, distinction can be earned in a number of ways and requires meaningful connections to both divine powers and fellow mortals. Moreover, while different *basileis* display the multifaceted aspects of Homeric rule, one can also locate similarities between rulers such as Zeus, Agamemnon, and Achilles in ideas such as self-possessed individuality and the relative equality among rulers. These ideas help carve a conceptual path for political egalitarianism and chip away at the more traditional, hierarchical model of ruling-over. As we will see in Hesiod, these elements of Homeric rule gesture toward more horizontal, proto-democratic, and human-centric strains of political thought.

This leveling of rule exhibits a very noteworthy development in early Greek thought, which we see epitomized in the tense situations between Thersites and rulers such as Agamemnon and Achilles. Such tensions arise partly due to a belief in self-possessed individuality and emerging egalitarian ruling ideas. The resulting agonistic individualism between rulers across both the divine and human planes exposes particular anxieties regarding the connectedness of rule. Aiming to distinguish themselves in pursuit of honor, glory, and reputation, rulers of various sorts do not appear *primarily* concerned with the well-being or interests of their broader communities whether it be on Olympus, in Troy, or in hospitable royal households. While critiques of hubristic hierarchy and critical-individualist conceptions of rule arise at particular junctures in Homeric works, these ruling ideas are not depicted as fully legitimate in the *Iliad* and *Odyssey*—at least not in any systematic and philosophical sense. Hesiod will attempt to shore up some of these tensions between self-interested rule and the interests of a broader community, although his innovations will also introduce new barriers for conceiving the connectedness of rule.

The final passage in the *Odyssey* supplies a useful hinge for transitioning from Homeric to Hesiodic political thought. At the end of book 24 following Odysseus's slaughter of the suitors, a brief confrontation ensues between two camps: Odysseus, Laertes, Telemachus and their compatriots, on the one hand, and the suitors' kinsmen led by Eupeithēs who are seeking revenge, on the other. Before this bloody confrontation escalates, Zeus hurls a lightning bolt that halts the disobedient Athena and battle-hungry Odysseus from advancing. Prior to this intervention, Zeus had told Athena that a pact of peace must be struck between the two sides so that the bloodletting would end (*Od.* 24.477–86). At this dramatic finale of the *Odyssey*, we observe two important points. First, we see what appears to be a less agonistic and more peace-loving Zeus. Second, it is two divine beings, Zeus and Athena, who end the conflict and not contentious groups of human beings reasoning with one another of their own accord. In this finale, we thus observe a moment of divine intervention predicated on cosmic hierarchical rule, command, and force—but importantly, an intervention that seeks to end antagonistic relations and establish conditions for peace. Zeus's behavior shows how we have not quite arrived at a significant development that we will see in Hesiod's thought: the belief that the best type of ruling-over requires distinguishing oneself not through mere force or command, but through soothing speech that mimics the poet's skill and has the capacity to diffuse conflict. While we leave Homer with what looks like the predominant model of distinction through agonistic contest (Zeus and Athena, Odysseus's band and Eupeithēs's band), we end with a peaceful resolution predicated on Zeus's direct intervention. Justice, however, is conspicuously missing in this scene. Peace reigns, and here we witness the end of the heroic age and beginning of *polis* politics,[40] which, as we will see in Hesiod, requires greater reliance on the concept of justice.

Turning to Hesiod, we can get a clearer picture as to why ruling as distinction facilitates greater interest in the concept of justice and, perhaps most significant from a broader historical perspective, a move toward the first political metaphysics in ancient Greece. In contrast to Homer, Hesiod's political thought will exhibit a sustained attempt to turn the Greek understanding of ruling as competitive distinction—along with the abuses and violence associated with distinction in Homer's highly agonistic cosmology—into one of goodness, peace, and interconnected harmony. Considered within the framework of the various models of rule I have outlined, Hesiod will strongly criticize aspects of ruling-over and place greater emphasis not only on the responsibility of ruling-for the interests of a broader community of human beings but also for ruling-in a more just and peaceful cosmos.

2 HESIOD

CRITIQUE, POETIC JUSTICE, AND THE INCREASING ANTHROPOCENTRISM OF GREEK RULE

Like the Homeric epics, Hesiod's *Theogony* (*Th.*) and *Works and Days* (*WD*) provide an intriguing glimpse into the political ideas of archaic Greece (ca. 700–500 BCE).[1] As I suggested in the previous chapter, these poets outline important starting points for thinking about rule, political power, and socioeconomic relations to which subsequent political thinkers respond—notably, Plato and Aristotle—when formulating some of their own political ideas. Both Plato's *Republic* and Aristotle's *Politics* explicitly and implicitly reference these early poets, as Homer and Hesiod supply both the conceptual backdrop and a comparative reference point for classical political philosophy. It is important, therefore, to examine both Homer and Hesiod to understand the historical-conceptual framework that served as a starting point for the most significant theoretical foundations of Western political thought and practice. Moreover, clarifying the relationship between these two Greek poets provides an illuminating counter perspective on rule with which to compare Vedic political thought in subsequent chapters.

This chapter examines Hesiod's political thought to show how Hesiod exhibits significant continuity with Homer, but also how he diverges from the Homeric understanding of rule in a few key respects. Both express similar beliefs about kingly rule, such as the traditional-hierarchical idea that Zeus is the most powerful ruler in the cosmos and can serve as a model for human rulers. However, Hesiod elaborates upon a foundational dilemma that was posed in Homeric works, which concerns how the Greeks can reconcile the traditional understanding of Zeus as a paradigm of distinction, on the one hand, with the idea that he is also deeply concerned with justice, on the other. How can *basileis* voraciously seek distinction while remaining caretakers of justice who are responsible for preserving the community's well-being? Is honor or justice the central aim of rule? Or can both be pursued simultaneously? A dilemma in archaic political thought thus concerns how the Greeks can coherently accommodate anti-hierarchical beliefs in rule with the belief that hierarchically situated, distinction-seeking *basileis* should rule. Hesiod's solution is evocative: akin to the figures Hesiod identifies as the first cosmic rulers, namely Ouranos and Kronos, human *basileis* may be crooked distinction-seekers but Zeus provides a new, alternative model because he distinguishes himself as a just and fair ruler in the most recent cosmic succession. I argue that Hesiod expresses the new belief that Zeus is a just decision-maker and not quite the competitive, glory- and honor-seeking *basileus* of Homer's portrayal. Developing this belief, and the idea that Zeus serves as the proper model for human rulers, allows Hesiod to conceive a cosmological model of hierarchical kingly rule while coherently retaining the belief that human *basileis* should rule. In turn, this conception indicates a slight shift toward an impersonal, natural standard for rule that is not necessarily grounded in self-possessed individuality. In these respects, Hesiod pushes the early Greek conception of rule from one predominantly anchored in relations of ruling-over others to a position that emphasizes ruling-for the well-being and interests of a broader human community. Interestingly, this shift also entails a more hierarchical and agonistic relationship to the nonhuman world.

In turn, I argue that Hesiod's justice is "poetic" in two respects: not only does it arise from his poetic abilities but it also explains why and how rulers' vices will be punished, and their virtues rewarded. Akin to Homer, Hesiod's poetry has the capacity to tap into his audience's emotions and alter them at an aesthetic, pre-rational level. Hesiod exhibits the attempt to shift his audience's emotions and dispositions (likely aimed at both common citizens and rulers) in ways that clear more affective and rationalist ground for the audience to accept his critique of bribe-eating rulers, including an account of poetic justice in which their vices would be punished. For example, Hesiod's cosmogony and theogony provide an enchanting, dramatic story about the origins of the cosmos that could prove rhetorically powerful from a political perspective, partly because they do not always seem to be pitched as overt polemics about good rule. In this respect, I will argue that his cosmogony and theogony are helpful devices for establishing a broader, seemingly apolitical framework that resonates with and supports his claims about the nature of rule and protests against abusive rulers. His *Theogony* acknowledges and grapples with the agonistic "DNA" of archaic Greek cosmology while also telling a story that softens some of its sharpest edges, which is a particularly important move during the transition to *polis* politics where stability, peace, and fair decision-making become increasingly important goals. By the time we arrive at Hesiod's explicit critique of corrupt rulers in *Works and Days*, an underlying political synchronicity is established, and a broader cosmological and theological context is set for justifying his criticisms. The poetic elements and presentation of Hesiod's political thought are also cross-culturally significant because they show interesting similarities to the Vedic tradition. Both Hesiod and brahmin poets claim special access to understanding the nature of the cosmos and use divine invocations as a means of expressing their central political ideas. These invocations often mark tense relationships with rulers, as these Greek and Vedic poets deploy poetry as a form of political critique and means of "putting rulers in their place."

In moving from the macro-cosmological level down to human communities—metaphorically descending the cosmic scale—my analysis and argument parallel the structure of the previous chapter. I begin by clarifying the major categories, concepts, and cosmological context for situating Hesiod's political thought. Here I explain how Hesiod's relationship to the Muses supplies many of the underpinnings for his critique of unjust modes of ruling-over—a critique that gradually emerges throughout his accounts in the *Theogony* and *Works and Days*. As I suggest above, my argument in this section treats Hesiod's works as forms of protest poetry in which Hesiod adopts the stance—sometimes subtle, sometimes not so subtle—of political protestor. He criticizes rulers' abusive behavior by introducing a cosmology that would provide grounds for justifying why human rulers should behave in a more just fashion. This results in a rather unique "cosmo-political" vision in which cosmology and rule are intertwined. In the next section I further examine this primordial cosmo-politics in Hesiod's major works by analyzing the agonistic challenges to hierarchical rule that lead to Zeus's emergence as cosmic ruler. While these challenges lead to a monarchical form of ruling-over, they also display a leveling trend in rule insofar as Hesiod emphasizes ruling-for and ruling-in a broader community of beings. The subsequent section delves further into these developments to analyze how Zeus ascends as a just ruler and provides a new model for human *basileis* to follow. I then examine how Hesiod views rule within human communities and his reliance on the concept of justice to criticize crooked, "bribe-eating" rulers. In the Conclusion, I explain how these developments in Hesiod's political thought lead to an increasingly human-centric conception of politics that severs any systematic connection between human and nonhuman well-being. This idea of a cosmological break provides a transition to the Vedic tradition, clarifying how ruling as distinction can be understood as an alternative to ruling as stewardship in early Indian political thought.

Cosmic Conflict and a Laboring Mortal Existence: Muses and Memory as Existential, Political Balm

As I argued last chapter, one of the defining characteristics of the Greek cosmos was its intensely agonistic nature, and Hesiod's conception of rule displays an additional characteristic: the importance of divine inspiration as a source of easing some of the cosmic tension we observe in archaic political thought more generally, as well as for protesting against abusive rulers. Both the *Theogony* and *Works and Days* begin with Hesiod invoking the Muses and tapping into their divine memory for song and inspiration:

> Let us begin to sing of the Heliconian Muses, who dwell upon the great, sacred mountain of Helicon, and dance with their tender feet around the violet-colored spring and altar of almighty Zeus.... Once they taught Hesiod beautiful song as he was tending to lambs beneath sacred Helicon.... [T]hey breathed divine voice into me so that I might glorify events of the future and the past. (*Th.* 1–4, 22–23, 29–34)
>
> O Muses from Pieria, those bringing glory in your songs, come hither, tell of your father Zeus as you are singing, by means of whom mortal men are both remembered and forgotten alike, by the mighty will of Zeus. (*WD* 1–4)

In the *Theogony*, Hesiod thus explains how the Muses help draw him from the drudgery of his pasturing into the role of inspired poet, teaching him beautiful song (*kalēn aoidēn*) and breathing into him divine voice (*thespin audēn*) so that he could glorify particular aspects of the past and future. Hesiod also tells us that the Muses commanded him to sing about the gods and their respective births (*Th.* 31–34), displaying how these figures rule over his poetic inspiration.

This point about divine command also draws attention to a broader theme that pervades Hesiod's political thought. That is, various nonhuman beings in the cosmos exhibit considerable agency, and one could argue that the first "political" agents are actually nonhuman beings such as Gaia and Ouranos (more on this later). Such beings set the tone for Hesiod's conception of politics from a cosmological perspective, especially when we get to a discussion of Zeus and the model he provides for human rulers. In short, not all nonhuman beings and parts of the natural world are completely passive or inert substances upon which human agents can exert their labor and bracket themselves as the sole political agents in the cosmos. However, while agency and power are distributed among a multiplicity of beings, this distribution tends to shrink somewhat when Zeus ascends as the sole cosmic monarch. For example, as I will explain in the third section of this chapter, Zeus's monarchy is dependent on the consumption of figures such as Mētis and subjugation of figures such as the Titans, Typhoeus, Prometheus, and even his daughter, Athena. Dependence on this multiplicity is a precondition for being a distinguished, just ruler, and as we saw in Homer, ruling-over requires various degrees of ruling-with and ruling-in a pluralistic cosmos. This point then elicits the idea that just, peaceful rule requires greater humility on the part of rulers and ruling-for the interests of those beings who make such distinction possible in the first place. In the next section I will elaborate on how the capacity to subsume a multiplicity of forces while drawing upon their respective abilities is a powerful tool for those engaging in rule. As I argued in the Preface and discuss at greater length in the Conclusion, concealing this capacity and overlooking its significance can facilitate a surreptitious, domineering form of ruling-over that has pervaded many Western traditions of political thought and made us overlook its potentially damaging consequences when applied to nonhuman nature.

To return to the Muses as cosmo-political agents, there are a number of important points to make about these figures as a starting point in Hesiod's major works. The Muses are the primary sources of Hesiod's knowledge about the past, and without them Hesiod would not possess his extensive knowledge of the gods and the nature of justice. Such knowledge comes from a plurality of nonhuman, feminine sources that inspire and command him to put this inspiration to work for political purposes.[2] This plurality includes Kleiō or Glorifying (derived from verb *kleiō*, to glorify, make famous, or celebrate), as well as Euterpē (well-pleasing), Thaleia (blooming), and Melpomenē (singing) (see *Th.* 75–89). By explaining how they govern his identity as poet, Hesiod also clarifies how they serve as a platform for his critique of human rulers and his account of justice. For example, he emphasizes the political importance of the ninth Muse, Kalliopē (beautiful voiced), because she accompanies only those rulers who are *worthy* of reverence (*Th.* 80). Kalliopē is of particular importance for rulers because she provides them with the ability for soothing (*meilichos*) speech, which allows them to ease agonistic tensions in the assembly. Kalliopē and her sisters also signal the importance of the ruler's *style* of speech: it is "beautiful" not because it is competitively successful but rather because it diffuses social and political tensions and does not exacerbate or create new conflicts:

> Whomever the daughters of mighty Zeus honor and notice at birth among kings who are nourished by Zeus, they pour sweet dew upon his tongue, and soothing words flow from his mouth. All the people look to him to settle disputes with straight judgments. Steadfastly, while speaking in the assembly, he quickly yet skillfully puts an end to a large feud. (*Th.* 81–87)

Memory (*mnēmosunē*) is the one who gives birth to the Muses, all of whom Hesiod portray as distinctly soothing or joyful in nature. Interestingly, the Muses' genealogical relation to Memory highlights the significance of knowing the past, which Hesiod does not depict as some dead weight but rather an inspiring part of what it is to be a member of the mortal human community. Here, one can also identify a connection to rule insofar as the Muses are born from the coupling of Zeus and Memory (*Th.* 50–55). This pairing displays the idea that good ruling is connected not only to remembering but also *delighting* in the past—or at least particular aspects of it. Such delights are necessary, Hesiod further suggests, due to a human condition characterized by strife and labor. Hesiod tells us that Old Age (Gēras) gives birth to Strife (Eris) (*Th.* 225), invoking a central theme in archaic Greek thought regarding mortality. Memory, and poetry as a means of remembering, can help alleviate anxieties over Old Age and the aging process, which serve as a constant reminder of one's mortality.

However, Hesiod also claims that there are two kinds of Strife, one good and one bad (*WD* 11–26). Hesiod associates the bad sort of Strife with human conflict and honor-seeking, including competitive public speaking (for its own sake) and distinction, while the good sort of Strife is associated with the earth and the individual's responsibility to labor upon it: "If the *thumos* in your chest longs for wealth, then do as I say, and labor at work upon work" (*WD* 381–82). This distinction between good and bad Strife is important because it exposes a crucial assumption concerning human ontology: humans are laboring beings that must fight for survival within a seemingly ambivalent, and often threatening, cosmos. For example, Hesiod provides detailed warnings and instructions about the proper time, place, and body positions for urination (*WD* 727–30, 757–59). Not only are mortals naturally laborers but the earth, somewhat paradoxically, is viewed as a fruitful combatant because she motivates mortals to work and survive. Hesiod claims this is how human beings make the best of a generally challenging existence, contrasting it with the useless speech-mongering that often predominates in the assembly (*WD* 27–29).

In explaining how good Strife is literally rooted (*en rizēsi*) in the earth (*WD* 19), Hesiod suggests a way in which humans are connected to the earth as part of an organic process requiring foresight, labor, and tools to garner the means for their survival. Good Strife as physical labor requires foresight and proper planning, which are necessary because mortals must contend with a treacherous natural world. One reason for the necessity of foresight concerns the limitations surrounding voice (*phōnē*) and communication between the human and nonhuman world. Hesiod explains:

> But a myriad of miseries roam among human beings, for the earth is full of evils, as well as the sea: various sicknesses descend upon human beings by day, and others by night, acting of their own will [*automatos*], stalking around in silence while carrying evils for mortals, since counselor Zeus removed their voice. (*WD* 100–104)

Here, Hesiod intimates that various evils used to possess voice, and thus could presumably speak or communicate with humans. In turn, this may have helped human beings explicitly identify, understand, and better evade various evils. Foresight and technology (such as farming tools) fill this gap: if necessity is the mother of invention, then lack of speech is its father.

In general, because evils no longer possess voice and roam silently, human beings of Hesiod's generation find themselves in an unpredictable natural world that taxes mortal existence in various ways:

> At another time the mind of aegis-bearing Zeus is different, difficult to discern for mortal men. . . . At one time it rains in the evening, at another time it gets very windy. . . . Finish your labor before the north wind arrives and return home, lest an ominous cloud from heaven envelops you at some point, soaking your skin and drenching your clothes. (*WD* 475–76, 544–48)

Employing foresight to overcome these challenges also involves the use of various tools, which further exhibits an urge to survive, and perhaps control, a physical world from which there is no escape. For example, Hesiod contends that the gods hid the means of life from human beings within the earth and that this is "much better for them" (*WD* 42), perhaps keeping them humbly occupied and out of the assembly where they might engage in bribery or meddle in others' affairs. Through the usage of various human implements such as ploughs and nonhuman animals such as cattle, Hesiod explains that part of the mortal condition is to uncover the means of life that remain concealed. Mortals will never completely escape labor and toil because something always remains hidden and is not handed directly over to them. Hesiod tells his brother Perses that this is the human condition: labor at work upon work. Hesiod's cosmology thus suggests that mortals can never be completely self-sufficient as a species or freed from a laboring, agonistic stance vis-à-vis the earth. As we will also see in the Vedic case, the poet accesses and expresses all of this profound knowledge of the cosmos and the human condition through the poetic skill.

There are two ways of viewing this relationship through the lens of rule. From one perspective, *basileis* would always be ruling-*in* a context where humans, as a particular type of (laboring) being, cannot be released from a human–nonhuman relationship of ruling-over the earth, as they are anchored in it "by the roots." However, from another perspective Hesiod suggests a way in which the earth governs, or at least has the potential to govern, human behavior through concealment. This latter perspective exhibits one way that the earth paradoxically engages in ruling-over from below through concealment, holding the potential to destroy whatever stands above it. In the next section I will explain how this idea re-emerges in the agonistic relationship between Gaia and Ouranos. Relatedly, Hesiod also explains how good Strife and anticipating hardship aims at human well-being and not any sort of co-constitutive, earthly well-being. Gaia may be the mother of humanity, but she does not merely hand things over to human beings without a labor cost. These ideas of good Strife, necessary labor, and appreciation for mortals' rooted, earthly well-being help to establish a unique framework for Hesiod's poetic protest and sense of justice.

Returning to the concept of memory, the idea of delighting in particular aspects of the past is deepened by the role of forgetfulness (*lēthē*). Born from Memory, the Muses can also serve the purpose of forgetting because they supply the capacity to forget, allowing human beings to remember the good things in order to help forget the bad. These divine beings make it possible for human beings not to dwell on past ills or present difficulties, further displaying how Memory and the Muses serve as a sort of existential balm for healing present anxieties and the human's condition as a laboring being. For example, with the power of memory human beings can choose to forget past pains:

> For even if someone experiencing sorrow in his freshly grieved *thumos* is parched from the grieving in his heart, when the poet-messenger of the Muses sings the glory of former human beings and the blessed gods who dwell on Olympus, immediately this person forgets his anxieties and does not remember his grief at all. For quickly the gifts of the goddesses have driven it away. (*Th*. 98–103)

Similarly, at the political level, the Muses allow Hesiod to remember how Zeus pours sweet speech into rulers, helping Hesiod explain how these rulers can settle bribe-inducing quarrels (*Th*. 81–87).

Tracking such claims, one can identify a subtle political message on Hesiod's part when it comes to his criticism of his brother, Perses, in *Works and Days*: forget many of the existing tales of Zeus as an individualistic honor-seeker and adopt a less agonistic image of Zeus, especially his role as just ruler and enforcer of justice. From Hesiod's perspective, the Homeric conception of Zeus may actually exemplify a "past pain" that he wants his audience to forget, especially if one pays close attention to the positive nature and meaning of each Muse. This interpretive point could further apply to ruling and justice because the Muses not only make possible a temporal connectedness with the past, and thus provide greater meaning for human beings within a cosmogonic context, but they also provide the capacity to forget rulers' past wrongs (perhaps even Zeus's) and remember the good they can accomplish. As I will argue in the next section, "remembering the good" will include recalling Zeus's just actions in distributing honors fairly to the other Olympians.

In sum, the Muses play an essential role in Hesiod's political thought, especially by helping establish a conceptual framework for his poetic protest against bribe-eating *basileis*. We can see how his relationship with these goddesses gives him the ability to grant glory to and within human communities as an inspired yet critically minded poet, which further suggests how greater political power and potential for critique can be found in the hands of the poet. In the next section, I will begin to explain how Hesiod diverges from Homer in significant ways. Hesiod puts this critical inspiration to work by recalling a cosmogony and theogony that provide the basis for a more peaceful resolution to ruling as hierarchical, individualistic distinction.

Cosmogony, Theogony, and Challenges to Hierarchical Rule

While Hesiod's cosmogony begins with Chaos, it moves through multiple stages of tension and conflict toward a justly ordered structure under Zeus's rule. To begin with, the Greek term *chaos* indicates a chasm, space, or clearing that would allow things to appear and exist as distinct entities. Within this space Gaia (Earth) is born (*Th.* 116–17), who is the mother and primordial feminine figure in Hesiod's theogony. She gives birth to the first major masculine being, Ouranos or Sky, whom Hesiod tells us is equal to herself and covers or envelops (*kaluptein*) her on all sides (*Th.* 126–27). We thus observe an initial hierarchical distinction between a higher and lower, with the masculine entity on top and female on bottom. Importantly, the nature of this primordial relationship is afflicted by tension because Ouranos despises his children and takes joy in hiding them within Gaia, not allowing them to manifest themselves and see the light of day (*Th.* 154–58). Although Hesiod does not explicitly use the language of ruling at this stage, if we draw on the political valence of similar scenes in the *Theogony* and *Works and Days*, this depiction of Ouranos shows him to be something of a corrupt ruler while Gaia remains the positive cosmic source (*archē*) of the Titans and other beings. To return briefly to a point I made in previous chapters, "lower" figures—whether male (e.g., *laoi* in the *Iliad*) or female (e.g., Penelope in the *Odyssey*)—provide the basis or ground for various sorts of ruling-over by male figures. As we will see, if this fact is not adequately acknowledged then agonistic tensions and violence can arise.

Hesiod implies that Ouranos's behavior is unfair and places undue pressure on Gaia, who groans from this constriction, and we therefore observe the first moment of cosmic leveling of rule with the figure of Kronos. Gaia fashions a sickle for her son, Kronos, who castrates Ouranos and "reaps" his father's genitals as Ouranos spreads himself over Gaia (*Th.* 173–82). The images of the sickle, reaping, and tossing his father's genitals (whose bloody drops become the seeds of subsequent growth, *Th.* 183–206) further illuminate an idea of the potential productivity stemming from agonistic, and perhaps even antagonistic, relations. From a ruling perspective, one idea we might glean from this primordial castration is that those below have warrant to claim fair treatment from those who may possess greater power, and that ruling-over always implicates relations of ruling-with and ruling-for others. Consequently, Ouranos nicknames his children Titans—literally, "strainers," or those who have stretched out and exerted themselves from below (unduly from the perspective of Ouranos) (*Th.* 207–10). While this straining exhibits an exertion of self-possessed individuality and Kronos's effort to fully realize his distinctive identity, Hesiod interjects the idea that this act remains wicked (*atasthalia; Th.* 209). Although Kronos was the first to possess the official mantle of cosmic ruler, he was also "crooked counseled [*agkulomētēs*]" and the "most terrible [*deinotatos*]" of Earth's children (*Th.* 137–38). One potential reason for characterizing Kronos in this manner is that it helps Hesiod explain how the eventual shift from Kronos to Zeus's rulership would be justified, even if it entails violent acts. As I will argue later in the chapter, these early stages in the cosmogony lay conceptual grounds for an anti-hierarchical move and critique of unrestrained ruling-over, as Hesiod implies that those in power must acknowledge a broader community of beings and relations that make their distinguished position possible.

Moreover, Hesiod's account supplies the transgressive idea that two female figures, Gaia and her daughter Rhea, rule with Kronos to some extent even though they stand below him. Importantly, Gaia holds the inner power and potential for unseating an unjust male figure insofar as she remains the primary *archē* (source) of beings and possesses the ability to hide things within herself. Ouranos is always exposed and does not possess the "inner depths" that allow Gaia to possess a sort of private domain, or a concealed space that is not exposed to a broader cosmic light. This ability to conceal things serves as a potent tool for ruling. Additionally, before Rhea gives birth to Zeus she seeks counsel with Gaia and Ouranos, who then counsel with one another and decide together. Here Hesiod uses the same verb, *sum-phrazomai*, that Homer uses when Achilles criticizes Agamemnon's failure to take counsel with his fellow *basileis* in the *Iliad* (*Il.* 9.374). This deliberative process results in what could be considered a ruling decision with major cosmic implications (i.e., the necessary conditions for Zeus's ascendance as ruler), and it is important to note that Gaia and Ouranos find themselves persuaded and obey (*peithein*) their daughter (*Th.* 468–74). Therefore, Zeus would not have been able to overcome his father Kronos without male and female figures ruling-with one another, and those ruling-over others (Gaia and Ouranos) making a decision to rule for the well-being of someone beneath them (Rhea and her children).

These macro-cosmic relationships between Gaia, Ouranos, Kronos, and Rhea prefigure not only a broader cosmological framework for understanding the various dimensions of rule, but they also serve as a starting point for Hesiod's belief that ruling should not revolve around individual distinction and the pursuit of honor, glory, or reputation. In other words, he does not propound a cosmos defined by agonistic relations that lead to hubris and violence, and in this respect, figures such as Gaia, Kronos, and Rhea provide the first models of critics who challenge domineering modes of ruling-over. At this stage in the cosmogony the main problem is that Kronos does not behave like a just ruler because he overpowers his sister Rhea and gobbles up his children as they are born. Up to this point, Hesiod's depiction of ruling appears to track the Homeric understanding of distinction insofar as a central male figure, Kronos, seeks to maintain the highest point in the cosmic hierarchy and remain the sole possessor of the "kingly honor," or *basilēida timēn* (*Th.* 462). Before moving to Kronos's downfall at the hands of Zeus, however, it is essential to highlight how the Fates also provide one of the earliest cosmological checks on hubristic, violent acts.

In Hesiod's theogony the goddess of Night or Darkness gives birth to Fate (*kēr*), the goddess of death. Fate is born before the Olympian gods, and soon thereafter Night bears a wide variety of Destinies (*moirai*) and additional Fates (*kēras*), including Klōthō, Lachesis, and Atropos (*Th.* 211–18). A central idea that Hesiod develops in this genealogy is that the Destinies and Fates check the transgressions of both mortals and immortals (*Th.* 220). In contrast to the Homeric account, these divinities appear to play a stronger role in punishing and monitoring the boundaries of proper relations among both human beings and gods. That is, the Fates help establish a cosmological structure that inherently possesses greater moral force than one observes in the Homeric structure, as they assist in policing the behavior of gods and humans. Such monitoring further implies that both divine and human beings can over-step (literally, *para-basis*) some sort of ethical boundaries. This elucidates part of the ethical foundation for Hesiod's cosmology and ontology, including nascent standards for good rule. Hesiod's political thought thus seeks to place fences around potentially destructive manifestations of agonistic individualism, which helps reduce the level of agonism that we see in Homer. For example, Hesiod explains how any Olympian can suffer a decade-long punishment for swearing false oaths, beginning with losing his or her breath and voice, suffering a divine coma (*kōma*, deep sleep) for one year. This coma is followed by a nine-year banishment from divine feasts and assemblies (*Th.* 793–803). One implication of the Fates' roles is that Zeus, even when he ultimately emerges as the cosmic monarch, must rule within certain ethical boundaries.

Although the Fates play a major role in Hesiod's political thought, Zeus plays the most significant role in the poet's understanding of rule. As I suggested earlier, the cosmic conflicts between Gaia and Ouranos, on the one hand, and Kronos and Rhea, on the other, lead toward the emergence of Zeus as the central ruling figure in Hesiod's cosmogonic and theogonic narrative. With the overthrow of his corrupt father, Zeus will enter the scene as the first just ruler. This transition from Kronos to Zeus also displays some of the Greeks' deepest anxieties about hierarchical modes of ruling-over, especially fears of being overtaken or ruled by someone else and having to share in ruling-over others (*Th.* 459–62). In short, the story of Zeus's ascendance as the sole cosmic ruler serves as the backbone of Hesiod's political thought.

The Ascendance of Zeus

Over the course of his *Theogony* and *Works and Days* Hesiod provides a new model of Zeus—what one might consider Zeus "2.0"—who possesses many of the central characteristics that we observe in Homer, especially strength and cunning. However, not all of Hesiod's ideas about Zeus are novel. For example, Zeus remains the strongest among the gods: "He is best [*pherteros*] among the gods and mightiest in strength [*kratos*]" (*Th.* 48–49). But contrary to the predominant portrait we get with Homer, Hesiod overtly describes Zeus as a just and fair ruler who faces serious challenges in his path to cosmic monarchy. Perhaps most important, Zeus's rule is not only predicated on the two central characteristics we saw in Homer, namely strength and cunning, but also on his relationship to justice and the fair distribution of honors: "He distributed everything fairly to the immortals and contrived their honors" (*Th.* 71–74). As we shall see, Hesiod characterizes Zeus as ruling-for the well-being and interests of others within a broader cosmic context, which is nicely captured with the verb *em-basileuō*: to be king *in* or *among* others.

The first major step in Zeus's ascendance as sole ruler in the cosmos begins with his leadership role in the Olympians' battle with the Titans. Significantly, the story of the Olympian victory begins with just, effective speech and not pure strength or action. Hesiod tells us that the battle largely remained a stalemate (*Th.* 635–38) until Zeus offered the hundred-handed Obriareus, Cottus, and Gyges "entirely fitting or appropriate things" (*armena panta, Th.* 639),[3] including a share of the gods' nectar and ambrosia. Echoing an important Homeric phrase, Zeus does what his *thumos* bids him to do, but in this case his *thumos*' command invokes kind friendship (*philotēs enēēs*) between the Olympians and Hundred Handers and draws attention to their interconnected interests (*Th.* 651). Zeus explains that he has taken these Hundred Handers' suffering into account, contrasting his concern with Kronos's confining them in Tartaros, which displays his good nature and provides warrant for siding with his Olympians against the Titans. In ruling-over others, Hesiod thus emphasizes how Zeus considers the interests of those who had been hierarchically mistreated and the honor of those who deserve it. Again, Hesiod's poetic justice suggests that virtues—here, the Hundred Handers' friendship and loyalty in battle—be rightly rewarded.

The Hundred Handers then recognize the effectiveness of Zeus's plea by praising his speech (*epainein; Th.* 664–65), which exhibits an essential aspect of rule that we saw in Homer: the significance of *epainos* (praise, approval) and communal compliance for legitimate political decision-making. Such fair treatment of the Hundred Handers helps lead to what Hesiod implies is a just resolution to the battle. Only after this speech and the Hundred Handers' assistance is Zeus's superior strength and lightning bolts, along with the Hundred Handers' epic boulder-tossing, successful in tipping the scales of battle (*Th.* 687–720). This is the first exhibition of Zeus's just nature as he enlists the assistance of the three previously dishonored Titans and puts an end to a destructive, earth-shaking conflict.

The next step in his ascendence involves both speech and physical strength, as Zeus confronts Typhoeus, Gaia's youngest and most frightening son. Zeus's just rule will not be fully instantiated until he defeats a potentially stronger and (somewhat) singular foe, which parallels a previous sequence of events when Kronos overthrew Ouranos. Depicting such a challenger helps Hesiod further highlight the central characteristics associated with the Olympian's supremacy as sole ruler, narrating an engagement that may finally end the string of bottom-up tensions and challenges to a ruler's supremacy. Here, one might also ask why Typhoeus is not potentially justified in overtaking Zeus. One reason concerns the nature of speech. Typhoeus is incoherent, depicted as frightening and brutish because of the multifarious heads and voices that emanate from his body. For Hesiod, speech should be clear and fair in order to be just and politically unifying, as strength alone does not provide a warrant for just rule. Moreover, Typhoeus's multilingualism is *animalistic*:

> And from his shoulders there were a hundred heads of a snake, a terrible dragon's, licking with their dark tongues. . . . And there were voices in all his terrible heads, sending forth all kinds of sounds, inconceivable: for sometimes they would utter sounds as though for the gods to understand, and at other times the sound of a loud-bellowing, majestic

> bull, unstoppable in its strength, at other times that of a lion, with a ruthless spirit, at other times like young dogs, a wonder to hear, and at other times he hissed, and the high mountains echoed from below (*Th.* 824–26, 829–35; trans. Most 2006)

Typhoeus thus represents a tremendous multiplicity of beings and voices, and therefore he could not be a "monarch" in the precise sense of the term—*monarchia*, rule of or by a *single* ruler. This aspect of Hesiod's political thought expresses a somewhat traditional conception of proper kingly rule as requiring a single ruler who can guide and command the multiplicity around and beneath him. Such a plurality of voices, some of which are nonhuman, threaten the order that just rule aims to achieve. As in Homer, suppressing chaotic "noise" serves as a precondition for having a legitimate assembly—especially an assembly of self-possessed individuals capable of rational speech. Typhoeus's association with animality thus elucidates the increasingly human-centric dimension of Greek political thought. Hesiod suggests that while animals can make noises, self-possessed individuals—particularly gods and human beings—can and should speak rationally and coherently by corralling an inner plurality of impulses, or internal noise. There is a subtle suggestion here that self-possessed individuals should rule over this potentially chaotic, animalistic dimension of their own inner plurality.

In this regard, Typhoeus's physical features represent the unpredictability of a plurality presumed to be internal and constitutive of self-possessed individuality—a plurality that requires a hierarchical ruling element to attain coherence. If we look at Typhoeus as a loosely unified yet plural self, Hesiod adds something to the Homeric conception of self-possessed individuality by implying that such plurality is dangerous because it is unpredictable. For example, after Zeus defeats Typhoeus and hurls him to Tartarus, Hesiod recounts how Typhoeus gives birth not only to "moist-blowing winds" but also random gusts of wind that create great miseries for human beings both at sea and on the earth, as the latter "blow randomly across the sea . . . causing great calamities for mortals, as they rage with evil, stormy winds" (*Th.* 872–74). Hence, Typhoeus's motley nature is partly to blame for the unforeseeable natural forces that lie outside human control, which Hesiod depicts as distinctly evil for mortal humans. These passages expose a key component of Hesiod's political thought: the desire for predictability and hierarchical control over the irrational and unpredictable aspects of the nonhuman world. The battle with Typhoeus, however, is not the final step in Zeus's ascension.

After the Olympians ask Zeus to assume the role of monarch among the gods and to rule over them (*Th.* 881–86), Zeus takes Mētis (wisdom and cunning) as his first wife. From the marriage of Zeus and Mētis/Wisdom, Hesiod explains, Athena would emerge as an equally strong and wise counterpart to her father (*Th.* 895–96). But most important, Athena is prophesied to give birth to a male child who would challenge Zeus, and because of this Zeus consumes Mētis and breaks the chain of potential challengers to his monarchical rule (*Th.* 899–900). This move also allows Zeus to subsume and possess an entity who would counsel him about both good and evil things (*Th.* 900), further adding to the plurality of his own selfhood. Following this, Zeus marries another politically significant female figure, Themis (customary law or ordinance; also, a judgment or decision given by a king or ruler), who gives birth to Eunomia (lawfulness, good order), Dikē (justice, right judgment), and Eirēnē (Peace). While these goddesses exhibit many of the standards for proper kingly rule on the mortal plane, Zeus's consumption of Mētis again displays how a male ruler depends upon and requires a female counterpart to rule effectively. In this particular passage, we observe how Zeus both rules over his fellow gods and goddesses but must also rule with the advice and internal counsel of the female Mētis. Hence, the cosmological model that Hesiod lays out suggests that ruling-over requires ruling-with—a relationship that can easily be obscured or forgotten if one focuses more narrowly on a single individual such as Zeus and more domineering modes of ruling-over.

Zeus's status as an all-powerful cosmic ruler is also put to the test by a less powerful yet equally significant figure, Prometheus, whose cunning comes close to matching Zeus's own. Prometheus is a Titan whose name means "forethought," and this name evokes the ability to cautiously anticipate or predict the future, and perhaps even control, what might take place as a result of one's actions. For example, he instructs his brother Epimetheus (Afterthought) "Never to accept a gift from the Olympian Zeus but rather to send it back, lest some evil emerges for mortals" (*WD* 85–89). From a philosophical perspective, Prometheus's capacity for "fore-thinking" is significant because it further displays the normative idea that individuals can take greater responsibility for their actions instead of shifting total (or predominant) responsibility to the Fates or various gods. In turn, both Prometheus's name and actions open greater conceptual space for a more humanistic and human-centric understanding of decision-making, which will include the responsibility for ruling. This nascent humanism would impact how mortals could view their own agentic capacities because Prometheus's infamous behavior is closely linked to humans and their well-being. In one respect, Prometheus provides an ontological model for humans by exhibiting a strong sense of individualism and the ability to use foresight to choose a more desirable future for human life. Consequently, he displays an orientation to life that reflects a deep responsibility for one's own actions, and even one's fate.

From Zeus's perspective, Prometheus (forethought) displays a hubristic threat partly because the Titan provides a model of someone who decides (*krinomai*) things on his own and does not simply obey higher powers such as Zeus. As Hesiod tells us, Prometheus directly challenges Zeus by quarreling and striving against the Olympian's counsels (*Th.* 534). In the context of Hesiod's cosmogony and theogony, this contention takes place while mortal human beings and immortal gods are being definitively separated from one another (*Th.* 535–37), thus signaling a cosmological break that will have major repercussions for Hesiod's political thought. Over the course of his works, Hesiod narrates two major agonistic episodes between Zeus and Prometheus. First, when the decision was being made as to the proper sacrificial gifts for the gods, Prometheus attempts to trick Zeus by letting him choose between attractive fat-wrapped bones and an unattractive stomach full of meat and fat. Zeus chooses the former option and allows Prometheus to swindle him out of the desirable portions, partly so that he could punish both Prometheus and human beings for the deception (*Th.* 535–60). Second, as punishment for Prometheus's deceptive behavior Zeus withdraws fire from the mortal world, which the Titan later steals from Olympus (*Th.* 561–67; *WD* 47–52). This rebellious act then results in the baleful "gift" of Pandora to humans (*Th.* 570–612; *WD* 53–89), along with Prometheus being chained to a rock so that an eagle could consume his immortal, regenerating liver day after day (*Th.* 521–25). While significant ground for this Promethean assertion of will was already laid in the idea of self-possessed individuality, within the context of a cosmological separation and Prometheus's agonistic episodes, the ability of foresight supplies a conceptual hook for explaining how and why mortal individuals can (and must) start taking responsibility for their own actions.

Within the broader cosmic schema, the employment of such foresight draws Zeus's ire and elicits some of his harshest behavior, which understandably raises questions about the Olympian's identity as a just ruler. For example, in contrasting the cosmic roles of Zeus and Prometheus, Robert Bartlett (2006, 183–84) has argued that Zeus does not consistently act for the benefit of human beings as Prometheus does, thus emphasizing Zeus's punishment of human beings for stealing fire, especially through the gift of Pandora. Bartlett also comments on how events surrounding the creation of Pandora challenge the idea of Zeus's power as being absolute. In his account of the "five ages of man" Hesiod holds up the fourth race of mortals, the heroes and demigods, as interested in the well-being of their communities (*WD* 157–60). Bartlett argues that these passages provide evidence of the "defective character of Zeus's reign in the fifth and present age" (2006, 190). He advances this interpretation by referring to the fact that some heroes and demigods live apart from the immortals, under the kingship of Kronos, in the idyllic "isle of the blessed."[4] Perhaps the strongest piece of evidence for Zeus's potential injustice is captured in the Olympian's willingness to punish a whole city due to the injustice of a single person, which would include innocent women and children (Bartlett 2006, 193). Indeed, these interpretations portray a Zeus that looks like the antagonistic character that I outlined in the previous chapter.

While Hesiod claims that Zeus is a just and fair ruler, Bartlett helps highlight some of the tensions in Hesiod's accounts. Bartlett is correct to point out that Zeus's punishments concerning fire and Pandora are harsh in some respects, but from Zeus's perspective, one might alternatively blame Prometheus for the harsh outcomes. For example, because of Prometheus's willful theft of fire from Olympus mortals are able to regain its benefit, but this is a benefit that mortals did not necessarily *earn*. Here one could say that Zeus's punishments aim to teach humans a degree of humility, interpreting this episode as an attempt to show mortals that they are not the most powerful beings within the cosmos and draw their attention to a greater set of powers outside their control. Even if Zeus's behavior could be judged unjust, both Prometheus and humans should have been able to predict potentially destructive consequences through the ability of foresight. This milder characterization of Zeus would also cohere with a broader ethic that we see in Hesiod's works: the principle of not receiving the benefit of something that was not freely given or rightfully earned through hard work. In the *Works and Days*, Hesiod goes to great length in explaining the importance of labor and Good Strife, especially in his critique of Perses for unjust thievery and bribery of *basileis* (*WD* 34–41). It may be because the modern mind wants to understand fire as something like a right and not a gift (rather human-centrically and hubristically, one might add) that leads to a harsher reading of Zeus.

Relatedly, Richard Hamilton (1989, 25) notes how Prometheus is called an *anax* (*Th.* 543), which means that Zeus must contend with two kings in his attempts to order the cosmos: Kronos and Prometheus. As *anax*, Prometheus could also be considered unjust because he challenges Zeus in attempting to usurp Zeus's kingly prerogative, which includes serving as the primary distributer of goods and honors. Prometheus's sly attempt to give Zeus fat-wrapped bones and human beings the better portion supports this reading (*Th.*

535–44). Jenny Strauss Clay advances a similar interpretation, explaining, "By taking over the function of distribution, Prometheus reveals his ambition to be the supreme god and to usurp Zeus's power and status" (2003, 108). Therefore, one could argue that Zeus is not necessarily unjust in punishing Prometheus, and human beings as a result, because Prometheus attempts to trick and challenge a stronger and just ruler. This situation exhibits another instance of Zeus suppressing a challenge to his authority, which one need not interpret as unjust. After all, Prometheus was the first to act deceptively, not Zeus. This interpretation would evoke the second sense of Hesiod's poetic justice insofar as an *anax*'s vices—here, Prometheus's deception—are rightly punished.

Similar tensions surround the gift of Pandora to mankind. Bartlett (2006, 184) argues that the passages concerning Pandora's construction at the hands of multiple gods suggests chaos is the "first and decisive principle" in the world. This communal assemblage certainly shows how Zeus's power is not absolute in a "tyrannical" fashion, but it is not quite as chaotic as Bartlett seems to suggest. While Zeus's precise instructions may not be followed to the letter, no agonistic infighting occurs as a result, which is what we consistently see in Homeric examples. If anything, Hesiod's account is evidence of the greater order and harmony among the gods since they can act on their own prerogative without antagonistically threatening and fighting with one another. In comparison to many of Homer's accounts, this is evidence of an orderly, less violent agonism. As I will also argue later in this chapter, this does not mean the relatively ordered Olympian condition and Zeus's rule guarantee similar order and justice in human communities. Nevertheless, the differences between the Homeric and Hesiodic Zeus appear to be more significant than their similarities.

Here a critic might respond by highlighting the fact that Zeus swallows Mētis and his would-be successor in the *Theogony* (897), citing this as evidence of violent behavior and strong agonism among the gods. Zeus's behavior undoubtedly resembles the previous unjust actions of Kronos and Ouranos, and while this is a reasonable point, Zeus's actions in this scenario could alternatively be interpreted as just because they help solve the succession problem and stabilize rule in the cosmos (see Hamilton 1989, 16).[5] In addition, if Zeus is already depicted as a just ruler in contrast to Kronos, then ending the succession issue makes sense because it puts a stop to events that always entail violence of some sort. As Hamilton aptly summarizes, "power is no longer to be passed violently from father to son but is permanently in the hands of Zeus" (41).

Nevertheless, Bartlett points out that Zeus appears quite capricious and cruel in his treatment of innocent women and children in communities that may harbor unjust individuals. For example, Hesiod states: "But far-seeing Zeus, son of Kronos, marks out justice for those who care only about evil arrogance and cruel deeds. Oftentimes even an entire *polis* suffers because of a wicked man, someone who sins and devises reckless deeds" (*WD* 239–41). One might alternatively read these passages as suggesting that the unjust behavior of a single person (for example, Perses)[6]—especially if such behavior begins to accumulate when not properly addressed by rulers—can result in the gradual decay or destruction of a political community. This is precisely the sort of behavior that de-legitimates existing ruling structures. The idea that Zeus is responsible merely follows from Hesiod's traditional-hierarchical belief in a single cosmic ruler who may be the most powerful but not sole causal mechanism in the cosmos. Such a powerful entity would at least be partly connected to events that take place on the human plane, even if it is only by overlooking certain transgressions. This is not necessarily evidence that Hesiod believes Zeus is a cruel or unjust ruler, although interpreters might judge him so from a more modern standpoint. Most important, Hesiod himself does not directly label Zeus as cruel or unjust, even if some passages may suggest as much to a modern eye. While Zeus does not always appear as a warm, kind-hearted cosmic ruler, in contrast to the Homeric Zeus and Hesiod's own accounts of a smothering Ouranos and wicked Kronos, Hesiod's Zeus should not be interpreted as negatively as Bartlett suggests. Ultimately, such negative accounts of Zeus do not outweigh the political significance Hesiod places on Zeus as a fair decision-maker in the divine realm and enforcer of justice in human communities, and the punishments following the Promethean challenges appear to extinguish the potentially violent agonistic competition that might disrupt Zeus's ruling power or prerogative.

Human Rule and Unjust *Basileis*: Justice and Critiques of Hierarchy

When turning our attention to human communities, Zeus is explained as the divine, cosmological model for, and source of, human *basileis* (see also Donlan 1997, 42). While *basileis* derive their inspiration for right judgment from the Muses, Zeus is the source of their kingly power and social status: "Singers and harpers are from the Muses and far-shooting Apollo, but kings are from Zeus" (*Th.* 94–96; see also Raaflaub 2000). This statement thus clarifies how Hesiod's cosmology—as a web of beliefs concerning how the cosmos arose in the first place, came to be ordered, and its subsequent ordered nature under Zeus's kingly rule—is linked to his conception of rule on the human plane. Hesiod depicts Zeus not only as ruling-over others but also as ruling-in and ruling-for a broader cosmic community of divine and human beings. The resulting link between cosmic and human *basileus*-rule follows: hierarchical kingly rule exists at the cosmic level, with Zeus at the top, while human kingship is an inevitable result of this cosmic hierarchy, Zeus's existence, and his role as ruler in the divine community. As long as Zeus exists and rules over the cosmos, Hesiod seems to believe that human *basileis* will inevitably, and perhaps should, rule over human subjects. As he suggests in *Works and Days*, common subjects such as he and Perses should not meddle in the affairs of the assembly but rather spend their time working and leave decision-making to the proper authorities (*WD* 27–32). Because Zeus's cosmic rule appears quite favorable and stable, Hesiod does not appear to believe that a ruling structure other than kingship is desirable, or even possible.

As a transition to Hesiod's critique of ruling as honorific distinction, I want to highlight a particular connection between Zeus and human rulers that also played an important role in Homeric thought. Hospitality's (*xenia*) relationship to *basileus*-rule exhibits an important link to Zeus. Insofar as hospitality is a central ethical custom in archaic poetry, and to the extent that it is connected to *basileus*-rule (cosmic or otherwise), Hesiod's understanding of hospitality is a somewhat traditional and hierarchical one. He states:

> It is the same for a man who mistreats either a suppliant or stranger, or a man who mounts his own brother's bed, secretly sleeping with his wife, doing something indecent . . . Zeus himself is angry with this man, and in the end places harsh recompense upon him for such unjust deeds. (*WD* 327–29, 333–34)

In these passages, Hesiod links hospitality to Zeus in such a way that when a guest violates the customs of hospitality, Zeus will purportedly punish this person. This point entails two significant implications. First, Hesiod believes his cosmic reign is all encompassing and that Zeus, as the rightful hierarchical ruler, will justly punish those who deserve punishment. Second, it exhibits the belief that both cosmic and human kingship are necessary to maintain order. For example, when Hesiod chastises his brother and mentions the gift-devouring kings, one reason he is so angry is because he believes kings should make fair, straight judgments. Hesiod expects straight judgments from kings because he believes making such judgments is their social responsibility. As Hesiod intimates in the quote, Zeus, who is a just *basileus* and model for all human *basileis*, provides straight judgments and rightly punishes those who deserve it (see also Raaflaub 1993, 62, 67). If *basileis* do not make straight judgments, then the social order will break down and the entire community will suffer. It thus makes sense that Hesiod tries to convince his brother that Zeus justly punishes those who deserve it. Here one can observe how hospitality is linked to a hierarchical notion of kingly rule and the straight judgments that such rule is supposed to provide. In sum, he believes hierarchical kingly rule is proper and necessary, as he condemns his brother by referencing Zeus's power and unquestioned protection of hospitality.

Such beliefs expose a degree of cosmic interconnectedness between human beings and gods similar to that found in Homeric works. This connectedness, however, is also tenuous as it was in Homer. Because the gods mix and mingle with human beings as beings who themselves have self-possessed individuality, an ontological tension exists between them. Beginning with the primordial yet strained relationship between Gaia and Ouranos, the gods already exhibit much of the agonistic behavior that we see reflected in Hesiod's conception of human rule and communal decision-making. Hence, while the divine and human planes intersect and overlap to some extent, the Greek cosmo-political landscape is full of agonistic, individualistic behavior.

Bribe-Eating Kings and the Issue of Interconnected Well-Being

As in Homer, human *basileis* attempt to distinguish themselves in pursuit of honor, glory, and reputation, albeit more indirectly. In *Works and Days*, the phrase "gift devouring" (*dōro-phagos*) indicates the sort of ruling behavior mentioned in Homer, though from a different perspective. Hesiod similarly characterizes human rulers as primarily interested in wealth and honor. The gift giving and devouring Hesiod chastises is part of the process that helps *basileis* increase their honor and reputation within their aristocratic circle. This process resembles the Homeric examples discussed in the previous chapter, where gift giving and receiving were associated with competitive contests and hospitality. In *Works and Days*, Hesiod describes similar gift giving, although it now appears to extend to the courts or assemblies. From the *basileus*' perspective, the opportunities available for enhancing his honor, wealth, and reputation in legal situations likely differ very little from the parallel opportunities I examined in Homeric works. However, instead of describing the wealth and tribute from a kingly or aristocratic perspective, Hesiod views it from a commoner's point of view. Hesiod thus believes *basileis* should aim for straight judgments and not focus on acquiring gifts, wealth, or tribute. In this sense, Hesiod criticizes precisely what is celebrated in Homer: *basileis* that aim to acquire the necessary means for hierarchical distinction in order to situate themselves above others, and do so to such an extent that they can neglect the interests of others without necessarily suffering the consequences of a successful revolt by those below (upon whom the rulers depend).

As we saw in Homer, such competitive relations between rulers and their subjects fueled efforts at hierarchical distinction, and as I explained in the first section of the chapter, Hesiod rejects this agonism early on in the *Theogony* by praising gentle speech that soothes social and political tensions. Relatedly, Hesiod understands good rule as ruling-in and ruling-for the well-being of the broader community, and we can partly define this well-being by a lack of disagreement and competition in the *agora*, particularly disputes that lead to bribery or violence. For Hesiod gentle, persuasive speech is precisely what makes *basileis* "conspicuous" (*prepein*, to be clearly identified, distinguished) in a positive sense within their communities (*Th*. 91–92). Interestingly, Hesiod suggests that kings are better or more just as rulers the more they resemble *poets* and the poet's skill of beautiful speech. This provides yet another way in which Hesiod's political thought levels the significance of ruling-over by emphasizing a more egalitarian conception of rule, explaining how essential attributes for ruling can be shared across social strata.

To begin clarifying Hesiod's critique it is helpful to ask why *basileis* make partial decisions and behave as gift-devouring individuals in the first place, especially if Hesiod's Zeus is to be understood as a threatening enforcer of straight judgments. For example, Hesiod tells us that Zeus has numerous immortals upon the earth that monitor cruel or abusive behavior:

> O kings, give serious thought to this justice yourselves. For there are immortal beings that exist among humans which identify those who trample over one another with crooked judgments and do not heed the gods' vengeance. For upon the much-nourishing earth there are thrice ten thousand of Zeus' immortal guardians for mortal humans, who keep watch over judgments and wicked deeds, clothed in haze, roaming about in all directions upon the earth. (*WD* 248–55)

This cosmic surveillance system appears quite comprehensive, as these immortal spies keep watch from all directions and remain rather imperceptible to the human eye.

However, contra Hesiod's warnings, one gets the idea that Zeus must not be very threatening to these *basileis* who, if one recalls the Homeric model, seem more interested in distinguishing themselves from each other and increasing their personal honor, glory, and reputation. Although *basileis* may believe in Zeus's ability to punish to some extent, it appears that in Hesiod's immediate social context they may possess a more Homeric understanding of Zeus; in this regard, Hesiod's poetic protest can be seen as aiming to change rulers' minds that the Homeric model is the proper one to follow. Either Zeus must serve as a positive model for distinction as glory- and honor-seeking, or beliefs in Zeus's constant involvement in human affairs is beginning to wane. But one could press the question further and ask: What is the basis for rulers viewing their sociopolitical roles in such a pervasively individualistic manner? Or, looking at the situation from another angle, why are *basileis* not as influenced by Hesiod's threats as one might expect? One important explanation may be found in beliefs concerning self-possessed individuality.

In *Works and Days*, Hesiod explains how *basileis* are not concerned enough with just decision-making and honoring Justice (i.e., the goddess, Zeus's daughter). This indicates that rulers do not understand themselves as deeply connected to their subjects, broader communities, or other types of beings who might be affected by their judgments. One explanation for rulers' indifference is the lack of cosmological and ontological beliefs that would support the idea that it is necessary to make fair judgments. Hesiod's political context parallels Homer's epic world insofar as it lacks a strong sense of interconnected well-being between human beings, let alone between human and nonhuman beings. A potential basis for such ontological disconnectedness can be found in Hesiod's *Theogony*, where all differentiated, existent things emerge from the void (*chaos*) individually as they are and will continue to be (more or less) in their basic essence. For example, the identity of Gaia, Ouranos, Kronos, and Zeus are quite clear from the start and their basic "stripes" do not change—only their cosmological positioning based on internecine conflicts. To clarify, on Hesiod's account all beings' identities appear to be consistently demarcated and closed off on a basic ontological level from other beings, which will contrast starkly with brahmanical thought.[7] This is not to say that existent things do not connect to other things in various ways, or that they do not grow and change over time, but rather that every being's identity, interests, and well-being are not fundamentally predicated on its interconnectedness to other beings to the extent one observes in brahmanical political thought.

While this somewhat atomistic understanding of identity provides a hurdle for any strong sense of interconnectedness pertaining to rule, one can locate an additional barrier in Hesiod's cosmogony, cosmology, and ontology. In the *Theogony*, proper *basileus*-rule arises well after the initial creation of the cosmos. While the cosmos undergoes a long creative process before settling into its current state, we also learn that *basileis* and kingship did not arise in the initial creative moments. Hence, Hesiod's cosmogony and cosmology describe how Zeus's just kingship arrives late on the scene. The fact that kingly rule is not built into the initial cosmic fabric—let alone a just form thereof—would presumably decrease any strong cosmological commitment or sense of duty to rule justly, because rulers would not perceive it as inherent in the natural order of things. This cosmogonic account thus leaves room for innovation and the belief that one can make self-determining choices, which weaken—but do not entirely eliminate, as I discussed earlier with the Fates—the potential deontological aspects of Hesiod's political ethic. This is one reason why cosmic kingly rule may not assure order on the human plane and why Hesiod must pester Zeus to straighten the rulers' crooked judgments. In Hesiod's cosmology one finds an ideal model for *basileis*, but this is not enough to assure they behave justly because it does not adequately balance or overcome a belief in self-possessed individuality, agonistic displays of self-worth, and corresponding motivations to earn greater honor. These conceptions of self and identity raise a formidable barrier for potential beliefs in a deeply interconnected, communal well-being. At this point in time, Hesiod's attempt to square the circle of distinction and justice appears coherent enough in theory yet stillborn in the practical affairs of rule.

Poetic Protest and the Standard of Justice

To address these issues concerning the disconnectedness of rule, Hesiod develops and appeals to a new understanding of justice as an alternative to focusing on distinction and honor gained through wealth and competition. He explicitly recommends that *basileis* turn their attention to Justice as a deity, and more obliquely, to justice as an abstract ethical concept. Since justice (*dikē*) had not undergone any systematic philosophical reflection or questioning as a concept up to this point in Greek history, Hesiod's ideas about justice focus more explicitly on the divine goddess, Justice, and her connection to proper *basileus*-rule. Again, Zeus plays a central role:

> Justice is a maiden, born of Zeus, treated as glorious and venerable by the gods who dwell on Olympus; and whenever someone harms her by crookedly scorning her, immediately she sits down beside her father Zeus, son of Cronus, and tells of the unjust mind of men so that he punishes the people for the reckless deeds of their kings . . . (*WD* 256–62)

In this passage Hesiod links justice and kingship, attempting to convince *basileis* that they are responsible for making straight judgments and protecting Justice. When scorned, Justice reports to her father, resulting in everyone—not just kings—suffering Zeus's punishment. Therefore, Hesiod first posits a theological and cosmological understanding of justice and its connection to *basileus*-rule. According to this account, justice is a revered goddess and Zeus's daughter, and when she is mistreated, the cosmic ruler enforces the necessary punishment. In this passage Hesiod not only suggests a direct, genealogical connection between rule and justice but also a more horizontal, leveled dimension of rule. Departing from more familiar images that we see in Homer when gods and goddesses kneel or cower before Zeus, here we see that Justice sits beside him, which creates a horizontal image regarding the relation between ruling power and justice. In this respect, Justice engages in ruling-with Zeus when it comes to human affairs. This is not the only image of leveling, as Hesiod explains: "She remains, weeping, in the city and common peoples' abodes" (*WD* 222). Justice thus experiences her pain and laments in the human community because of what happens there, and not on Olympus or elsewhere. In contrast to Homer, these passages provide evidence of leveling in ruling responsibilities as human rulers possess a clear, weighty obligation to rule for the well-being of their communities.

The image of Justice's lament also captures a natural-communal element, suggesting that rulers and judges should understand themselves not necessarily as ruling-with the *laoi* or *dēmos* but rather as ruling-for their interests. In the passage that follows, we see a subtle shift from the goddess Justice (Dikē) to justice (*dikē*) as a general, abstract concept. Not only does this signal the transition to a more general ethical point that Hesiod may want to advance, but we can also observe how ruling-for the interests and well-being of others involves an earthly agency:

> But those who provide straight judgments for both foreigners and citizens, and do not deviate from justice (*dikē*) at all, their city thrives, and the people within it blossom. Peace, the nurse of children, exists upon the earth, and far-seeing Zeus never ordains that there be baneful war for these people: at no time does famine or recklessness accompany these straight-judging people, and in their festivities they share the things they have cared for in their labor. And Gaia then brings an abundance of life for them, as the mountain oaks bear acorns on the tips of their branches and honey bees in the center of their trunks; their woolly sheep are heavily laden with flocks of wool; and men's

> wives give birth to children who resemble them; they continuously thrive with good things. (*WD* 225–36)

Hence, when Justice is cared for, the earth/Gaia responds kindly, implying a certain level of connectedness between rule and the natural world. However, this conception also places human beings in the driver's seat as Hesiod suggests that humans can partly control the Gaia–human relationship through the activity of rule. Just forms of ruling-over and ruling-for human communities thus lead to more peaceful relations of rule within a broader natural context. Nevertheless, many *basileis* must not find this sort of account convincing. If they had strongly believed in its truthfulness, then one would expect Hesiod to be applauding *basileis'* decisions rather than scorning them. This passage clearly displays one of Hesiod's central criticisms of *basileus*-rule as distinction. The passages also exhibit how Hesiod views the community's well-being as a measuring-stick for proper *basileus*-rule (*WD* 238–47). In sum, Hesiod challenges precisely the type of *basileus*-rule described and generally accepted as justified in the Homeric epics.

While Hesiod focuses more explicitly on Justice as a goddess, his political thought also suggests that justice (more broadly construed) contains a natural, normative aspect that is proto-metaphysical in orientation. The first important point to highlight is that Zeus ends up serving Dikē, who is both younger and female. It follows that rulers must always be responsive to Justice within the human community and of service to those who are politically weaker than them, as Zeus (the ruler) will purportedly enforce his daughter's concerns. Second, justice also operates as an impersonal standard for explaining why Zeus is a good ruler, which contrasts markedly with Homer's Zeus. Aside from and before the birth of Justice (his daughter), Hesiod implies that a standard exists even for Zeus, which is the most radical implication of Hesiod's innovative move toward the first discernable political metaphysics in Greek thought. That is, Zeus is just due to the nature of his achievements and how he distributes honors. In order for Hesiod's claim to make sense, an impersonal criterion must exist to judge his actions as just—a criterion that is not merely self-referential or predicated on his distinguished, self-possessed individuality. The larger lesson here is that rulership, power, and force should be in the service of justice, further meaning that kingly rule is now itself governed by justice to some extent.

To unpack this idea a bit more, for Zeus's actions to be deemed as just vis-à-vis his Olympians and fellow victors there must be a standard that exists independently of Zeus by which Hesiod could make such a judgment. In this respect, Zeus does not determine what justice is, as Bartlett (2006, 181) suggests. Bartlett's interpretation relies more on Justice as a goddess and daughter of Zeus, and here I agree that she could not precede Zeus since a daughter cannot precede a father. Justice as fair, straight decision-making is another matter. The tricky thing here is that Zeus is the first to act justly and dole out fair judgments and honors, so it can appear that *he* determines what justice is. But this could not be the case because then justice could only exist after a purportedly just decision was made, which is both incoherent and ill-suited to the idea that justice revolves around fair, straight decision-making as such. Also, if this was plausible, there would be no way to discern whether or not Zeus's actions and decisions were just, as they would only be bare commands predicated on power. Hesiod does not explain how such commands could be just merely as a result of coming from Zeus rather than simply being just in and of themselves. I do not want to suggest the complete lack of inconsistency or incoherence in Hesiod's thought, but I think it is wise not to overlook Hesiod's bifurcated (Justice/justice) understanding of the concept because justice as a normative standard can be logically prior to Zeus, even if the goddess cannot be.

In this regard, Bartlett rightfully claims, "surely it is impossible to say of Zeus that he would ever make crooked the straight" (2006, 181–82), which further implies a natural standard and proto-metaphysics of some sort. On the one hand, if Zeus really could determine what justice is, then making crooked the straight would not be an impossibility. Although logically possible, this situation is highly unlikely and counterintuitive given Hesiod's overarching portrayal of Zeus. On the other hand, one might contend that this scenario would be eminently possible if one were to accept the interpretation of Zeus as an all-powerful and capricious ruler, as Bartlett does. However, this counterfactual scenario would be highly implausible because Zeus must follow a standard to earn the mantle of "just." Deforming the straight would not make sense precisely because it is unjust, and if Zeus were to make a straight person (or ruler) crooked, surely Hesiod would deem this behavior unjust and akin to the behavior of figures such as Ouranos and Kronos. Contra Bartlett, it appears that Zeus cannot determine what is just and unjust.

Nevertheless, Bartlett (2006, 180) draws important attention to Hesiod's account in the proem about Zeus's power in crushing the mighty, bringing down the conspicuous, and withering the proud. He also points out how these accounts "fail to mention explicitly either the goodness or the justice of Zeus" (180). He then uses this point to argue that Zeus stands prior to justice as such, contending "justice is the 'law' given to human beings by Zeus

[*WD* 276]" (181). This interpretation of the passage, however, can be misleading. The moral thrust here is that Zeus ordains (*dia-tassein*) that this law (*nomos*), justice, be followed. Indeed, this is the gist of Hesiod's entire argument concerning justice: it exists as an independent entity (both goddess and normative concept), and while Zeus (supposedly) enforces it as a standard for human beings to follow, he does not necessarily determine its substantive content. As I explained earlier, one gleans this point from Justice's behavior insofar as Zeus does not tell her what to think or how to feel concerning the decisions of human rulers. Rather, she tells him how and why she has been wronged, and then Zeus gets involved. This process also displays how Justice participates in a sort of ruling-over from below when it comes to human affairs, carrying forward the theme of potent feminine figures and their ability to combat potentially domineering modes of ruling-over. Interestingly, there is precedent in Greek thought for this relationship between Zeus and Justice: in Homer, Zeus recognizes Fate as something apart from him that possesses a power he must observe.[8]

Here it pays to recall how a predominant characteristic of distinction had been its exclusive hierarchical character. Beginning with Zeus and extending downward to Agamemnon, ruling as distinction was understood in a distinctly hierarchical fashion and was associated with a specific group of individuals, namely *basileis* and *anaktes*. Hesiod's challenges to hierarchical kingly rule as distinction become increasingly stark at this juncture. While Hesiod does not argue that common people or citizens should rule, he suggests that ruling practices are deeply intertwined with the well-being and interests of the *dēmos*. Instead of understanding rule and the exercise of power (*kratein*) as hierarchically disconnected from the interests of the many and grounded in the concerns of a small few, Hesiod's political thought exhibits a new avenue for understanding rule. Hesiod supplies the first systematic challenge to the traditional aristocratic ruling model based on a notion of justice that is *not* predicated on distinction through honor, glory, or reputation. While we do not see the rule *of* the *dēmos* quite yet, we begin to see justifications for the idea of ruling *for* the *dēmos*.

The first major move in Hesiod's challenge is his dismissing the automatic assumption that *basileis* will be good rulers and decision-makers for the broader community.[9] This idea is primarily found in *Works and Days*, where he critiques *basileus*-rule by employing his unique conception of justice (*dikē*). Here it would help to clarify a broader context in which to distinguish the Homeric and Hesiodic conceptions of justice. For the most part, in Homer *dikē* means something like a right decision or judgment arrived at orally and according to proper custom(s).[10] In the *Iliad, dikē* tends to center on whatever *basileis* decide is right according to customary considerations of honor, contest, and rank between two or more individuals disagreeing on a particular matter. In the *Odyssey*, as Havelock points out, the notion of *dikē* entails an even broader ethic: "Homeric *dikē* . . . symbolizes what one has a 'right' to expect, what it is 'just' to expect, of given persons in given situations . . . fitting with the kind of behavior that pragmatic common sense would view as normal in specific cases" (1978, 183). Therefore, contra Hugh Lloyd-Jones (1983, 5–6) and Charles Segal (1994, 195–227), Homeric *dikē* is not necessarily grounded in *basileus*-rule as such, nor is it accompanied by a specific understanding that *basileis* must protect communal concerns and citizens' well-being. This is not to suggest that one does not see any evidence in Homer of accountability to a broader community, or that Homeric rule is merely a form of ruling-over in which aristocratic claims (in council) and the common peoples' needs (in the broader assembly) are completely neglected. For example, the trial scene on Achilles's shield suggests the audience plays a role in approving the straighter decision, and during the funeral games for Patroclus, Achilles must recognize the appeals and negotiate the concerns of others with an eye toward present circumstances.

However, in Hesiod justice becomes a moral and normative focal point for rule in response to the existing meaning of *basileus*-rule as distinction.[11] To sharpen this view of justice, he views ruling-for the interests of others as central criteria for kingly rule by explicitly connecting justice's existence with rulers' responsibilities to a broader community of human beings. Consequently, Hesiod's understanding of *dikē* is perhaps more "political" in a historical sense because it extends *basileus*-rule's meaning and applicability to all free individuals living in a *polis* or *astu* (city, town), as well as to strangers (*xenoi*) who depend on *basileis*' judgments and decision-making (*WD* 225–27). Such beliefs about rule are unique for two reasons. First, they highlight the importance of justice for ruling as such, as Hesiod expresses the idea that they cannot and should not be decoupled. By contrast, in Homer relations of rule often operate without any explicit regard for justice. Second, Hesiod's justice is conceptually applicable to a broader group of people and not just a small circle of rulers. This increasing concern with justice and its relation to the broader community is perhaps the most significant change one can observe in moving from Homeric to Hesiodic political thought, and one that places greater emphasis on ruling-for and ruling-in the *human* community. Significantly, those who are "in" this community require justice, but those who are "out" do not.

Following these observations, two additional anti-hierarchical dimensions of justice present themselves. The first is a *communal* one, whereby justice (*dikē*) applies to everyone in the community, including citizens (*politai*) and strangers (*xenoi*). He states: "But those who give straight judgments to strangers and fellow citizens and do not deviate at all from justice, their city flourishes, and the people in it flourish" (*WD* 225–27). Throughout *Works and Days*, Hesiod comments on the importance of "straight judgments" for maintaining a community's well-being and highlights the crucial role *basileis* play in enforcing justice in the *polis*.[12] Hesiod also makes this point using the allegory of the hawk and nightingale (*WD* 202–12). In this allegory he warns kings not to be like the hawk, which asserts its strength over the weaker nightingale and tells the smaller bird: "Woman, why do you shriek? Indeed, one far better holds you. You are going wherever I lead you, though you are a singer. . . . He is foolish who wishes to vie against those who are stronger; he is deprived of victory and suffers pains in addition to disgrace" (*WD* 207–8, 210–11). This allegory presents an implicit critique of distinction as it concerns the broader community.[13] Instead of applauding superior strength and the pursuit of honor amidst other "hawks" (*basileis*), Hesiod warns kings not to prey on weaker individuals, calling this *hubris* (arrogant pride, insolence, or wanton violence) (*WD* 213–24). His depiction of the hawk and nightingale thus stands as a vivid symbol of poetic protest.

Justice's communal dimension is also expressed in Hesiod's frequent label of kings as "gift-eating/eaters" (*WD* 38, 220, 263). This label shows how Hesiod views gifts and prizes from a communal perspective as a critical individual. From this perspective, gifts and honorific prizes influence kings to make crooked judgments rather than just, straight judgments. As I mentioned earlier, *basileis* are responsible for making sure Dikē or Justice (the goddess) is not "dragged around," which can result in Zeus punishing the entire community for the kings' crooked judgments (*WD* 218–73). This image of Zeus punishing the human community for driving out *dikē* due to crooked decision-making first appears in the *Iliad* (16.386–88). However, contra Segal's (1994, 195–227) suggestions, aside from this passage no sustained portrayals of Zeus as a protector of justice arise in the *Iliad* or *Odyssey*. This communal belief about *dikē* is novel in Hesiod because it exhibits an understanding of rule that does not simply assume hierarchical *basileus*-rule will assure proper rule. Rather, Hesiod's notion of proper rule depends upon *basileis*' recognition and protection of the community's well-being in accordance with a refined conception of justice. Finally, justice's communal component is novel because it provides a critical, agonistic individual—in this case,

Hesiod—with criteria that is conceptually distinct from *basileus*-rule, which could then provide an external standard by which to judge the quality of hierarchical *basileus*-rule.

The second anti-hierarchical dimension of Hesiod's justice is one of *fairness*, or justice's link to fair, straight judgments predicated on equality. In *Works and Days* Hesiod expresses his frustration at what he believes were unfair judgments in the case with his brother: "For already we had divided up our inherited lot, but snatching more you carried off a large amount for honoring gift-devouring kings, those foolish ones who wish to pronounce this [unfair] judgment" (*WD* 37–40). Here, a fair judgment would also be a straight one. A straight judgment, which is also just (i.e., in accordance with *dikē*), is a judgment that does not unfairly favor one side over another. Hesiod thus assumes that a basic equality between litigants exists and expects impartial decisions for litigants who appeal to *basileis* for judgments. In Hesiod's case a fair and just decision had been made on a division of goods assuming that the brothers were, and still are, more or less equal. After an allotment was made, Hesiod's brother evidently snatched more than the agreed upon amount and used some of it to bribe the *basileis*. Hesiod believes the *basileis*' subsequent judgment was crooked because it favored his brother and allowed his brother to receive more than their prior, agreed upon amount.

The significance of this point about bribery and attending the assembly is one that Aristotle later addresses in his *Politics* when discussing democratic polities. The best democracies, Aristotle tells us, are agricultural ones composed of farmers such as Hesiod:

> The best kind of [democratic] populace is one of farmers. . . . Such people, since they do not have a great amount of property, are busily occupied; and they have thus no time for attending the assembly. Because they [do not] have the necessities of life, they stick to their work, and do not covet what does not belong to them; indeed, they find more pleasure in work than they do in politics and government—unless there are large pickings to be got from having a finger in government. (1318b9–16; trans. Barker 2009)

Farmers are the best democratic citizens precisely because they do not frequent the assembly, as their lack of virtue or goodness limits their ability to engage in ruling well. Connecting this idea to Hesiod's criticism of Perses, we might say that the increased presence and involvement of common citizens in the assembly and public affairs facilitates the political bribery that

Hesiod detests. Like Aristotle, Hesiod suggests farmers spend most of their time engaging in labor and procuring the necessities of life, which ties back to Hesiod's conception of good Strife: such strife helps to keep farmers busy and productively focused on their own affairs. Of course, without such "democratic" accountability, this situation places tremendous weight on Hesiod's claims that Zeus will be the final arbiter for fair, straight judgments and that he serves as the model for *basileis'* proper behavior (*WD* 34–37). For Hesiod, it is therefore essential that Zeus distributed honors fairly—for example, to Styx's children (*Th.* 386–403) and Hecate (*Th.* 412–52)—and guaranteed the distribution of appropriate honors that were not distributed by his father Kronos (*Th.* 392–96) (see Hamilton 1989, 20–21). While Hesiod maintains a hierarchical conception of *basileis* ruling over common citizens, the connection between ruling, fair decision-making, and justice also exhibit the anti-hierarchical idea that citizens and non-citizens alike deserve to be judged according to impersonal standards of fairness and equality.

The next anti-hierarchical dimension of Hesiod's thought lies in the connection between two ideas: divine inspiration and *dikē*. In *Works and Days*, Hesiod makes an important move. As a bard, he links his ability for divine inspiration to the possibility of questioning kings' behavior, and does so while maintaining his novel conception of justice. The Homeric epics, in contrast, do not provide any examples of a poet or seer personally and explicitly critiquing a king or his decision-making, including Homer.[14] Hesiod, however, makes this move directly:

> O Muses from Pieria. . . . Come hither, tell of your father Zeus . . . easily he straightens the crooked and dries up the arrogant, high-thundering Zeus who dwells in the highest palaces. Listen, Zeus, as you see me and give me your ear, as you straighten judgments with justice [*dikē*]. Meanwhile, I would explain truths to Perses. (*WD* 1–2, 7–10)[15]

Hesiod personally asks Zeus to straighten things out in accordance with a communal notion of justice because, as this passage implies in light of Hesiod's later comments, human rulers have failed to do so.[16] In making this request Hesiod assumes that he, by means of divine inspiration, can hear or understand what is proper regarding rule. This inspiration will then allow him to speak truths to both Perses and arrogant *basileis* who make crooked judgments.[17]

Here it is also important to note how particular cosmogonic and theogonic ideas in the *Theogony* have helped to establish a broader framework and justification for Hesiod's protest. Such crooked behavior hearkens Kronos's behavior, and therefore, Hesiod implicitly aligns himself with figures such as Gaia, Zeus, Justice, and any other just critic from "below." Moreover, he assumes that he can understand Zeus's will, which entails punishing the wicked in accordance with justice and fair, straight decision-making. Perhaps most importantly, this appeal is made to a source lying outside the human institution of kingship. Divine inspiration thus provides a new method that a critical, agonistic individual can employ to challenge or question *basileis'* decisions.

This new method of political critique is crucial for subsequent developments in Greek political thought, as it expands the scope of agonistic individualism so that it would justifiably include non-*basileis*. This is a significant move because it presents a new way in which preexisting beliefs about rule can be questioned or challenged—a method that does not simply rely on human, hierarchical kingly rule. Hesiod achieves this by linking divine inspiration with his understanding of justice. Drawing these two together provides a powerful means for protesting against existing forms of rule, and in Hesiod's particular case, for challenging the belief that individuals must accept *basileus*-rule and *basileis'* judgments as inherently right or best. This link between the ability and willingness to access external criteria by which to judge existing forms of rule, accompanied by an impersonal, proto-metaphysical conception of justice, exhibits a historical model that passes to Socrates and Plato later on in the Classical period.[18] As last chapter's analysis made clear, this development is not apparent in Homer. In the *Iliad*, fellow rulers Achilles and Odysseus are Agamemnon's most persistent critics, and their critiques rely primarily on notions of wounded individual honor and lack of respect for the agonistic conditions that make distinction possible in the first place. However, in *Works and Days* Hesiod personally criticizes kings as "gift-devouring" and alternatively appeals to notions of justice accessed through divine inspiration. This link between the poet's divine inspiration and ability to criticize *basileus*-rule displays an important leveling trend in Hesiod's thought.

From a theoretical perspective, this method of critique provides an overarching framework for justifying challenges to unmitigated assertions of ruling-over. To begin with, we can see how Justice is becoming increasingly de-personalized and unmoored from criteria decided upon by self-possessed individuals, partly through making a critical framework accessible to those below. Interestingly, we can see how Hesiod's theogony helps lay the foundation for this conceptual shift insofar as he depicts Kronos as justifiably throwing off the yoke of Ouranos, with Zeus following suit, and now it is

Hesiod making the critical move from below. Because Hesiod is a commoner and not a ruler or potential ruler, he must appeal to alternative standards—whether the goddess Justice or some natural conception of justice—to justify the move. He adds further ammunition to his critical arsenal by drawing up a new model of Zeus that would help justify his rejection of a more agonistic and glory-mongering Homeric model. In these regards, his cosmogony and theogony narrate a series of events (supported by the Muses as witness) of taming corrupt rulers from below and simultaneously soften the radical move he is making by laying out a series of ethical and conceptual precedents for his critique.

However, I do not wish to overemphasize these anti-hierarchical ideas and neglect some of the traditional-hierarchical aspects of his thought. As Hamilton (1989, 20–21) points out, Hesiod's vision of cosmic rule differs from Homer's insofar as it does not end with an agonistic plurality on the divine plane. As I have suggested at various points in the chapter, Hesiod's Zeus gradually becomes an absolute monarch, even if he ends up being more just than Homer's Zeus. This is reflected in the final exhibition of Zeus's power and authority when he single-handedly defeats Typhoeus, a monster who would have been "king of men and gods" had he overtaken Zeus (*Th.*, 837). Such evidence not only throws into relief the more robust agonistic and leveled elements of Homer but also provides an additional example of how Hesiod attempts to reconcile hierarchical kingly rule with the idea that justice—and not mere distinction in pursuit of honor, glory, and reputation—is central to the meaning of rule. In effect, Zeus's rule as cosmic monarch tends to suppress or subsume some of the agentic capacities of nonhuman beings and forces in the cosmos that might otherwise share in less hierarchical forms of ruling-with.

While I argued earlier in the chapter that Hesiod does not ultimately abandon an understanding of ruling-over in the form of kingship, his cosmological ideas and arguments about just decision-making remain significant because they shift the line of questioning and potential criticisms of *basileus*-rule. In both the *Theogony* and *Works and Days*, the origin of the cosmos (cosmogony) and its general structure (cosmology) do not guarantee just decision-making through human kingship. Hesiod's critique implies that human kingship as an institution is deeply flawed, as he places his trust in Zeus but has little faith in human kings. Unlike what we will see in the brahmanical case, Hesiod does not assume the social structure is linked to specific, ritualized social group functions and elaborate sacrificial ritual that might allow kingship to assure cosmic order and proper rule in human communities. Hesiod's political thought thus elicits an innovative line of questioning. Is there perhaps a better, more effective form of rule than kingship, especially when justice is so important? Could another form of rule achieve a better distribution of fair and just outcomes than *basileus*-rule can provide? As is evidently the case, if kingship is flawed and Zeus cannot (or simply does not) always enforce just outcomes through the institution of *basileus*-rule, upon whom does it fall to figure out a better set of practices? Thersites's and Achilles's critiques in the *Iliad* do not elicit the same questions because there is no impersonal or natural criterion superseding Zeus that may provide a distinct alternative for envisioning good rule. All Homer offers is kingship and an agonistic, honor-hungry Zeus.

In *Works and Days*, Hesiod's skepticism of kingly rule emerges quite starkly, as he simultaneously laments Zeus's potential lack of enforcement. Hesiod explains:

> Zeus' eye both catches and apprehends everything—if he wishes—and he looks upon these things [i.e., evil plans contrived by evil planners], and he does not forget which kind of city this is that has justice enclosed within it. At the moment, I myself would not want to be a just person among human beings nor would I want my son to be, since it is treacherous for a man to be just, if the more unjust man will procure greater justice. Nevertheless, up to this point in time I hope that the counselor Zeus would not allow this to come about. (*WD* 267–73)

While Hesiod warns Perses about Zeus's power, we also see Hesiod admitting that behaving justly appears unwise because it simply would not pay in this context. Hesiod's belief in Zeus's authority thus reflects a deep skepticism about justice's actual enforcement. Moreover, punishment for injustice is purportedly enforced after the abuses take place and is not automatically assured, which exposes justice's reactionary dimension and suggests some distance between the divine and human. Because Zeus only appears when needed, if human rulers were doing what they should be doing then human communities would apparently never need Zeus in the first place. Zeus's presence, therefore, is also marked by a conspicuous absence.

These are precisely the types of questions that set Greek political thought on a more skeptical, human-centric path. Hesiod's ideas thus anticipate subsequent developments in Greek thought, as he suggests an un-fixable fracture in the cosmic order when it comes to rule. If the cosmic structure does not guarantee just decision-making and Greek society cannot secure proper rule through ritualized mechanisms such as sacrificial practice, then human beings would appear responsible for finding answers to ruling questions and ultimately ruling themselves. While Hesiod does not directly pose or answer these questions, his comments and ideas clearly elicit them. By explicitly connecting particular ideas (justice, communal well-being, fair or impartial decision-making) with kingship and rule, Hesiod's thought could then influence—and was also likely influenced by—non-traditional, proto-democratic inquiries and ways of conceiving good rulership. I am not claiming that Hesiod necessarily intended to formulate a radical and systematic break with traditional-hierarchical ideas. Rather, his thinking and innovative use of particular concepts and terminology helps establish textual-poetic precedent for new challenges to preexisting ruling ideas. Hesiod's political thought thus paves new avenues for political inquiry and answers to the ruling questions: Who rules? Who should rule, and why? What does it mean to rule? While his conception of rule remains cosmologically hierarchical in some respects, he also develops novel anti-hierarchical ideas. Definitive answers may not be obtainable concerning the extent to which Hesiod's political ideas are a symptom, cause, or combination of both for subsequent changes in Greek conceptions of rule. Nevertheless, when one compares the political ideas found in Hesiod with those found in Homer, Hesiod's cosmology and critique of bribe-eating rulers introduce novel grounds for believing that hierarchical kingship may no longer be the necessary or proper form of rule.

Conclusion: Strong Individualism, Anthropocentrism, and the Disconnectedness of Greek Rule

While Hesiod's political thought exhibits a significant leveling of hierarchical ruling ideas and emergent conception of political equality, his conception of rule also entails a narrower cosmological and ontological scope. Before I unpack this point, I should reiterate the positive implications of Hesiod's thought. Through his conception of justice, he attempts to shore up a rift in communal connectedness that had been opened by beliefs in self-possessed individuality and agonistic individualism. A culture of agonistic behavior partly results from acknowledging plurality and can help to foster healthy disagreement between human beings, as exhibited in Thersites's challenge to Agamemnon's hubris and Hesiod's critique of gift-eating kings. In Homer, however, such behavior tends to support the model of ruling as hierarchical distinction and systematically neglects the deleterious impact of overactive pursuits of honor, glory, and reputation within various communities. Hesiod's divergence from Homeric political thought thus highlights one potential avenue leading toward democratic thought and practice. That is, Hesiod explicitly connects concepts of equality and justice to rule, further emphasizing a leveled dimension of ruling-for those outside a tight-knit circle of *basileis*.

While Hesiod's natural standard of justice seeks to enhance human interconnectedness and a leveled sense of political self-worth, it does so while simultaneously narrowing the scope of ruling-in a broader cosmological and ontological framework. As I have suggested at various points in the chapter, Hesiod's conception of rule drives a wedge between human and nonhuman beings in a more explicit fashion, thus preventing a potentially broader understanding of community and interconnected well-being. The first issue here is a strongly demarcated sense of individuality, which cultivates a somewhat atomistic political ethos that stunts potential conceptions of identity and flourishing as more porous in nature. The selfish Perses, the irritated Hesiod, and the bribe-eating rulers all exhibit this outlook as they view each other quite skeptically. These figures express ambivalence toward the nonhuman world or, as we see in Hesiod's case, view it primarily as an obstacle to overcome through good strife, astute seasonal planning, and trudging labor. While Justice complains and Zeus is supposed to punish the wicked, common folk such as Hesiod are left with nothing but (perhaps vain) hope for straight judgments and sweaty labor to ward off the trials introduced by various seasons.[19] Interestingly, agonistic individualism not only characterizes inter-human relations but also human beings' relations to the environment and nonhuman beings. This cosmological break and antagonism between human and nonhuman beings in archaic political thought undergirds the conceptual framework that Val Plumwood (1993) identifies with a "master identity" narrative in Western political thought, especially as it manifests in later Platonic thought.

Two examples of such human–nonhuman agonism stand out. In Homer the combat between Achilles and the river Xanthos (*Il.*, book 21) displays agonistic individualism vis-à-vis a particular environmental entity:

> But when they came . . . to the river of whirling Xanthos. . . . Now swift Achilles would have killed even more Paionians except that the deep-whirling river spoke to him in anger and in mortal likeness, and the voice rose from the depth of the eddies . . . "the loveliness of my waters is crammed with corpses, I cannot find a channel to cast my waters into the bright sea since I am congested with the dead men you kill so brutally." . . . [defiantly] Achilles leapt into the middle of

> the water.... And about Achilles in his confusion a dangerous wave rose up, and beat against his shield and pushed it. (*Il.* 21.1–2, 211–13, 218–20, 233–34, 240–41; trans. Lattimore 1961)

When the river groans due to all the dead bodies that are piling up within it, and thus attempts to persuade Achilles to take his fighting onto dry land, Achilles scoffs at the request and carries on. Achilles's subsequent combat against the river exhibits two important ideas: first, the general disinterest in the interests of nonhuman entities expressed throughout Homer's epics, especially when such entities stand in the way of some fervent human purpose (e.g., Achilles's everlasting glory in the *Iliad* and Odysseus's homecoming in the *Odyssey*); second, the willingness to fight the entity and treat it as something that can and should be defeated in physical contest. In the *Odyssey*, for example, the ocean is generally characterized as a buffer between gods and human beings—especially the god Poseidon, who frequently uses it as a barricade or device for punishing Odysseus as he attempts to return to Ithaca.

As I argue earlier in the chapter, in Hesiod we observe the idea that human beings must labor over and against an ambivalent, even threatening, natural environment. The human activity of ruling and human interests have little stake in nonhuman well-being, as Hesiod specifically states that good rulers are a "holy gift" for human beings (*Th.* 93). It may also be the case that any agonism spilling into nonhuman relations is a result of well-established beliefs about the behavior of humans and gods. If the Greeks treat each other as agonistic individuals, then why would they treat nonhuman beings and environment any differently? Ultimately, Greek beliefs do not display any explicit, positive treatment of the interconnected nature and well-being of human and nonhuman beings as neither Homer nor Hesiod, two of the earliest and most important educators of Greece, provide any explicit model for interconnected well-being.

From a cross-cultural perspective, the most important point for my argument is that Hesiod's notion of justice moves further in a human-centric direction, isolating human beings from nonhuman beings by conceiving a politics which has its normative standard lodged almost entirely within the human community and a concern for its own interests. To start, the strong ontological demarcation expressed in self-possessed individuality supports an understanding of justice applicable only to gods and human beings. Because Hesiod's justice concerns decisions made by human beings and gods for human beings and gods, and both types of beings are those who share the special characteristic of self-possessed individuality, justice is now caught (in an "ideal" sense) within a god–human feedback loop, while all other beings lacking this characteristic are left out. This loop then disconnects gods and human beings—at least when it comes to rule and justice—from all other nonhuman beings. Because things such as plants and animals lie outside the loop of justice, mortals must engage in a type of ruling-over such nonhuman beings in a manner that precludes direct relations of justice.

Hesiod's tale of the hawk and nightingale exhibits some of these ideas and further clarifies Hesiod's departure from Homer. For example, Hesiod places something like the Homeric understanding of rule *in the mouths of animals*, showing how the powerful hawk draws on the language of shame and an honor-based political ethic. He does this partly to highlight a distinction between the law of animals and human beings, telling us that human rule possesses a different standard (*WD* 276–80). The law (*nomos*) of strength and force govern the animal world, but this is not the law proper to human beings and gods. Hence, the tale provides a critique of human rulers who, when behaving like animals, apparently exhibit an ontological mix-up in their understanding of rule.

This alone would not make justice entirely human-centric, as gods remain an important part of the picture. However, because Hesiod tells us that Zeus has taken care of things on the divine plane and put a final, just stamp in the divine realm, dilemmas concerning the application of justice are now primarily (if not solely) applicable to human communities. This logic not only narrows the ontological scope of justice by parsing it from the nonhuman world, but it also leads human beings such as Hesiod to dwell more intently on the problems and connectedness of ruling-in the human community alone. Hesiod's justice, therefore, conceives nonhuman relations as materially instrumental, resulting in a humanistic solipsism concerning two important dimensions of rule: increasingly, ruling-with and ruling-for begin and end within the human community and their interests. At minimum, there is no systematic effort in either Homer or Hesiod to explain how this might be otherwise, or an effort to explain how self-possessed individuality might fundamentally level the interests and well-being of gods and humans to that of a broader community of nonhuman beings and entities. The gods thus recede further into the political background and nonhuman beings such as plants and animals are left entirely out of the sphere of justice, becoming instrumental to the health of the polis' human inhabitants.

Interestingly, this political disconnect between the human and nonhuman entails a leveling of hierarchical rule on the human plane. This cosmological break, however, also makes it increasingly difficult to conceive how central political concepts like justice might apply across cosmological and ontological boundaries. At an early stage in Greek political thought, these ruling beliefs effectively sever divine and human politics from a non-self-possessed world of beings. To better understand the historical and cultural significance of this Greek development, the next two chapters provide an evocative comparative vantage point in early Indian political thought.

3 VEDIC POLITICAL THOUGHT

HIERARCHY, CONNECTEDNESS, AND COSMOLOGY

The turn to ancient Indian political thought will bring most Western political theorists and historians of political ideas into an unfamiliar landscape. While pre-Classical Greek thought has not received nearly as much attention as Classical thought, early Indian political thought has received even less attention in Western academic circles. In transitioning from Greece to India, I begin by critically surveying the existing scholarship on ancient Indian political thought. Literature in this area not only exhibits significant interpretive problems and unanswered questions but also a paucity of fresh approaches to Vedic texts in recent decades. In directly addressing such problems and questions, my analytic approach will help clarify novel aspects of Vedic political thought as they concern human–nonhuman political relations. Correspondingly, because political theorists have not critically examined much of the existing literature on ancient Indian political thought, I briefly summarize the predominant analytic approaches and notable debates in studies of early and middle Vedic political thought in the first section of the chapter. Here I address some of the major interpretive issues confronted in this and the following chapter, along with the stakes of my interventions in existing debates. As I will explain, the overarching problem has been that the scholarly literature is not grounded in any consistently and clearly defined debates and issues. In turn, this has prevented rigorous argumentative analysis from developing around particular interpretations of important texts and concepts.

Since these interpretive issues require an approach that is more attentive to central brahmanical categories, concepts, and terminology, this chapter focuses on outlining a new Vedic analytic framework that draws upon the relevant scholarship in Indology and South Asian studies. This synthetic, interdisciplinary approach integrates methods and analyses developed by scholars who are generally more familiar than political theorists with these Vedic works. In the remainder of the chapter I explicate the categories, concepts, and terminology pertinent to the meaning of kingly rule in three different layers of Vedic works. These layers, I argue, expose an interesting development in early Vedic thought that contrasts sharply with early Greek political thought—namely, a simultaneous hierarchizing of rule on the human plane (ruling-over) and horizontal interconnection of rule across human and nonhuman registers (ruling-in and ruling-for). This chapter thus clarifies ancient Indian political thought such that political theorists unfamiliar with these early works can begin to understand this tradition based upon a conceptual framework found within the tradition itself.

Before providing my introduction to ancient Indian political thought, I should explain the reasoning behind differences in analytic organization of the Greek and Indian chapters. Because the Vedic Saṃhitās and Brāhmaṇas differ from Homeric and Hesiodic works insofar as the Indian texts are (more or less) not singular, self-contained epics or narrative poems, I take a slightly different approach to mapping out change and continuity in them. While the structure of my analysis may differ in some respects due to stylistic differences between the texts (and my general analytic approach is predicated on sensitivity to such differences), I should emphasize that the basic "unit of analysis"—namely, beliefs about rule—remains the same. Parsing textual layers provides the necessary conditions for diachronic explanation by supplying an analytic framework capable of pinpointing developments in the meaning of rule across different Vedic works. The first layer consists of two categories: the early Ṛg-Veda Saṃhitā, books 2 through 7 (the Family Books), 8, and 9; and the later Ṛg-Veda Saṃhitā, books 1 and 10. The second layer consists of the liturgical Saṃhitās—the Sāma-Veda Saṃhitā and Yajur-Veda Saṃhitā—and the Brāhmaṇas, while the third layer consists solely of the Atharva-Veda Saṃhitā.[1] Each layer, while sharing many similarities in terms of categories, concepts, and terminology, exhibits significant differences that must be located to understand continuity and change in the meaning of kingly rule.[2] Organizing the analysis in this fashion provides a more nuanced approach than those found in the existing scholarship, further allowing me to examine the central yet unidentified dilemmas that instigate changes in the Vedic understanding of rule.

Ancient Indian Political Thought

Political theorists and historians of political ideas might initially be inclined to ask why they need to know anything about these ancient brahmanical works. In addition, those who are more familiar with Indian traditions may ask how ideas found in these works are relevant to our understanding of more prominent Hindu political texts such as the Śānti Parva (Mahābhārata), Dharma-Sūtras, Dharma-Śāstras, and Kauṭilya's *Arthaśāstra*. To start, the Vedic Saṃhitās and Brāhmaṇas are the first Indian works to address ruling questions, and thus express the earliest tradition of political thought that can be discerned from texts on the Indian subcontinent. They also contain the earliest exposition of many of the most important categories, concepts, and terminology that would later be adopted, developed, or criticized by post-Vedic Hindu and non-Hindu traditions. The categories of ritual and sacrifice as well as concepts such as *dharma* first appear in these Vedic works, gradually becoming canonical in a historical sense as they help establish the foundational beliefs to which many subsequent traditions of Indian political thought respond in one way or another. In comparative perspective, the Saṃhitās and Brāhmaṇas play similar historical and cultural roles to those played by Homeric and Hesiodic texts in Greek and Western traditions. This is important to highlight because political theorists generally do not have sufficient knowledge of this Indian backdrop, which is necessary for understanding a broader history of Indian and Hindu traditions comparable to what we possess for Western traditions.

Providing one helpful entry point, Anthony Parel has claimed that "Indian political thought had a canon of its own at least since the time of Kautilya's *Arthasastra* (end of fourth century BC)" (2008, 40). Parel is one of the foremost experts on Indian and Hindu traditions of political thought, yet he leaves open the possibility that Kauṭilya's *Arthaśāstra* may not be the earliest, or perhaps even the most important, text for locating a canon of Indian political thought. Here I want to advance an argument similar to the one I advanced in the Greek case for Homer and Hesiod, namely that scholars' attention should extend further back to locate the origins of these important and influential traditions. Because political theorists like Parel often refer to texts such as the Manu-Smṛti and *Arthaśāstra* as starting-points for locating a canon, one aim of my analysis in this and the following chapter is to explicate the earliest identifiable tradition of Indian political thought—one that predates these texts. This will help enhance scholars' future understanding of a variety of subsequent Indian thinkers, texts, and ideas, including where (or even if) the term "canon" can be appropriately applied.

The next task is to explain why a broader audience of political theorists would be interested in this subject matter. First, a better understanding of the history of Indian political thought provides the only way of knowing whether or not past Indian traditions, thinkers, and ideas can contribute to our general understanding of politics in both India and abroad. I will argue that ancient brahmanical ideas can make such a contribution to our understanding of rule, just as others have made cases for ancient Greek thinkers such as Plato and Aristotle. Here I suggest it is a logical step for political theorists to extend their attention to ancient Indian thinkers just as they have to Greek thinkers and texts. Such non-Western traditions should not be written off a priori, before knowing whether or not they have something to teach us. These lessons or contributions, of course, are predicated on an adequate understanding of such traditions in the first place. As questions about the meaning of rule remain relevant in contemporary political thought and practice, I argue that ideas expressed in ancient Indian political thought can reveal new, creative avenues for understanding the connectedness of rule.

Gandhi provides a useful example to show how one can draw upon or be inspired by past ideas so as to address contemporary political issues without necessarily adopting an entire web of beliefs. It is well known that Gandhi was inspired by concepts in the Bhagavad Gītā (ca. 200 BCE) and developed them as a partial basis for critiquing modern political and economic practices, thus exhibiting what the Gītā might have to teach us about politics (see Alter 2000; Godrej 2011, 2012; Gray and Hughes 2015; Parel 2006). Many have lauded Gandhi's achievements in this regard but have failed to appreciate fully how he was able to achieve such things. That is, he made a sincere effort to understand a non-Western text (Gītā) and its central ideas, then used this understanding to question the world around him. It may be true that Gandhi was not particularly interested in historical meaning or gaining a solid understanding of historical context. Nonetheless, much of the power of Gandhi's political thought resides in the fact that he looked outside a Western tradition and contemporary context, allowing him to locate differences and an effective cross-cultural vantage point from which he could critique modern and contemporary practices. Similar to my historical-comparative approach, Gandhi's method depends upon one's ability to access and critically employ normative differences between ideas anchored in various linguistic and cultural locales. As I have already suggested, it may also simply be a worthwhile intellectual exercise for political theorists to be pulled from their cultural and historical comfort zones in order to see familiar political ideas and practices from a fresh perspective.

A related warrant for Vedic and Indian political thought's broader relevance is that a rigorous history of Indian political ideas provides the only way of understanding if and how this history has some connection to both contemporary Indian and non-Indian political practices and experience. At minimum, my analysis will show how India possesses its own non-Greek and non-European categories, concepts, terminology, and beliefs that it can draw upon to understand both its past and present political problems. In contemporary Indian politics, categories such as *varṇa* (social group) have helped shape conceptions of caste, as political parties and electoral issues addressing the status of *dalit*s and untouchability are related to *varṇa* distinctions that are initially delineated in the Saṃhitās and Brāhmaṇas. Here, Bhikhu Parekh eloquently articulates some of the most important reasons to examine native Indian political ideas in a historically inflected manner, noting how the "non-Western world exports the raw material of its experiences and imports the finished theoretical products from the West. . . . [as] indigenous traditions of thought remain unexplored and unfertilized by its novel political experiences" (1989, 2–3). Not only has this "import-export" model deprived countries such as India of opportunities to reflect critically upon its indigenous traditions, but it has also denied Western traditions the opportunity to be confronted and challenged by various cross-cultural vantage points. As Parekh further explains, "even as an individual fails to develop fully without constant interaction with an equal, a tradition of thought loses vitality and lacks the capacity for rigorous self-criticism without the probing presence of an authentic 'other'" (3). Political theorists should therefore be concerned about the absence of non-Western traditions that can provide such opportunities for self-criticism.

Now turning to the existing scholarship, a fairly large but under-examined body of literature has addressed ancient Indian political thought, including the early and middle Vedic periods. Due to the size and diversity of this literature, my review here is not intended to be completely comprehensive. Studies of kingship and political thought in ancient India can be found in multiple disciplines and take a wide variety of methodological approaches. Here I simply seek to organize and examine the most notable approaches and positions on the subject matter for an audience of political theorists and historians of political ideas. Therefore, I focus on scholars who are political theorists themselves, or at least address issues familiar to political theory as a field of study.

Much of the scholarship on ancient Indian political thought centers around Hindu texts and traditions, which are heavily influenced (especially early on) by the brahmanical tradition. Even with this overlap, theorists have taken very different approaches to the texts and historical evidence. These approaches can be parsed into two general categories: chronological and topical. Those such as N. C. Bandyopadhyaya, Charles Drekmeier, and U. N. Ghoshal approach ancient Indian political thought chronologically, beginning in the Vedic period and ending in the early Hindu period (ca. 200 BCE–500 CE), medieval Hindu period (ca. 500–1200 CE), or Muslim period (ca. 1200–1750 BCE) (e.g., see Bandyopadhyaya 1980; Drekmeier 1962; Ghoshal 1966).[3] Other scholars such as A. S. Altekar (1958), Jan Gonda (1966), K. P. Jayaswal (1967), and B. A. Saletore (1963) approach the material topically, in which case analyses of Vedic political thought are scattered throughout studies that focus on a variety of topics such as the state, republics, assemblies, or sovereignty.[4] While I take the former approach and examine the texts chronologically, my temporal focus is narrower and thus provides finer distinctions than those found in previous studies. This more nuanced chronological approach, combined with a focus on a smaller body of texts, ultimately allows for greater analytic precision. Finally, theorists have undertaken two general types of studies: on the one hand, broad overviews of many texts and traditions across a long period of time (ranging anywhere from the sixteenth century BCE up to the eighteenth century CE),[5] and on the other hand, more narrow examinations of a particular time period,[6] thinker and text,[7] concept,[8] or some combination thereof. This and the following chapter constitute the latter type of study, organized around a specific time period, set of texts, and concept.

When one attempts to identify a consistent set of scholarly debates in studies of early and middle Vedic thought, a significant difficulty arises. The scholarly literature is not centered on any consistently or clearly defined debates and issues. Most studies of Vedic political thought are predominantly exegetical and descriptive in nature, and thus do not attempt to defend specific arguments about the meaning of terms with reference to a particular ongoing debate or scholarly conversation. As broader surveys, most of these studies fail to offer systematic, critical analysis in defense of a single thesis.[9] Because this scholarship is not organized around clearly defined theses, positions, and ongoing debates, it has developed in a rather idiosyncratic manner and addresses an incredibly broad variety of topics. Drawing such a distinction between the type of study one generally finds in the literature and the present study, I craft an argument that addresses a single question, defends a clearly delineated position, and references some of the more pressing debates in the literature when appropriate.

Although most existing scholarship is quite broad in focus, a few notable debates regularly surface. For example, theorists have debated whether or not there were popular, deliberative—sometimes depicted as "democratic"—assemblies with ruling and judicial functions that were socially inclusive.[10] Another debate concerns whether or not kings were "elected" either by the people (*viś*) or other kings.[11] Finally, some have argued about whether or not the king's (*rājan*'s, *rājanya*'s, or *kṣatriya*'s) power was independent and superior to the priest's (brahmin's) power.[12] The first problem with these sorts of questions as they arise in the literature is that they presume all sorts of misleading or inaccurate cross-cultural similarities to Western traditions, categories, and concepts (see Gray 2010). While I address these debates when appropriate, I want to point out that such cross-cultural comparisons are often premature and require greater reflection on the part of scholars. Because this type of critical reflection is generally lacking, political theorists' analyses have not arrived at an understanding of ancient Indian political thought by means of Indian categories, concepts, terminology, and beliefs.

The second issue related to these questions concerns how previous scholars generally attempt to answer them. Scholars usually do not provide straightforward answers to these questions but simply point out that the texts say one thing in one place, and something else in another. This mode of textual analysis frequently gives the impression that the Saṃhitās and Brāhmaṇas merely present a hodge-podge of inconsistent claims. I take a distinctly different approach to analyzing these texts, and one that uncovers a relatively consistent but complex framework of beliefs that contextualizes a coherent meaning for kingly rule.

While I can address many of these aforementioned issues by narrowing the chronological, textual, and conceptual focus of analysis, a few current debates invoke issues that lie outside the temporal scope of the present study and will require future research on the topic. First, by taking a more narrow chronological focus I am able to analyze ruling, kingship, and hierarchy according to more precise temporal distinctions. Because most scholars have examined texts and ideas across a very broad chronological spectrum, they have not been able to isolate text- and genre-specific meanings in particular time periods. This tendency to take a broad chronological focus then leads scholars to note broad similarities and trends over incredibly long periods of time. This customary chronological approach does not allow scholars to understand subtle yet significant historical continuity and change. Second, focusing on a smaller body of texts helps prevent the common interpretive problem of hastily jumping from genre to genre over long periods of time.

This tendency neglects the fact that each genre is a world of its own and contains categories, concepts, and terminology that may be shared across genres but nevertheless have different meanings and varying degrees of significance in each. For example, while some mention that books 1 and 10 of the Ṛg-Veda Saṃhitā are composed later than books 2 through 9, political theorists have failed to do anything analytically useful with this observation. As I will argue in chapter 4, this tendency has led scholars to gloss over the most significant developments in early brahmanical political thought. Finally, by focusing on rule I am able to advance a specific argument about the meaning of the most important political concept in early and middle Vedic political thought. Thus examining the meaning of kingly rule allows me to address ongoing debates in the literature when they are pertinent to my analysis without losing argumentative coherence along the way.

The Vedic Period: Hierarchy and Cosmology in Brahmanical Political Thought

I begin my analysis of the Vedic Saṃhitās and Brāhmaṇas by providing a brief overview of the texts, their general content, and a critical introduction to pertinent Indological and South Asian literature. This overview helps show how the paradoxical yet simultaneous development of hierarchy and horizontal (human–nonhuman) interconnectedness provide the proper conceptual context in which to understand Vedic political thought and meaning of rule. This review will also explain how I diverge from scholars such as H. N. Sinha (1938, 1–30) who argue, or at least imply, that the earliest form of kingly rule in the Vedic period was "secular" in orientation and only later became religious and theological (see also J. P. Sharma 1968, 15–80). Such secularist readings greatly obscure the depth and nuance of the interconnected nature of Vedic political thought, especially the degree to which Vedic rule differs from more familiar Western conceptions.

The word Veda means "knowledge," from the Sanskrit root *vid*, "to know," and refers to brahmanical texts that are classified as *śruti*, or "that which was heard."[13] The Saṃhitās (ca. 1500–800 BCE) are collections of verses, chants, sacrificial formulae, and charms or incantations, which fall into the following categories: Ṛg-Veda Saṃhitā (ca. 1500 BCE), a collection of verses (*ṛcs*) that are recited by the *hotṛ* priest; Sāma-Veda Saṃhitā (ca. 900 BCE), a collection of chants (*sāmans*) that are chanted by the *udgātṛ* priest; Yajur-Veda Saṃhitā (ca. 900 BCE), a collection of sacrificial formulae (*yajus*es) spoken by the *adhvaryu* priest when performing sacrificial actions; and Atharva-Veda Saṃhitā (ca. 1100–800 BCE), a collection of charms, incantations, and imprecations (*atharvāṅgiras*es or *atharvan*s) that can be invoked by the *brahman* priest, if necessary, during the sacrificial rituals. Finally, the Brāhmaṇas (ca. 900–650 BCE) are sacrificial manuals attached to the Vedic Saṃhitās that describe the Vedic fire sacrifices (*yajña*s), providing rules for the performance of each ceremony as well as explanations of the purpose and meaning of the sacrificial acts and *mantra*s (Holdrege 1996, 44).

It is important to highlight that these texts, which have been recited and memorized through a strict tradition of oral recitation for over three thousand years up to the present day, are not "traditional" political treatises. These works mostly consist of hymns to gods and instructions for sacrificial rituals. Therefore, claims regarding kingship and ruling must be understood within this context. The existing literature on ancient Indian political thought has largely failed to appreciate this, plucking passages from their sacrificial ritual contexts and interpreting them as if they were found in a treatise on political theory in some familiar Western sense. While this de-contextualized mistreatment of the texts largely stems from scholars' desire to make very different texts sound more familiar, it is precisely this attempt at familiarization that has obscured a proper understanding of their political thought in the first place. To reinvoke the Procrustean issues surrounding cross-cultural comparison, all non-Western texts and traditions do not fit a "Western bed," nor should they be forced to do so.

Due to the nature of these texts, much of my analysis revolves around the central category of sacrificial ritual. In the early Vedic context the most important general category to understand is sacrificial ritual. This category is also useful insofar as it helps distinguish early and middle Vedic thought from later ascetic traditions that question the earlier priestly sacrificial tradition. Sacrifice, in this context, generally refers to *yajña*, the material offering or oblation given to the gods, or *deva*s.[14] *Mantra*s (verses) are also offered as oblations, or sound offerings.[15] *Yajña* can also refer to the Vedic fire sacrifice or sacrifice in general. As Laurie Patton has pointed out regarding the *havir-yajña* (a sacrifice involving material offerings such as rice cakes and clarified butter), the *yajña* was so important in the Vedic context that "time was measured by these regular *haviryajña*s," marking such things as "the morning and evening of each day" and "the spring, rainy season, and autumn" (2004, 41). Given these categories' central importance in early and middle Vedic thought, claims regarding rule and kingship should not be interpreted as disconnected from them. Rather, interpreters must figure out what rule and kingship mean within the network of categories, concepts, and terminology surrounding sacrificial rituals.

Because of their long-standing engagement with this subject matter, the work of a number of Indological and South Asian scholars is important to consider for the arguments I advance. First, Georges Dumézil has argued for a tripartite social organization that existed within ancient Indo-European societies. In these societies, he identifies a "hierarchically-ordered, tripartite social organization, each stratum of which was collectively represented in myth and epic by an appropriate set of gods and heroes . . . with the three social strata including, in order of precedence, [the] priestly, warrior, and herder-cultivator" (Littleton 1982, 4).[16] According to his thesis, the priestly stratum was the most important, in large part because it "concerned itself with the maintenance of magico-religious and juridical sovereignty or order" (4–5). Dumézil's work on hierarchically ordered, Indo-European social groupings provides a broad yet useful entry point for an analysis of Vedic political thought. As I argue below, a distinctly hierarchical conception of society exists in the Ṛg-Veda and intensifies in the later liturgical Saṃhitās and Brāhmaṇas, and human typology plays an incredibly important role in distinguishing the early Indian and Greek traditions of political thought.

While Dumézil's position proves useful as a starting-point, Louis Dumont's *Homo Hierarchicus* further contributes to our understanding of hierarchy as an analytical category in post-Vedic brahmanical traditions. Dumont (1970, 66) argues for an ideology of *jāti* (caste) that is fundamentally religious and anchored by the hierarchical opposition of purity and impurity. In part, Dumont frames his thesis by distinguishing between individualism and holism—that is, the sociological viewpoint privileging an empirical and rational agent or individual versus privileging the society as a whole and its overall "good" or highest values (8–9). While he further posits this distinction as one between traditional and modern societies, in chapter 5 my comparative analysis will show how such a distinction overgeneralizes, and thus misses, important similarities between (traditional) Greek and modern conceptions of the self and related notions of rule (9). Categorized as a form of traditional holism, brahmanical hierarchy positions the brahmin at the top and *śūdra* at the bottom of the social stratum. He explains that this differentiation exists in the classical *varṇa* (social group) theory.[17] Therefore, Dumont argues that hierarchy, anchored by a fundamental opposition between purity at the top and impurity on the bottom, is the essential element in traditional brahmanical Hinduism and is opposed to any modern egalitarian theory or assumptions that we may find in Western societies (2). As this and the following chapter will show, the general trajectory of Dumont's thesis appears accurate.

However, I will elaborate on Brian K. Smith's work to explain why Dumont's thesis regarding the hierarchical categories of purity and impurity are overly simplistic, and how scholars' understanding of brahmanical political thought must account for complex taxonomic schemas that appear throughout the Vedic Saṃhitās and Brāhmaṇas. Before examining Smith's work I want to clarify a few key points. Smith's interpretation of the political dimension of these early Vedic works presses an assumption of brahmanical ideology that cannot be convincingly proven nor disproven given the general paucity of dependable historical evidence during the early and middle Vedic period (see also Gray 2016). Therefore, in the present and subsequent chapter I will critically extend Smith's political commentary in a number of ways, partly because his research in Vedic taxonomies has not been adequately appreciated and applied to scholars' understanding of ancient Indian political thought. My systematic engagement with Smith's work also aims to bridge a significant gap in interdisciplinary knowledge between religious studies and political theory. For example, I will explain how various "religious" ideas are quite political in nature and influence some of the most important developments in Vedic political thought.

Most important, Smith's analysis of Vedic works helps highlight the centrality of, and complex relations between, categories such as hierarchy, sacrificial ritual, cosmology, metaphysics, and ontology. In his earlier work, Smith (1989) argues that Vedic ritual ideology and practice are governed by hierarchical resemblance between different types of beings and entities. Building upon this innovative work, Smith later argues that within brahmanical thought the universe is "composed of mutually resembling and interconnected, but also hierarchically distinguished and ranked, components" (1994, vii). Accordingly, brahmins posit ritual as a constructive, classificatory activity that was capable of connecting the universe's constituent parts (vii). Smith thus elaborates upon the importance of *bandhus*, or connections. He explains how *bandhus* help brahmins conceptually classify the universe in a vertical *and* horizontal fashion, tying it together as an immense cosmic network of meaningful relationships in which most conceivable phenomena are included. In contrast to the conceptual framework we observe in archaic Greek thought, *bandhus* clarify how the brahmanical conception of rule entails a different understanding of ruling-in a broad, interconnected community of both human and nonhuman beings. Such relations of rule are precisely what I seek to clarify and examine in elaborating on Smith's work. Nevertheless, his research uncovers a fairly coherent set of cosmological claims—accompanied by a particular metaphysics and ontology—that provide the basis for the brahmanical understanding of the cosmos and human beings' role within it. His collection and analysis of cosmogonic material in the Saṃhitās and Brāhmaṇas signal a monumental achievement in the field of Vedic studies because he is among the first to show that brahmanical thought in these works is not haphazard, though it may seem so at first glance. Cosmological beliefs expose a thorough classification of the universe that undergirds brahmanical political thought and provides a coherent basis for the meaning of its ruling ideas.

While I take a historical-comparative approach to these texts and conduct a textual analysis of concepts therein, I will also address Indological and South Asian scholarship—most of which utilizes different approaches and methodologies—for the following reasons. Political theorists and historians of political ideas, because they have focused predominantly on Western traditions of political thought, have not closely studied the Saṃhitās and Brāhmaṇas. However, these works have been studied for over a century in a combination of fields such as Indology, Indo-European studies, South Asian studies, and religious studies. It would thus be a mistake to ignore scholarship in these disciplines, some of which directly bears on political theory scholarship. While difficulties arise in choosing which studies to address in this cross-disciplinary horizon, I hope to show that the benefits resulting from thoughtful examination of such material outweighs the risks of blurring traditional disciplinary boundaries.

Ṛg-Veda Saṃhitā 1: *Rājans*, Early Cosmology, and Metaphysics

The most important political terms in this early layer are *rājan, rājanya,* and *kṣatriya.* The term *rājan* is the earliest and most frequently used term for a king, generally interpreted as a chief, ruler, or tribal king. However, as Hartmut Scharfe (1989) cautions, the translation "king" can be misleading. He explains that early Ṛg-Vedic *rājan*s should be understood more as communal protectors or guardians and not permanent political rulers (74, 93). Also, in the earliest layer of the Ṛg-Veda Saṃhitā, *rājan* is a title given to *deva*s (gods), or divine kings. While scholars have traditionally assumed that the title of *rājan* applies equally to human rulers throughout the Ṛg-Veda, references to human *rājan*s are quite rare (e.g., see ṚV 4.50.7–9). As I explain in more detail in the next chapter, recognizing this fact is crucial for explaining changes in the meaning of kingly rule. In contrast, a human ruler or communal chieftain is usually referred to as a *pati* (father, lord) of some sort, such as *viśpati* (lord of the people). Early Vedic rulership was sometimes hereditary but not always so, and while *rājan*s are sometimes referred to as "chosen" (verb root, *vṛ*) in the later Ṛg-Veda, A. A. Macdonell and A. B. Keith (1967, 2:211; see also Drekmeier 1962, 24; Scharfe 1989, 58) rightly note that *rājan*s were not likely "chosen" by the *viś* (people, subjects) but merely accepted by them.[18] The next important term, *rājanya*, refers to a king, ruler, or member of a royal family and does not appear until Ṛg-Veda Saṃhitā 2, in the Puruṣa-Sūkta. However, in later texts *rājanya* is generally replaced by the term *kṣatriya* as a designation for a member of the ruling class (Macdonell and Keith 1967, 2:216). In subsequent textual layers, the term *kṣatriya* refers to a king and warrior, the ruling social group, or a family to which a king or ruler belongs.[19] Therefore, while the terms *rājan, rājanya*, and *kṣatriya* can all refer to a king or ruler in some capacity, the earliest human rulers—generally referred to as *pati*s (lords, fathers) of various sorts—are transient tribal chiefs and guardians, not permanent, institutionalized rulers.

The context surrounding the predominant term for a king or ruler, *rājan*, is rather unique in the early books of the Ṛg-Veda because *rājan* is reserved predominantly for *deva*s (gods) as opposed to human rulers (see also Scharfe 1989, 74, 93). A good example of this is found in the seventh book of the Ṛg-Veda: "O kings, guardians of mighty order [truth, *ṛta*], lords of rivers, *kṣatriya*s, come hither, O Mitra and Varuṇa, shed refreshment and rain upon us from the heavens, you two whose fluid is speedy" (ṚV 7.64.2).[20] In this verse dedicated to the gods Mitra and Varuṇa, the terms *rājan* and *kṣatriya* refer to *deva*s, who are also referred to as *gopṛ*s (guardians, defenders). The fact that the earliest *rājan*s are *deva*s and referred to within the context of a broader cosmology highlights the importance of cosmological beliefs for the meaning of kingly rule throughout the Saṃhitās and Brāhmaṇas, including key dimensions of ruling-over and ruling-in a broad cosmological context.

One can begin to observe how such divine rulers are connected with human rulers in this early layer by focusing on the term *bandhu*. A *bandhu* is a connection, bond, or fundamental relation between one thing and another.[21] In this layer of the Ṛg-Veda, *bandhu*s can indicate either abstract relationships or concrete (e.g., familial) relations. As a concept, interconnectedness is central to brahmanical beliefs. Throughout this and the following chapter I will discuss the belief in cosmological interconnectedness, and the *bandhu*s that support it, in greater detail. But here I want to point out that even in the earliest Vedic works the belief in interconnectedness, made possible through *bandhus*, plays a central role in the meaning of kingly rule. While the connection is not yet elaborated and systematized in this textual layer, divine and human rulers are already understood as primordially related to one another through *bandhus*. Such connectedness will also help explain how brahmanical thought conceives both vertical and horizontal connections between human and nonhuman beings.

Moving from cosmology to metaphysics, one of the most significant terms appearing in the Saṃhitās is *kṣatra*. This term generally denotes the metaphysical essence underlying a *kṣatriya* as an individual human being and the social group as a whole. Here, metaphysics refers to claims regarding the nature and structure of reality. The term *kṣatra* is a neuter term, which in the Ṛg-Veda frequently indicates an abstract, impersonal essence underlying something else. The term *kṣatriya* (masculine) is a nominal derivative of *kṣatra*, thus expressing the relationship between an abstract, neuter principle and a specific type of being existing in the world. More specifically, *kṣatra* can indicate one of two things. While it can indicate "the general sense of 'dominion,' 'rule,' [or] 'power' exercised by gods and men" (Macdonell and Keith 1967, 1:202), it can also denote an abstract power underlying a given *rājan* or *kṣatriya*. This latter meaning denotes a power that makes possible ruling relations on both the divine and human planes. Taken together, these meanings clarify how *kṣatra* pervades both the divine and human realms and connects rulers in these separate realms. *Kṣatra* also helps provide a conceptual explanation for how divine and human rulers, to a certain degree, must rule with one another as cosmological kin.

While cosmological, metaphysical, and ritual terminology abounds in these early Vedic works, the terms *ṛta* and *dharma* possess special significance. In one sense, *ṛta*, as the earliest term for truth and order in the Ṛg-Veda, is the underlying structure or order upon which the entire cosmos rests.[22] As Barbara Holdrege explains, *ṛta* is the "principle of cosmic order that ensures the integrated functioning of the natural, divine, human, and sacrificial orders" (2004, 215–16).[23] Therefore, in addition to denoting an underlying cosmic structure, *ṛta* supplies a regulative principle that operates in four different orders of reality and pervades everything imaginable. *Dharman*, on the other hand, refers to a sacrificial ordinance, rule, or custom that maintains *ṛta*.[24] In the Ṛg-Veda, *dharman* is connected with *ṛta* in a number of different contexts, especially in sacrificial rituals (216).[25] In this early Vedic layer *dharman* thus functions as something that actively supports *ṛta*, highlighting how human beings participate in sustaining the interconnected well-being of a broad cosmos through ritual activity.

Ṛg-Veda Saṃhitā 2: Cosmogony, Metaphysics, and Hierarchical Rule

In the subsequent layer of Vedic works, books 1 and 10 of the Ṛg-Veda, one observes more explicit cosmogonic accounts that elucidate how the cosmos came into being and how its constituent parts relate to one another at both micro- and macro-levels. In this layer, brahmanical thought begins to conceive an ordered social hierarchy as emerging during the initial creation of the cosmos, thus justifying ruling-over as a pervasive feature of human relations. In contrast to the Greek tradition this development supplies an emerging set of beliefs that legitimate ruling hierarchies on the human plane, which then prevents brahmanical political thought from conceiving a strong ontological individualism and corresponding political egalitarianism. Importantly, developments in this layer also open additional avenues for conceiving cosmological connectedness between the human and nonhuman.

In books 1 and 10, a few terms begin to grow in political significance. First, *varṇa* refers to the social group or class to which an individual belongs: brahmin, *kṣatriya, vaiśya*, and *śūdra*.[26] These four groups are mentioned together for the first time in Ṛg-Veda 10.90, the renowned Puruṣa-Sūkta, or hymn to Puruṣa. This hymn provides a cosmogonic narrative addressing each group's origins from the primordial "cosmic person," Puruṣa. In this account, Puruṣa is sacrificed to create a manifest and differentiated reality, and from the different parts of its body the four social groups eventually emerge:

> When they [i.e., the *deva*s and *ṛṣis*] divided Puruṣa, into how many parts did they apportion him? What was his mouth? What were his two arms, his two thighs and his two feet called? His mouth became the brahmin, his arms were made the *rājanya*, his thighs were made that which was the *vaiśya*, and from his two feet the *śūdra* was born. (ṚV 10.90.11–12)

Beginning with this Ṛg-Veda hymn, four separate social groups are understood as emanating from the original cosmic creation. In this hymn the rulers (*rājanya*) are clearly delineated and understood as embedded in the cosmic framework. Brahmanical thought from this period onward clearly posits a hierarchical conception of rule whereby kings are the only and proper rulers. As with the Greeks, ruling-over is ingrained within the cosmology. The next important question for brahmanical political thought involves the specific means by which these groups came about.

In this layer sacrificial ritual begins to achieve prominence as *yajña*, the sacred offering or sacrifice, now plays a central role in the brahmanical understanding of rule. In early Vedic works the term *yajña* generally refers to the fire sacrifice. For example, in the *soma* sacrifice, *soma* (elixir of immortality and sacrificial libation from the *soma* plant) is offered to the gods, which is the seminal offering that provides *devas* the strength needed to defeat their enemies.[27] Agni, both the god of fire and the sacrificial fire itself, is the messenger who transfers the *soma* offering to the gods. Not only is *yajña* a means of feeding and honoring divinities, but in four separate cosmogonies *yajña* is also the means by which the cosmos is created (ṚV 10.81–82; 10.90; 10.130). In fact, *yajña* can even be understood as a means of constructing reality itself (Smith 1989, 50–51). In a broader sense, *yajña* is a manifestation of the open and interconnected relationship that brahmanical thought perceives between gods and men. One reason *yajña* is so important is because it is understood as an efficacious means of appreciating the overarching power of the *devas* within the cosmos. *Yajña*, as offering, signifies a deep respect and humility vis-à-vis the cosmos and the *devas*' roles within it. On these points, brahmanical beliefs show distinct similarities to Greek, and especially Homeric, sacrificial beliefs. While *yajña* exhibits the idea that human beings play a significant role in an open and interconnected cosmos, it also involves them in a process that, by the time of the Brāhmaṇas, deepens an ongoing role in cosmological maintenance through ritual.

Although sacrifice is one of the primary means of cosmic creation, there are other means as well. In many respects, the tenth book of the Ṛg-Veda is the foundational text for both Vedic and post-Vedic creation narratives. However, no single comprehensive cosmogonic hymn exists in the Ṛg-Veda. Multiple cosmogonic hymns can be found in this book and each can be understood as describing a different *aspect* of the original creation.[28] The Vedic *ṛṣis*, or seers, because they simply record what they discern at the moment of creation, are not understood as fallible in this recording, even if their accounts differ. Rather, each *ṛṣi* cognizes a different aspect of what takes place. Therefore, as Holdrege (1996, 35–40) observes, there are as many as five major creative principles and five creative means included in these cosmogonic hymns.[29] While each of these hymns expresses a variety of cosmological, ontological, and metaphysical beliefs, the most relevant hymn for early brahmanical political thought is undoubtedly Ṛg-Veda 10.90.

Ṛg-Veda 10.90 establishes, for the first time in Vedic literature, a coherent account of how the proper rulers in Vedic society (*rājanyas* or *kṣatriyas*) emerge and how they fit within the broader cosmic framework. This hymn provides a foundational expression of what the Brāhmaṇas will elaborate in greater detail: a vast, interconnected cosmic network filled with entities that fit together in a coherent and, rather paradoxically, both a hierarchical and horizontal manner. The hymn begins with Puruṣa, who "possesses a thousand heads, eyes, and feet, and pervades the earth on all sides, extending beyond it the distance of ten fingers" (10.90.1). Not only is Puruṣa the lord of immortality, he is "all this—that which was and is to be" (10.90.2). Already we have the first "lord" (verb root *īś*, to be lord or rule over), Puruṣa, from whom a group of human rulers (*rājanya*) will soon be born. Later in the hymn Puruṣa is offered as the sacrifice, with the gods (*sādhyas*) and *ṛṣis* serving as sacrificial officiants (10.90.6–7). After the sacrifice gives birth to animals and sacrificial sounds (10.90.8–10), the social groups are born (10.90.11–12). As mentioned earlier, Puruṣa's mouth becomes the brahmin, his arms the *rājanya*, his thighs the *vaiśya*, and his feet the *śūdra*. Following the social groups, the natural elements, major divinities, a three-tiered cosmic structure, and cardinal directions are born (10.90.13–14).

I want to make two observations regarding this particular cosmogony. First, the *rājanya* (ruling social group) emerges during the initial stages of creation and emanates from the body of the cosmic person, Puruṣa. A ruling group is thus built into the very fabric of the cosmos. Here one does not observe elections, deliberations, nor human or divine choice. This ruling group is simply part of a cosmic whole that the *ṛṣis* discern at the very beginning. This is a powerful and influential claim in brahmanical thought. The hymn, in mentioning the four social groups together for the first time in Vedic literature, asserts the proper rule of one group of individuals as a cosmic reality anchored in a cosmogony. This hymn also hierarchically situates the *rājanya* vis-à-vis the other social groups: below the brahmin yet above the *vaiśya* and *śūdra*. The fact that the ruling group emerges after the priestly group in this hymn is also significant, because it clearly establishes the brahmin's central importance not only in the cosmos but also as superior to the ruling or political power of the *kṣatriya*.

This point is underemphasized in the existing literature, which often interprets kingship as if it was a "secular" political institution and fundamentally separated from the brahmins' otherwordly, "spiritual" realm. Scholars sometimes explain the *kṣatriya* as a purely political or "temporal" power, categorically separate from the priestly and sacerdotal power. For example,

Dumont claims, "the king in India has been [was] secularized. It is from this point that a differentiation has occurred, the separation within the religious universe of a sphere or realm opposed to the religious, and roughly corresponding to what we call the political" (1970, 68). While Dumont is correct to highlight a distinction between earlier "religious" forms of kingship—what he calls "magico-religious," such as Ancient Egyptian or Sumerian kingship—and Vedic kingship, I think he pushes this distinction too far. In an attempt to explain how ancient Vedic kingship is different from earlier "magico-religious" forms, he overdraws similarities between Vedic kingship and later political developments, relying upon a Westernized notion of a secular/religious divide. He himself claims that whatever this "political" sphere was, that it existed "within the religious universe." Therefore, it is misleading when Dumont claims, "in India the king has lost his religious prerogatives" (68), because it is precisely the "religious" (brahmanical) perspective mapped out in the Vedic Saṃhitas and Brāhmaṇas that establishes the cosmic necessity of kingly rule and contextualizes the meaning of such rule. In order for his argument to work, Dumont would need to explain how a distinctly secular form of kingship could exist within a theological framework that posits various truth claims accessible only by oral scripture and directs kingship toward non-secular ends. Secular dichotomies, while they may work well as distinctions within various Western traditions, can be quite problematic when applied to Indian and Hindu traditions (e.g., see Bhargava 2006, 2010).

Second, the *rājanya* is also connected and corresponds to other elements born from Puruṣa. This system of correspondence within a broader cosmic framework influences a conception of interconnectedness that one can identify throughout later brahmanical traditions in the middle, late, and post-Vedic periods. In particular, the later liturgical Saṃhitās and Brāhmaṇas posit a tightly woven, interconnected cosmic network of entities in which the *rājanya* (eventually, *kṣatriya*) is not only precisely situated but is also correlated in a hierarchical manner with other entities and elements in other cosmic categories, which include: body part, deity, space, time, animal, plant, tree, Vedic meter, and metaphysical essence. These correspondences allow for a highly complex and interconnected cosmic network in which everything has its proper place. Having clarified a conceptual inroad for examining this network of entities, I now turn to the layer of texts that maps out this elaborate cosmic structure in greater detail and properly contextualizes the meaning of kingly rule.

Liturgical Saṃhitās and Brāhmaṇas: Solidifying Sociopolitical Hierarchy and Horizontal Interconnectedness

Some of the most significant developments in early Indian political thought can be identified in this layer of Vedic works. In distinguishing this layer from the previous two layers, I begin by reiterating the importance of such "layering" for our understanding of the history of Indian political thought. Because existing scholarship on ancient Indian political thought has generally failed to analyze these works and their subject matter in a nuanced fashion, I will provide a brief overview of the liturgical Saṃhitās and Brāhmaṇas to clarify for political theorists their subject matter and significance within the brahmanical tradition.

Whereas Ṛg-Veda hymns provide the foundational *mantra*s for brahmanical thought and do not primarily focus on ritual, the liturgical Saṃhitās (ca. 900 BCE)—that is, the Sāma-Veda and Yajur-Veda Saṃhitās—describe a complex system of sacrificial rituals that explain how to conduct these rituals as well as their meaning and purpose. In this later period there is a system of *śrauta* sacrifices utilizing three fires (*gārhapatya, āhavanīya*, and *dakṣiṇa*) and four categories of priests (*hotṛ, udgātṛ, adhvaryu*, and *brahman*). Each one of these priests is associated with a particular Saṃhitā and plays a particular role in the sacrifice, ranging from verse recitation to uttering sacrificial formulae (Holdrege 1996, 33). The Saṃhitās are thus mainly concerned with sacrificial ritual, and any examination of kingship or rule in these works must be attentive to this sacrificial ritual context. The Brāhmaṇas (ca. 900–650 BCE) are sacrificial manuals attached to the Saṃhitās that discuss the rules (*vidhi*s) for ritual performance as well as the purposes and meanings of the sacrificial acts and *mantras*. Holdrege explains how these sacrificial manuals are not only concerned with correct performance of Vedic rituals but generally have two purposes: first, to help the patron of the sacrifice (*yajamāna*) attain particular worldly ends and construct a divine self (*daivātman*) to convey him to the world of heaven (*svarga loka*); second, to regenerate and maintain the cosmic order (43). While such rituals appear to express some distinctly individualistic beliefs and goals, the next chapter will clarify how these beliefs open the individual's ontological boundaries to a broader nonhuman world in ways that we do not see in the Greek tradition.

Panning out for a moment, these ritual texts are tremendously important for India's history of political ideas. Embedded within these works are the foundational concepts, terminology, and beliefs that are subsequently adopted, reworked, and critiqued to address changes in brahmanical society and in a variety of Hindu traditions. While sifting through these works and explicating concepts and terminology relevant for early brahmanical political thought can be a tedious task, this is necessary if scholars want to gain a better understanding of India's broader history of political ideas, especially Hindu traditions of political thought. For example, this approach immediately dispels confusion about whether or not the ruler's power was independent and superior to the brahmin priest's power(s). Drawing attention to the nature of the liturgical Saṃhitās and Brāhmaṇas shows how the brahmin's and *kṣatriya*'s powers and social roles cannot be understood as independent of one another. Recognizing the encompassing nature of sacrificial rituals in brahmanical thought and how brahmins have ultimate control over these rituals displays how their power was understood to encompass the *kṣatriya*'s power. Therefore, the *kṣatriya*'s identity remains distinct while simultaneously being connected to the brahmin's within a broader cosmological framework. It would thus be misleading to think that either one of them is completely independent. I also emphasize the significance of ritual because it invokes rule's early connection to ritual as a process of world-making. The brahmin's relation to the ruler reflects the hierarchical relation of ritual to rule because it is through ritual, especially sacrificial ritual, that the world is made and remade in an ongoing fashion. The general idea is that ritual, rule, and cosmic construction always walk hand-in-hand with one another.

Cosmogony and Cosmology

Although numerous cosmogonies and cosmological claims appear throughout the Saṃhitās and Brāhmaṇas, Smith has shown that they all express a similar taxonomic schema. What this taxonomic schema indicates is a complex and interconnected conception of the cosmos in which all phenomena are allotted their proper places within vertically and horizontally linked categories. Smith's work on this topic, therefore, will help me explain how beliefs about society, *varṇa*, and kingship fit within a broader taxonomy encompassing the entire cosmos and mapping the parameters for ruling-in. This broad framework also helps display how brahmanical conceptions of rule become increasingly hierarchical on the human plane while simultaneously horizontal and interconnected across human–nonhuman registers.

By examining thirteen separate cosmogonies found primarily in the liturgical Saṃhitās and Brāhmaṇas, Smith (1994, 60) shows how Vedic cosmogonic myths variously describe the world as divided into four, five, or six parts. While variations in the cosmogonies and cosmologies arise, what is striking is the overall consistency in the accounts. The horizontal categories include: social group, body part, social function and trait, elementary metaphysical power, essential power, deity, space, time, animal, tree, sacrificial fire, priest, Vedic work, and meter. The *varṇas* (social groups) are then horizontally connected to other entities in these categories through *bandhus*. For example, a *kṣatriya* is linked to the following: chest and arms (body part), rulership (social function), *kṣatra* (elemental metaphysical power), *virya*/virility and *bala*/strength (essential powers), Indra (deity), mid-regions and southern direction (space), midday and summer (time), horse (animal), banyan (tree), *dakṣiṇa* (sacrificial fire), *adhvaryu* (priest), Yajur-Veda (Veda), and *triṣṭubh* (meter) (Smith 1994). In the liturgical Saṃhitās and Brāhmaṇas, a *kṣatriya* is thus understood as fundamentally connected to each of these entities, as each helps fill out the *kṣatriya*'s broader onto-cosmological identity. These categories and all the entities found in them emerge during the initial moments of cosmic creation so that everything fits together co-primordially. In other words, rulers enter the world in a particular way and do not get to choose how they enter it, and in turn, they are understood as responsible for all these connections and meaningful relationships. The brahmanical account thus differs in significant ways from Homer's and Hesiod's more agonistic accounts, which, as we saw in the previous two chapters, lacked such structured, taxonomically precise connections and relationships.

In addition to horizontal relationships, vertical hierarchies also exist in which the various entities in a particular category are hierarchically ranked. For example, among the social groups a brahmin—associated variously with the mouth and head (body part), priesthood (social function), and *brahman* (metaphysical power)—is hierarchically situated above the *kṣatriya, vaiśya*, and *śūdra*. Due to this taxonomic schema, which is made possible by *bandhus*, everything in the cosmos relates to everything else through both horizontal and vertical connections. First and foremost, everything exists as a categorized being, entity, or phenomenon that has its proper place within a broader community of beings and arises at a particular point during the creation process in conjunction with other cosmic elements. Therefore, brahmanical cosmology conceives the origin, structure, and nature of the cosmos as characterized by an interconnected set of relationships that have existed from the very beginning. In turn, sacrificial ritual is concerned with maintaining this structure through enlivening the *bandhus* that connect various categories of beings and phenomena, because order and hierarchy are always in danger of slipping into disorder (*nirṛti*) and untruth (*anṛta*).[30]

Metaphysics

Conceptions of reality and the forces that disrupt an ordered reality further explain how brahmanical rule differs from more familiar Western conceptions, especially the Greek beliefs examined in the previous two chapters. The brahmanical conception of reality expresses a two-tiered metaphysics, with the first being un-manifest and the second manifest. First I will examine the manifest tier, then I will work my way down to the un-manifest level. I partly agree with Smith that manifest reality consists of what is fundamentally created or constructed,[31] and my interpretation of reality on this tier involves two distinct components: first, that which is constructed within a cosmogonic context and discernible by the Vedic *ṛṣis*, and second, that which is subsequently connected to and resembles something else through *bandhus* on the horizontal and vertical planes of existence. As Holdrege (1996, 33–34) has shown, this reality can also be parsed into four general categories or orders: *adhibhūta* (natural order, relating to the material world), *adhidaiva* (divine order, relating to the gods), *adhyātma* (human order, relating to the self), and *adhiyajña* (sacrificial order, relating to the sacrifice). Following from these claims about reality, the cosmos forms a coherent whole in which everything is connected to everything else, either directly or indirectly. Although there may be separate orders of reality, entities found in each order have correspondences in the other orders (see Smith 1989, 46–81). A *kṣatriya*, for example, resembles or corresponds to a banyan tree (*adhibhūta*) and Indra (*adhidaiva*).

This metaphysical system entails a related conception of prototypes and counterparts. Metaphysical prototypes (*pramās*) and counterparts (*pratimās*) characterize this cosmic structure insofar as everything that is real possesses a prototype and counterpart in another order. Put another way, there is nothing manifestly real in the cosmos that stands completely independent from everything else, or is not primordially connected and related to something else. While this may initially sound similar to Plato's theory of the forms in the *Republic*, one must keep two things in mind: first, that the brahmanical system posits an additional *horizontal* connectedness between beings, made possible through *bandhus*; second, that individual beings and entities are understood in more interrelated, categorical terms than as particular, atomistic applications of abstract forms. An important example of this relationship of prototype and counterpart arises between the creator Prajāpati and sacrifice. As Smith argues, sacrifice has Prajāpati (who is identified with the primordial Puruṣa) as its prototype, or that which makes it real: "Sacrifice also, then, is the *pratimā* of the Cosmic One in that the composition of parts into wholes achieved within the ritual resembles the body of Prajāpati, a similarly constructed whole and the prototype to all others" (1989, 74). To summarize: if something is manifestly real, it is constructed, connected to, and resembles something else across both horizontal and vertical registers of existence.

Shifting from a manifest to un-manifest tier of reality, the metaphysical concept of *brahman* takes center stage. *Brahman* serves as the un-manifest absolute at the basis of all existence and must be separated from those things that are manifest in the cosmos. In this brahmanical context, that which is utterly un-manifest provides the foundation upon which everything else rests. *Brahman* thus provides the fundamental "from which" and "in which" manifest reality occurs as it does (see also Smith 1989, 71–72). Because *brahman* is un-manifest, unchanging, non-active, and formless it is not any "thing," nor does it exist in the way manifest things exist. In this sense, *brahman*'s mode of existence is non-manifestation, understood in brahmanical thought as the wellspring of everything that is manifest. This two-tiered metaphysics must then be seen as contextualizing claims about kingly rule and the role *kṣatriya*s play vis-à-vis reality.

In turn, ritual ties this metaphysical system more explicitly to the concept and practice of rule. Smith has emphasized the centrality of sacrificial ritual for reality in these texts, explaining how "ritual was the workshop in which all reality was forged," and how "sacrifice was displayed as a constructive activity, creating the human being (ontology), the afterlife (soteriology), and the cosmos as a whole (cosmology)" (1989, 46, 50). Sacrificial ritual replicates and continues Puruṣa's and Prajāpati's original sacrifice, ensuring the cosmos continues to operate in an organized, interconnected manner. Ritual thus sustains the two-tiered metaphysics through ritual labor, or *karman*. Within this two-tiered metaphysics, ritual action gives phenomena and entities their meaning by naming them, claiming what they are, how they exist, what they are connected to, and how they fit within a cosmic whole that requires ritual for its ongoing construction and maintenance.

Ontology

As one might anticipate, these cosmogonic, cosmological, and metaphysical beliefs are connected to a unique set of beliefs about what, and how, things exist. While I will discuss gods and animals intermittently throughout my analysis, here I want to focus on human beings and how they exist according to brahmanical thought. First, as I explained earlier, human beings fall into one of four major groupings. Elaborated in the Vedic *gṛhyasūtras* and *dharmasūtras*, the first three social groups—brahmin, *kṣatriya*, and *vaiśya*—are "twice born" (*dvija*) in Vedic ritualism, meaning that members of those groups are required to undergo rituals that result in a second birth and complete their respective identities.[32] Not surprisingly, any discussion of Vedic ontology invokes sacrificial rituals. Unlike the self-possessed, agonistic individualism observed in Homer and Hesiod, individual ontology in this liturgical layer operates in a strikingly different manner and expresses very different beliefs. Vedic ontology presents a group-based understanding of individuality that is further embedded within a holistic cosmological and metaphysical framework.

To begin with, an inextricable relationship exists between brahmanical ontology, identity, and ritual. In the example provided below, identity and its relation to ontology operate at three distinct levels: natural or real, ascribed, and inscribed. On the first level, a human being is born a particular type of being, and this aspect of identity is understood as completely natural, reality-based, and in accordance with *ṛta* (cosmic order, truth). In addition, this ontological aspect of identity exists prior to birth and any *ex post* linguistic classification. On the second level, a person is born into a particular classification (e.g., *kṣatriya*) that constitutes the ascribed aspect of one's identity. This aspect of a one's identity will dictate the particular practices and responsibilities associated with being this or that type of human. On the third level, the inscribed aspect entails the proper, particularized practices associated with the ascribed classification. A *kṣatriya*'s inscribed identity is thus forged through particular ritual practices, which properly solidify the ascribed identity and are distinct from those of a brahmin or *vaiśya*. Therefore, while *ṛta* and cosmology predetermine a fundamental aspect of who one naturally is, ascription subsequently classifies the human being while inscription completes the identity-formation process. Ritual, then, sustains and completes what *ṛta* and cosmogony have already established.

The *upanayana*, a ritual of initiation into Vedic study and sacrifice, reflects these pervasive ontological claims regarding human beings and the central importance of sacrificial ritual. Smith (1989, 86) clarifies additional ontological dimensions of Vedic identity by explaining how twice-born individuals are understood as incomplete, and thus require ritual action to realize their true identities. Since individuals born into the three twice-born *varṇa*s are born incomplete, they must be "born again" through the proper ritual to realize their inborn ontological status and "inherent proclivities" (86).[33] While one is born *as* a particular type of person, this initial existential condition is unstable because one's ascribed and inscribed social status have not yet been fully achieved. At this stage uninitiated individuals are "prohibited from the cultural act par excellence of sacrifice" (87). Smith's analysis shows how someone who has not undergone the *upanayana*, or the proper initiation and realization of one's ascribed social group status, remains permanently deficient. Those from the twice-born *varṇa*s must go through the *upanayana* in order to perform proper sacrificial activities, and only then can they fully become who they naturally are. This process of identity formation is thus inherently constructive and ritualistic. Young males were ritually constructed as particular types of human beings, displaying a process that connected physical practices, embodiment, and the person's inherent identity. Rituals thus serve an ontological function wherein one becomes a *varṇa*-inscribed being: what type of being one is depends partly upon the ritual practice one goes through. However, only a twice-born goes through such a ritual, with each type of person going through a specific, tailored version depending on his inborn status.

The twice-born designation, therefore, is quite significant. Being reborn through ritual is important because "this 'birth from the Veda' is explicitly contrasted with the merely biological birth from the mother and is called the 'real' birth—a blatant move to devaluate the products of women and extol the cultural/ritual labor of men" (Smith 1989, 93). This twice-born status expresses the belief that biological birth is a defective and incomplete birth. While the ascribed identity may appear quite determinative, as one looks closer at the role ritual plays it becomes clear that only ritual can provide the necessary means for becoming who one is and should be. Smith explains, "this second birth was thus a socio-ontological birth standing in radical opposition to the defective natural birth, and was designed to rectify biological faults and construct a higher ontological existence for the young boy" (93). Therefore, no guarantee is made at birth because ritual must complete or fulfill this human being through inscription. An inscribed social identity remains unfulfilled and incomplete without the inscriptive and constructive function that ritual practice provides, placing the male-controlled "womb of sacrifice" at the forefront of identity formation. A *kṣatriya*'s *upanayana* fulfills his identity, for example, by having him undergo highly specified ritual actions according to season, sacrificial garment, and garment color (e.g., see Smith 1989, 94–96). Each of these specifications indicates the ways in which a *kṣatriya* is related to his broader world. As someone who is born into the ruling social group, these activities thus teach *kṣatriya*s that ruling is not individualistic in nature and requires a whole host of interconnected activities and entities to participate in an ongoing process of identity and world-formation.

In addition to guaranteeing individual ontological completion, ritual practice also poses particular threats if not completed. As Jan Gonda originally explained and Smith reiterates, "there were consequences for failing to undergo the ritual. . . . Those who failed to undertake the *upanayana* ceremony were condemned, and he [Gonda] concludes that the ritual was 'more or less a compulsory institution' in Vedic India" (Gonda 1965, 391; Smith 1989, 94). A significant consequence thus arises from the fact that ritual activity provides an instrument for constructing a world for oneself, in both this life and the afterlife (Smith 1989, 115). Even someone who is born a brahmin can fail if he does not perform the proper rituals, thereby creating and eventually falling into a quite horrendous place after death—what Smith dubs a "specifically contoured hell" (1989, 113–14). One general lesson we glean from these beliefs is that individual human beings and communities are always in the process of creating a broad, interconnected world for themselves through their particular ritualistic activities. In this respect, ruling beliefs and assumptions about the "self" help craft both a present world and one that lasts beyond one's individual death. This provides a sober reminder that current political and economic activities—many of which have become ritualistic and flown under critical awareness—will have a lasting impact and shape an entirely new world for future generations. Brahmanical political cosmology suggests that altering ruling rituals may be a prerequisite for realizing more sustainable modes of world-building.

It should also be clear from this analysis that brahmanical thought posits a deeply embedded social and political hierarchy. Whereas an explicit social hierarchy expressed in cosmogonic narrative does not appear in the earlier layer of the Ṛg-Veda, the tenth book of the Ṛg-Veda and the liturgical Saṃhitās and Brāhmaṇas clearly express such hierarchical beliefs. Within this social hierarchy, kingly rule (rule by *rājan*s or *kṣatriya*s) is embedded in an interconnected cosmic structure. For example, kings are depicted as created from the body of the cosmic person, Puruṣa or Prajāpati. Not only is kingly rule built into the cosmic framework, but kings also have essential metaphysical characteristics allowing them to rule. *Kṣatra* supports and enlivens the *kṣatriya*'s ruling characteristics, such as strength and virility. In addition to the cosmogonic and metaphysical beliefs supporting kingly rule, ritual inscribes a particular identity in *kṣatriya*s and reinforces many of the cosmogonic and metaphysical beliefs that sanction ritual's legitimacy. As I explained, the *upanayana* ritual tells young *kṣatriya*s who they are, how they are, how they fit into the broader scheme of things, and what they must do with their lives. This layer of Vedic works thus presents a rather coherent context within which to examine and interpret kingly rule in the next chapter.

Atharva-Veda Saṃhitā: The Question of Assemblies, Democratic Deliberation, and Election of Rulers

The final layer of Vedic texts consists of the Atharva-Veda (ca. 1100–800 BCE) and is somewhat unique. As mentioned earlier, this collection of works consists of charms, incantations, and imprecations (*atharvāṅgiras*es or *atharvan*s) that can be invoked by the *brahman* priest, if necessary, during the sacrificial rituals. These charms and imprecations are not the cosmos-ordering *yajña*s I have been discussing thus far but rather minor charms that aim to achieve more limited personal goals, such as guarding a pregnant woman from demons, appeasing jealousy, or strengthening a man's virility. In this regard the Atharva-Veda exhibits a different ritual world than the one I have been discussing, and it is not unlikely that these *atharvan*s either arose from, or were heavily influenced by, popular non-brahmanical sources. Nevertheless, in most regards the cosmogonic, cosmological, metaphysical, and ontological context in this collection of hymns is commensurate with those in the liturgical Saṃhitās and Brāhmaṇas. More important, a somewhat unique set of claims arises in the Atharva-Veda that may initially appear to challenge my interpretation of brahmanical rule. A number of scholars have argued that this text provides proof of political deliberation and election of kings. As I will argue at more length in chapter 4, this is a problematic position to hold for a variety of reasons. In this section I simply want to provide a critical overview of some major debates regarding political thought in these works.

Many scholars paint a rather secular political picture of kingship in the Atharva-Veda, highlighting terms that seemingly indicate a more democratic, deliberative form of rule. Debates on this topic tend to revolve around two important terms. The first term, *sabhā*, is an assembly, assembly hall, or communal meeting-place. Macdonell and Keith (1967, 2:426) point out that the *sabhā* was a multipurpose assembly where dicing and gambling took place, along with conversation regarding general communal affairs. Ghosal concurs with this interpretation, explaining, "The gambler's addiction to the *sabhā* (ṚV 10.34.6) makes its sense and purpose clear" (2006, 62). The second term is *samiti*, an assembly or place where members of the community gather.[34] The central question is this: In these assemblies, did a type of political deliberation take place, and were communal ruling decisions made according to such deliberation by a relatively free and equal community of individuals? I contend that scholars cannot definitively answer these questions. Such questions have predominantly been asked as empirical-historical questions, with scholars arguing about what did in fact happen in these assemblies. However, because we do not have reliable historical documents for this time period, historical questions such as these cannot be answered in any precise or definitive way. While attempting to reconstruct an accurate history from these texts is a tenuous exercise, most scholarly arguments regarding these terms are veiled—if not explicit—empirical-historical arguments.[35]

Setting such historical questions aside for a moment, there is not sufficient textual evidence to provide a clear view of these assemblies' character and purpose within the works themselves. As Ian Mabbett (1972, 22–23) helps point out, scholars have wrongly argued that these *sabhās* and *samitis* were democratic assemblies wherein participants exercised popular sovereignty. For either or both of these assemblies to have a significant ruling character or role, scholars must be able to marshal enough textual evidence to show that people in these assemblies ruled over the community, or at least participated in making ruling decisions. Previous scholars have not been able to make this argument without tremendous speculation and interpretive liberties, and the textual evidence currently available likely precludes scholars from doing so. Some scholars notice and rely upon the increased occurrence of the terms *sabhā* and *samiti* in the Atharva-Veda, using this to argue for a democratic, deliberative element in early Vedic society (e.g., see Jayaswal 1967, 12–20; R. S. Sharma 1968, 78–108). The *sabhā* is mentioned eight times in the Ṛg-Veda and seventeen times in the Atharva-Veda, while *samiti* is found nine times in the Ṛg-Veda and thirteen times in the Atharva-Veda. While the increased occurrence of these two terms is noticeable it is not so statistically outlandish that it provides an argument in and of itself.

Finally, in making these arguments scholars have largely neglected the context in which claims about *rājans* and their supposed accountability to the *viś* (common people) in the assembly are in fact made. Ritual chants and imprecations surrounding *rājans* always focus on or include deities. One is hard-pressed to find any hymn in the Atharva-Veda that, in mentioning kings and their relationship to the people, does not invoke *devas* or a particular *deva*. For example, a charm uttered at the consecration of a king states:

> Let kingly domain [*rāṣṭra*] come to you with its brilliant power: Ascend forth! Rule the people as the lord and sole ruler. O king [*rājan*], let all four quarters call you; become one who is revered and deserving of

> homage. Let the people and these regions, as five goddesses, accept you for kingship [*rājya*]. . . . Let the kinsmen invoking you, go to you; the agile Agni shall accompany them as messenger. . . . First, the Aśvins, both Mitra and Varuṇa, all the gods, and the Maruts—let them invoke you. (AV 3.4.1–4)

This particular *atharvan* invokes a variety of *deva*s, and this is not uncommon. Ruling claims involving *sabhā*s, *samiti*s, kings or rulers, and *viś* never appear without the belief that human beings, at the most fundamental level, do not rule in any human-centric sort of way. Rather, people are naturally ruled by being caught up in a preexisting and interconnected cosmic network—the network I have attempted to clarify throughout this chapter. In this sense, ruling on the human plane takes place within a larger cosmological "flow." Human beings are not understood as the fundamental, meaning-giving center of the cosmos, especially with respect to rule. Rather, human beings are understood as ontologically open to receiving meaning from within a broader network of entities and relationships. By undertaking narrowly focused analyses of particular verses (or parts of verses) and hymns that mention assemblies and kings, scholars have generally neglected the broader contexts in which ruling claims make sense. As I explain in chapter 5, these contexts are important to clarify because they provide a very different vantage point from which to assess problematic Western beliefs and commitments concerning rule and human–nonhuman relations.

Conclusion: Laying the Groundwork

In this chapter my primary goal has been to explicate the necessary categories, concepts, and terminology for understanding early brahmanical political thought. The framework outlined in this chapter provides a more nuanced and textually responsive analytic framework for examining the meaning of kingly rule in the Saṃhitās and Brāhmaṇas. A better understanding of this brahmanical context can help prevent political theorists who are unfamiliar with these texts from unduly employing Western concepts, terminology, and assumptions during the interpretive process, as well as provide a coherent cross-cultural vantage point for a comparison with the Greek tradition. This analysis also provides scholars a better historical foundation for examining the broader history of Indian political thought, especially Hindu traditions of political thought. While the category of sacrificial ritual plays a central role in these analyses, hierarchy also proves to be an important category. Finally, addressing relevant South Asian scholarship helps bridge a gap that has traditionally existed between such scholarship and the political theory literature. In sum, this analytic framework now allows me to locate the most significant continuity and change in brahmanical political thought during the early and middle Vedic periods.

4 VEDIC SAṂHITĀS AND BRĀHMAṆAS

RULING AS STEWARDSHIP

Providing a coherent analytic framework for the immense collection of material found in the Saṃhitās and Brāhmaṇas is a challenging first step, and finding the proper entry point for examining rule also presents difficulties. In comparison to Homer and Hesiod, these brahmanical works do not offer the same sort of coherent narratives through which one might follow particular characters and their thoughts, actions, and consistent engagement with other rulers. The later Indian epic, the Mahābhārata, stands closer to the Homeric and Hesiodic texts in this respect. As I argued last chapter, one must take a somewhat different approach to this early Vedic material to locate the change and continuity in the meaning of rule.

Following the layers I parsed in the previous chapter, this chapter examines the meaning of kingly rule in early and middle Vedic thought. Beginning with Ṛg-Veda Saṃhitā 1, I examine the initial meaning of kingly rule as divine guardianship because, as I argued in chapter 3, the title "*rājan*" is predominantly applied to the *deva*s (gods) in this layer. I then explain how this understanding appears to influence an understanding of human kingship as stewardship beginning in Ṛg-Veda Saṃhitā 2. An apparent dilemma arises in this later layer of the Ṛg-Veda: human kings are not divine kings, and hence they cannot rule exactly like them. In other words, they cannot be the cosmic guardians that Varuṇa, or Mitra-Varuṇa, and Indra appear to be in the early Ṛg-Veda. If brahmanical thought wants to retain an understanding of kingly rule as the only or proper form of ruling, then it must formulate a new understanding of rule. In the early and middle Vedic context, brahmanical thought achieves this by formulating the belief that human kingly rule was part of the cosmic framework from the very beginning. While the prior meaning of divine kingly rule as guardianship influences the new meaning of human kingly rule as stewardship in some respects, the new meaning signals a major change as brahmanical thought begins to formulate a more nuanced account of rule on the human plane. The simultaneous hierarchizing of human rule and horizontal interconnectedness between the human and nonhuman, I argue, is the most important development in the early stages of brahmanical political thought.

Ṛg-Veda Saṃhitā 1: Divine *Rājan*s and Guardianship

In the earliest layer of Vedic texts deities receive the title of *rājan* almost exclusively. The frequent references to *rājans* in the early Ṛg-Veda are to divine *rājans* such as Indra, Varuṇa, Mitra, Agni, and Soma.[1] Throughout various hymns the Vedic *ṛṣis* (seers) give each of these deities the title of *rājan*. The second book provides a good example. Hymn 27 is offered to the Ādityas (celestial *deva*s, offspring of goddess Aditi), in which Aryaman, Varuṇa, Mitra, and Bhaga are all invoked as *rājans*. Among these deities, the most important *rājan* is Varuṇa, frequently referred to as Mitra-Varuṇa, who is invoked as the ruler of other *deva*s and the protector of *ṛta*.[2] Varuṇa (or Mitra-Varuṇa), as the upholder of the moral order and cosmic law, embodies what could be considered the judicial and administrative functions associated with *rājan*-ship (see Macdonell 1897, 24–29; Söhnen 1997, 236). Therefore, contra John Spellman (1964, 2), the earliest conception of kingship was partly but not predominantly militaristic. Indra, on the other hand, is primarily invoked as the warrior god, hero (*śūra*), and ever-important slayer of Vṛtra.[3] Indra and Varuṇa thus constitute a ruling pair, and hymn 41 of book four exemplifies the early Vedic understanding of this divine pair's cosmic rule. In this hymn dedicated to Indra and Varuṇa, the two deities are mentioned together as a cosmic ruling force that protects human beings, defeats enemies in battle, and bestows wealth (ṚV 4.41–42). One can thus identify two distinct aspects of rule in this early pairing: while Varuṇa oversees and protects cosmic order and truth (*ṛta*), Indra displays courageous leadership and strength in battle. Together these two deities provide the earliest Vedic understanding of what it means to rule.

Because divine *rājans* are the beings predominantly designated as *rājans* in early Ṛg-Vedic cosmology, one must examine their role as it is invoked throughout the early hymns. Divine *rājans* are guardians in a cosmos that is even more uncertain and potentially dangerous than the Greek cosmos, at least in some respects. Most of the hymns in the early books invoke figures like Indra, Agni, and Mitra-Varuṇa as protectors or guardians of some sort (Scharfe 1989, 93). These divine *rājans* protect the cosmos, cosmic order and truth (*ṛta*), as well as human well-being. In the fifth book, hymn 63 celebrates Mitra-Varuṇa as "guardians of *ṛta*, you whose ordinances (*dharmans*) are true" (ṚV 5.63.1). In this hymn Mitra and Varuṇa are consistently invoked as *rājans*. In the sixth book, Agni is called both *rājan* and *gopṛ* (protector) of immortality (*amṛta*) (ṚV 6.7.1/7). In addition, these divine kings work both alone and in unison to fight forces of darkness, destruction, and constraint but not against each other like Homeric gods.[4] For example, in the third book a hymn dedicated to Indra mentions that he has overcome the *dāsas* (demons) and valiantly defeated Vṛtra (ṚV 3.34.1–3; 6.26.3–5). These types of invocations are common. As Gonda explains regarding *rājans* and *kṣatriyas* in general, "The idea of protecting the people was central" (1966, 2). In this early layer of the Ṛg-Veda, however, ideas of cosmic protection and guardianship are not yet associated with human kings to the degree one observes in subsequent Vedic layers.

Moreover, divine *rājans* and the principle of guardianship are linked in the early Ṛg-Vedic hymns to a number of cosmological and metaphysical beliefs discussed in the previous chapter. Last chapter I argued that *bandhus* (connections) help explain how divine *rājans* are connected to human beings. An example of this connection can be found in the seventh book in a hymn dedicated to the Aśvins: "There are paternal friendships and a common connection (*bandhu*) between us—acknowledge this" (ṚV 7.72.2).[5] This verse shows how inherent connections of friendship and kinship can exist between *devas* and human beings. A term analogous to *bandhu*, with its specific Vedic meanings and associations, does not appear in Homer or Hesiod. The closest similarity may be found in accounts of the direct kinship relation between various gods and their human children—for example, Thetis and Achilles. However, the term *bandhu* exhibits a broader understanding of cosmic and metaphysical kinship that is not limited to specific genetic cases. While gods and human beings also interact with one another in a variety of ways in Greek poetry, and this interaction clearly implies some sort of connectedness, neither Homer nor Hesiod formulates or elaborates a particular abstract concept to explain this connection in a way that might undercut the strong ontological individualism of self-possessed individuality.

In the previous chapter I explained that the term *kṣatra* provides a metaphysical connection between divine and human rulers. In this early layer, *kṣatra* generally refers to a *deva*'s dominion or scope of rule.[6] However, the term *kṣatra*, in its agentive sense and relation to the underlying verb root *kṣi-* (to rule), can also denote a means or instrument for ruling. Therefore, implied in *kṣatra*'s earliest meaning is the understanding that a *deva*—Indra, for example—possesses a fundamental characteristic necessary for rule. This characteristic also suggests a metaphysical principle associated with *kṣatra*, which will be further elaborated in the liturgical Saṃhitās and Brāhmaṇas. On this reading, *kṣatra* implies some cosmological and metaphysical constant that serves as a condition of possibility for rule. One can thus interpret *kṣatra* as a fundamental connection, or *bandhu*, between rulers on the divine and human planes. Insofar as human rulers possess characteristics and responsibilities associated with *rāj-* and *kṣi-* (ruling), the metaphysical principle of *kṣatra* making these ruling attributes possible underlies both divine and human rulers. As I will explain later, this "divine king–human king" connection in the earliest layer of the Ṛg-Veda makes it sensible for brahmanical thought later to assign *kṣatriyas* some of the characteristics and responsibilities associated with divine *rājans*. This cosmic relationship exhibits one way in which an understanding of divine guardianship can sensibly influence the subsequent understanding of human stewardship, which further helps provide explanations of change and continuity in the meaning of rule.

The other important cosmological and metaphysical terms that are linked to divine *rājans* in this early layer are *ṛta* and *dharman*. As I explained in the previous chapter, *ṛta* is the earliest Vedic word for truth, further implying a cosmo-metaphysical structure and ordering principle that regulates the cosmos. Not only are *devas* consistently associated with *ṛta*, they are also understood as its guardians and overseers.[7] As mentioned earlier, Mitra and Varuṇa are invoked as such: "Guardians of *ṛta*, you whose ordinances (*dharmans*) are true, standing in (your) chariot you ascend to the highest heavens" (ṚV 5.63.1). *Dharman*, as sacrificial ordinance, not only supports *ṛta* but also provides a means by which humans and *devas* are connected to each other. Agni is invoked in this manner during ritual as "being kindled following the first *dharmans* to bring the gods for worship" (ṚV 3.17.1). In the seventh book the poet asks for Varuṇa's forgiveness should he and others transgress Varuṇa's *dharmans* (ṚV 7.89.5). Therefore, *dharmans* provide a mechanism that directly connects human beings to other beings such as *devas* in the broader cosmology and indirectly connects human beings to *ṛta*. This indirect connection then evokes the concepts of hierarchy and interconnectedness.

A hierarchical conception of the cosmos and early assumptions about interconnectedness can both be found in this layer. First, divine *rājans* are the most prominent beings bearing a ruling title. These *rājans* clearly stand above human rulers and heads of households (*viśpatis*), and are therefore understood as ruling-over both. Second, while these divine *rājans* protect *ṛta*, *dharmans* help ensure that human beings are connected to and assisting *devas* in their cosmic struggles against forces of darkness and death, which constrain the flow of life-giving elements such as the waters (*ap*). For example, in the ninth book a hymn to the deity Soma exhibits how humans are responsible for preparing *soma* libations, which Indra enjoys and needs for strength: "Thus, flow towards us after purification, bestowing wealth: come with Indra, bring forth weapons. . . . Set down *soma* vessels abounding in ghee as the most intoxicating and joyous drink of Indra" (ṚV 9.96.12–13). These verses display a fundamental interconnectedness between human beings and *devas*: neither gods nor humans are alone in the cosmos, and they need each other to preserve their well-being.

In addition to sacrificial ordinances, divine ordinances (*vratas*) also regulate the cosmos. Here an important cross-cultural distinction can be made. While the Greek gods may enjoy and expect sacrifices from human beings, Vedic gods *require* sacrifices from human beings. This requirement constitutes a key aspect of divine *vratas* because the Vedic gods, unlike their Greek counterparts, are not self-sufficient. As Mahony (1998, 125) explains regarding the Vedic case, interconnectedness and reciprocity characterize human–divine relations, especially as depicted in the divine need for *soma*. This reciprocal relationship between human beings and *devas* is celebrated at great length in the ninth book, where the Vedic *ṛṣis* recount how provisions of *soma* libations in sacrificial rituals allow humans to help the *devas* defeat their enemies and maintain cosmic order. Therefore, within this hierarchical and interconnected cosmos, divine *rājans* (with the help of their human kin) guard against threats coming from a variety of directions and nonhuman forces. As we will begin to see in the next layer of Vedic works, the meaning of the term *rājanya* does not entirely dismiss this understanding but rather builds upon it in novel ways.

Admittedly, the role and meaning of *human* rulership is more ambiguous in this layer of the Vedas. As I explained in the last chapter, the Vedic *ṛṣis* do not cognize and communicate these hymns as political treatises in any straightforward Western sense, nor are these hymns primarily intended to explain the duties of human rulers in early Vedic society. Any textual examination of human rule in this layer involves a fair amount of inference and speculation. Moreover, while such beliefs found in these works may help us understand the early brahmanical view of kingly rule, they do not necessarily reflect historical actualities or describe historical events.[8]

Early Vedic hymns predominantly portray human rulers as leaders and social notables involved in assemblies and battles. The earliest term for a human ruler in the form of a chief or community leader is *viśpati*, which can refer to the chief of a settlement or the master of a house.[9] The term, however, does not express many relevant beliefs about ruling relations and serves more as a social title that one can usually translate as a "head of household" or "tribal leader." Although analytic emphasis should remain on the term *rājan* in this layer, leadership and social notability remain important characteristics of early Vedic, human rulers (ṚV 4.50.7–9). As Gonda explains, "an ancient Indian chief or king was often designated by the name of the tribe or people which had accepted his leadership" (1966, 48). While human rulers' specific duties in early assemblies are uncertain, these individuals are represented as prominent in the assembly's various proceedings (ṚV 9.92.6). For example, in the fourth book, a hymn dedicated to Indra states: "You [Indra] whose resourcefulness (*kratu*, or inventiveness) is like the *samrāṭ* (king, chief, sovereign) of a religious assembly (*vidathya*)" (ṚV 4.21.2).[10] The analogy in this hymn implies that a *samrāṭ* is clearly distinguished in early assemblies, although we are not told the specific reasons why this is so. In contrast with the Greek case, we do not find descriptions or narrative accounts of kings giving orders, making specific ruling decisions, or arguing with one another over honorific prizes. Human rulers also appear important for battle purposes. A hymn in the eighth book associates ruling power (*kṣatra*) with men of war (ṚV 8.35.17). However, like much of the evidence regarding *rājan*s in this layer, most battle evidence must be inferred from exploits associated with divine *rājan*s such as Indra (e.g., see ṚV 4.26.3, 6.26.5). Therefore, political theorists and historians of political ideas should circumscribe their claims about human rulers, chiefs, or kings in this layer since these early texts do not regularly or systematically express beliefs about human kingly rule.

Ṛg-Veda Saṃhitā 2: Cosmogony and the Emergence of Human Kingship

In this layer of Vedic works, the earliest and most important conception of *rājan*-rule undergoes a significant change. Here a gradual shift in terminology from *rājan* to *rājanya* and *kṣatriya* displays both change and continuity in the brahmanical understanding of rule. Looking ahead briefly, I will argue that a belief in *rājan*-ship as guardianship by *deva*s helps explain the later belief in human kingship as stewardship by *rājanya*s and *kṣatriya*s. The terminological focus thus moves from *rājan* (Ṛg-Veda 1) to *rājanya* (Ṛg-Veda 2), and finally, to *rājan* and *kṣatriya* (liturgical Saṃhitās and Brāhmaṇas). In the course of this development a belief in kingly rule as the only and proper form of ruling emerges in brahmanical thought. Particular cosmological and metaphysical beliefs strongly influence brahmanical conceptions of kingly rule in this early Vedic period and highlight a central contention of this historical-comparative study. That is, Vedic political thought exhibits the inverse development from the one I identified in early Greek political thought. As opposed to a leveling of rule on the human plane paired with individual demarcation and disconnectedness between human and nonhuman beings, Vedic political thought expresses the simultaneous hierarchizing of human rule and an increasingly complex horizontal interconnectedness between human and nonhuman beings.

Within books 1 and 10, the latest books of the Ṛg-Veda, divine *rājans* remain the most prominent *rājans*. Hymns continue to invoke deities as *rājans*, a term connoting guardianship in this layer as well as in the earlier Ṛg-Vedic hymns. Agni, Varuṇa, Indra, Soma, and Viśvadevas are all called *rājans*,[11] and deities such as Mitra and Varuṇa remain guardians and overseers of *ṛta* (ṚV 1.23.5). Mahony (1998, 125), for example, explains how Varuṇa's *vratas*, as solemn vows or obligations, include maintaining *ṛta* (see ṚV 1.24.10, 1.25.10). Those offering hymns to the gods are also called *deva-gopṛ*, or those whose protectors are the gods (ṚV 1.53.11). The gods thus remain the primary guardians (*rājans*) in the cosmos within this later portion of the Ṛg-Veda. At this point in Vedic textual chronology, brahmanical thought continues to express a belief in *rājan*-ship as guardianship, which exists primarily at the divine level. One also observes, however, an important transition with the occurrence of a particular cosmogonic hymn in the tenth book.

In Ṛg-Veda 10.90 for the first time *rājanya*, a term associated with the term *rājan*, is applied to human kings in a cosmogonic context. This development is tremendously significant from a historical standpoint because, beginning with this hymn, brahmins express novel cosmological beliefs while also invoking the term *rājanya* to identify the existence of an inherent ruling group on the human plane. Here, some brief comments are in order concerning the term *rājanya* and its historical-textual significance. This term does not appear in the earlier layer of the Ṛg-Veda, which is something previous political theorists have failed to notice.[12] Its first appearance is in Ṛg-Veda 10.90.12. By now we are familiar with the term *rājan*, but the suffix "*–ya*" added to the term can indicate an adjective of relation, a masculine patronymic, or a neuter abstract noun (Macdonell [1916] 2005, 263). The term *rājanya* appears to straddle the first (adjectival) and second (masculine patronymic) categories, indicating someone who is "*rājan*-like" or perhaps the son (or descendent) of a *rājan*. Therefore, a significant change and elaboration takes place in this cosmogonic account: the transition from a belief in divine (*deva-*) *rājan*-ship to a belief in a human king who is *rājan-ya*, or *rājan*-like. This development displays how the term *rājan* provides a conceptual hook in the inherited web of beliefs for a new belief in *rājanya*. In this hymn we thus begin to see a move away from earlier terms for a human chief or communal leader, such as *viśpati*, to a term directly related to *rājan*, which previously had been associated with divine kings such as Indra and Varuṇa. This development also helps explain why brahmins adopt a belief in the (human) kingly rule of *rājanya*s and *kṣatriya*s: they draw upon preexisting beliefs in divine *rājan*-ship in order to accommodate a new belief in human kingship, resulting in the term *rājanya*.

These observations suggest that a particular dilemma arises in brahmanical thought—namely, a new belief that human rulers should be king-like and more than mere *pati*s. Brahmins appear to retain the term *rājan* because it expresses their preexisting understanding of kingly rule. However, this term had been applied predominantly to *deva*s in the preexisting web of beliefs, and it is quite evident that human beings are not *deva*s. A human king could not have the same powers as his divine ancestors and his cosmic role could, at best, only approximate the *deva*'s powers and role. Human kings could thus only be *rājan-ya*, or *rājan*-like. Therefore, the dilemma appears to be: How could one move from a conception of divine kingship to human kingship without starting all over and completely reconceiving what it means to rule and be a king or ruler? Or, how could brahmins develop an understanding of human kingly rule that would cohere with their preexisting beliefs about what it meant to be a *rājan*? Their answer is: human kings could not be guardians in the sense that Indra and Varuṇa are guardians, but they could be stewards of the ruling function by protecting the brahmin's ability to conduct sacrificial ritual and maintain the emergent *varṇa* (social group or class) system. They could be guardians of a sort, just not the same kind as Indra and Varuṇa. This, I argue, is an incredibly significant development in early and middle Vedic political thought and provides a central hinge for subsequent conceptions of human rule.

I have explained how *rājan* is the most important term to focus on when analyzing rule in the first Ṛg-Vedic layer, and if we track this term into the next layer, the significance of *rājanya*'s emergence within a cosmogony (ṚV 10.90) becomes clearer. Because cosmogonies provide a foundational account of the origin, structure, and nature of the cosmos, any ruling beliefs expressed within them are incredibly important. In the previous layer, words associated with the verb root *rāj-* (to rule) are primarily associated with deities, but in Ṛg-Veda 10.90 the term *rājanya* now distinguishes a particular group of human beings associated with *rāj-* who stand in particular relation to other social groups emerging from Puruṣa. While human kings took a back seat to divine kings in the previous layer, this hymn provides the first account of the origin of an important type of human being associated with *rāj-*. As we will see in the liturgical Saṃhitās and Brāhmaṇas, brahmanical thought will elaborate on human kingly rule and responsibilities associated with *rāj-*, albeit with new reference to *rājan*s, *rājanya*s, and *kṣatriya*s.

This cosmogonic interpretation of the origin of kingly rule contrasts with most existing accounts, as scholars generally highlight a variety of possible origins and do not argue for the priority of any particular one (see Altekar 1958, 27–36; Drekmeier 1962, 245–52; Ghoshal 1966, 29–30). Spellman (1964), for example, argues for a number of existing theories about the origin of kingship and the "state," including: a fear of anarchy (*mātsyanyāya*), an organic theory, a sacrificial theory, kingship through *karma*, divine appointment, the king as appointed by *ṛṣi*s, and theories of social contract. Spellman is not completely off base here, as a variety of these types of claims about kings or rulers arise over the course of Vedic and post-Vedic works. Nonetheless, this analytic approach and type of argument, which accurately represents the majority of scholarship in this area, face problems that scholars have not sufficiently addressed.

To begin, such analytic approaches examine too much material in surveying texts that extend over incredibly long periods of time. If in the same analysis one treats texts ranging from the early Vedic period (ca. 1500–900 BCE) to the early Hindu period (ca. 200–500 CE), one must necessarily gloss over many important details and distinctions between texts and genres. This analytic tendency generally leads to oversimplification and forecloses the possibility of good synchronic and diachronic explanation. In addition, such analyses display the predominant descriptive, broad-ranging exegetical approach most scholars take to the Indian material. This usually results in arguments and positions that lack a higher degree of scholarly rigor, and I presume previous scholars have taken more descriptive approaches for two reasons.

First, like most political theorists who have written on this subject matter, they aim to provide general introductions to the topic. However, the usefulness of such introductions has waned because they generally provide similar—and often identical—summaries of material in the texts, which fail to provide critical, rigorous analyses that employ specific theories or arguments. Simply put, such introductions no longer advance scholarly understanding in significant ways. Second, political theorists present brahmanical political thought as complex, and rightly so, but also as somewhat unsystematic and disorganized. They seem to assume we cannot explain much and are necessarily left with descriptive exegetical projects on the subject matter. We are then left with a meandering about in this large, diverse forest and (more or less) randomly pointing things out that might look interesting to us. Spellman, who has actually written one of the better introductions to this topic, captures the spirit of this predominant yet problematic approach when he states: "This book attempts to describe and in some cases interpret aspects of ancient Indian political theory" (1964, xxi). While I do not want to overstate this critique, instead of undertaking more descriptive projects that cover incredibly broad periods of time, what we need in this area are more focused, rigorous interpretations and attempts at explaining historical meaning, change, and continuity.

My interpretation of rule in this layer can be summarized as follows. Although deities are still invoked as the most prominent *rājan*s in the cosmos, in ṚV 10.90 the first explicit account of a group of individuals who will inherit many of the responsibilities associated with divine *rājan*-ship starts to emerge. Belief in guardianship on the divine level possesses tremendous significance to those reciting the hymns. After all, the cosmos is viewed as a very dangerous place and plagued by uncertainty, so *deva*s need all the help they can get from human beings to defeat enemies such as the *dānava*s and Vṛtra. Because divine *rājan*s are incredibly important in early Vedic cosmology and metaphysics, brahmanical thought does not entirely strip them of their cosmic importance but transfers some of their most significant attributes and responsibilities to a specific group of human beings—*rājanya*s, or *kṣatriya*s. This transference of ruling responsibility from divine to human agents signifies the first major development in brahmanical political thought, as the understanding of kingly rule as guardianship gradually morphs into an understanding of stewardship on the human plane. While rule had previously been conceived almost entirely along a vertical (divine to human) scale, it now entails a more distinct horizontal dimension (human to human). This transference in ruling responsibilities from divine *rājan*s to human *rājanya*s thus displays how rule is increasingly associated with human as opposed to divine kings. In comparative perspective, an important question to keep in mind is how brahmins can pull this off without simultaneously becoming more human-centric, as we saw happen in Hesiod's political thought. In the next layer of Vedic works, I explain how *kṣatriya*s are responsible for protecting brahmins, *vaiśya*s, and *śūdra*s and become stewards responsible for maintaining all beings, worlds, and the cosmos as a whole.[13] This leads to an incredibly robust conception of ruling-in and ruling-for a broader cosmic well-being and the interests of a wide variety of nonhuman beings and phenomena.

Liturgical Saṃhitās and Brāhmaṇas: Human Rule as Stewardship

In this section I explicate the meaning of ruling as stewardship in the liturgical Saṃhitās and Brāhmaṇas by employing an analytic framework that draws upon the cosmological, metaphysical, and ontological beliefs presented in the current and previous chapters. First, I consider kingly rule's relation to a broad web of cosmological beliefs, examining the king's origin and positioning in the cosmic hierarchy. Here I rely on a collection of thirteen separate cosmogonies and cosmological frames that Smith has carefully culled from this layer of Vedic texts, which provide a useful base of textual material for examining *kṣatriya*s within a broader cosmic framework. Second, I show how important metaphysical concepts and beliefs express an understanding of kingly rule as stewardship, which entails ruling-in and ruling-for a vast array of beings within the cosmos. Third, I examine how particular ontological concepts and beliefs deepen this understanding. At the end of the section I summarize the *kṣatriya*'s stewardship relations to the community as a whole, including the brahmin, *vaiśya*, and *śūdra* social groups.

Cosmogony, Cosmology, and Stewardship

As we see for the first time in the Puruṣa-Sūkta, the *rājanya* emerges from Puruṣa's arms. In the liturgical layer one can now observe significant elaborations of this initial cosmogonic move. As a disclaimer on origins, however, Smith (1994, 80) explains that multiple cosmogonies and cosmologies are presented in the texts, some of which include the body of the primordial creator god, ritual, or various elements of the natural world. While the liturgical Saṃhitās and Brāhmaṇas may present multiple cosmogonic narratives and sources, I believe the most important point here is that some initial, primordial act of creation does in fact take place, and regardless of the particular source presented in the texts, the result is a consistent hierarchical and horizontal account of beings within the cosmos. *Kṣatriya*s, regardless of their particular source, are produced at some point in the creative process, and thus a specified group of human beings responsible for ruling emerges during the earliest creative stages. Consequently, these cosmogonies maintain that kingly rule is built into the cosmic framework and not an issue to be decided or debated among human beings in assemblies or some "public" venue. In other words, human beings are not understood as having a choice in the matter. I should also point out, as Smith (1994, 80–81) does, that brahmanical thought does not consciously privilege the brahmin social group over other groups of entities—for example, meters, divinities, flora, or fauna—as the origin of these other groups. *Varṇa* (social group) is only one among many categories within the broader cosmic schema and thus embedded in the same cosmogonic process as all the other categories. In this regard, human beings are not understood as exceptional or privileged over other groups of entities.

According to the consistent tripartite cosmology Smith identifies in the Śatapatha Brāhmaṇa, Aitareya Brāhmaṇa, and Jaiminīya Brāhmaṇa, *kṣatriyas* (rulers) are connected with the following: *kṣatra* (metaphysical essence), greatness (essential power), humans (ontological entity), Indra/Vāyu (deity), mid-regions (cosmological world), wind (natural element), midday (part of day), breath (body function), Yajur (Veda), *bhuvas* (primordial utterance), *triṣṭubh* (meter), *adhvaryu* (priest), and *āgnīdhrīya/anvāhāryapacana* (sacrificial fire) (1994, 67). Regarding the *kṣatriya*'s connection to *kṣatra*, during the Puruṣamedha (human sacrifice, or sacrifice of Puruṣa), where victims from each social group are offered to their respective elemental quality, the Śatapatha Brāhmaṇa states: "For the *kṣatra*, he seizes a *rājanya* [*kṣatriya*], for the *rājanya* is the *kṣatra*" (ŚB 13.6.2.10; Smith 1994, 29). Here an important cosmo-ontological claim is made: the *rājanya* (or *kṣatriya*) is *kṣatra* (*kṣatram vai rājannyaḥ*), as his identity is equated with the essential power that makes him what he is.[14] The *kṣatriya varṇa*, like the other *varṇas*, is thus considered to have intrinsic connections (*bandhus*) with particular essences and entities within the cosmos.

The *kṣatriya*'s correspondence to Indra is clearly significant in light of the earlier Ṛg-Vedic hymns in which Indra is the penultimate warrior god. The *kṣatriya*'s association with force, strength, and Indra express the understanding that *kṣatriyas* are natural rulers.[15] The ruler's connection to Indra is made clear in the *mahābhiṣeka* (great anointing of Indra) ceremony described in the Aitareya Brāhmaṇa (8.12), a ceremony that serves as the divine prototype for a human king's consecration. Because Indra, and a human king by extension, cannot display his strength (*vīrya*) unless he is properly consecrated, the ceremony establishes the following:

> The gods proclaimed him [Indra, the king] as the unified ruler and unified rulership, as ruler of uncommon attributes and lord of such rulers,

> as ruler over himself and self-rulership, as a wide ruler and wide rulership, as king and lord of kings, as possessing supremacy and supremacy itself. [Hence] The ruling power [*kṣatra*] was born, the *kṣatriya* was born, the overlord of every being was born, the consumer of the people was born, the breaker of establishments [*pur*] was born, the slayer of the *asuras* was born, the defender of the brahmin (or priest) was born, and the defender of *dharma* was born. (AB 8.12)

The significance of this passage is manifold. First, it lists most of the major titles associated with a ruler found in both earlier and later texts, providing a terminological roadmap for identifying beliefs about rule. The variety of terminology in the passage surrounding the term and verb root *rāj-* provides grounds for synchronic explanation stretching back to the earliest layer of the Ṛg-Veda. Second, the passage outlines the necessary qualities of a ruler and his social role as a defender of brahmins (*gopṛ*), a dependent consumer of his subjects (*viś*, of which *vaiśya* is a nominal derivative), and a slayer of enemies (*asuras*). Contra R. S. Sharma, passages such as these do not intimate a "contract theory of the origin of the state . . . [which] refer to the origin of kingship through election among the gods on account of the compelling necessity of carrying on successful war against the Asuras" (1968, 64). There is no election here and no talk of obligations on Indra's part or obedience on the gods' part. The emergence of kingly rule among the gods in this passage is simply the result of Indra's (and by extension, a *kṣatriya*'s) natural attributes, which are based upon particular metaphysical beliefs about essences, such as *kṣatra*, elaborated upon in this layer. Cosmologically, due to a connection of essences through *kṣatra*, here we can see how brahmanical thought posits one way human rulers engage in ruling-with divine rulers such as Indra. In addition, contra R. S. Sharma (65) and Ghoshal (1966, 11, 24), kingly rule's emergence does not automatically entail some sort of electoral procedure or any corresponding conception of obligation on the part of the ruler. Terminology and concepts for obligation and obedience cannot be justifiably located in these passages, especially the modern (Western) language of contract theory that scholars such as R. S. Sharma tend to suggest.

The passage directly precedes and is part of the *mahābhiṣeka* of a human king, thus establishing a cosmological connection between Indra's divine rule and the human king's rule. Preexisting beliefs about kingly rule stretching back to Ṛg-Veda 1 thus constitute an inherited tradition for ruling beliefs in the liturgical Saṃhitās and Brāhmaṇas. Here one observes the belief that a *bandhu* exists between a god who is a divine ruler in the inherited tradition and a particular type of human ruler. One also notices that, in contrast to the Greek case, ruling beliefs do not revolve around a strong notion of individuality or individualistic motives. Rather, brahmanical rule revolves around beliefs about a type of individual—namely, *rājanya* or *kṣatriya*. While Indra is distinctly identified, the passage indicates that becoming a "unified ruler" does not have anything to do with self-enactment or striving for individual distinction, as we see in the Greek example of Zeus. Indra does not become a ruler out of motivation for distinguishing himself from others and earning glory or honor among his peers.

Varuṇa's connection to human kings, and kingship more broadly, is also tied to such sacrifices: "Now Varuṇa, whose desire was for kingship (*rājya*), established this [sacrificial fire]. He thus attained kingship. Therefore, whether one [i.e., the sacrificial patron, householder] knows this or not, they say, 'Varuṇa is king'" (ŚB 2.2.3.1). Here one observes how kingly rule is necessarily connected to sacrificial ritual, and by association should be connected to the ritual's role in maintaining cosmic order (*ṛta*). In this context, beliefs about a human king are linked to beliefs about Varuṇa's judicial and administrative associations as the upholder of order, which extend back to the earliest layer of the Ṛg-Veda. Finally, in the Śatapatha Brāhmaṇa the Vājapeya (drink of vigor) ritual bestows ruling power upon the sacrificial patron, in this case the human king or ruler, by connecting him with the creator Prajāpati (lord of creatures) and allowing him to come back down to earth as ruler after the connection is properly established:

> Then he [the brahmin officient] spreads out the skin of the he-goat. This he-goat is truly Prajāpati, since these goats are most perceptibly from Prajāpati—because, when these goats are giving birth three times per year, they birth two and three. Thus he makes him [i.e., the sacrificial patron] out to be Prajāpati. Therefore, he spreads it out, declaring, "This is your kingship," and bestows this kingship upon him. So then he [the brahmin] makes him sit down, declaring, "You are the ruling leader," and he makes him the ruling leader, so ruling over his people. "You are lasting, and steadfast," and thus he makes him [the king] lasting and steadfast in this world. "You are made so for ploughing, for communal safety, for wealth, and for prosperity." Thus he has said this to mean, "You are made so for the good of the people." (ŚB 5.2.1.24–25)

In this passage, we see an example of how a connection and correspondence are made between the he-goat, Prajāpati, and kingly rule within the context of a broader cosmic framework. Access to the he-goat allows for ritual access and manipulation of various cosmological entities—for example, Prajāpati—that are not immediately or tangibly available (I explain this process in more detail later). As I explained last chapter, such access and manipulation are made possible through a system of interlinked prototypes (*pramās*), counterparts (*pratimās*), and connective resemblances (*bandhus*). Through this ritual process, kingly rule is then bestowed through a cosmological connection to Prajāpati. An important aspect of stewardship also arises in this scene because all this is done, and kingly rule established, as a means of ruling-for "the good of the people."

Kṣatriyas also fit within four-, five-, and six-part cosmologies. Smith (1994, 65–79) has shown how brahmanical thought expands the basic tripartite cosmology, further classifying the cosmos as well as its basic phenomena and characteristics. According to the quadripartite scheme found in the Pañcaviṃśa Brāhmaṇa, Jaiminīya Brāhmaṇa, and Taittirīya Saṃhitā, *kṣatriyas* also correspond to virility (socio-ontological quality), horse and sheep (animal), summer (season), chest/arms (body part), *bṛhat* (chant), and the fifteen-versed hymn of praise. In this quadripartite taxonomy the *kṣatriya*'s warrior and ruling characteristics are more clearly established because he is now associated with the chest and arms, the hot summer season (matching his suspected hot-tempered nature), and virility (Smith 1994, 70). These warrior-like characteristics help link the *kṣatriya* to his divine counterpart, Indra, "for the *kṣatriya* has the nature of Indra" (TS 2.4.13.1). In the subsequent pentadic scheme Smith (1994, 75) locates in the Śatapatha Brāhmaṇa, Taittirīya Saṃhitā, and Maitrāyaṇī Saṃhitā, *kṣatriyas* are also correlated with the south (direction), mind (bodily function), *prauga* (recitation), *antaryāma* (soma cup), Bharadvāja/Sanātana (*ṛṣi*), two-year-old cow (type of cow), and *treta* (throw of dice). While these correlations may not initially appear significant for explicating the meaning of kingly rule, they exhibit the increasingly complex classificatory nature of brahmanical thought in the liturgical context. These correlations also exhibit the various entities and phenomena that brahmanical thought considers most important. These taxonomic schemas can thus be seen as attempts to connect *kṣatriyas* and kingly rule with other elements in their broader web of beliefs. These correlations and classifications are relevant because they display the tremendous scope and interconnectedness posited within brahmanical thought and, as we shall see, help highlight what is at stake in kingly rule as stewardship. Finally, in the six-part cosmological schema Smith (1994, 79) locates in the Maitrāyaṇī Upaniṣad (a text lying outside the liturgical layer explicated here) and Kauṣītaki Brāhmaṇa, *kṣatriyas* also correlate with circulation (breath) and moon (astronomical body). According to these various cosmologies, *kṣatriyas* are connected to a wide range of cosmic phenomena and characteristics, displaying the vast extent of brahmins' cosmological classification and interconnectedness.

Within these cosmologies, *kṣatriyas* possess unique characteristics and are situated in a very specific way vis-à-vis other entities and phenomena. As I have already explained, *kṣatriyas* are connected to Indra, the warrior deity, as well as greatness (essential power) and virility (socio-ontological quality). A king's connection to Indra is important to note because the king's duty to protect the community requires defeating external aggressors in battle—a duty which has its prototype in the belief that the *devas* require Indra to lead them in defeating the *asuras*: "The gods and *asuras* were engaged in battle. As such, Prajāpati hid his best son, Indra. . . . The gods, having met with Prajāpati, said: 'We need a king in battle. Thus, we desire Indra to be king (*rājan*)' " (TB 1.5.9.1–2). In a sacrificial context the brahmin also asks: "May our king here, having become the Vṛtra-slaying king [i.e., Indra], slay the enemy" (TB 1.7.3.5; TS 1.8.9.2). Therefore, the Brāhmaṇas clearly express the belief in a cosmic kinship between the earthly ruler and divine kings, as explained during the *rājasūya* (kingly consecration) ritual: "Now, the *kṣatriya* has Indra as his divinity" (AB 7.23.1).

Importantly, *kṣatriyas* are not closed off from their surrounding cosmic environment but rather fundamentally connected—either directly or indirectly—to a multiplicity of beings and phenomena. Here one might ask how someone can be "fundamentally" yet "indirectly" connected to something in the manner I am suggesting. In addition, to invoke Hesiod as a comparative vantage point, one could point out that human beings in Hesiod's cosmos were not fundamentally closed off from their surrounding environment either. How would this claim about fundamental, indirect connections differ from the Hesiodic case? While I argued that different entities affected one another in both Homeric and Hesiodic political thought, I also explained how no particular cosmology, metaphysics, or ontology establishes any deeper links between different beings.[16] For example, Hesiod's farmer is undoubtedly connected to and affected by the seasons, but Hesiod does not claim that farmers have an essential connection to a particular season, let alone a particular animal, plant, or time of day. Of course, these sorts of linkages may appear absurd through a more individualistic and human-centric political lens, but that does not make them inherently irrational.

To further address the question about fundamental yet indirect connectedness, brahmanical taxonomies explain how a *kṣatriya*'s well-being, even if he is not directly connected to the brahmin's immediate kin (animal, plant, season, etc.), depends upon the brahmins' direct connections with these things for his own well-being, as will soon become clearer. Put another way, the category of *varṇa* provides the direct link, or hinge, for indirect connections between a *kṣatriya* and the myriad beings that are variously connected to brahmins, *vaiśyas*, and *śūdras*. Contra Hesiod's position, there is no fundamental distinction—political or otherwise—between human and nonhuman "loops" when it comes to things like rule and justice. There is only one broad, interconnected framework, and there is no way out of it.

This interconnectedness thus clarifies what is at stake in brahmanical rule. *Kṣatriyas* have a heavy responsibility as rulers because they play an integral role in helping maintain the order and integrity of this expansive community of beings and phenomena. The cosmic dimension of such stewardship can also be observed in the Aitareya Brāhmaṇa, which explains that when a king is consecrated he is born as the "defender of the brahmin and defender of *dharma*" (AB 8.17.6). In the liturgical Saṃhitās and Brāhmaṇas, this elaborately interconnected cosmos survives due to brahmins' Vedic knowledge and ability to conduct sacrificial rituals. As I will discuss in more detail at the end of this section, *kṣatriyas* are the human beings responsible for protecting brahmins' ability to perform the necessary rituals in the proper fashion.

The *kṣatriyas*' general positioning in this cosmology thus facilitates a belief in kingly rule as stewardship. Their connection to Indra and Varuṇa establishes them as a new type of guardian of cosmic order. As such, they have the characteristics necessary to fulfill this function, such as strength and virility. These beliefs about guardianship are inherited but also elaborated in both the Taittirīya Brāhmaṇa and Jaiminīya Brāhmaṇa. In these particular works, Indra and Varuṇa are alternatively depicted as becoming rulers of the gods due to their power, might, and superiority, which allows them to defeat enemies (Indra) or maintain cosmic order (Varuṇa).[17] On the human plane, this guardianship becomes a form of stewardship whereby the human *rājan* is the sustainer of the realm (*rāṣṭra*: realm, kingdom, or dominion): "Kings are sustainers of the realm [*rāṣṭrabhṛts*], they alone uphold the realms" (ŚB 9.4.1.1). As I will explain, *kṣatriyas* achieve this aim by protecting *vaiśyas*' and brahmins' abilities to undertake their own proper functions. Nevertheless, their most important role as ruler is to protect brahmins and the latter's ability to conduct sacrificial ritual. It is not only the order of the human realm that is at stake but also the fragile, interconnected cosmic structure. While the earlier meaning of divine *rājan*-ship as guardianship passes to human *kṣatriyas* in this liturgical layer, the newly elaborated cosmological structure and *kṣatriyas*' positioning within it make them its stewards. Whereas divine *rājans* were direct guardians in the earlier layer, *kṣatriyas* are also guardians, but in an indirect sense. Due to the increased centrality of sacrificial ritual in this layer, rule by *kṣatriyas* becomes a tertiary activity: a means (protection and promotion) to a means (sacrificial ritual) to an end (maintenance and construction of the cosmos and reality). The term stewardship, I argue, best captures this indirect or tertiary aspect of kingly rule. I have also shown how this change in the meaning of rule relies increasingly on complex cosmological speculation, which situates *kṣatriyas* in a specific position vis-à-vis other entities. These developments place a profound responsibility upon *kṣatriyas*, for what is now at stake is a more delicately balanced, complex, and interconnected cosmos than we observe in the Ṛg-Veda.

Metaphysics and Stewardship

Revisiting the metaphysical concepts and beliefs introduced in the previous chapter, I can now examine their connection to kingly rule as stewardship. I explained how *kṣatra* is a metaphysical essence or power underlying a *kṣatriya*'s ability to rule.[18] If *kṣatriyas* are responsible for upholding the ordered cosmos by protecting sacrificial ritual and defending the community, and *kṣatra* allows them to do so, then *kṣatra* provides the metaphysical support for stewardship. As a passage from the Śatapatha Brāhmaṇa quoted earlier explains: "For the *rājanya* (*kṣatriya*) is the *kṣatra*" (13.6.2.10). The *kṣatriya*'s underlying essence of *kṣatra* also links these rulers to their proper weapons: "The *kṣatra*'s weapons are the horse-drawn chariot, armor, and the bow and arrow" (AB 7.19). Finally, *kṣatra* anchors the *kṣatriya* as the proper ruler in the human community:

> Among the trees, the Nyagrodha is the ruling power, and the *rājanya* is the ruling power because the *kṣatriya* dwells here in the kingdom as stretched down into it, as it were, and becomes rooted in it like the Nyagrodha, which is rooted in the earth by its roots. (AB 7.31)[19]

In this passage one observes how the *kṣatra* essence connects the *kṣatriya* to a particular type of tree (banyan, or Nyagrodha) within the broader community of entities. Therefore, kingly rule as stewardship entails an important metaphysical belief. Underlying a *kṣatriya*'s *varṇa*-duty is a metaphysical power allowing him to fulfill his broader cosmological role as steward as he engages in ruling-in this overarching structure.

In addition to *kṣatra*, a *kṣatriya*'s role in sacrificial ritual expresses metaphysical beliefs associated with stewardship. In the previous chapter I explained how the manifest tier of reality is constructed and therefore does not fall into the more familiar (Western) "appearance/reality" distinction. This constructed form of reality, as we also saw, can arise through multiple means—for example, through desire, *yajña* (sacrifice), *tapas* (meditative heat), procreation, or speech (*vāc*). In the liturgical layer, the creator god Prajāpati is understood as the immediate source of all existent things. As Smith (1989, 50–69) points out, sacrificial ritual rectifies Prajāpati's initial procreative acts by ordering and maintaining manifest reality through ritual action, or *karman*. Smith further explains how Prajāpati's creative acts result in two metaphysical excesses: excessive resemblance, similarity, or non-differentiation (*jāmi*) and excessive differentiation, disconnectedness, or over-diversification (*pṛthak, bahutva*, or *nānātva*) (52). From the standpoint of these brahmanical beliefs about excessive differentiation, the Greek belief in self-possessed individuality would fall under the category of *pṛthak* (etc.), which further highlights Greek conceptions of disconnectedness. The ritual rectifies such excesses by "connecting the inherently disconnected, and healing the ontological disease of unreconstructed nature, the state toward which all created things and beings perpetually tend" (51).

Brahmanical ritual alleviates these metaphysical excesses by positing resemblances that operate in the following way. Because cosmic prototypes (*pramā*s) and counterparts (*pratimā*s) exist within the cosmos, the ritualists can access and manipulate prototypes by accessing and manipulating their counterparts in the ritual (Smith 1989, 53–54). The Vedic ritualists thus posit a theory of resemblance and connectedness that allows them to manipulate—physically, through ritual action and labor—counterparts to those things that might not be immediately accessible. Here *bandhu*s provide the necessary connections between prototypes and counterparts that allow for this ritual ordering and manipulation. As Prajāpati's initial creation is plagued by both excessive similarity and differentiation, sacrificial rituals allow brahmins to continually reconstruct and renovate Prajāpati's faulty procreative acts. As the protector (*gopṛ*) of the brahmins, *kṣatriya*s must safeguard their ability to conduct these incredibly important rituals (AB 8.17). Therefore, *kṣatriya*s are also stewards insofar as they maintain the cosmic order by protecting brahmins' abilities to perform sacrificial rituals that rectify metaphysical similarity and excess.

The final metaphysical aspect of stewardship pertains to the distinction between an emerging conception of *ātman* (self) and *brahman* (un-manifest

Absolute). Here I want to further clarify my claim that a belief in self-possessed individuality does not appear within brahmanical thought. I want to be clear on this point because this belief in self-possessed individuality presents one of the major differences between the meaning of kingly rule in ancient Greece and India. In the liturgical layer, *kṣatriyas*, as individual persons, are not believed to possess a self-contained, demarcated, and unitary personhood that is *prior to* and *more fundamental than* its connections with anything outside itself. As I explain in chapter 1, self-possessed individuality assumes that individual personhood possesses boundaries that fundamentally demarcate or separate it, at the most basic ontological and cosmological level, from other entities such as plants and animals. Because the term *ātman* is frequently translated as "Self," I want to explain how this notion of Self differs from the notion of a plural yet self-possessed individuality discussed in the Greek case. Because *ātman* lies at the core of every individual person or entity, including the creator Prajāpati,[20] it is tempting to interpret a *kṣatriya*'s *ātman* as an individual personhood that, like self-possessed individuality, possesses boundaries fundamentally separating it from other entities. However, this would be incorrect for a seemingly simple reason. At the most fundamental level, *ātman* is *brahman*. This means that at the most basic ontological and metaphysical level, the Self that is the innermost core of every being is identical with the un-manifest Absolute that is the basis of all existence.

The figure of Prajāpati will help clarify this point. In the Śatapatha Brāhmaṇa, Prajāpati is said to possess an *ātman*, and he is interested in putting his creation, or beings, back into his *ātman* (ŚB 10.4.2.3). One might be tempted to misinterpret this as meaning that the *ātman* is the most fundamental, essential aspect of an individual entity, separating it from other entities. However, as Smith points out, Prajāpati is commonly referred to as "this all" (*sarvam*) and identified with the unifying, neuter cosmic force, *brahman*. Smith explains, "the *Brahman* is not different from Prajāpati himself and has the same creative and ontologically formative powers" (1989, 69; see ŚB 7.3.1.42, 13.6.2.8). Although Prajāpati seems most concerned with his *ātman*, Smith rightly points out that the most essential aspect of Prajāpati is his identification with "this all" (*idam sarvam*), or with the all-encompassing, impersonal *brahman*. This identification provides the proper context for understanding *ātman*'s relation to *brahman* and the framework within which a *kṣatriya*'s individuality should be interpreted.

As is frequently the case, beliefs about deities provide a glimpse of how human beings understand themselves. Therefore, as Homer's Zeus clearly exhibits the belief in self-possessed individuality, so the brahmin's Prajāpati exhibits the model of, and belief in, a more universal Self. Like Zeus, Prajāpati also provides a model for kingly rule, although this brahmanical model continues to revolve around the category of sacrificial ritual. For example, connecting passages from the Jaiminīya Brāhmaṇa (3.152) and the Pañcaviṃśa Brāhmaṇa (13.9.20) shows how a king—with both Varuṇa and Prajāpati as exemplars—must secure *vāja* (generative power, vigor) through ritual to obtain royal power and kingship. The Śatapatha Brāhmaṇa (5.2.1.25) also claims that the Vājapeya (the drink of vigor) ritual bestows ruling powers upon the king. *Kṣatriya*s, then, should not be interpreted as possessing a "rock-bottom" individuality that fundamentally separates them from other entities. Rather, any individual boundaries that appear to separate beings are porous and ultimately dissolve at a metaphysical level in these beings' identity with *brahman*, the un-manifest Absolute, which is the impersonal source and basis of all individual beings.

Ontology, Ritual, and Stewardship

Having outlined the cosmological and metaphysical dimensions of stewardship, this section examines the *kṣatriya* as he passes through the ritual process, first, to clarify the ontology operating in this layer, and second, to show how this ontology supports a conception of ruling as stewardship. I begin by revisiting the *upanayana* ritual in which a *kṣatriya* passes through the first phase, or "womb," of sacrifice and fulfills his twice-born (*dvija*) status.[21] At age eleven a young *kṣatriya* undergoes his particularized version of the *upanayana*, which includes wearing garments of a particular material and color (spotted deer upper garment and a red cotton or linen lower garment), carrying a staff (*daṇḍa*) made out of a specific type of wood (*nyagrodha*), and chanting the Sāvitrī verse in a particular meter (*triṣṭubh*) and in a particular season (hot season) (Smith 1989, 95). As I explained in the previous chapter, this ritual holds the threat of ontological delinquency if it is not performed in a timely manner, or if it is performed incorrectly. In such cases a young *kṣatriya* would not become who he was born to be because his natural identity would fail to achieve proper inscription. Importantly, in this ritual a young *kṣatriya* is inscribed as a particular type of human being. Ontologically, this means the boy is told that he is not some unique "so-and-so" but rather a particular type of person who falls into a particular category—the *varṇa* of *kṣatriya*. First and foremost, rather than existing as a self-possessed individual, the *kṣatriya* thus exists as an individual defined (more fundamentally) by social group status and not some robust form of self-enactment. Stewardship, therefore, is not based upon a belief in individual choice or autonomy, as *kṣatriyas* are born with a necessary and categorical cosmic responsibility.

The second important ritual is the *rājasūya*, a king's royal consecration ceremony.[22] One term frequently analyzed in relation with the *rājasūya* is *ratnin*, a dignitary or member of the royal household (see Heesterman 1957, 49). Because *ratnins* are translated as "givers" (*pradātāraḥ*) and "takers" (*apādātāraḥ*) of a kingdom (TB 1.7.3), some scholars find this and other evidence to imply a representative, deliberative assembly and perhaps even political principles of accountability, election, or popular control over kingship (e.g., see Jayaswal 1967, 196–97; R. S. Sharma 1968, 146–47; Singh 1993, 43–44). Unfortunately, much of this work devolves into historical speculation that is difficult to support with textual evidence. Heesterman (1957, 49) explains that the *ratnins* are simply individuals who possess *ratnas*, which are ritual functions held by royal dignitaries and royal household members. Accordingly, I think it best to interpret *ratnins* as extensions and necessary parts of kingly rule and strength, and not as individuals who somehow control or "have a say" in ruling. As Heesterman further explains, "Like Prajāpati, the king integrates the dispersed elements, the 'limbs' [i.e., *ratnins*] of the kingship, tying them together in his person" (51).

Revisiting our young *kṣatriya*, while the *upanayana* established his initial ontological identity, the *rājasūya* now consolidates this identity. As Smith (1989, 110; PB 18.10.10) points out, the *rājasūya* offers both transcendence and immanence for a king: while a king ascends to the world of heaven through this ritual, he must also return to this world, which is his "firm foundation" (see also AB 4.21; PB 5.5.4–5). The *rājasūya* ritual requires the *yajamāna* (sacrificial patron), here a *rājan*, to return to this world where he is invested with vigor and strength: "There are eleven royal *sāmans*; the *triṣṭubh* is of eleven syllables; the *triṣṭubh* is vigor and strength; in vigor and strength he is inaugurated" (PB 18.10.7, trans. Caland). This ritual also explains how Indra lost his strength when he slew Vṛtra, likening this to the king who loses his strength when he himself slays an enemy (*vṛtra*) in the *rājasūya* (PB 18.11.1). The king's return from the heavens, together with his association with vigor, strength, and Indra, invoke the king's duty to protect his subjects and the brahmins who are conducting this ritual.

Because the king is understood as a steward with an important set of responsibilities, he requires periodic renewals of strength—adult versions of ritual rebirth—through the womb of sacrificial ritual that the *rājasūya* provides. Heesterman (1957, 6–7) makes the important point that the sacrificer must undergo ritual rebirth in an ongoing fashion, which reminds us how this royal consecration ceremony differs from more familiar modern versions. Stewardship thus entails a constant reacquisition of the strength needed to fulfill a ruler's responsibilities, and such strength must be periodically renewed through ritual. This ritual again displays the central importance of both brahmins and sacrificial rituals for the meaning of kingly rule. Moreover, the *rājasūya* expresses the belief that *kṣatriya*s need rituals to fulfill their *varṇa* duties—in this case, to acquire vigor and strength in order to emulate Indra, the paradigmatic warrior-king. This ritual thus elaborates how kings require participation in a life-long series of rituals that continually re-establish their identities as *kṣatriya*s.

Ruling-Over and Ruling-For Others: Stewardship Relations between the Kṣatriya, Brahmin, Vaiśya, and Śūdra

I can now summarize the *kṣatriya*'s stewardship relations within the human community, particularly their relation to the other *varṇa*s (social groups). Following one of his primary divine counterparts, Indra, the *kṣatriya* is a warrior who protects the entire community. As Indra killed the demon Vṛtra with his powerful *vajra* (thunderbolt), so "the king of the *rājanya* [fights] with the chariot and the arrow" (ŚB 1.2.4.2). While Indra was characterized by might and virility in the earlier layers of Vedic works, now the *kṣatriya* (here, *rājanya*) is also characterized in this manner: " 'So the *rājanya* accomplished this'—'he fought and won this battle'. [These are the things] The *rājanya* sings. Truly, war is the *rājanya*'s strength" (ŚB 13.1.5.6; TB 3.9.14.1–2). As Smith (1994, 37) explains, the ideal *kṣatriya* is described as "an archer, a hero, and a great charioteer,"[23] who alone among the other social groups wields physical and military power and is associated with war and violence. A *kṣatriya* is the type of human being that "kills and desires to defeat his enemies" (ŚB 2.1.2.17). This warrior possesses strong arms and legs, which are fitted with armor, and services the community by performing virile (*vīrya*) deeds (Smith 1994, 37; TB 3.8.23.3).[24] Therefore, the *kṣatriya* is clearly associated with battle, military functions, and impetuous strength or virility. Brahmanical thought understands the *kṣatriya* as a warrior who protects the community by defeating external enemies with his inherent might and force of arms.

As my analysis has already suggested, the *kṣatriya*'s relationship to the brahmin social group and sacrificial rituals is one of protection and complementarity. First, being a steward entails protecting brahmins and allowing them to complete the *kṣatriya*'s identity as a human being. For example, the *kṣatriya* needs the brahmin's help to become stronger than his enemies:

> Then a brahmin gives the sacrificial sword [*sphya*] to him [the king]—either the *adhvaryu* priest or his domestic priest [*purohita*]—stating: "You are the thunderbolt of Indra; with this you become subject to me." This sacrificial sword is indeed the thunderbolt, and by means of this thunderbolt the brahmin makes the king weaker than himself; the king who is weaker than the brahmin truly becomes stronger than his enemies. In this way, he [the brahmin] makes the king stronger than his enemies. (ŚB 5.4.4.15)

This passage, taken from a king's consecration rite, explains how the brahmin has a wooden sword (*sphya*) he uses simultaneously to subordinate the *kṣatriya*'s power to his own and make the *kṣatriya* stronger than his enemies. Here one might ask why the *kṣatriya* must be encompassed or subordinated in such a way by the brahmin, and the answer lies in the cosmological, metaphysical, and ontological beliefs examined thus far. The cosmological hierarchy, beginning with the cosmogony expressed in Ṛg-Veda 10.90, places the brahmin above the *kṣatriya* as Puruṣa's mouth is situated above his arms.[25] Metaphysically, the brahmin's essential power (*brahman*) supersedes the *kṣatriya*'s essential power (*kṣatra*). Given the brahmin's impulse for precise taxonomies, this hierarchical metaphysics parallels the hierarchical cosmology and ontology. Finally, on the ontological level, the brahmin oversees a number of rituals—for example, the *upanayana, rājasūya*, and *vājapeya*—that assign the *kṣatriya* his identity and tell him that he exists in a specific way because he is a particular type of person. These rituals express the belief that the *kṣatriya* necessarily follows the brahmin because he needs the brahmin to conduct the proper ritual in the proper way. Hence, the brahmanical conceptual framework situates the *kṣatriya* below the brahmin. This does not mean, however, that the two groups do not require each other's unique identity and abilities to sustain their own.

While the *kṣatriya* is linked to and situated beneath the brahmin in the broader cosmic-taxonomic schema, this is not a situation of utter dominance but rather one of complementarity and co-dependency. The *kṣatriya* ruler needs a brahmin *purohita* (personal priest) because the *purohita* is considered to be a "half part of the *kṣatriya*" (AB 7.26). On this point I disagree with Smith, who argues that the brahmins "As the ontologically complete form of the human being, present themselves in the Veda as ultimately self-sufficient, and the Kshatriyas as dependent on priests . . . Brahmins can live without rulers, but rulers cannot adequately carry out their tasks without the aid of Brahmins" (1994, 42). Smith's first claim is clearly not accurate because, like the other twice-born groups, brahmins require the proper initiation rituals to become complete human beings. Therefore, they are not inherently complete. I also believe his second claim is misleading. For example, the Taittirīya Saṃhitā states: "By means of the *brahman* he quickens the *kṣatra*, and by the *kṣatra* the *brahman*. Therefore a brahmin [priest] who has a *kṣatriya* [patron] is superior to another brahmin; and therefore a *kṣatriya* [king] who has a brahmin [*purohita*] is superior to another *kṣatriya*" (TS 5.1.10.3, trans. Smith). This passage explains that one brahmin is superior to another if he has a king as a patron, suggesting that while brahmins might be more self-sufficient than *kṣatriya*s in some respects, they are not completely self-sufficient if having a *kṣatriya* patron makes one brahmin superior to another. While a brahmin *could* live without a ruler, it appears that he is better off if he does not do so. Ultimately, if sacrificial rituals require patrons, then a brahmin who makes a living by conducting and overseeing such sacrificial rituals cannot be utterly self-sufficient.

In addition, the Aitareya Brāhmaṇa (3.11) explains that the *kṣatra* (ruling power) and *brahman* (priestly power) should be united, and that "the *kṣatra* is established upon the *brahman*, and the *brahman* upon the *kṣatra*" (AB 8.2; see also ŚB 1.2.3.2, 2.5.4.8, 5.4.4.5). The Śatapatha Brāhmaṇa likewise explains that the *purohita* perfects or completes "both his *brahman* and [the] *kṣatra* powers" when he assumes office:

> Concerning the *purohita*, he places it upon him, stating, "My *brahman* [priestly power] is completed, the *vīrya* [strength, vigor] and *bala* [power, might] are completed. The victorious *kṣatra* of he whose *purohita* I am, is completed." He [the *purohita*] thus completes both his *brahman* and *kṣatra*. (ŚB 6.6.3.14)

Therefore, both the king's and the priest's powers are perfected when the priest takes his office, and thus full realization of both *kṣatra* and *brahman* powers depends upon them completing one another. In addition, the king is the protector (*gopṛ*) of the Brahmins (AB 8.17) because the latter must be safeguarded from injury as the origin, or womb, of the other social groups: "*Kṣatriya*s were born from brahmins. Fire arose from the waters, *kṣatriya*s from brahmins, and iron from stone" (TB 2.8.8.9, trans. Smith). A divine prototype for this *purohita*/ruler relationship also exists in the form of the relationship between the divine priest Mitra and *kṣatriya*-king Varuṇa (ŚB 4.1.4.1). In sum, although the *kṣatriya* needs the brahmin, the reverse is also true.

Lest I overemphasize the idealized brahmanical understanding of harmonious co-dependence, I must draw attention to textual evidence indicating tensions between brahmins and *kṣatriya*s, which displays important political tensions in these works. To begin, while their powers and social functions are understood as co-dependent, only the brahmin can subdue the sacrifice. Brahmins' overt claims that their power is superior to the *kṣatriya*'s expose anxieties about the *kṣatriya*'s physical supremacy. Brahmins thus claim for themselves the power to tame the all-important sacrifice and its corresponding cosmic, metaphysical, and ontological powers:

> The sacrifice fled from them; the *brahman* and *kṣatra* pursued it—the *brahman* with its weapons and the *kṣatra* with its weapons. The *brahman*'s weapons are those of the sacrifice, and the *kṣatra*'s weapons are the horse-drawn chariot, armor, and the bow and arrow. This ruling power [*kṣatra*] returned, not having obtained it [the sacrifice], for it turns away from its [the *kṣatra*'s] weapons, trembling. Then the *brahman* pursued it and obtained it. . . . Therefore, even now the sacrifice is situated in the *brahman* and in the brahmins. (AB 7.19)

Here we see brahmins defending their power as supreme—a power that would undoubtedly be fragile since the *kṣatriya* commands horse-drawn chariots, armor, and the bow and arrow. Smith has identified a number of passages where tensions and power imbalances arise between the two groups: *kṣatriya*s possessing particular powers over the brahmins, including the power to subordinate them (TS 2.5.10.1; JB 1.285); the brahmin being depicted as someone who merely follows the *kṣatriya* ruler around (ŚB 1.2.3.2); the *kṣatriya* being characterized as harsh (*krūra*) (TB 6.2.5.2) while the brahmin is a friend (*mitra*) (KS 7.11); warnings to *kṣatriya*s about the consequences of appropriating a brahmin's property (AV 12.5.5–11, 5.18.1–4); warnings to the *kṣatriya* about cheating his brahmin priest and consequently losing his kingdom and life (AB 8.23); brahmins and *kṣatriya*s being portrayed as outright competitors, and even enemies (ŚB 13.1.5.2–3).

Unfortunately, we do not have access to the *kṣatriya*'s voice in the same way we have access to rulers' voices in Homer and Hesiod. We thus do not know the extent to which *kṣatriya*s are critical of brahmins and each other. Nonetheless, a variety of textual evidence indicates that brahmins made their best effort to restrain the apparent might of this warrior-king group. We have already seen how brahmanical thought faced a dilemma regarding ruling questions. While they believed divine *rājan*s ruled in the divine sphere and were guardians of the human sphere, there was no apparent body of beliefs elaborating upon the nature of the proper human ruler and what human kingly rule might mean. This dilemma instigates an elaboration of beliefs in human kingly rule that draws upon, but also diverges from, earlier beliefs about divine kingly rule. This elaboration eventually results in an understanding of human kingly rule as stewardship. New beliefs about sacrificial ritual and the brahmin's power over them further explain how brahmins contextualize and restrain the *kṣatriya*'s new role as steward by placing him under the brahmin in a broader cosmic framework. In this regard, *kṣatriya*s rule *beneath* the poetic-priestly group, which displays some parallels to Hesiod's privileging of poets' abilities, yet diverges from Homer's emphasis on the near-absolute strength of the ruler. As the evidence indicates, the underlying tensions associated with subordinating the *kṣatriya* were definitely acknowledged.

J. C. Heesterman supplies further insight into the potential conflicts, social and otherwise, that underlay the apparently serene and controlled sacrificial ritual. Heesterman's work is incisive on this topic because it provides a counter-argument (albeit highly speculative) to aspects of my argument and textual focus, as he attempts to reconstruct the pre-classical world of agonistic sacrifice that he claims preceded the emergence of the classical Vedic ritual. On his account, sacrifice was intensely agonistic and reflected a contentious, broken world, while the classical Vedic ritual was employed "to control the passion and fury of the sacrificial contest and to keep such [destructive, agonistic] forces within bounds" (Heesterman 1993, 2–3). Therefore, while sacrifice is agonistic by nature and emphasizes the highest "stakes of the game," ritual is controlling by nature and represents the "rules of the game" (3). He then contends that a "monistic doctrine of ritual," based upon the conceptual formulation and employment of equivalence (discussed earlier), ends up "invalidating the agonistic dualism of the sacrificial contest" (3). Heesterman thus concludes his thesis where I began in the liturgical layer, explaining that by the time of the Brāhmaṇas the ritual system was quite coherent and sophisticated (4). This thesis poses an interesting theoretical reconstruction of an intensely dualistic and competitive process that may have originally existed in the pre-classical sacrifice. His analysis also draws the political theorist's attention to potential conflicts and tensions in ancient India and how, even if one does not find his conclusions fully convincing, a fair amount of contestation likely existed between brahmins as priests and *kṣatriya*s as rulers. In the end, Heesterman's thesis suggests that although brahmanical thought formulates a tightly woven hierarchical framework full of *bandhu*s and feverish attempts to sustain this framework through ritual, underlying questions about rule and the brahmin's relationship to *kṣatriya*s consistently arise. This reminds us that ruling beliefs, even when the preexisting web of beliefs is quite determinative and hierarchical, always involve questions and that these questions can perhaps never be settled once and for all by any thinker or group. Heesterman's analysis thus shows how brahmanical thought likely did not stamp out all social conflict, despite its best efforts to do so in conceiving an all-encompassing cosmology.

It is also important to clarify the dimensions of ruling-over and ruling-for in the *kṣatriya*'s relationship to the other two social groups, the *vaiśya* and *śūdra*. If we recall Ṛg-Veda 10.90, we observed that the *vaiśya*s are made from Puruṣa's legs and consequently constitute the commercial sector and productive capacities of Vedic society. As Smith (1994, 31) explains, the *vaiśya*'s essential quality is *viś* (metaphysical power), and this group is associated with characteristics and powers such as: *puṣṭi* (material prosperity), *ūrj* (nourishment), *paśu*s (livestock or animals), *anna* (food), and *annādya* (nourishment). The *śūdra*s, being fashioned from Puruṣa's feet, constitute the service sector of Vedic society and were thus understood to serve the three higher *varṇa*s.[26] The *kṣatriya* rules over these two groups and encompasses them just as the brahmin does the *kṣatriya*. While the higher group encompasses the lower group, the latter are always understood as distinct foundations for the higher groups. Interconnected dependence thus runs along the vertical human register as well as across the horizontal human–nonhuman register.

Using Puruṣa's body as the cosmic paradigm, while the higher faculties may be seen as residing in progressively higher parts of the body, these higher parts are nonetheless dependent upon the functions performed by the lower parts. The head (brahmin) and arms (*kṣatriya*) have no foundation or stability without the legs (*vaiśya*) and feet (*śūdra*). This is why one finds passages explaining how the *kṣatriya* and his ability to rule properly are dependent upon the basic material well-being provided by his *vaiśya* subjects (ŚB 12.7.3.8–12/15). As Smith has remarked, the *kṣatriya* can thus be understood as the "offspring" (*garbha*) of the *viś* (ŚB 5.3.4.11), and just as "Indra is the *kṣatra* and the Maruts are the *viś*, the *kṣatriya* becomes powerful by means of the *viś*" (1994, 43; ŚB 4.3.3.6/9). Revisiting the cosmogony found in the Puruṣa-Sūkta again proves useful, as the "cosmos body" exhibits the earliest beliefs about how human beings are differentiated and the role each type of person plays in the larger social body. The *kṣatriya*'s relationship to the *vaiśya* and *śūdra* is best understood in accordance with this image since the ruler serves as the arms to defend the functional capacities of the legs (production) and feet (service). The king or ruler is not only a steward insofar as he protects the brahmins' ability to conduct sacrificial rituals, but also because he protects the two lower *varṇas'* abilities to sustain and service the community. Therefore, while the *kṣatriya* rules over these two groups, his rule is also grounded in ruling-for their well-being and capacity to undertake their distinctive social responsibilities.

To summarize, cosmogonic and cosmological beliefs provide an essential starting point for examining the meaning of kingly rule and the *kṣatriya*'s relationship to the other *varṇas*. Because the cosmos was created with complex, interconnected vertical and horizontal registers, the metaphysics and ontology operating in these works—given the brahmanical tendency to classify everything in this liturgical layer—coheres with this meta-level framework. The liturgical Saṃhitās and Brāhmaṇas elaborate upon this cosmological framework in greater detail than both the Ṛg-Veda Saṃhitā and Atharva-Veda Saṃhitā. Going against the general grain of existing political theory scholarship, a systematic examination of this framework has allowed me to clarify and sharpen the meaning of *kṣatriya*-rule in the middle Vedic period. This analysis also exposes how *kṣatriya*-rule as stewardship includes two distinct components. First, it entails a warrior component that requires rulers to defeat external enemies, influenced by earlier beliefs about Indra's *rājan*-ship. Second, it includes a judicial and administrative component that requires keeping order within Vedic society, influenced by earlier beliefs about Varuṇa's (or Mitra-Varuṇa's) rulership.

While this understanding of human kingship stretches back to the earliest layer of the Ṛg-Veda and displays a fair amount of synchronic consistency in brahmanical political thought, various elaborations found in the liturgical layer display important diachronic developments. The mechanism for change and elaboration in the later liturgical layer, I have argued, points back to the dilemma presented in the Puruṣa-Sūkta: granting a new belief in human kingly rule, what is the role and meaning of such rule, since human kings are not *devas* and hence cannot be understood as ruling in the same way? Focusing on the *rājanya* and *kṣatriya*, I examined how liturgical works begin to pose answers to this question by elaborating upon a cosmic framework that possesses distinct yet interconnected categories. For example, the category of *varṇa* includes a belief in particular metaphysical essences and expresses a relational harmony between the social groups. The concept of *bandhu*, apparent though less significant as a cosmological concept in the Ṛg-Veda, becomes a way of envisioning connections between these distinct categories (cosmological, metaphysical, and ontological) in the later liturgical works. Accordingly, each *varṇa* has its intrinsic connections to various nonhuman entities. In this later layer, brahmins also elaborate how sacrificial rituals enliven those connections, according to which counterparts (*pratimās*) are used in ritual to access and manipulate their cosmic prototypes (*pramās*). Beliefs about *bandhus* and sacrificial rituals allow brahmins to conceive connections between the human ruler and numerous nonhuman beings, and to depict the ruler—as the "arms" of Vedic society—as the steward for protecting and maintaining such connections. Clarifying the general taxonomic schema depicted in the Saṃhitās and Brāhmaṇas to organize my analysis of kingly rule in the liturgical layer allows me to achieve two things. First, I am able to locate the *kṣatriya*'s positioning within this framework and explicate the meaning of kingly rule in a more textually responsive manner. Second, I am able to identify the most important continuities and developments in early and middle Vedic political thought, including the change in the meaning of kingly rule from *deva*-guardianship to *kṣatriya*-stewardship.

Atharva-Veda Saṃhitā: Assemblies and Stewardship

As I explained in the previous chapter, the Atharva-Veda's significance for brahmanical political thought lies primarily in the increasing mention of two particular terms: *sabhā* and *samiti*. Some have argued that these two terms indicate popular assemblies, public deliberation, and election of kings. I maintain these claims cannot be adequately substantiated by textual evidence and analysis alone, and that the phrase "popular assembly" is quite misleading. I do not deny that these assemblies may possess various "public" characteristics,[27] but I argue that scholars cannot, based on textual evidence alone, accurately deduce what type of ruling functions (if any) they may have undertaken. Therefore, in this section I argue against common interpretations of *sabhā* and *samiti* in the existing scholarship and conclude by discussing the role of stewardship in the Atharva-Veda.

Interpretations of *sabhās* and *samitis* as popular assemblies are sometimes based on a problematic interpretation of the term *vidatha*, variously meaning divine worship, household, or sacrificial establishment. Both Jayaswal (1967, 20) and R. S. Sharma (1968, 78–95) locate the earliest form of the *sabhā* and *samiti* in this frequently used Ṛg-Vedic term. Because the *vidatha* is often glossed as a public gathering of some sort, some scholars prematurely deduce that it must have possessed popular, deliberative characteristics. However, Bloomfield (1898, 13) has explained how the *vidatha* did not entail a public cult or religious sacrifice with a public assemblage, but was rather a private affair. Bloomfield argues that while the term *sabhā* can generally be associated with communal matters, *vidhatha* is associated with domestic affairs (13).[28]

Linking Bloomfield's interpretation to Macdonell's ([1917] 2010, 248) translation of *vidatha* as "divine worship" helps clarify the important sacrificial connotations of the term. As Bloomfield explains, insofar as the sacrifice is a private event, the *vidatha* understood as a domestic sphere helps makes sense of its connection to *yajña*. That is, the fact that the term *vidatha* is mostly used in the locative case while *yajña* appears in other cases indicates that the sacrifice took place in the *vidatha* and should thus be interpreted as a sacrificial establishment that would have been the home, given the context (Bloomfield 1898, 16). Finally, Bloomfield contends that *vidatha*'s meaning sometimes "advances from the meaning '(sacrificial) establishment, until it reaches the meaning 'sacrifice' ... [which] may preferably be assumed for some of the passages relating to Agni" (17).[29] *Vidatha*'s translation as "sacrifice" is then close to Macdonell's translation as "divine worship." Given these meanings and qualifications, attempts to establish textual and historical connections between *vidatha* and *sabhā* or *samiti* should be tempered. The primary interpretive mistake in the political theory literature has been the move to find historical continuities, especially regarding would-be political institutions, by suggesting that India possessed one of the earliest forms of deliberative—if not democratic—assembly.[30] These motivations must be set aside for more careful analyses of the text, which may end up showing how Vedic political thought has unique conceptual contributions to make that do not necessarily cohere with a contemporary desire to find democratic rule in India's ancient past.

Scholars have attempted to draw a number of problematic connections between the *vidatha, sabhā*, and *samiti*, arguing that they represent popular assemblies in the Atharva-Veda.[31] Perhaps the most notable proponent of this interpretation is Jayaswal, who argues: "The *Samiti* and *Sabhā* were not the only popular institutions of the Vedic times ... the '*Vidatha*' ... seems to have been the parent folk-assembly from which the *Sabhā, Samiti* differentiated ... associated with civil, military and religious functions" (1967, 20). One problem with this claim is that Jayaswal makes a firm interpretive distinction between civil, military, and religious functions when it is not clear that such distinction are made (or make sense) in the text itself.[32] Regarding the *samiti*, Jayaswal claims that it "was the national assembly of the whole people or *Viṣah* ... [who were] electing and re-electing the *Rājan* or 'King.' The whole people were supposed to be present in the assembly" (1967, 12; see AV 3.4.2, 6.87.1, 6.88.3). In my translation, the passages he cites as evidence are as follows: "Let the people accept you for kingship, as well as these five divine regions (of the sky)" (AV 3.4.2); "Let all the people desire you: do not let the kingdom fall away from you" (AV 6.87.1); "Let all the cardinal directions be unanimous, pursuing the same goal: here let the *samiti* accommodate itself to you, the steadfast one" (AV 6.88.3). If one pays close attention to Jayaswal's language and the context of these passages, the problems with his position become clear.

First, he draws upon the language of "national assembly" and "election" to interpret the *samiti*. He chooses to interpret the Sanskrit word *jana* as "nation," failing to adequately qualify his usage of this term, which gives the word an overly modern interpretive slant. A translation carrying less modern and contemporary connotations, such as "tribe"—which Jayaswal also mentions as a possible translation in a footnote—is more appropriate within this context. Second, the language and interpretation of human "election" is completely unsubstantiated in the passage he cites. In the first (3.4.2) and third (6.88.3) passages, if the people are interpreted as electing the king, then the divine regions of the sky and cardinal directions must also be considered electors. But what would this mean? It is difficult to imagine how the cardinal directions can behave like people with a voice and a vote.[33] The context is deeply cosmological, and Jayaswal's attempt to bracket this context in order to privilege some sort of human-based election of a king is quite problematic. Rather confusingly, he also cites a particular Atharva-Veda passage (5.19.15) as evidence for the people *viś* electing the *rājan*. This passage states, "The rain, belonging to Mitra and Varuṇa, does not fall upon the person who oppresses the brahmin; the *samiti* is not fit for him, and he subjects no friend to his will."[34] No terminology for "election" in any modern sense exists in these Atharva-Vedic passages. Jayaswal chooses this terminology because he believes the people possess the sovereign ruling power, which he contends is channeled by and exhibited in the *samiti*. (1967, 12–16; see also Altekar 1958, 107, 143). However, there is no clear textual evidence supporting this claim. Altekar also helpfully points out how the term *rājakṛt* (literally, "king-maker") can misleadingly be interpreted as an elector (81–82). These *rājakṛt*s were not king-makers in any electoral sense (perhaps based upon some belief in free choice) but rather conductors of the necessary coronation rituals that were required for a king to become a king. *Rājakṛt*s may help make a king or ruler by serving as part of the ceremony, but they do not elect him.

The language of elections, in the sense that Jayaswal employs it, would require that he find some evidence of the following: the belief in some sort of equality between members of the community (or at least a subset thereof), and a belief that this equality makes the freedom of choice possible within clearly expressed decision-making and ruling practices. However, no clear claims about equality, freedom of choice, or institutionalized ruling procedures can be found in the passages of the Atharva-Veda he cites.[35] Jayaswal believes he can identify such beliefs in statements such as "*tvām viśo vṛṇatām rājyāya*" (AV 3.4.2). This phrase should be translated, "let the people accept you for rulership." Jayaswal's problematic interpretation is based on a translation of the verb root *vṛ*, which he prefers to read as "choose" and subsequently interprets as "elect." However, in this context I agree with Macdonell and Keith that it makes more sense to translate this verb as "accept" (1967, 2:211). To translate this verb as "choose" in this context, and on this basis interpret free choice and an elective procedure, is both overly speculative and anachronistic. Jayaswal must be able to provide sufficient textual evidence that expresses a belief in something like "free elections" to make this interpretation work. I do not believe he provides this evidence, nor do I think it can be provided based on the available material. As I have explained throughout this and the previous chapter, the Atharva-Veda and other Vedic works are not primarily intended to be political treatises and should not be stripped of their cosmological, metaphysical, and ontological framework when advancing claims about rule. Foisting a secular-political reading upon these passages, Jayaswal offers misleading, de-contextualized interpretations that neglect broader webs of belief as well as central categories, concepts, and terminology.[36]

While other scholars are more restrained in their claims about popular forms of participation, representation, and sovereignty in these Vedic assemblies, their interpretations also present problems. R. S. Sharma (1968, 78–92), one of the most notable defenders of deliberative assemblies in the Vedic period, argues that the *vidatha* was the earliest "folk assembly," which included women, deliberative and distributive functions, military functions, and religious functions. His position in these debates is useful for pointing out the types of interpretive problems that consistently arise in the existing scholarship. For example, Sharma interprets a deliberative function from the phrase, "He who is the giver of life, the giver of strength, whose command all beings and the gods obey; he who rules over this two-footed and four-footed world. . . ." (AV 13.3.24). Extrapolating from this passage, he claims "we learn that people aspired for talking big there" (82).

Three comments are in order here. First, this Atharva-Veda passage is taken directly from a creation hymn in the Ṛg-Veda (10.121.2–3). Therefore, this passage's proper context is a cosmogonic narrative and has nothing to do with a *vidatha*, assemblies, or deliberation. Second, the passage does not actually contain the term *vidatha*. Finally, one could ask how "aspiring to talk big" has any relevance for ruling concerns and the meaning of kingly rule. Does "aspiring to talk big" necessarily indicate deliberation about who should rule, why, or what it means to rule? Kings are assumed to be the proper rulers in Vedic works, and references to the *sabhā* in the Atharva-Veda do not contradict the account I have provided. One problem with interpreting the *sabhā* as relevant for ruling concerns is that statements made about it neither prove nor disprove anything distinctly relevant about kingly rule. That is, this assembly assumes an institutionalized king, and none of its functions overlap with or contradict the king's apparent *varṇa* duties. In one example, R. S. Sharma cites a passage (AV 7.12.1–3) as evidence that the king considered the advice of the *sabhā* as "supremely important" on "hotly discussed proposals" (1968, 101). These verses, however, actually emphasize agreement and harmony in the *sabhā* and not the type of disagreement or agonism that one observes in the ancient Greek assemblies. Sharma translates one of these verses as stating, "We know thy name, oh, *sabhā*, thy name is interchange of talk; let all the company who join the *sabhā* agree with me" (AV 7.12.2). As Sharma himself suggests, this verse indicates that agreement, not disagreement, is valued (101). In addition, Sharma admits that the subject of deliberations in the *sabhā* "can be known only vaguely" (82).[37] This admission is one reason that treating *vidatha*s and *sabhā*s as ruling bodies is of limited use for understanding the meaning of rule. In sum, not enough supplementary evidence exists to warrant an interpretation of *vidatha* as a term of crucial importance for our understanding of ruling in the Atharva-Veda.

R. S. Sharma also argues that the *sabhā* carried out judicial functions, which included "influential men" being accountable to their peers (1968, 99–100; AV 7.12.3). He tellingly explains how "it *seems* that the richest men had to submit to the decisions of their peers" (99, emphasis mine), thus indicating the speculation involved when one attempts to make historical claims about whether or not "judicial functions" were carried out in this body. In addition, Sharma speculates that the *samiti* was an assemblage of individuals who "transacted tribal business" and busied itself with "religious ceremonies and prayers" (102–103). His tentative discussion of the *samiti* indicates the uncertainty surrounding the *samiti*'s functions as well, most of which must simply be guessed at. In the end, scholars cannot know precisely who—that is, which *varṇa*s and those perhaps outside the *varṇa* system—constituted these assemblies or how they operated, because the texts do not clarify such things. Due to the lack of clear textual evidence showing that either of these assemblies shared ruling responsibilities with the king, I believe scholars have generally overstated these assemblies' importance for understanding the meaning of kingly rule in the Atharva-Veda.

Drawing upon these critiques, I want to summarize the most important qualifications and conclusions regarding these assemblies' potential ruling functions. First, these gatherings or assemblies cannot be interpreted as secular or purely political in nature. Insufficient evidence exists from which to argue that individuals in these assemblies made ruling decisions themselves or assisted the king/ruler in making particular ruling decisions. Second, this qualification should lead scholars to temper the empirical-historical claims they tend to make about these assemblies. Just as these texts are not overt political treatises, they are also not composed to present accurate historical accounts. Finally, Jayaswal's analysis displays a common yet problematic practice in this literature: employing modern and Western political terminology to interpret ancient brahmanical ideas about rule. Language of "state(s)," "elections," "national assemblies," "popular representation," and "accountability" simply do not make sense within this ancient brahmanical belief system. Modern practices, beliefs, and assumptions associated with this type of political terminology are not compatible with those expressed in these Vedic works. As I have argued, scholars can begin to appreciate this fact by using the categories, concepts, and terminology found within the works themselves. A more attentive textual approach can help prevent the misleading and anachronistic interpretations that frequently arise.

These critiques aside, stewardship can also be located in the Atharva-Veda. To explain how this is so, a brief overview of the development from guardianship to stewardship is in order. In the earliest layer, Ṛg-Veda 1, the most prominent *rājan*s are deities, and *rājan*-ship means guardianship. Then, in Ṛg-Veda 2, we observe the first cosmogonic speculations explicitly positing a specific group of human beings (*rājanya*s) as proper rulers and inheritors of responsibilities associated with *rāj-*, or rule. However, in this layer the most prominent *rājan*s remain deities, and an understanding of *rājan*-ship as guardianship continues largely unchanged. In the following liturgical layer, we see a transition from guardianship to stewardship as the meaning of kingly rule. While various beliefs about divine *rājan*-ship as guardianship influence beliefs about human *rājan*s and *kṣatriya*s, we can also identify an important change. Due to the interconnected nature of the cosmology posited in the liturgical layer, which includes the system of *bandhu*s and the manipulation of prototypes and counterparts in sacrificial rituals, human kings begin to adopt some heavy ruling responsibilities. The responsibility for rule thus passes to *kṣatriyas* (or *rājanyas*), and because of the increased importance of sacrificial rituals and increasing level of cosmic classification, rule by *kṣatriyas* becomes a tertiary activity that is best understood as stewardship: a means (protection and promotion) to a means (sacrificial ritual as well as productive and service sectors of society) to an end (maintenance and construction of the cosmos and reality). Hence, *kṣatriyas* act as stewards and not as direct guardians in the manner of previous divine *rājans*.

Now, the Atharva-Veda provides a clear picture of the outcome of these developments. In the Atharva-Veda kingly rule is fully assumed as the only and proper form of rule, exemplifying the trajectory toward the increasingly hierarchical conceptions explicated in the liturgical layer. To begin, N. C. Bandyopadhyaya (1980, 53) has argued that Atharvan coronation hymns display how kingly rule was becoming increasingly consolidated and hierarchical. In this layer of Vedic works hierarchical kingly rule was increasingly understood as a legitimate ruling structure, as the dimension of ruling-over by *kṣatriyas* receives increasing emphasis. Coronation hymns in the Atharva-Veda express a more thoroughgoing set of ruling claims and privileges for human kings than those found in earlier Vedic works such as the Ṛg-Veda, which also exhibits an increasing sense of responsibility for ruling-in and ruling-for a broader array of beings. For example, Bandyopadhyaya highlights a passage in the fourth book where the human king is described as the "sole lord and friend of Indra who feeds on the people" (AV 4.22). This passage expresses the belief that the people must support the king, or that a king rightfully subsists (or "feeds") on the people in a hierarchical manner. One also observes the association with Indra, who, as we saw in previous layers, is one of the most important divine *rājans* and whose attributes, as well as responsibilities, are increasingly associated with human rulers.

Textual evidence indicates beliefs in an established, hierarchical form of kingly rule, as no systematic counter-evidence arises in the Atharva-Veda challenging the idea that kings are the rightful, proper rulers. The most pertinent passages for explicating kingly rule in this layer concern the king's consecration and ruling attributes,[38] as well as the general desire for harmony between the king and people.[39] A good example of this desire for harmony and agreement with brahmanical speech in social gatherings can be found in book seven:

> Let the *sabhā* and *samiti*, the two daughters of Prajāpati, who together know, assist me. Whomever I shall meet, may he be helpful to me.

> (Let my) words be esteemed in the gatherings, O Fathers. We know your name, O *Sabhā*: indeed, you name is "socializing" [*nariṣṭā*]. And let all those who are sitting in the *sabhā* employ similar speech to my own. I have won splendor and knowledge from those seated together here. O Indra, make me prosperous among this entire group seated together. Whether your mind [i.e., those sitting in the *sabhā*] has gone elsewhere, or whether it is caught up here or there, we bring this, your mind, back: let your mind come to rest on me. (AV 7.12.1–4)

In this passage the *sabhā* and *samiti* are invoked as the two daughters of Prajāpati, and the speaker makes no claims about ruling matters (presumably, however, the king is present in the gathering). Rather, the brahmin speaker emphasizes something more general, indicative of most passages involving gatherings or assemblies: agreement and the wish that those assembled delight in what the brahmin says. From this passage one can glean two additional points.

First, the assembly does not appear to be a place where argument and individualistic reason-giving are highly valued. It is not agonistic in the Greek sense. Second, it displays how, whether scholars like it or not, interpreters of Vedic texts only have access to the brahmanical viewpoint. The Atharva-Veda communicates a brahmanical understanding of the world and thus posits a king as the rightful ruler of human beings. One must also remember that brahmins perceive themselves as crucial for maintaining both social and cosmic order, and because of this privilege, many Atharva-Veda charms are aimed at preserving and protecting the interests of brahmins.[40] This belief in the need to protect brahmins brings us back to stewardship because the king is responsible for protecting brahmins' abilities to conduct sacrificial rituals. Through knowledge of the Vedas and sacrificial rituals maintained by brahmins a king is able to properly protect his kingdom: "Through study of the Veda (*brahmacārya*: studenthood, disciplehood) and fervent practice, the king (*rājan*) protects the kingdom" (AV 11.5.17).

Stewardship, therefore, can be located in this layer of Vedic texts as well. However, lest one overstretches claims about the meaning of kingly rule in the Atharva-Veda, scholars must remember that this text does not focus solely on explaining how and why kings rule. This Vedic work is a collection of charms and imprecations, and kingly rule is only one of the many topics it addresses. While the trajectory of ruling ideas points distinctly toward hierarchical kingship in earlier layers of Vedic works, it appears—given the available evidence—fully instantiated in the Atharva-Veda.

Conclusion: Cosmology and the Issue of Human–Nonhuman Scale

Like early Greek conceptions, early Indian rule was steeped in cosmology. But this brahmanical tradition also shows us how political cosmologies can differ quite drastically from one another, along with their accompanying ontologies and metaphysics. Early and middle Vedic political thought provides a fascinating comparative vantage point because it conceives such a tight-knit, interconnected relationship between human beings and a wide variety of nonhuman beings and phenomena. The catalyst for this move is a concerted effort to taxonomize and connect nearly every meaningful entity in the surrounding environment. This is astonishing from predominant Western standpoints since rule—especially in the wake of Greek conceptions—is generally understood as a human-centric affair. As we saw in Hesiod, rule and an attendant understanding of justice are entirely humanistic, or, as we see later in Aristotle, the ability to rule places humans in a staunchly hierarchical and domineering relationship to the nonhuman. In contrast, brahmanical political thought flattens and "de-humanizes" rule to a significant degree by embedding its theory of rule within a grand cosmological, metaphysical, and ontological narrative predicated on interconnectedness.

In this regard, I argue that early Indian political thought comes up with a very different idea of how to rule within human society that could help mitigate potential abuses by rulers.[41] This is an issue that Hesiod is also concerned about, and he attempts to address it by formulating a novel political position centered on the concept of justice. In contrast, a key feature of the brahmanical understanding of rule could be stated: whether human beings like it or not, ruling necessarily involves broader considerations for the nonhuman world. While Hesiod's move fundamentally excludes the nonhuman, brahmanical thought suggests that narrowing one's cosmological perspective to the human estate may increase the abusive behavior stemming from agonistic individualism. That is, cutting human beings off from a broader and interconnected community of beings tends to highlight and dramatize what are often minor differences in human affairs and attitudes, and exclude broader concerns about cosmic well-being. Such differences are important because they help us recognize and cultivate the plurality and diverse richness of human identity and ideas, which is an incredibly valuable aspect of distinction and the early Greek tradition. But when such differences are magnified under the microscope of a relatively human-centric view of politics, we can easily lose our sense of scale, and this narrower view can facilitate violent attempts to suppress such differences in order to create a greater degree of unanimity and identity. As we saw in the Greek case, a more human-centric and strongly individualistic view can lead to hyper-competitive attempts at distinguishing oneself from others at the cost of the interconnected well-being of a broader community of both human and nonhuman beings. Cosmology is important for politics for this very reason: it can help human beings retain and cultivate a healthy sense of scale.

The resulting logic of brahmanical human–nonhuman leveling, while not necessarily elaborated by brahmins themselves, could be unpacked in the following way. In drawing attention away from our particular human differences, human–nonhuman leveling pushes us to set our sights on a broader landscape, which then helps contextualize our differences and minimize the potential resentment and violence that can stem from them. Brahmanical taxonomies achieve this effect by extending ruling concerns outward and linking them to other beings and phenomena, stretching human attention in more radical horizontal directions. Rule, or our ability to rule, then becomes a *bandhu* that quite literally binds (Sanskrit verb root, *bandh*, "to bind, tie, fasten") us to the nonhuman world and prevents us from conceiving of politics in a human-centric fashion. Ruling can thus be understood, in the most primordial sense, as binding us to the world in such a way that we cannot extricate ourselves as much as the Greeks had hoped. Consequently, because our ability to rule binds us to the earth and cosmos it is not an ability that allows us to "swing free" as some unique, disconnected political species. Here we should remember that Hesiod left his hawk and nightingale—along with the entire animal kingdom—to its own devices and *nomos*: mere force and "rule" of the strongest. In contrast, brahmins conceive an entire system that prevents humans from understanding rule in such a detached fashion.

In viewing multifarious relations between human and nonhuman beings, brahmanical political thought provides reasons for considering, with greater intensity, how humans may better integrate themselves within a broader, interconnected community of beings and phenomena. Another way brahmins pull this off is to develop cosmological recognition of human uncertainty and existential fragility in a larger cosmos. Indeed, a strong sense of existential and cosmological fragility is also apparent in Homer and Hesiod, especially the former. In response to such uncertainty, brahmins alternatively suggest that sacrifices (personal, social), and perhaps a more reflective system of sacrificial political rituals, might enhance our recognition of interconnectedness and ability for integration. More narrow human disagreements are then more likely to recede into the background, at least on occasion. Of course, this is a move that would have made little sense to Hesiod and Homer, given the tradition they inherited. As I argued in the Introduction, this is a central reason why a historical-comparative approach to political theory is useful: it helps us identify gaps and implausible possibilities in one tradition by using a comparative vantage point that draws out a meaning, idea, or implication that another tradition may not be able to find when consulting its own conceptual resources. As I will also suggest in the next chapter, however, these brahmanical ideas have their own limitations. This Indian tradition approaches the connectedness of rule in problematic ways by conceiving a static, anti-egalitarian typology of human rule (ruling-over) and a naïvely harmonious conception of human–nonhuman connectedness (ruling-in and ruling-for). Using brahmins' own terminology, if Homeric and Hesiodic political thought fall prey to cosmo-ontological and metaphysical *pṛthak* (excessive differentiation), then the brahmanical tradition saddles too closely to *samatva* (excessive similarity) in formulating its taxonomic schemas. The next chapter will elaborate on these countercultural critiques by placing the two traditions in direct contact with one another.

5 COMPARATIVE CONSIDERATIONS ON THE MEANING OF RULE

Having examined each tradition's understanding of rule independently, this chapter undertakes a direct comparison of Greek distinction and Indian stewardship. Here I consider how each tradition helps expose unique aspects and unforeseen background assumptions of the other by looking at (sometimes seemingly) shared categories and concepts, thus increasing cross-cultural intelligibility while also providing a cross-cutting perspective on the meaning of rule. I begin at the "micro" level of the individual to consider how the openness and complexity of a ruling self plays a central role in each tradition's beliefs about rule. I then broaden my perspective to examine how each tradition views micro-level rule within a particular cosmological context, primarily through categories understood to bridge the human and nonhuman such as religion, sacrifice, and ritual. In these first two sections, I argue that ancient Greek and Indian political thought have much less in common than it may appear, at both the individual and cosmological levels. In the final section of the chapter, I clarify the major similarities and differences in each tradition's understanding of justice. Their diverging conceptions of justice, I argue, highlight how brahmanical political thought supplies unique non-Western insights into the relationship between ruling and the nonhuman world. In turn, this comparative analysis will provide many of the conceptual strands that I will pull together in the Conclusion to outline an alternative vision of ruling as world-building, which is inspired by insights drawn from both traditions.

As I explained in the Introduction, comparative analysis of two distinct traditions is not without its dangers and limitations, and one reason I have taken care to examine each tradition on its own terms in prior chapters is to help prevent any cultural reductionism.

Since each tradition is deeply concerned with the meaning of rule, I believe neither tradition has been domesticated in broaching this comparative analysis. Nevertheless, emphasizing differences instead of similarities raises two related sets of concerns. First, does this general approach suggest an Orientalist-type belief in fundamental cultural differences between the "East" and "West"? I would hope my careful attention to each tradition's web of beliefs would relieve the critic's concern here. But, more important, mapping out the differences helps us locate and clarify important conceptual developments that have been overlooked in each tradition, which then exposes each tradition's unique attributes and strengthens a platform for cross-cultural intelligibility. Finally, understanding significant differences deepens our ability to undertake more balanced forms of cross-cultural critique, concept formation, and theory building. While there is nothing inherently wrong with examining similarities, the differences will prove especially intriguing for historical and theoretical purposes.

This attention to difference, however, might raise broader methodological concerns. By emphasizing difference, have I brought the analysis around to a more Greek (and thus Western) mode of political thinking? Namely, does the historical-comparative approach inherently privilege a Greek political ethos insofar as it gestures toward an agonistic plurality of beliefs and the idea that one tradition's understanding is superior to, and should thus "defeat" the other? On a methodological level, does this approach domesticate the brahmanical mode of political thinking, or conversely, fetishize this Indian tradition by placing it on some sort of normative pillar? To begin, I will not argue that one tradition's understanding is superior to the other's *tout court*. As I see it, each tradition has its respective strengths and weaknesses when conceiving the meaning of rule. Concerning the point about agonism, I concede that a historical-comparative approach stands somewhat closer to a Greek ethos. But comparative political theory, if it is going to live up to its "comparative" moniker, must not run from difference and its comparative implications (e.g., see March 2009). Evaluating a comparative engagement need not be a zero-sum game but rather an opportunity to think through multiple webs of belief in an effort to recognize a multiplicity of cultural blind spots and to cultivate greater intercultural understanding.

The Openness and Complexity of a Ruling Self

We can begin this comparison by considering how each tradition understands the self, or the nature of individuality. As I argued in chapters 1 and 2, the Greeks expressed a belief in self-possessed individuality, which could be characterized as an inwardly sealed yet complex conception in comparison to the brahmanical self, which is conceived in an outwardly porous yet inwardly uniform fashion. I argued that Hesiod's critique of Homer centered on the idea that distinction should not be fundamentally concerned with enhancing individualistic glory, honor, and reputation in pursuit of hierarchical standing. Rather, Hesiod believes that rulers should aim at being just and fair decision-makers within the human community. Nevertheless, both Homer and Hesiod saw individuality as characterized by agonistic competition, which facilitates some of the abusive behavior resulting from efforts at distinction. I suggested that agonistic contests in Homer and bribe-eating scenarios in Hesiod abound partly because *basileis* such as Agamemnon and Achilles assume a firm individualist ontology. This ontological boundary then supports the belief in agonistic individualism, a political concept that possesses two distinct components: a strong sense of individuality and self-worth that are not grounded in a holistic metaphysics or cosmology, and a practical extension of this self-understanding to challenge existing ruling practices and communal decision-making processes. I also explained how Hesiod develops the Greek concept of justice and emphasizes ruling-in and ruling-for the interests of a broader human community, which he believes could help to address some of the negative repercussions that follow from an individualistic and agonistic ontology.

In contrast to the Greek case, brahmanical beliefs about how human and nonhuman beings exist entail a belief in interconnectedness, whereby the grounds of an individual's being are not as demarcated as they are in Homer or Hesiod. By the time of the liturgical Saṃhitās and Brāhmaṇas, the *kṣatriya*'s ontological connection to a wide variety of nonhuman beings and phenomena are increasingly seen as constituting *who* he is, just as much as his association with the other *varṇa*s or types of human beings (brahmin, *vaiśya*, and *śūdra*). In short, his own human-ness (i.e., the *kṣatriya* aspect of his identity) is only one among multiple categorical delineations that determine who he is, making the brahmanical conception of individuality much less (if at all) human-centric. In addition, with the emergent conception of *brahman* as the underlying reality of all things, one's individuality is even less significant in light of a broader cosmology and metaphysics. This results in a conception of stewardship that is much less individualistic than the understanding of distinction.

A direct comparison of these conceptions indicates the following. For Homer and Hesiod, what is most essential about oneself as an individual is something one does not and cannot owe to anyone or anything else, nor can it ultimately be reduced to some sort of social construction. On the other hand, in brahmanical thought, whatever is most essential about oneself is more diffuse. Brahmins claim that one's identity is inherited in the form of a natural identity, and thus not self-enacted from the bottom up. While Zeus and the Fates play a significant role in determining the life course of Greek rulers, their identity as this or that sort of person is gradually realized and enacted over the course of their lives. Even if their fates are predetermined, they do not know exactly what these fates entail and thus behave in all sorts of impulsive and unpredictable ways. Within Greek thought there is significant allowance for enacting one's identity throughout one's life, which means one must accept greater responsibility for who one has become and what they have enacted. Put another way, I owe myself *to* myself to an extent that is not sensible within the brahmanical conceptual framework.

The *kṣatriya* is a much more situated being than the *basileus* because the *kṣatriya*'s identity and roles are bound by a multitude of relations that extend outside the human plane and cut across nonhuman registers. Since the brahmanical ruler is not isolated in his individual being in the manner of a Homeric or Hesiodic ruler, the *kṣatriya*'s responsibility for his being is distributed among a broad network that includes his ancestors, brahmin priests, productive and service groups (*vaiśya* and *śūdra*), and a large host of nonhuman entities. However, the Greek tradition understands the individual ruler as almost entirely responsible for his own being. If I am a Greek ruler, even though my identity and life course may have something to do with Zeus's jars and the Fates' threads, this "who" is ultimately mine and thus my responsibility because, as we see with both Agamemnon's and Achilles's ghosts in Hades (*Od.*, book 11), through my *psuchē*, my identity is grounded in self-possessed individuality. As these examples from the *Odyssey* show, the Greek conception of individuality is so strong that not even death can demolish it or relieve me of it. A basic or core self-possessed individuality as such cannot be fundamentally altered. While this Greek understanding has a somewhat closed-off, fatalistic feel, it is also more open-ended insofar as it leaves more room for self-enactment and change, particularly while one is still living. While there is an element of openness in the brahmanical conception insofar as the self can be constructed properly or improperly, ultimately the brahmanically ascribed identity shuts down any deeper notion of self-enactment.

I would like to revisit the *kṣatriya* to further clarify this point. A Vedic ruler's identity as a particular individual was determined by a broad swath of cosmological, metaphysical, and ontological claims. To start, this ruler was born—as his cosmic brethren were so born—as a particular type of individual. The underlying essence of *kṣatra* goes back to the cosmogonic account of Ṛg-Veda 10.90, where the *kṣatriya* originally emerged as the arms of the cosmic person, Puruṣa. Here we can recall that Hesiod's cosmogony and theogony do not posit rulers, let alone just ones, as built into the cosmic fabric *from the very start*. Not only does the metaphysics of *kṣatra* reinforce the *kṣatriya*'s identity as the member of a particular *varṇa* (social group), but I also showed how this identity was inscribed through a lifelong series of rituals and conceptually reinforced through taxonomic schemas that situated the ruler in a very particular way within a wide community of beings and phenomena. If one were to press on the concept of *ātman* as a potential comparison with *thumos*, I also explained how this *ātman* found its ultimate grounding in *brahman*, which serves as the unmanifest substrate for all manifest reality. The *ātman* may delineate a ruler from others to some extent, but as soon as one begins to fill out the ruler's identity and motivations, one must consider concepts such as *varṇa, bandhu* (connection, resemblance), and *upanayana* (constructive initiation ritual).

Still, one might ask whether the term "*basileus*" implies similar roles to the term "*kṣatriya*," as both seem to delineate a particular type of person. However, *basileus* does not have the cosmological or metaphysical associations with, and connections to, an extensive network of nonhuman entities. The extensive connectedness in the Vedic case facilitates a greater degree of situatedness, which greatly reinforces the power of social roles. The closest Greek example is surely the connection that Homer and Hesiod make between Zeus and human rulers, expressed in the idea that *basileis* come from and are modeled after Zeus. But, as I argued in chapters 1 and 2, this connection is wrought with tension and presumes a strongly demarcated self on both the divine level (in the figure of Zeus) and human level (in the various human *basileis*). Vedic social roles run much deeper and ultimately trump one's individuality understood as utterly distinct and unique in contrast to others' individuality. Put another way, the importance of a *kṣatriya*'s individual personhood is predicated more on his *kṣatriya*-ness, and not who he happens to be in a more individually demarcated sense. After all, it is the category of *varṇa* that establishes one as a *kṣatriya* and thus connects one to a broader world of beings and phenomena. This is a crucial part of what makes the world meaningful in brahmanical thought, as the concept of *varṇa* draws attention away from a distinguished individuality towards connective resemblances with the nonhuman world. In moving from particularity to a greater degree of generality or commonality, the designation of *kṣatriya* de-emphasizes particular differences and stresses abilities that are shared and connective in nature, not merely "one's own."

In contrast, one's demarcated individuality establishes a meaningful world for the Greeks more through the concept of personalized death, accompanied by the potential to be remembered and thus achieve personal, eternal fame through lyric poetry. That is, individual life draws much of its meaning from the idea that my death cannot be shared in any deep sense, which makes the possibility of being remembered a more distinctive and illustrious enterprise. Alternatively, in the Vedic case my indebtedness and ability to play a *role* deepens my commitments to a broader community of beings and phenomena. Vedic individuality thus draws more of its meaning—comparatively speaking—from the idea that the weight of my existence and death is fundamentally intertwined with the existence and well-being of other human and nonhuman beings, and can thus be shared in a certain sense. While a Vedic ruler acts as a *yajamāna* (sacrificial patron) to create a world for himself in the next life and experiences this life somewhat individualistically, the ruler is never cut off from nonhuman beings and phenomena in the process. Responsibility for one's individual being is rather porous and distributed while self-boundaries remain fluid and constructed. Therefore, while an individual's death is important in Vedic thought, it entails much more in terms of connectedness to the nonhuman world and relies upon the poet's ability to cognize a deeper a-human reality, whereas Greek distinction through eternal fame pivots around connectedness to other *human* beings per the poet's ability to pass memories along to subsequent generations. When linked to the idea of rule, this Vedic understanding of individuality helps make possible the idea of ruling as stewardship, accompanied by thicker notions of ruling-in and ruling-for the well-being of a broader, human–nonhuman community.

These comparative differences can be further clarified if we revisit a passage that I discussed in chapter 4 concerning the kinship relation between a ruler and the Nyagrodha tree. The early Vedic notion of interconnectedness, as it pertains to rule, is clearly expressed in the Aitareya Brāhmaṇa (AB 7.31). *Kṣatra*, as a particular type of power or ability, anchors the *kṣatriya* as a ruler within a broader community and draws upon ideas of correspondence between beings such as humans and trees. The *kṣatriya*'s likeness and correspondence to a Nyagrodha tree is intriguing for numerous reasons. First, this resemblance displays a nonhuman-centric conception of rule by suggesting that particular nonhuman entities possess corresponding abilities and serve similar purposes in other types of communities, such as forest communities occupied by trees, plants, and soils. While my primary focus is the human ability to rule, one could further explore the implications of extending abilities such as rule to nonhuman beings, which might further allow us to conceive how purportedly human-centric abilities could extend to various nonhuman entities. Such a move may help enhance human empathy toward a variety of nonhuman beings.

Second, the Nyagrodha association highlights how rule entails a stretching outward into rulers' sources of nourishment, becoming firmly rooted in these sources. This passage shows how rulers are rooted in the *viś* (people, productive part of society) and depend upon them for nourishment in the same way Nyagrodha trees are rooted in and depend upon the soil. Homer and Hesiod do not express such sympathetic intra- and inter-species beliefs about rule. In addition, the ruling ability does not stand alone and stabilizes those things to which it is connected, as do the roots of a tree in soil. While the tree's (or individual ruler's) base or trunk first appears individualized, unitary, and cleanly demarcated on the surface, upon further investigation it displays tremendous plurality insofar as it splays downward into so many small, intricate roots beneath the surface. What appears to be a rather unitary entity is thus fractured and polycentric at its roots, and vulnerable due to this polycentric dependency. This brahmanical belief and image not only help us visualize a pluralized, interconnected environment but also highlight an internal complexity associated with the self that orthodox brahmanism tends to downplay and, in this respect, resembles the internally plural self exhibited in Homer.

Most important, this example of rule displays a twofold sense of interconnectedness: first, the well-being of rulers and those affected by rule are intricately intertwined, thus leading to an incredibly thick notion of ruling-in and ruling-for others; second, rulers are deeply connected to a type of tree that displays a similar ability and vital relationship to a variety of different entities. This second point would radically destabilize any Hesiodic-exceptionalist connection between human beings and rule because the human capacity for rule and making just decisions for the well-being of a community parallels the Nyagrodha's capacity to do the same. Brahmanical political thought thus posits a way in which rulers share such capacities and engage in ruling-with members of different species. From a comparative perspective, this idea would help unsettle the human-centric belief that Hesiod develops in response to the Greek understanding of rule as distinction. Not only does this relation shrink the conceptual and ontological distance between the human and nonhuman by expanding the cosmological scale for rule—especially the dimensions of ruling-in, ruling-for, and ruling-with the nonhuman world—but it also provides a reason, and thus greater sensibility, for rulers to care for various nonhuman entities, since they are understood to share particular capacities and remain equally vulnerable in terms of their interdependent well-being. Now we can address the sorts of beliefs and practices connecting these complex, interdependent human selves to the nonhuman world.

Bridging the Human and Nonhuman: Religion, Ritual, and Sacrifice

Previous chapters displayed how each tradition's respective understanding of rule is linked to religious, ritual, and sacrificial beliefs. When considering these topics, one might contend that these traditions have quite a bit in common. While such beliefs and their corresponding practices are important in both traditions, I will argue that they do not play as central a role in Homeric and Hesiodic political thought as they do in brahmanical thought. Consequently, their differences offer unique insights on various ways of conceiving the connectedness of rule and open new conceptual avenues for imagining different ways of approaching the topic.

To start, in both Homer and Hesiod one observes the general importance of religious beliefs, ritual, and sacrifice.[1] Jan Bremmer points out that "in ancient Greece, too, religion was totally embedded in society—no sphere of life lacked a religious aspect" (1994, 2). In fact, Richard Seaford (1994, 21) has argued that ritual and reciprocity both exhibit and play a central role in early state/*polis*-formation in Homeric works, further contending that being a *basileus* entailed managing tensions in reciprocity relations. Because he is not primarily interested in defending a specific interpretation of Homeric rule, however, Seaford does not explain any necessary connection between ritual and the meaning of rule per se. Walter Burkert also explains how "there is no priestly caste" in Greek religion and how the *basileus* plays an important institutional role in religious ceremonies later in Athens (1985, 95),[2] further discussing how ritual is of central importance in Greek religion. Regarding changes in Greek religion and sacrificial ritual during the Early Iron Age, Burkert (1985, 53) argues that the collapse of pre-archaic palace culture helped lead the Greek understanding of sacrifice and ritual away from more hierarchically ordered social divisions and ruling relations toward a more leveled and humanistic conception.[3] At the conceptual level, his analysis thus supports my argument for the leveling of ruling ideas discussed in chapters 1 and 2, including an emerging notion of equality in Greek society. Burkert also highlights some general similarities and differences between Greek and

"Eastern" sacrificial ritual, with one important similarity being the fire sacrifice that connects human beings and gods. The most important difference is a comparative lack of hierarchy in the Greek case, which, Burkert explains, exhibits the Greek belief in a basic equality among mortal human beings in contrast to the immortal gods.

Further arguing for a connection between sacrifice and politics in the late archaic and early Classical periods, Marcel Detienne claims that sacrificial rights correspond to political rights and that "political power cannot be exercised without sacrificial practice. Any military or political undertaking . . . must begin with a sacrifice followed by a meal. All citizens holding civil posts regularly offer sacrifices" (1989, 3). Below I will argue that an essential connection between sacrifice and politics does not appear prevalent in Homeric and Hesiodic beliefs about rule, but to make a brief note here, I would suggest that connections between sacrifice and rule appear to be more formal in nature and show greater similarity, for example, to congressional proceedings that open with a prayer led by the Senate and House chaplains in the US Congress. Like Detienne (1989, 8–9), Vernant (1989, 21, 24) emphasizes the distance and tenuous, agonistic relationship between gods and human beings that can be observed in sacrificial ritual. Examining Hesiod's "foundation myth of sacrifice," Vernant explains that "the distance separating mortals from Immortals is begun in sacrifice and perpetuated in sacrifice" (1989, 27). For example, he investigates the rivalry and competition between Prometheus and Zeus, explaining how "sacrificial practice is present as the first result and most direct expression of the distance created between gods and men on the day that Prometheus started his road to rebellion" (27). Here Vernant claims that Prometheus's "allocation of the meat reflects his desire to subvert the distributive order embodied by Zeus the sovereign" (27). Hesiod's portrayal of such competitiveness and Prometheus's attempt to subvert Zeus's rule displays the agonistic individualism I examined in both Zeus and Prometheus. Comparatively speaking, however, *basileis* are not understood as cosmologically, metaphysically, or ontologically responsible for either conducting sacrificial ritual themselves or protecting those (such as priests) who conduct them. At most, *basileis* are socially and economically responsible.

These comments are not meant to imply that sacrifice and sacrificial ritual are unimportant in Homer and Hesiod. In Homer, one observes both individuals and larger groups of people sacrificing to particular gods for a variety of reasons. For example, in the *Iliad*, the Achaeans, led by Odysseus, return Chryseis to her father and make sacrifices to Apollo to appease him in an attempt to ward off the plague he sent to the Achaean camp. Nevertheless, these sacrifices do not appear to have a *direct* connection to ruling practices or beliefs.[4] In the Ṛg-Veda Saṃhitā, individuals also sacrifice to gods such as Indra for things such as strong sons, cows, and rain. In both traditions, sacrifice exhibits and serves as a connection between gods and humans, yet the following differences can be identified between the two traditions.

As I explained in chapters 3 and 4, in the liturgical Saṃhitās and Brāhmaṇas, sacrifice (*yajña*) and sacrificial ritual become increasingly elaborate and of central importance in brahmanical thought. In contrast, for Homer and Hesiod, sacrifice (e.g., *thusia; hiereion*, the sacrificial animal or offering) and sacrificial ritual do not have the same cosmic implications they have for brahmins. Rather, brahmanical political thought posits a pervasive connection between rule, sacrificial ritual, the cosmic structure, the nature of reality, and identity construction. Sacrifice was a central method for creating the cosmos, and in the liturgical Saṃhitās and Brāhmaṇas, sacrificial ritual becomes crucial for maintaining the existing cosmic framework. In contrast, for Homer and Hesiod, sacrificing to a god may be a good idea when one wants something done on one's behalf, but it is not cosmologically or ontologically necessary as it is in brahmanical thought.[5] As I have already suggested, the gods enjoy and frequently expect sacrifices, but they do not *need* them in the same way that Vedic gods do. Of course, lyric poetry is necessary for remembering the Greek gods' divine glory, but sacrificial rituals themselves play a less significant onto-cosmological role. Comparatively speaking, the Greeks conceive human beings and the gods as less interdependent. One must certainly acknowledge that *basileis* such as Agamemnon are generally the proprietors of sacrifices, especially major ones, since *basileis* are the wealthiest individuals and possess the greatest amount of sacrificial fodder such as bulls and goats. In this, Vedic and Greek rulers have much in common. Homer and Hesiod do not, however, clearly or systematically express the following brahmanical idea: ruling itself entails an inherent, ongoing responsibility to maintain a system of sacrificial ritual that sustains the well-being of an interconnected community of beings and entities.

Cosmological Justice and the Connectedness of Rule

Both Greek and Indian cosmologies include ideas about the proper ordering of human–nonhuman relations and how rulers should treat others, which leads to my final comparative assessment of justice. The concept of justice is rather difficult to compare between the two traditions partly because it is difficult to find a Sanskrit equivalent to the Greek term *dikē*. As I explained in chapter 2, the meaning of and connotations surrounding the term *dikē* develop over the course of Homeric and Hesiodic works. Its initial meaning in Homer is simply a judgment in a particular case. At most, *dikē* is the right judgment made by judges (*istōres*), elders (*gerontes*), or kings (*basileis*) based upon considerations of honor and rank between two or more individuals that disagree on a particular matter. Perhaps the closest Sanskrit/brahmanical equivalent to this conception would be *vrata*, which originally means a divine ordinance, command, or rule and was associated with divine *rājans* such as Varuṇa.

On the Greek side, it is in the *Odyssey* where *dikē* first appears as meaning something like "right custom" or "justice" and carries more abstract, moral connotations. Hesiod's conception of *dikē* exhibits an important development insofar as he emphasizes the moral and communal dimensions of *dikē* and their connection to proper *basileus*-rule. I argued that Hesiod understands *dikē* to provide a moral criterion lying outside human kingly rule as such, by which *basileis*' or rulers' judgments could be judged as better or worse. This Hesiodic notion is based upon the belief that a *basileus* must help preserve the broader *human* community's well-being and make fair judgments. The brahmanical concept that comes closest to Hesiod's *dikē* is perhaps *ṛta*, which denotes both truth and the underlying cosmic order.[6] At first glance, it may appear that a *basileus*'s relationship to *dikē* is quite similar to a *rājanya*'s (or *kṣatriya*'s) relationship to *ṛta*. As rulers, both a *basileus* and *rājanya*/*kṣatriya* are responsible for protecting an underlying moral principle that serves as a standard for proper rule.

However, while *ṛta* possesses a moral dimension akin to Hesiod's *dikē*, the two terms and their relationship to ruling beliefs differ in significant ways. As a cosmic ordering and moral principle, *ṛta* is more fundamental than *dikē* in a cosmological and metaphysical sense because it contains an inter-species, integrative component. While *dikē* provides a moral and political criterion by which to judge proper kingly rule it does not, in contrast to *ṛta*, denote some underlying regulatory principle holding a complex and interconnected cosmos together. For example, I explained how *dikē* does not apply to animals and pertains only to beings with self-possessed individuality—namely, gods and humans. As the daughter of Zeus and Themis, Dikē ultimately stands beneath Zeus in the cosmic hierarchy and is not part of the original cosmic framework.[7] While Hesiod's Dikē is a goddess, brahmins' *ṛta* is not a god or goddess of any kind. *Ṛta* does not stand below some superior regulatory force or principle. Rather, *ṛta* itself is the superior, abstract, and preexisting principle that even the most powerful gods, such as Indra, must follow and sustain.

As we saw in the Ṛg-Veda Saṃhitā, *rājans* such as Indra and Varuṇa are responsible for ruling in accordance with *ṛta*. A central difference here is that Dikē is inferior to the overarching cosmic ruler, Zeus, while rulers such as Indra and Varuṇa are alternatively inferior to *ṛta*. Only in Hesiod do we see *dikē* begin to develop as a transcendent normative principle standing above any particular self-possessed individual, whether human or divine. Not only do these contrasts expose the deeper metaphysical aspects of *ṛta* but also the comparatively high level of individualism in early Greek political thought. The Greek understanding of rule as distinction is reflected in the fact that even Hesiod's Zeus-*basileus* (let alone Homer's model), as a self-possessed individual, stands above the predominant depiction of Dikē/Justice as both her progenitor and protector. In contrast, extending back to Indra and Varuṇa in the earliest layer of Vedic texts, brahmanical political thought expresses a belief in rulers as guardians and eventually stewards of a ruling responsibility that entails maintaining a preexisting, ordered cosmic structure in accordance with a superior principle. This cross-cultural contrast thus shows how a potential brahmanical conception of justice transcends human–nonhuman boundaries and invokes a thoroughgoing political cosmology. These points then bring us to the idea of interconnectedness, particularly the brahmanical notion of *bandhus*.

The brahmanical concept of interconnectedness expressed by the term *bandhu* (connection, resemblance) displays the belief that all entities in the cosmos, either directly or indirectly, are connected and relate to one another in some fundamental way. The taxonomic schema in the liturgical Saṃhitās and Brāhmaṇas maps out the vertical and horizontal connections between all beings and phenomena in the cosmos. However, *bandhus* are also found in the earliest layer of Vedic texts, the Ṛg-Veda Saṃhitā, where they generally refer to kinship relations between two or more things. For example, the term *rājanya* exhibits the brahmanical belief that the human ruler is related to divine *rājans*, who are the earliest and predominant *rājans* in brahmanical thought. According to brahmanical cosmology, not only are human rulers such as *rājanyas* and *kṣatriyas* connected to divine rulers such as Indra, they are also connected to the mid-regions (cosmological world), wind (natural element), midday (part of day), and breath (body function). *Bandhus* make all these connections possible. The brahmins' desire to discover and map out such connections between a wide variety of entities and phenomena is clearly absent in Homer and Hesiod. One of the best examples of this, as I also suggested, can be observed in the Aitareya Brāhmaṇa, where brahmins posit a metaphysical connection and kinship between the Nyagrodha tree and the human *rājanya*.

There does not appear to be any clear Greek equivalent to the Sanskrit term *bandhu* and such pervasive interconnectedness. The belief in self-possessed individuality undermines a potentially similar belief in a fundamental interconnectedness and kinship between gods and human beings, especially between these self-possessed beings and nonhuman beings such as plants and animals. While some kinship relations between gods and human beings do exist—for example, Thetis is the mother of Achilles—such relations are the result of isolated and relatively rare instances of gods and humans coupling with one another. Most human beings portrayed in Homer have no direct genealogical connection with a particular god. This further reflects the belief in self-possessed individuality because these Greek kinships are highly individuated genealogical relations. Such kinships or resemblances are not shared by means of possessing similar metaphysical capacities (e.g., *kṣatra*), nor constructed through mechanisms such as sacrificial ritual (e.g., *rājasūya*). As we see in both the *Iliad* and *Odyssey*, gods appear to be connected to human beings only insofar as they intermittently interact with them and influence various human affairs. Moreover, gods generally participate in human affairs only when it suits some private interest or impulse, and human beings generally perform sacrifices and seek the gods' help for the same reason. Because self-possessed individuality applies to both gods and humans, thus establishing basic ontological boundaries between them, the belief in this demarcated selfhood is another reason why individuals are not understood as cosmologically, metaphysically, or ontologically connected to beings such as plants and animals. Furthermore, this condition is a reason why the latter sorts of nonhuman beings, comparatively speaking, are mere fodder for human desires and interests in Greek political thought. Not only does an ontological rift exist between self-possessed gods and humans, but an even larger one exists between these types of beings and those who do not share self-possessed individuality.

Here a critic might ask about the cosmic resemblances between divine and human rulers. More particularly, in both the Greek and Vedic case, don't divine and human rulers have something very important in common—namely fame, glory, and a shining reputation that distinguishes them from others on their own cosmic plane? Isn't distinction an important ruling characteristic for Indra and Mitra/Varuṇa? I do not want to suggest that concepts for glory (e.g., *dyumna*) and reputation are completely absent from Vedic works, and two Sanskrit terms stand out in comparative analysis.[8] The first term is *śravas*, meaning "fame, glory, renown," which derives from the verb root *śru*, "to hear." Therefore, *śravas* is that which is heard about someone and relates the exploits of a notable god or person. In this respect, *śravas* resembles the Greek adjective *klutos* (famous, renowned, glorious), which derives from the verb *kluein*, meaning "to hear." The second comparable Sanskrit term is *kīrti*, which similarly means "fame, renown, or glory." This term derives from one of the many meanings of the verb root *kṛ*, meaning "commemorate, or turn one's thoughts or heart toward." Hence, it would be overly rash to suggest that terms and concepts that communicate some idea of fame, glory, and a notable reputation never apply to kings or rulers (see also Scharfe 1989, 175–86). For example, Indra is indeed "famous" and has earned a glorious reputation for defeating cosmic foes such as Vṛtra. Indra's greatness (*mahan*) among the gods is well established. I also do not want to suggest that militaristic and agonistic attributes of Vedic rule, especially as they apply to gods such as Indra, do not contribute to ideas of distinction and glory.[9]

Such similarities aside, important differences arise between each tradition's understanding of kingly rule on the topic of fame, glory, and reputation. In Homer, Zeus, who provides the closest parallel to Indra, actively seeks glory and honor to distinguish himself from the other gods and solidify his status as the supreme king, or ruler. This is partly due to the fact that glory, honor, and reputation are never guaranteed and must constantly be earned in agonistic physical and verbal contests. Indra, on the other hand, does not appear to pursue such things for their own sake (at least not to the extent that Zeus does), nor as a highest good. It is more in Indra's nature to do such things—it is who he inherently is. An expression of this idea can be found in the earliest layer of the Ṛg-Veda Saṃhitā, in a verse dedicated to Indra: "The god who, as soon as he was born, was preeminent in his possession of wisdom and surpassed the (other) gods in power" (ṚV 2.12.1). In this verse the particle *eva* follows and emphasizes the past passive participle *jāta*, thus laying stress on the idea that Indra was who he was as soon as he was born. In contrast, neither Homer nor Hesiod claims that Zeus was as preeminently and fully developed at the moment of his birth. Zeus had to grow and mature, protected by his mother, in order to eventually earn his glory and reputation through a series of acts, and must continue to do so. Although Indra may sometimes behave like Zeus, he does not appear to do so for the same reasons. This belief that a ruler possesses specific, inherent characteristics allowing him to rule properly can be located in each layer of the Vedic Saṃhitās and Brāhmaṇas. In the liturgical Saṃhitās and Brāhmaṇas, *kṣatra* becomes the metaphysical power that makes proper rule possible and connects divine and human rulers. Such characteristics are part of the cosmic framework and constitute *kṣatriyas*' and *rājanyas*' identities as a specific type of human being. In addition, Indra's glorious deeds accord not only with his inherent characteristics but also with the preexisting cosmic order, *ṛta*. As I argued above, no god is superior to *ṛta*.

The closest similarity between Zeus's and Indra's distinction and renowned acts, perhaps due to some of the shared Indo-European mythological roots between ancient Greek and Indian cultures, can be observed in a Ṛg-Vedic account of Indra's birth (ṚV 4.18). This verse explains that Indra's mother hid him away from his father because she feared that the father would kill the strong son (Indra) who might overtake him. Indra ultimately fulfills his father's suspicion and kills his father. Indeed, this verse displays some cross-cultural similarity to Hesiod's agonistic account of Zeus's birth in the *Theogony*, albeit with a few important differences. First, in Hesiod's version, Zeus does not actually kill his father but defeats him in an all-out battle that includes a host of combatants composed of Titans and Olympians. In the Ṛg-Vedic account, Indra only has the help of Tvaṣṭṛ and Viṣṇu, and it is largely a personal, family matter. Second, there is no systematic corroborating evidence that Indra's act was for the purpose of distinction and achievement of honor, glory, reputation, or justice. Contra Hesiod's account of Zeus, we also do not see Indra distinguish himself by fairly distributing honors to a cohort of victorious combatants and community of fellow gods. Finally, the verse further reiterates that Indra was who he was immediately at birth and thus exhibits that he was born as a particular *type* of individual (ṚV 4.18.5/10). Not only do important differences arise between the two accounts but the similarities are more broad and generic in nature. In contrast to Zeus, Indra and Mitra/Varuṇa do not consistently seek to distinguish themselves from other *deva*s, nor do they appear fundamentally concerned with their reputations and achieving honor or glory to uphold that reputation. There is a wider purpose to Indra's militaristic actions and achievements: he is playing his cosmic role as the type of individual he is, which is aimed toward maintaining the broad, interconnected well-being of the cosmos. Both Indra and Mitra/Varuṇa have their proper functions and responsibilities in the larger cosmic structure, so their rule does not fundamentally revolve around the distinguished status of each one's demarcated selfhood.

While these differences may initially appear minor or cosmetic, they highlight important differences in ideas about the connectedness of rule. In the early Greek tradition, justice does not appear to be effective glue for maintaining communal well-being. In Homer, it does not play a central normative role in the meaning of rule and remains overshadowed by agonistic pursuits of honor, glory, and reputation. For Hesiod, justice begins to play an important role, but in so doing it parses a human-centered politics from a broader nonhuman community. Brahmanical political thought, however, increasingly conceives the well-being of human and nonhuman beings as intertwined, and rule plays a central role in its web of beliefs. If we consider how brahmins formulate this conception of stewardship, we begin to notice the centrality of sacrifice and ritual, especially insofar as such activities involve a broad array of nonhuman beings and phenomena. Any conception of justice that might support the connectedness of rule and remain attentive to brahmanical ideas must account for these categories and consider their potential value.

As a final point about justice, speech plays a significant role in each tradition. First, Hesiod explains that the evils confronting humans no longer have voices (*phōnai*), expressing the idea that there is a lack of direct, sensible communication between human and nonhuman beings, and thus a significant onto-cosmological demarcation that demands tremendous labor and foresight. Second, for Hesiod the ability to speak and discuss what is just seems to further justify his claim that human beings possess the capacity for justice as their ontological-moral law (*nomos*), while nonhuman beings do not. Bringing Homer into the picture, one might argue that it is the ability to speak coherently and authoritatively that allows self-possessed individuals to communicate with one another and differentiate themselves from other types of beings. As John Heath explains: "More than any other ancient culture, the Greeks knew both that we are like the beasts with whom we share space, and in some fundamental way different as well. They did not tend to confuse either the human or divine with animals" (2005, 24).

In contrast, brahmanical political thought holds speech as important but does not privilege it as differentiating the human from nonhuman to the same extent. For example, I explained how brahmanical thought places special significance on roles. This difference is incredibly important because it allows brahmins to conceive of things like rule and justice as connected and shared across nonhuman registers due to the relative capacities and roles that various sorts of beings have within their communities. What connects a *kṣatriya* and Nyagrodha tree is a kinship per a metaphysical essence (*kṣatra*) and ability, which provides grounds for a parallel role that this tree plays within the broader cosmic framework. Something like speech may be particular to human beings insofar as humans are placed into social groups or *varṇas*, but as I have also explained, this is only one aspect of their identity and not the defining category for their existence. Because of this overlap in roles, one can locate a greater degree of moral recognition and respect of various nonhuman entities and phenomena, since they all play an important part in facilitating each other's well-being. In the Vedic case, one might say there is greater emphasis on a more general capacity to relate, communicate, and understand something's responsibility to other beings with which it is connected, and not merely to parse and privilege something based on the question of whether or not it can speak. Human beings may communicate through speech and Nyagrodha trees through alternative means, but for brahmanical thought the most important point is that they do in fact communicate in some way and play their respective roles within the cosmos. In the case of rule, this would also mean that various nonhuman beings and not only *kṣatriya*s serve a stewardship function, helping to hold communities of shared interest(s) together and assist in their flourishing. The *kṣatriya* and Nyagrodha tree are not, therefore, entirely distinct in ontological terms when it comes to their ability to rule. Moreover, this shared ability entails a responsibility to act as stewards of those other beings who may not possess the capacity to rule in the same way (e.g., through speech) yet fulfill other essential roles in responding to the needs and interests of those to which they are connected. In these respects, speech is not the central aspect of what it means to rule.

Conclusion: Reconsidering Ancient Greek and Indian Conceptions of Rule

In this chapter, I undertake a direct comparison of Greek and Indian conceptions of rule to explore some of their most important similarities and differences. Using each as a critical, comparative vantage point, I structured my analysis by starting with the individual and working outward to broader, human–nonhuman relations. In the first section, I investigated how micro-level beliefs about the individual or self inform various beliefs concerning human and human–nonhuman relations. This comparative analysis shows how each tradition responds to the connectedness of rule in unique and informative ways. In the subsequent section, I examined how religion, sacrifice, and ritual reflect each tradition's beliefs about the connectedness of rule. Here I argued that sacrifice and ritual do not play as central a role in Greek political thought, yet in both traditions these categories help to explain how Homer, Hesiod, and brahmins conceive a bridge between human and nonhuman beings in both belief and practice. This comparative analysis opens new conceptual avenues for imagining different ways of approaching and thinking critically about the meaning of rule. Further warrant for emphasizing sacrifice can be located in reconsidering the meaning of justice in an interconnected world. Therefore, in the third section of the chapter I examined justice to clarify the comparatively human-centric conception of the Greeks and its emphasis on distinction, especially when viewed in light of concepts such as fame, glory, or reputation.

Building on these points, in the Conclusion I will articulate a new vision of rule that emerges from a comparative analysis of ruling as distinction versus stewardship. Shifting from historical and conceptual analysis to concept formation and theory building, I will revisit the normative justification for this project and critically rework what I take to be some of the most important strengths and weaknesses of the Greek and Indian conceptions of rule. This will allow me to outline a cross-culturally hybrid, normative understanding of rule that can inform contemporary thought and practice. As I have already begun to suggest, this new vision of rule will revolve around the category of cosmology and require viewing rule as a form of world-building that involves duties of stewardship for the interests of nonhuman nature.

CONCLUSION

PANOCRACY AS A NEW VISION OF RULE

Locating cross-cultural difference enhances our understanding of rule, especially in contexts that are distinctly cosmological in nature. In turn, this historical-comparative approach articulates a new conceptual groundwork for re-theorizing the concept of rule. Such a project is necessary because major underpinnings for moral hierarchies between human beings and nonhuman nature in the West extend back to the earliest traditions of Greek political thought. Western instrumentalist conceptions of rule have played a central role in justifying these hierarchies. Not only do problematic beliefs about human–nonhuman relations continue to impact how we interact politically with nonhuman nature in the contemporary world but the historical and cultural contingency of these beliefs can easily be forgotten, thus leading us to overlook reasons and potential means for altering damaging political ideas and practices that are neither inevitable nor "natural." Admittedly, challenging some of our basic assumptions about rule is no easy task because many modern economic and political institutions are built on the edifice of these assumptions. Therefore, I will argue that re-envisioning the nature and meaning of rule will require a gradual yet systematic reconstruction of long-held beliefs along each of the four dimensions that I have discussed in previous chapters.

The first step entails drawing greater attention to the complexity of rule by examining its cosmological dimensions in Greek and Indian thought. We often overlook this complexity in favor of assuming a more simplistic, human-centric understanding of rule that emphasizes ruling-over and ruling-with other human beings. Consequently, democratic and republican traditions have celebrated ruling-with, privileging the horizontal and participatory aspects of rule wherein humans are understood as ruling-for human interests. Focusing predominantly on these dimensions and their pertinence for human relations has led us to neglect one of the most important yet underappreciated elements of ruling: the *connectedness* of rule that fundamentally links human and nonhuman interests. Historical-comparative analysis has sought to expose these ideas to elucidate the narrowness of current conceptions and provide a more nuanced understanding of the complexity of rule.

Modern societies have largely ignored the questions of whether and to what extent (human–nonhuman) connectedness is intrinsic to the concept of rule, helping lead to the perilous environmental scenario in which we currently find ourselves. Therefore, we have something valuable to learn from premodern traditions: we must recover the idea that human–nonhuman connectedness and duties of stewardship are essential to rule. A central aim of this Conclusion is to explain how we can begin to think in more consequentially fruitful ways by expanding the cosmological landscape for conceiving the moral and political stakes of rule. As I mentioned in the Introduction, this aim also involves clarifying hinges for communication across differing theoretical and practical perspectives in environmental political theory. In sum, outlining an alternative vision of rule allows us to challenge our predominant instrumental conception and develop a more descriptively accurate, and normatively valuable, understanding of rule for contemporary politics.

Ruling-Over: Interdependence, Polycentrism, and the Rejection of Instrumentality

Ruling-over captures the vertical dimension of rule and evokes the question of who or what rules over someone or something else. In Greek political thought, we saw that rule entails ruling-over both human and nonhuman beings but also that various nonhuman beings or forces can rule over human beings. For example, Hesiod contends that human beings are organically tied to the nonhuman world through work and labor. These capacities trigger ruling relations that cannot be shirked and that humans ignore to their own detriment. Hesiod explains that Gaia (earth) and those aspects of the natural world that we find "below" us, if not cared for, can also end up ruling-over us. Both Ouranos (Sky) and Kronos fall from their ruling pedestals because they fail to account for the needs and interests of those beneath them. In both Hesiod and Homer we also see how ruling-over entails a degree of agonism and tension, and this is something we must learn to cope with in a way that does not lead to either violent attempts at mastery or indifference to the interests of beings who do not appear to share self-possessed individuality. Nevertheless, in some respects the Greeks possessed greater humility than the brahmin poets in the face of such cosmological fragility insofar as they did not believe the cosmos could be ordered, and largely controlled, through the precise application of particular sacrifices and rituals. In brahmanical thought, we also see the idea that we are deeply embedded beings within a community of complex, meaningful relations in which the welfare of all community members is fundamentally intertwined. Brahmins appreciate the human capacity to rule as part of an ongoing process of building this interconnected world, and categories of sacrifice and ritual provide important insights for re-theorizing the dimension of ruling-over.

Following particular brahmanical insights and rejecting self-possessed individuality, we can begin by adopting a more porous, "polycentric" conception of the self. A polycentric conception of the self is one in which the integral parts of a self are connected to multiple nodal points outside one's individual person. From Indian thought, I draw inspiration from the following concepts: *ṛta*, which evokes a more holistic conception of integral well-being and connectedness; *bandhu*, which elicits relations of care or connective resemblances, acted on physically and materially, whereby we view parts of ourselves in other people or nonhuman beings outside our immediate person. Such concepts elucidate the idea that one is always entwined in a diverse and open, multi-nodal network that situates and provides a partial basis for a self. This further means human beings never find themselves in a static or atomistic location.

In a parallel manner, Stefan Dolgert has recently drawn on Platonic ideas regarding metempsychosis, along with literature in post-humanism (Latour) and radical democracy (Rancière), to argue for a "trans-ing of the self" that views nonhuman beings such as animals "potentially as other parts of *our own* beings . . . thus extending our self into other bodies"; importantly, such trans-ing can be conceived both spatially and temporally (2015, 85, emphasis in original). On the topic of space, Peter Cannavò has also argued that our identities are partly constituted by "place," wherein the "boundaries between place and identity are not absolute" (2007, 33). Here I would add that the concept of rule helps to clarify the explicit political dynamics of such porous identities and well-being. On my polycentric account, one's identity is intertwined with the geographic location in which one lives, the region's climate, loved ones, workplace and co-workers, pets, garden, electronic devices, and so on. For example, if my pet or a loved one becomes sick, the care and time I extend to them exposes aspects of my polycentric identity. This not only applies to specific living beings but also to things such as geography and climate: living in one geographic region versus another alters my daily, lived experience and what I care about, as does living in a rural versus urban environment.

While geographic context partially determines the nodal points of one's polycentric identity, it is important to note how these nodal points are not only proximal but include distant points, both human and nonhuman, that provide many of goods and services that we depend on in our daily lives. Connecting these ideas to recent debates about political obligations or duties to others, ruling-over and polycentric identity lend support to Andrew Dobson's defense of ecological citizenship. For example, Dobson (2003, 106–27) highlights the asymmetric impact that citizens in affluent nations have on others through their ecological footprints, which generate non-territorial political obligations extending across national boundaries. Here we can see how identities and actions are not "self-contained" and always (or merely) private because they tend to impact those providing grounds for one's well-being. On consequentialist reasoning, this creates political responsibilities of stewardship based on the rule of connectedness.[1] As Dobson explains, such conceptions of transnational obligation run against liberal contract theories insofar as they must be understood as non-reciprocal and non-contractual.[2] Nevertheless, my position differs from liberal and democratic positions that ground obligations on a theory of rights or the maximization of liberty.[3]

We can also draw conceptual inspiration and support for such polycentrism from Greek thought, particularly Homer. As I explained in chapter 1, Homeric political thought posits a significant degree of complexity within the self (*thumos, kradiē/kradia, noos*, etc.) and does not attempt to police it through a rigorously ordered typology. This complexity at the personal level suggests that an internally plural self will likely remain open, in different ways and at different times, to a wide variety of beings and phenomena from which human beings derive meaning in their lives and conceive their identities. Following insights from both Indian and Greek thought, we must therefore resist attempts to typologize human beings and place them in static, hierarchically ordered groupings.

Polycentrism presents important normative implications for our understanding of rule. First, internal plurality helps open us to external plurality and muddies the boundaries of one's identity. Each of these parts of the self—for example, our gut instincts, anger or spiritedness, and ability for mental reflection and ethical critique—help open us to a pluralistic world and disclose various aspects of it that we might otherwise neglect if we pre-define identity by privileging any single aspect. At one moment I may plausibly think or act based on a gut reaction to some event, while in the following moment I may reflect on why and how I reacted this way, including how I might act differently as a result. This speaks to the co-constitutive nature of polycentric identity and the multidimensionality of the world in which we are porously embedded. Second, because everyone possesses this internal complexity, we also have greater reason to believe in political equality when it comes to ruling capacities. That is, the Greek conception of the self can help facilitate a leveled conception of self-worth because everyone is relatively equal in having a pluralistic and tumultuous interior that exposes us to different aspects of the world, in different ways, at different times, and in different moods. We must then reject any hierarchical human typologies such as those we find in brahmanical thought, especially when it comes to the capacity to rule with others.

Here one might ask how the polycentric nature of the self necessarily discourages human hierarchy or typology. After all, Vedic thought provides a clear counterexample of polycentric identity that retains both human and nonhuman hierarchies in ṚV 10.90 (Puruṣa Sūkta). As we saw, this hymn conceives hierarchically arranged social groups that come from different parts of Puruṣa's body. While polycentrism does not logically exclude the possibility of hierarchy or typology, it does not follow that recognizing polycentrism necessarily encourages or commits us to particular human hierarchies or typologies. In the following ways, polycentrism can actually encourage a more fluid and egalitarian conception of rule.

Various relations of ruling-over are inevitable, and it is this inevitable hierarchical dimension of rule that should give us reason to pause and pay more attention to the "rule of connectedness." That is, polycentrism assists in making connectedness the ordinary and necessary condition of human life, and ruling will always impact our connectedness. Because of this, I argue that we have good reason to understand rule as entailing a consequentialist, normative duty for stewardship whereby humans have pragmatic responsibilities to care for nonhuman nature and preserve it. We are equally responsible and capable of fulfilling our own particular, context-based duties in this sense. Understanding human identity in a polycentric fashion not only helps us recognize our porous interdependence on nonhuman nature, but it should push us to better appreciate the various hierarchies that exist within this web of relations. Finally, the polycentric nature of the self emphasizes the different roles each of us can play vis-à-vis nonhuman nature due to our ability to fulfill a variety of functions, which includes reasoning and deliberating, laboring, and providing service to others—each of the capacities associated with the different body parts of Puruṣa (more on this later). If this multiplicity of roles predicated on polycentrism were properly acknowledged and various modes of participation were flattened or distributed more evenly, then existing human hierarchies and typologies could be challenged. In fact, such ruling hierarchies and typologies tend to proliferate when we forget or fail to acknowledge peoples' multifarious abilities to engage in ruling-over, ruling-for, ruling-with, and ruling-in a broader network of human and nonhuman beings.

Importantly, the nodal points of a polycentric self would not simply be other human beings. We get an example of how this works in the brahmanical case in its notion of interconnectedness: what it means to be an individual person is inextricably caught up in one's connectedness to a whole host of entities within a broader human–nonhuman community. Polycentric individuality would thus be a constantly shifting yet "sticky" site through and against which a rich diversity of beings and events converge and orient themselves as one's (always open and contestable) identity is forged within a broader nexus of nodal points. In addition, these beings and events that help constitute one's identity in terms of positioning need not be current or present. Due to the manner in which multiple modes of temporality overlap and fold into one another (e.g., see Connolly 2011), polycentrism can also be poly-temporal.

This poly-temporal aspect of rule speaks to debates about cross-generational justice, resource conservation, and representation yet does not rely upon existing democratic or liberal conceptions of rule. For example, as a polycentric ruler my identity is partly constituted by my connection and relationship to future generations, which will inevitably be impacted by my present thoughts and actions. While I can choose to remain ignorant of this connection and poly-temporal aspect of my being, I cannot shirk its brute reality. As I will argue further along, ruling implicates us in a type of stewardship applicable in both the present and future, whether we know it or not. Present modes of ruling-over extend into the future, which means that human beings always find themselves engaging in ruling-over in the present as well as ruling-over both future human and nonhuman beings that do not yet exist. Similar to nonhuman nature, future generations (both human and nonhuman) cannot appear in *propria persona* to defend their interests, so ruling-over calls for stewardship of their interests as well. This is yet another reason to adopt a non-reciprocal and non-contractual approach to our contemporary political responsibilities: both nonhuman nature and future generations cannot voluntary reciprocate and agree to contracts with the present generation, so both groups depend upon our conscious recognition that we are always in the process of ruling-over them, and thus possess responsibilities to rule in their interests as much as possible.

In lacking the ability to reciprocate and contract in the aforementioned manner, nonhuman beings cannot demand rights in the ways humans can. This means that humans must shoulder particular responsibilities to rule for their interests. Granting universal human rights to beings such as animals, as Donaldson and Kymlicka (2011) have done, faces distinct challenges in this respect. For example, the existence of modern rights are partly the result of historical struggles by specific groups of people who were pressed into demanding, undesirable work conditions at the hands of other groups and early capitalist modes of production. While nonhuman beings and forces might resist domineering and instrumental modes of ruling-over—for example, by exhibiting increased destabilization and fragility—this is not the same thing as a human proletariat making demands and earning concessions from the wealthy entrepreneurial classes and political elites. This is not to say that rights discourse does not or could not play an important role in reforming existing practices and institutions, only that extending rights faces important practical challenges and thus offers a limited action-oriented form of social change.[4]

The fact that ruling-over impacts those who cannot directly defend or represent their own interests applies to a particularly pressing contemporary issue involving the environment and future generations: population growth and control. Acknowledging the significance of ruling-over and responsibilities it triggers toward those who cannot appear and vote or verbally protest in person would provide reasons to support increased social services such as family planning and greater access to contraception.[5] Not only should governments pursue such aims domestically but developed nations like the United States should bear the greatest financial burdens and responsibilities of supporting these efforts across the globe, for at least two reasons. First, such nations enjoy comparatively unequal access to primary goods such as clean air and water, partly due to their ability to export increasing amounts of environmental risk associated with industrialization to poorer, more economically vulnerable countries. Second, as Dobson (2016, 296) argues, wealthier countries are more responsible for resource scarcity because their lives are more resource-intensive—for example, per capita carbon emissions are greater in rich countries.[6] These points also help explain why claims about ruling-over and responsibility need not reflect a neo-Malthusian position that would divert blame and responsibility for ecological problems from rich, powerful countries to poor, dispossessed ones.

Returning to the nature of polycentric identity and its relation to ritual and sacrifice, rather than seeking to dissolve all boundaries between human and nonhuman beings to achieve a more unitary and harmonious whole, it is more helpful to view human identities as sites that are unpredictable, fractured, shifting, and constructed. While the boundaries of identities constantly shift, they do tend to stick and tack on different connections and relations over time. In the Vedic context, this conception of identity as open, constructed, and requiring perpetual inscription can be found in rituals such as the *upanayana* (initiation into Vedic study and sacrifice). This ritual demonstrates that identities are partly constructed and stabilized through various ritualistic practices and habits involving the types of garments we wear, how we interact with others, and how we treat our physical surroundings and nonhuman nature. The *upanayana* helps form a *kṣatriya*'s identity by employing particular upper garments (spotted deer), meters of a Sanskrit verse (*triṣṭubh* meter) with suitable officiants (brahmins), a nonhuman instrument (staff made from the wood of a Nyagrodha tree), and initiatory season (summer). Modern rituals that are particularly relevant for our relationship to nonhuman nature include the production and purchase of food and clothing. These rituals, extending from the micro-level of the individual and household up to the macro-level of nation-state and international trade, must be seen as contributing to the ongoing construction not only of political identities but also to the construction of the world around us that will extend into the future. Moreover, rituals help highlight the importance of sacrifice.

For example, the Puruṣa-Sūkta depicts ruling as a necessary, ritualistic, and potentially laudable activity that involves self-sacrifice. First, this particular hymn portrays the sacrifice of a singular, demarcated self and the adoption of an outwardly porous conception of selfhood. Second, Puruṣa, the primordial person and ruler, is perpetually sacrificed so that an ontological plurality of beings could emerge and sustain itself over time. Rule thus entails ongoing ritual activities that must constantly be performed to sustain the welfare of an interdependent human–nonhuman world. Contemporary examples of sacrifice might include sacrificing our overreliance on fossil fuels such as coal and oil as primary sources of energy, as well as economic and population growth, in exchange for more sustainable practices associated with de-growth.[7]

Both rituals and sacrifices that involve ruling-over should be refashioned in ways that better account for our duties as stewards. A specific example drawn from the Aitareya Brāhmaṇa (7.31) may help tie together these ideas about polycentrism, stewardship, and ruling-over. In brahmanical thought, *kṣatra*, as a particular type of power or ability, anchors the *kṣatriya* as a ruler within a broader community and draws upon ideas of correspondence between beings such as humans and trees. The *kṣatriya*'s likeness and correspondence to a Nyagrodha tree is intriguing for numerous reasons. As I mentioned last chapter, this resemblance displays a nonhuman-centric conception of rule because nonhuman entities possess corresponding abilities and serve similar purposes in other types of communities, such as forest communities occupied by trees, plants, and soils. The Nyagrodha—and by the cosmological and metaphysical associations within Vedic texts, the *kṣatriya* or ruler—is something that stretches downward and outward into its source of nourishment, becoming firmly rooted within and growing increasingly dependent upon sources that it rules over and helps stabilize in various ways. In chapter 5 I explained how this passage also exhibits the idea that rulers remain equally polycentric and porously dependent as the Nyagrodha tree at their "roots." This example of rule displays a twofold sense of interconnectedness: first, the well-being of rulers and those affected by ruling-over are intricately intertwined; second, rulers are deeply connected to a type of tree that displays a similar ability and vital relationship to a variety of different entities. This second point destabilizes any exceptionalist connection between human beings and rule because the human capacity to rule stands ontologically equidistant to the Nyagrodha's capacity to do the same. Not only does this relation shrink the distance between the human and nonhuman, but it also cultivates a sensibility in rulers to care for various non-human entities with which they share particular capacities. The *capacity* and relationship matter most, less so the type of being that exhibits the capacity.

These ideas intersect with new materialist and post-humanist arguments about the overlooked agentic capacities of the nonhuman world, especially ideas about distributive agency. Recent examples include Jane Bennett (2010), who explores the "thing-power" of object-agents and heteronomous assemblages, and Catriona Sandilands (2016), who provides vivid accounts of plants as biopolitical subjects (see also Coole 2013; Coole and Frost 2010). Samantha Frost (2016, 178–92) has recently provided an insightful overview of multiple philosophical approaches to this topic, explaining how humans have been decentered as the sole political actors in the world. Her critical overview not only provides us with reasons for adopting greater respect and care for the interdependent, shared capacities that supply the necessary resources for our integrated welfare, but it also helps supply a descriptive correction to the idea that nonhuman nature is merely inert matter meant for our instrumental use and consumption.

An additional aspect of this leveled, interconnected stewardship in Indian thought finds expression in the liturgical Saṃhitās and Brāhmaṇas. These works elaborate a metaphysics whereby manifest reality is always in the process of being constructed and remains fundamentally interconnected. One observes this idea in the figure of Prajāpati (the lord or father of creatures), who is identified with the primordial Puruṣa in later Vedic works. As I explained in chapters 3 and 4, ritual action plays a role in constructing what is manifestly real, and sacrificial ritual in particular replicates and continues Puruṣa's and Prajāpati's original sacrifice. This ongoing ritual action ensures the cosmos continues to operate and flourish in an organized manner, while sacrificial ritual, understood as contributing to the maintenance of the manifest world, sustains the world through ritual labor, or *karman*. The liturgical Saṃhitās and Brāhmaṇas thus express a deep sense of interconnectedness and stewardship in emphasizing how the processes of sacrifice and ritual assist in creating the world and how ruling entails responsibility for participating in these processes. Ruling is then understood as an ongoing activity characterized by sacrifice and ritual labor. In sum, ruling requires facilitating and protecting sacrifices and rituals that help maintain the interconnected well-being of the cosmos, as the connectedness of rule pervades Vedic thought and provides a theoretical basis for polycentrism and stewardship as a form of "panocracy," as we will see later.

Bringing Hesiod's conception of rule back into the picture, this brahmanically inspired conception of stewardship differs in important ways. Through a network of *bandhus* (bonds, connections, kinship), the brahmanical vision levels ruling relations and carves more open, interconnected space for considering the interests of nonhuman nature. In doing so, it further levels—by means of *dharmans* (sacrificial customs) and *yajña* (sacrificial and ritualistic reality-construction)—what it means to rule by taking into account the constitutive well-being of more than just a deliberating citizen body. Hesiod's conception of justice and its connection to rule, as I argued in chapter 2, is largely a human-centric activity that only entails considerations for nonhuman well-being insofar as the nonhuman world plays an instrumental role for human interests and well-being. For example, Gaia and the natural world are not viewed as possessing humanistic subjectivity and equal interests to flourish on their own terms. Rather, for Hesiod the natural world is managed through human labor and foresight in such a way that human beings can live moderately comfortable lives. The role of speech is also telling insofar as Hesiod does not consider alternative ways in which nonhuman beings can communicate with humans. If one is open to a broader, constitutive body of nonhuman beings, then one can become open to more diverse forms of communication. A brahmanical vantage point helps show how Hesiod problematically asserts that good rule is more about speech, especially the ability to communicate through human language about what is just and unjust, than it is about the capacity to engage in ruling-over and fulfill the role of steward for the interests of those who are impacted by this ability. Examining the figure of Puruṣa, for example, one sees how this cosmic individual is made up of interconnected parts and abilities, and that each part depends on other parts/abilities for its proper functioning and flourishing. These parts and abilities then correlate with and serve particular sociopolitical functions. While Puruṣa's arms (*rājanya*, rulers) are responsible for protecting the broader communal body of beings and entities, this community includes not only a human sociopolitical body but also numerous nonhuman beings and phenomena that constitute a larger *cosmic* body.

In our contemporary context, an increasingly vulnerable and unstable cosmic body would include the natural environment and various non-living things such as mountains and rivers, as well as nonhuman beings such as plants and animals. If we understand the self as outwardly porous and interconnected within a larger cosmic body, then we can begin to shift our understanding of rule in a nonhuman-centric, or polycentric, direction. As I have suggested, the cosmic body is a political body. Drawing upon the Vedic concept of *kṣatra* as an ability that always keeps humans open to the nonhuman world, we can begin to see the importance of understanding ruling as stewardship whereby each person is responsible for protecting the well-being of a larger, interconnected community of beings. Compared to this vision the more narrow, human-centric nature of Homeric and Hesiodic rule becomes more evident. Neglecting our roles as stewards of the varied interests of nonhuman nature, members of which cannot present and defend their interests in *propria persona*, can create an increasingly unstable cosmological environment. In turn, this instability increasingly threatens human welfare. Recent examples such as super-storms, rising sea levels, and severe droughts may only be the beginning of a more tempestuous relationship between nonhuman nature and human communities, placing the natural world in a position of increasing power over human interests and welfare. Advanced weather tracking systems and various biotechnologies expose human beings' anxiety over this very fact. For example, human beings increasingly want to know when, where, and how nonhuman nature will "strike." Here we can note a feeling of antagonism similar to what we see in Homeric and Hesiodic political cosmology. The ability to rule over something else can easily entice us into an instrumental understanding of nonhuman nature, especially because it involves the power to control or manipulate the nonhuman world in various ways to serve our own interests. In fact, an instrumental mentality may even be more tempting in an age when humans feel threatened as a species in the face of things such as climate change.

Moreover, we must reject instrumental approaches that grant sole agentic status to human beings, situate us in a position of master, and objectify nonhuman nature as a passive resource for our consumption. If we do not reject these destructive and inaccurate tendencies, then human beings may assist in building a world so fragile and unstable that interdependent, necessary agonism becomes an antagonistic contest for hierarchical specieist distinction, domination, and potential counter-dominance at the hands of nonhuman nature. Some degree of agonism or competition is inevitable because our response-ability as rulers will necessarily involve considering various trade-offs between conflicting needs and interests of a wide variety of beings. As stewards and fellow rulers, human beings must think carefully about what are oftentimes mutually incompatible goods and act accordingly. Good stewardship thus entails dealing with this tragic aspect of rule in such a way that agonism does not turn into a combative form of antagonism whereby human beings—or any other being for that matter—possesses the ability to eradicate all competition and engage in outright domination.

To summarize, we should view ruling-over as co-constitutive of human and nonhuman well-being and adopt a heightened awareness of the need for stewardship, including greater respect for our cosmological embeddedness. This would entail shifting from predominant Western conceptions that humans should merely use or employ nonhuman nature in an instrumental fashion (especially since it cannot defend its interests through reasoned speech), and altering our conception of this relationship to one of rule. This would further require us to level our conception of rule to one of ruling-with, ruling-for, and ruling-in the interests of nonhuman nature.

Ruling-With: The Need for Double-Leveling

In contrast to the hierarchical dimension of rule, ruling-with constitutes a horizontal dimension and evokes the question: *With* whom do rulers rule, if anyone? Building on my claims from the previous section, I want to suggest that ruling-over always entails various modalities of ruling-with and co-participation on the part of both human and nonhuman beings. That is to say, our concepts of ruling-over always include an element of ruling-with, and our practices of ruling-over cannot escape the issue of ruling-with because we are always in danger of failing to sustain the conditions of our own survival and hierarchical impact on nature.[8] Re-theorizing rule demands that human beings view themselves as ruling-with not only their fellow human beings (single leveling) but also with and among various nonhuman beings in at least two ways (double leveling).

First, both Greek and brahmanical thought express the idea that nonhuman beings and entities affect human life in myriad ways, and to some extent, each tradition also holds that this affect can become destructive if rulers do not accept their responsibility to rule thoughtfully in an interconnected world. While human beings might possess some unique abilities that other species or natural phenomena do not,[9] the opposite is also true. For example, Vedic thought views the Nyagrodha tree as possessing a slightly different yet parallel capacity to the one that *kṣatriyas* possess insofar as it protects and stabilizes the soil beneath it, further providing various services for plants and animals that depend upon it for food, shade, or shelter. In this respect the Nyagrodha tree engages in ruling-with by serving as a steward for the needs and interests of different types of beings to which it is connected. In turn, if common citizens attempt to evade their stewardship duties and shift all responsibility to laws, elected representatives, or macro-level institutions, then citizens actively contribute to endangering nonhuman beings that possess the parallel capacity to act as stewards in their respective environments. Second, ruling-with should reflect the recognition that human lives, interests, and relations of rule are inextricably entangled with the nonhuman, its diverse agentic capacities, and a "push/pull" relation to human needs and interests. Here the preposition "with" can be understood in two senses: first, there are ways and moments in which the nonhuman world expresses power over us and thus akin to a co-participant in ruling; second, "with" highlights the simple fact that human beings exist among nonhuman beings and entities in such a way that we cannot bracket ruling, politics, and human flourishing from our impactful immersion within and dependence on the natural world.

Again, we can draw on some of the dominant categories in ancient Greek and Indian political thought for imagining how we could engage in ruling-with in a more thoughtful fashion. First, rituals provide one tool for building greater consideration of nonhuman beings' interests into our personal and public decision-making. While many of our daily rituals, such as those involving our dietary and consumptive routines, often go unexamined and thus turn into rote practices and thoughtless habits, they nevertheless have a cumulative effect on the world around us. As Barry argues, infusing rituals of gratitude and generosity into practices of food production and consumption create "occasions to pause and reflect upon our connections with one another and the non-human world. It also evokes a sense of reintroducing 'mindfulness' into these everyday activities" (2012, 110). Not only do our personal and communal rituals have cumulative impacts on nonhuman nature, but they are also grounded in meaningful relationships and practices such as shared meals with family or friends, which, if altered in various ways, could help slow us down and adopt "natural/agricultural conceptions of time against unilinear economic/industrial-capitalist conceptions of 'clock time'" (111). Following the seasons and shifting our consumptive rhythms away from industrialized, mass-produced food systems and rituals of food production could help initiate more sustainable food practices.

Reforming existing practices draws our attention to both "negative/privative" and "positive/additive" elements of sacrifice. Sacrifice can be understood as giving up something of value to particular human beings or communities for the sake of something that is of value to various nonhuman beings or communities whose well-being is a constitutive element of our own. In a privative sense, stewardship would then require sacrificing some of our personal comforts for the sake of various nonhuman interests in the same way that we might do so for another human being or member of the human community. However, as Paul Wapner (2010) has argued by drawing on the work of Wendell Barry, Barbara Kingsolver, Bill McKibben, and Michael Pollan, it is entirely possible to view environmental sacrifice not simply as a privation but as gain and enrichment: "Knowing where one's food comes from; interacting with producers through community-supported agriculture efforts; rejecting fast, institutional food . . . one gains a sense of knowledge, control, and appreciation for one's meals" (55). Relatedly, such "positive sacrifices" in food consumption would lend support to grassroots food movements like Food Democracy Now!, which exhibit ways of decentralizing rule by providing common citizens means for developing more sustainable relationships and exercising response-ability to nonhuman nature. Importantly, grassroots food movements also facilitate more direct, meaningful relationships with the people in local and regional communities that make something like "food democracy" possible: that is, greater local control and more equal distribution of healthy foods grown and produced in sustainable ways.[10]

This understanding of sacrifice aligns with a polycentric conception of identity and not an atomistic one. On the one hand, because human beings do have personal interests that coincide with their individualized physical embodiment, sacrifice will entail a negation or giving up various objects of personal pleasure and gratification, and not instrumentally expecting anything in return. On the other hand, sacrifice will involve a validation, or giving to nonhuman nature by focusing on aspects of ourselves or things surrounding us to which we often pay little or no attention. This would include beings and phenomena that help constitute or nourish our polycentric identities, whose identities and interests we must nourish in turn. Such nonhuman beings might range from particular living things like the plants and animals we consume, to something more diffuse such as the ecosystems in which we live. In this latter regard, sacrifice means acknowledging and serving the interests of different parts of a porous self that comprises both the self narrowly construed and other beings to which we are connected yet have their own distinctive identities.

For example, although industrialization in a particular locale may create more jobs and increase the affluence of various members of the human community, such projects may have to be sacrificed due to the impact they would have on the native habitat and its nonhuman inhabitants. Agreeing with those who argue for the limits of growth and de-growth, here we would sacrifice our insatiable desire for anthropocentric economic growth. We should ask ourselves questions such as: Will this industry serve the interests of local bird or plant species, making them more affluent in resources they need for survival and long-term growth, which would also be understood as part of future generations' welfare? As a corollary to this point, individuals should not attempt to shift the responsibility for stewardship to others. As much as possible, we should understand ourselves as ruling-with one another as fellow "citizen-rulers" in a leveled fashion and not think of rule as the sole responsibility of elected representatives in distant institutions. Rule is a personal matter for all citizens. Because rule is personal yet embedded within a web of human–nonhuman relations that differ from place to place, considering one's impact on nonhuman interests will be relative to local and contextual considerations such that we cannot determine a priori whose interests are most important or have priority in a given case. The "who" may sometimes be a particular plant or animal species, but it may also be a natural body such as a river whose needs or welfare has priority. Importantly, this conception of rule must also converge in collective efforts and movements to instigate change.

This argument for both personal and collective efforts of ruling-with resonates with arguments made by "green civic republicans" concerning the need for greater local governance and decentralization of political deliberation and decision-making. Part of the aim here would be to create conditions in which human beings could better understand and address their common interests and goods in ways that facilitate more sustainable relations to nonhuman nature. A more localized conception of ruling-with requires exercising personal responsibility for the stewardship of nonhuman welfare, which could be pursued in a number of ways. For example, John Barry (2012, 89–112) has explained how the international Transition movement exhibits green republican ideas and strategies aiming at sustainability, flexibility, and resiliency. These towns exemplify an experimental ethos and "concrete utopianism" that remains crucial for altering and reforming existing ruling practices, especially as they pursue the following goals: increasing flexible, open-ended ecological management at the local level, and consequently reducing traditional state-centered and market forms of management; transitioning to a low-carbon economy and reducing energy consumption in general; localizing adaptive capacities for renewable energy and sustainable rituals of food production, preparation, and consumption.

An aim of such movements, which accords with the new vision of rule that I have been outlining, is to construct new practices and institutions that render explicit human–nonhuman interconnectedness. These practices and institutions would allow people to participate more directly in constructing more sustainable, resilient practices of rule in the face of our material vulnerabilities in an era of increasing ecological vulnerability. However, this move toward political decentralization, greater local governance, increased citizen participation in the ruling process, and coproduction of public goods, services, and projects need not dismiss entirely governance at the national level. Rather, these aims must draw upon ruling capacities in a more distributed, integrated fashion that extends from the local and regional levels to the national and international levels.

As Carmen Sirriani (2009) has suggested, policymakers at the national level can help take the lead in actively promoting "collaborative governance," which integrates policymakers in a collaborative process of problem solving that draws upon the knowledge and ruling capacities of average citizens, including non-elected citizens' and private sector groups' potential contributions to progressive policies. Robyn Eckersley (2004) has also defended the ability of governments to promote, guide, and sustain more ecologically attentive forms of citizenship. For example, she argues that rethinking principles of ecological democracy can "serve to cast the state as an ecological steward and facilitator of transboundary democracy" (3). Eckersley thus explains how reforming the liberal democratic state based on normative criteria provided by critical political ecology could lead to a "green state," wherein future generations' and nonhuman nature's interests are better represented based on a principle akin to the one I defend—namely, those who cannot defend their interests in *propria persona* should "otherwise be represented in the making of the policies or decisions that generate the risk" (111).

Nevertheless, tremendous potential for re-envisioning how we can rule with one another in more sustainable ways lies outside traditional political institutions and procedures. David Schlosberg and Romand Coles (2016, 160–81) explore non-traditional calls for collective change by examining how "bottom-up" activist groups offer novel solutions for altering our material relations to nonhuman nature. They explain how activist groups have aimed at reconfiguring and developing more sustainable material flows—that is, flows that do not undermine the stability and predictability of environmental processes and systems. Examples of such movements include the following: food movements such as farmers' markets, community supported agriculture and food policy councils; energy movements that increase their use and distribution of more sustainable forms of energy in preparation for a post-carbon future; crafting and making movements oriented around a "new domesticity" that includes canning, sowing, mending, trashion, and upcycling (162–66).

Sustainable materialist strategies and procedures that aim at reconfiguring material flows could provide a valuable way of enhancing our stewardship capacities and, moreover, better reflect care for human–nonhuman connectedness and leveled forms of ruling-with. The food justice movement exhibits another example. As Schlosberg (2013, 49) argues, humans must collectively challenge and redesign problematic institutions and practices that surround basic needs such as food consumption. This would not simply entail "buying organic veggies at a natural foods megamart, but getting more involved in growing and sharing food in community supported agriculture, collective gardening, urban farms, and farmers markets" (49). Transforming our relationship with material flows such as food consumption, production, and transportation entails altering many of our existing relations of ruling-over nonhuman nature and ruling-with one another. Decentralizing and leveling rule along these dimensions will likely require combining electioneering, law making, and direct forms of contestation with less traditional forms of grassroots activism that establish local practices and institutions capable of altering the flow of food and clothing in more sustainable directions. In this respect, activist groups would likely need to focus on building multilevel coalitions and political power capable of protecting and expanding their new practices and institutions against powerful counter-interests. In short, new institutions, procedures, and methods of ruling-with are necessary for us to exercise fully our capacities for stewardship.

Still, ruling-with does not require us to collapse moral distinctions and duties between humans and animals across every dimension of rule, for example, by viewing particular animals as co-rulers or sovereigns within overlapping communities of interests.[11] To explain why this is the case, clarifying the nature of humanistic stewardship is essential. Can and to what extent do various types of animals possess the capacity to critically reflect and deliberate, personally and communally, on how they should protect *human beings'* needs and interests in the same way that humans are capable of doing for *their* interests? This question re-raises the point about our non-reciprocal duties to nonhuman nature. Because we have good reason to be skeptical about the potential and/or likelihood for animals to exercise this sort of capacity, at least at the moment, we must acknowledge that the duty for stewardship exhibits one way in which human beings are somewhat unique and thus possess a greater burden of response-ability. However, just because humans differ in ways that suggest potential inequalities as a species in one respect, this does not mean that we are necessarily unequal in other or all respects—especially to such a degree that it would justify complete political exclusion. This pervasive yet mistaken assumption in Western traditions of thought extends back to the Greeks and provides an apparent justification for instrumental approaches to nonhuman nature that have gotten us into serious environmental trouble in the contemporary world.

For example, claiming human beings are unique and unequal in this regard should not lead us to conclude that there is a fundamental break and moral distinction between human and nonhuman beings in terms of species dignity, as George Kateb (2011) suggests. As I have argued, human beings do not and cannot break from nature in any strong sense. Such arguments for a species break tend to overprivilege the human species and implicitly reinforce a hierarchical anthropocentrism that we must challenge. Rather than arguing that we can be stewards I contend that our understanding of ruling always places us in various relations of stewardship, partly because we always find ourselves ruling-over and ruling-with others, as well as ruling-in a deeply interconnected world. Human beings should not start by conceiving themselves as self-demarcated, ontologically dignified, rights-bearing individuals and thereafter as potential stewards of nature. Rather, our ruling capacity and beliefs always place us in a fleeting and limited hierarchical relationship to the nonhuman world in at least one crucial sense: ruling-with other human beings inevitably impacts how we rule over, in, and for a broader environment and community of beings. Ruling-with is always entangled with the other dimensions of rule.

As I have intimated in my critique of Hesiod, the problem is that many Western understandings of rule have situated human beings above the animal world and environment in a rather dominant, instrumentalist fashion. Such essentialist hierarchies have increasingly come under attack due to the environmental issues facing human beings on a global scale. I thus contend that we do not have the absolute freedom or leverage to parse our ruling beliefs and response-abilities from their application and broader effects. Indeed, this is one of the central reasons why each person's capacity to rule triggers the duty for stewardship: the rule of connectedness means that human beings should not be understood as having the freedom or choice to act as stewards or not. It is more accurate to say that humans are always already stewards, and the most pressing question is whether or not they are acting as such, in more or less sustainable ways that are attentive to our interdependence and vulnerability. Consequently, many of the standards for judging effectiveness will remain localized, contextual, and circumstantial. While they may have greater power to craft and enforce public policy, the duty for stewardship does not merely fall on macro-level institutions and elected representatives. Such institutions and figures generally sit at great distance from most peoples' daily, lived experience and remain largely outside citizens' immediate influence. In making this move I wish to downplay the notion of human dignity and sublimate human–nonhuman interconnectedness, partly because our capacity to rule always places us in a position where we do not have the absolute freedom or leverage to parse this capacity from its application and broader effects.

Ruling-For: Panocracy and Expanding the Cosmological Scope of Interest

It should now be clear how reconceiving what it means to rule over and with will lead us to a different understanding of ruling-for. This third dimension captures the depth of interests considered and impacted in making both personal and collective decisions, eliciting the question: *For* what or whose interests and well-being do rulers rule? As I have already begun to suggest, the ability to rule implicates everyone in ruling-for the interests of not only other human beings but also a wide variety of beings that are impacted, both directly and indirectly, through our daily decisions, habits, rituals, and communal practices. Here I wish to take the next step in my argument by suggesting that we move away from the concept of democracy as an ideal conception of rule and begin thinking more in terms of what I call "panocracy."

This is an understanding of rule that extends across both human and nonhuman registers, drawing on the Greek terms *pan* (neuter form of adjective *pas*, meaning "all") and *kratein* (to rule, hold sway). We can combine these two terms to elucidate the idea that all human beings have the power and response-ability to rule as stewards, and that the ability to rule affects an incredibly broad array of human and nonhuman beings. As a form of rule, it can be viewed as ruling by all and ruling-for the inclusive interests of the human and nonhuman. This alternative, more capacious conception of rule captures the idea that ruling "pans out" in multiple directions, along with our ability to gauge the effects of rule that reverberate cosmologically and impact everything from living beings to non-sentient things. The polycentrism that I have outlined at the individual level suggests that we understand stewardship as gesturing toward a more inclusive conception of rule that does not merely refer to and measure its success by the quantity of rulers and breadth of human political participation (humanistic ruling-with). Rather, panocracy would measure its success by considering the scope of interests and well-being of both human and nonhuman beings who are impacted by each citizen's ongoing ability to rule.

Drawing upon a brahmanical notion of stewardship and the idea of a polycentric self helps fill out this alternative conception of panocracy. To start, stewardship is not necessarily a form of ruling whereby ruling power and response-ability is distributed equally to nonhuman beings, resulting in something like a democracy writ large that is full of human and nonhuman beings as demarcated, rights-bearing individuals. Rather, the version of stewardship that I defend supports a panocratic vision insofar as ruling beliefs and practices would be considered more expansive in terms of their impact and affect. As John Barry (2012) similarly argues from a green republican standpoint, recognizing this impact should spark greater appreciation of our vulnerability due to our dependency on nature, which should press us to adopt a disposition of care that informs stewardship ethics. Instead of focusing solely or predominantly on the question of who rules (i.e., who possesses the ruling power and responsibility), we now focus equally on the broader communal, nonhuman impact of our ruling beliefs and practices. It is important to note that polycentrism supports this notion of panocracy in two regards. First, panocracy is grounded in the notion of a polycentric self and its porous, interconnected identity. Second, panocracy focuses more intently on the meaningful entities within our surrounding environment that our ruling beliefs and practices inevitably impact. In this way, panocracy involves polycentrism and stewardship, both of which can help us envision a nonhuman-centric form of rule whereby ruling citizens govern based upon an acknowledgement of the impact their ruling ideas and practices have within a broader community. This form of rule does not focus solely on human rulers and ruling-with in the human community but increasingly on the implications of human beings' response-ability as rulers for maintaining the well-being of other types of beings within a broader community and environment.

I can further clarify this part of my position by returning to the idea of a "common good." Initially, it may seem that the conception of rule I defend relies on some conception of a common good or goods. However, I want to reject any generic or universal idea of a common good or pre-specified common goods that may serve as criteria for judging exactly how and when we should rule for the interests of various nonhuman beings. Due to our diverse positionality, contexts, and circumstances as porous beings, it is unlikely that we would ever be able to identify a particular, unchanging common good a priori. What is good "for everyone" is hardly ever so. For example, what I see as good for me in my private life may have significant impact or consequences on others and their interests, making it both private and public in different senses, and to different degrees. As Raymond Geuss explains: "We do not have a clear grasp, not even a rough-and-ready nontheoretical grasp, of the two categories of public and private as marking out two clearly distinct domains. Rather, each of these categories is a disordered jumble of different things" (2001, 109). Of course, this does not mean we cannot make any distinction between a private and public good because "it does not follow that we cannot come to a rationally well-supported view that gives us reason to distinguish them for particular purposes in particular contexts," and "it follows that the 'reason' we will use will be a contextually located human power, not some abstract faculty of reading off the moral demands of the universe from the facts of the case" (Geuss 2001, 113). Consequently, we must sustain a thoughtful attitude about when and for what purposes we seek to make such distinctions in our personal and collective lives. The porous, polycentric conception of the self that I defend fits this type of sensibility not only because it does a better job of describing the nature of our situated identities but also because it serves as a healthy reminder that we should extend gratitude and care to various nonhuman beings and phenomena that make our ways of life possible. Homer, Hesiod, and brahmanical poets all felt the importance of such cosmological porosity, albeit to varying extents and for different reasons.

This means that one should consider the circumstances, information, and stakes that seem to be most pertinent at any given time. This will entail ruling-for the good or interests of those impacted by a potential action, or deciding to do A versus B, or C as opposed to A or B, and so on. Stewardship must remain sufficiently contextual so that we do not fall prey to a major weakness that we see in brahmanical thought: the urge to delimit and typologize human beings' ability to exercise their capacity to rule by structuring all human behavior through tightly specified rituals or procedures based on predetermined social groupings.

Concluding this section, perhaps the best way to approach "ruling-for" is to flip some of our predominant assumptions on their head. Because humans need a wide variety of nonhuman beings to survive and flourish, instead of adopting the Hesiodic conclusion that these beings should be in service of us, we should alternatively conclude that we should be in service of them. As we saw in Hesiod, effective ruling-over and ruling-with has as a precondition ruling-for the interests of those over whom someone (or something) exercises various powers. Because our existence relies upon the nonhuman world to a much greater extent than nonhuman nature relies on our existence, we owe the nonhuman world more than it owes us and have a duty to act as stewards. Such a panoramic field of response-ability would be an essential component of a panocracy.

Ruling-In: There is No "Out"

While distinct from the other dimensions, in some respects ruling-in encapsulates the others by elucidating the spatial dimensions for rule. This dimension evokes the fact that human beings rule not only within the context of human communities but also in a broader, more expansive context of human–nonhuman communities of interest. Following aspects of both Greek and Indian political thought, ruling-in invokes the idea of cultivating greater humility in the face of beings, phenomena, and forces that supersede the capacities of human agency, and ultimately, approaching rule in a more cosmological fashion.

As we saw in the case of Hesiod, tremendous significance hangs on the question of who and what is "in" versus "out" of the purview of justice. First, we must reject something akin to Hesiod's ethico-political distinction between the human and nonhuman in our cosmological landscape, especially as it concerns relations of justice. Second, in doing so we could view justice in an alternative way that draws upon particular insights in brahmanical political thought. One facet of justice understood within a context of ruling-in would be to understand it as involving something like *bandhus*—that is, affective bonds, kinships, or connections to various nonhuman beings. Accordingly, justice would signal contextual and relational duties of care to both human and nonhuman beings as opposed to being grounded in a single, predefined normative principle that tells all citizen-rulers how they should treat others in any or all cases. We could then speak of justice*s* and injustice*s* predicated on a more holistic and contextual, yet no less pluralistic, conception of ruling-for the interests of those beings who are impacted by our ruling decisions. Most important, this must include nonhuman interests.

Paralleling this position on affective connections and justice, Schlosberg (2007, 2012) has defended a capabilities approach to environmental justice that emphasizes recognizing and resiliently adapting to human–nonhuman connectedness. His approach helps us to better appreciate the importance of maintaining the integrity of our ecological support system by drawing our attention to the myriad ways in which a working environment provides the basis for social justice. My theory of rule is compatible with this approach and provides additional conceptual support by supplying a reinterpretation, and corresponding modification, of a deeply entrenched historical concept that has contributed to our unjust treatment of nonhuman nature. I would also argue that adapting to climate change requires a corresponding adaptation in how we look at rule. That is, we must shift our focus from democracy as the ideal form of rule and adopt a panocratic vision as a precondition for any successful form of democracy. As an alternative vision of rule, panocracy helps clarify—both conceptually and practically—our connectedness to and dependence on nonhuman nature, which includes both primary goods that are a precondition for meeting basic needs and accompanying conceptions of distributive and social justice.

Due to the connectedness of rule, both human and nonhuman beings always exist in the world together, and thus rely on relations of care that we often overlook due to our humanistic hubris. Cosmologically speaking, nothing is "out" when it comes to the connectedness of rule and considerations of justice in the contemporary world, even if people live and rule in the world in differing ways and locales. Human beings therefore possess not only a response-ability to care for nonhuman interests but also duties of stewardship due to humans' existence as ruling-in-the world. Predominant Western conceptions of rule, elements of which stretch all the way back to archaic Greek thought, have deluded us into thinking we can bracket rule as an activity that merely involves human relations.

As I argued in the previous section, reconceiving our understanding of ruling-in complicates liberal distinctions between a public and private sphere because one could not theoretically predefine or antecedently specify what constitutes a private versus public thought or action. For example, purportedly private decisions that are often understood to pertain solely to household life cannot be so easily or statically parsed. Many private decisions end up having broader, potentially public repercussions. If I have the monetary resources to purchase a new vehicle, then my choice between a large, gas guzzling truck and a small, gas efficient hybrid car is not merely a private choice with personal consequences. Even if it was the case that I chose to view it as a private affair, it is nevertheless one that will have an impact on the environment—so will my choice to buy a car as opposed to using public transportation, or riding a bike.

Now, if I do not merely view myself as an individuated citizen making a private choice that bears only on my personal affairs, but rather view myself as a polycentric ruler and panocratic steward who is making a decision and undertaking various actions that impact the interests of many other human and nonhuman beings, then my perspective begins to shift. In making this point I do not want to imply the following: first, that every thought or action will have considerable consequences for some broader community and its members' interests; second, that all my actions are publicly consequential to the same degree; third, that I could accurately know or predict all of the consequences that might follow from a particular thought or action. I only want to emphasize that it would be a step in the right direction to think about rule in a more interconnected, cosmological fashion and consistently consider the various layers and "impact zones" in which we inevitably find ourselves. Following insights drawn from both Homer and Hesiod, we should also admit that these layers and impact zones could be quite unpredictable and often agonistic in nature. Because of this fact, however, we should not neglect the need for consistently reminding ourselves that each of us always finds our self ruling-in a broader network of beings and interests that we often take for granted.

The dimension of ruling-in highlights the need to adopt what Schlosberg calls a "politics of sight" for the Anthropocene, which builds on a politics of receptivity centered around listening to the nonhuman and brings "attention to the previously hidden, and visualize the ongoing human relationship with the non-human" (2016, 202). We can easily lose sight or appreciation of ruling-in due to the ways in which modern industrialization obscures many of our dependencies and effects on nonhuman nature, resulting in an "immersive ignorance." For example, industrialized agriculture and slaughter hide from view the processes that lead to the tidy packaged goods we find on supermarket shelves or in freezer bins. As Barry explains, we must learn to adopt practices that "render explicit those forms of relations of dependence on nature and fellow humans that have been occluded, forgotten, or otherwise hidden away in modernity" (2012, 28). In order to comprehend and critically reflect on such dependency, Schlosberg makes two important points. First, conceptions of environmental justice require practices of deconstructive and affirmative *recognition*. Building on the work of Nancy Fraser, Schlosberg explains how "in the context of climate change, recognition is not only about the effects on place and culture but on the *relationship* between the processes of the natural and social worlds" (2012, 451, emphasis in original). Importantly, this would include recognizing the varying levels of vulnerability facing different communities around the globe as well as how ecological processes support human beings' basic needs at both the individual and communal level (452). Second, adaptation planning can integrate impact studies that "visually illustrate drought range, sea level rise, urban heat islands, etc" (Schlosberg 2016, 205). I agree with Schlosberg and argue that more sustainable forms of ruling-in require national, state, and local governments to use visualizations that draw attention to and prompt reflection on the broad interconnectedness between human and nonhuman welfare. Cultivating virtues of receptivity and mindfulness along these lines can stir us from more narrow anthropocentric visions of ruling-over and ruling-with to a more complex and multidimensional vision of rule that I am defending.

Finally, representation would be understood as a modality of ruling-for the interests of nonhuman nature, thus requiring a shift in the meaning of representation within a panocratic system. At the theoretical and normative levels, representation would first be understood as non-reciprocal because nonhuman beings and phenomena do not and will not represent our interests in a like fashion (at least in any traditional sense), and non-contractual because they cannot enter into voluntary contracts with the present generation. Second, representation would entail thoughtfully ruling-for the interests of future generations of humans and nonhuman nature in accord with a polycentric and poly-temporal conception of identity. The result of neglecting such intergenerational and nonhuman ruling-for must be acknowledged as leading to dire consequences and unsustainable, non-resilient forms of ruling-in. Third, such representation is not something we could freely or voluntary choose to do; as I explained earlier, the modality of ruling-over automatically implicates us in relations of ruling-for, world-building, and stewardship. In a practical sense, representation would become increasingly, and more efficaciously, practiced at the local and regional levels through decentralized processes of governance. It would be practiced in both individual and more locally collective ways, while exhibiting mindful efforts by all citizens to act as better stewards of nonhuman nature. These aims can draw inspiration from a number of strategies and practices that I have mentioned in this chapter, especially those exhibited by grassroots food movements and the Transition movement, which include greater decentralized and local control in creating and participating in more sustainable material flows that involve basic needs of human life such as food and energy.

Thus far I have sought to explain how my historical-comparative analysis helps bridge conversations in comparative and environmental political theory. I have also begun to show how a new vision of rule, panocracy, can address the four major dimensions of rule in ways that help us better attend to human–nonhuman connectedness. Moreover, this conception of rule provides a theoretical framework broad enough for synthesizing valuable lessons not only from Greek and Indian thought but also contemporary environmental theories, thus explaining how we might draw upon ideas, practices, strategies, and institutions associated with liberalism, democracy, civic republicanism, or post-humanism.

Ruling in an Interconnected World: Stewardship, Panocracy, and the Process of World-Building

If we re-theorize the various dimensions of rule in the aforementioned ways, where does this lead us in terms of a new understanding of what it means to rule? I would like to conclude by pulling these four dimensions together to explain how an alternative vision of rule justifies stewardship of nonhuman nature and coheres with ideas of panocracy and world-building. Going back to the earliest Greek ideas about the nature of rule, we find a number of fascinating yet problematic beliefs. Perhaps the most problematic aspect of early Greek thought is something that we see Hesiod develop in a more systematic way: namely, the idea that just rule pertains only to human beings, and nonhuman beings appear either irrelevant or solely instrumental to human purposes. One reason for this conception, Hesiod suggests, is that nonhuman beings such as animals and plants do not possess human speech and the ability to defend their interests in the same way that Hesiod can deploy poetry to challenge the behavior of corrupt rulers. More broadly, assuming some form of strong individualism further prevents us from developing a sense of interconnectedness and responsibility for the interests of various beings or entities that cannot assert something like self-possessed individuality in the agon of politics. If we find that a politics and understanding of rule based on ideas we inherit from the Greeks are problematic, partly because they cause problems that appear to be based on commitments to strong individualism and moral hierarchies between species, then we might find some help for rethinking them from the Vedic tradition. Contrasting Greek and Vedic conceptions of rule should press us to rethink the meaning of rule in a manner that better addresses contemporary environmental predicaments that extend across numerous boundaries.

Nonhuman beings and entities have interests that we must take into account by viewing ourselves as stewards and members of interwoven local and global panocracies. This remains an especially pressing task when these beings cannot speak, defend, or represent these interests in a verbal manner. Human beings must reflect more carefully on the ability they possess *as humans* to participate in the various dimensions of rule, especially on what this ability means for their relationship to and impact on the nonhuman world. Because this ability does have impact extending from the micro-level of the individual to the macro-level of national and international institutions, we need to think more carefully about how we can act as stewards for the needs and interests of those beings, entities, and phenomena that may not be able to speak, reason, and defend themselves in humanistic ways. This is an essential aspect of panocracy. Yet, unpacking and rethinking how we approach the various dimensions of rule also requires understanding how ruling constitutes part of a larger process of building the world.[12]

Following the connectedness of rule, we not only find ourselves embedded within a broader political cosmology but we continually alter, construct, and enact this cosmology. The connectedness of rule thus entails the capability to put new relations into motion and invokes the creative side of ruling. Because we can change how we are embedded in a broader human–nonhuman community, we are not resigned to human-centrism. Through daily practices and rituals, citizens can and oftentimes do alter their relations to the nonhuman world. Moreover, leveling many of the hierarchical dimensions of rule between both human and nonhuman beings—while appreciating the fact that we cannot eradicate all relations of ruling-over—could help develop panocracy by clarifying how rule is something all people exercise on a daily basis. Under this conception of citizen-rulership, one need not serve as an elected representative or be an influential media figure to feel politically empowered. If Homer and Hesiod teach us anything, however, it is that we must resist the associated problems that can stem from assuming fundamentally unequal moral stature and the resulting urge to distinguish ourselves from and over both human beings and nonhuman nature in pursuit of permanent hierarchical standing.

Briefly revisiting a few brahmanical ideas can help clarify a second point about ruling as a form of world-building. In possessing and exercising their ability to rule, people are bound to the process of building a world into which they will be born on a day-to-day basis and others will soon be born, which is an idea we observe in the Vedic *upanayana* ritual. However, contra the brahmanical belief that we can perfectly harmonize this process, we should see our rituals and sacrifices as assisting in—but never mastering—the creation of our shared world. We are just as much under its influence as the other way around. To borrow a Heideggerian locution, we are constantly in the throw of a world that we are always already in the process of helping to build. This idea of "*helping* build" is crucial because, as Steven Vogel points out: "The constructed world we live in isn't one we've constructed 'by ourselves' . . . we're never by ourselves, we're always active in a world *with other entities* that themselves are active. To build is to *co-build*: no building can happen without the cooperation of thousands or millions of non-human entities in the world" (2016, 156, emphasis mine; see also Vogel 2015). Relatedly, in brahmanical thought we also saw the idea that human beings participate in constructing their world and realities through multiple means, which include ritual, sacrificial, meditative, and reasoning practices.

Finally, through such means we assist in changing how the world operates and how we operate within it, but we do not and cannot fully control this process from the ground up. In this respect, the brahmanical conception of rule is deeply mistaken. This also means that we can never fully know or foresee all the ways in which we assist in creating the world, which is an idea that comes closer to how the Greeks conceive gods, goddesses, and the Fates as providing boundary conditions for human knowledge and mastery. Drawing on both Greek and Indian thought, an intercultural approach to the connectedness of rule is one that views human beings as bound to an open-ended process of world-building in which there is no ultimate blueprint for coming to know, and thus following, a soteriological path to deliver humans from death and the threat of natural degradation. Nevertheless, this view of open-ended world-building does not mean that humans are powerless because it leaves considerable space between a naïve belief in techno-scientific progress and the possibility of utter predictability or control on the one hand, and resigned fatalism on the other. Remaining thoughtful of the ways in which our rituals, roles, and willingness for personal and collective sacrifice impact the world around us, we can always alter our existing ruling practices and create new habits and institutions that are more attentive to the connectedness of rule.

A conception of rule predicated on stewardship, panocracy, and world-building is not intended to be exhaustive for all of the ways human beings can have duties to nonhuman nature. Nevertheless, paying closer attention to the various dimensions of rule is crucial for debates over human treatment of nonhuman nature because our predominant conceptions of rule in the West have served as roadblocks for reconceiving a more sound human–nonhuman political ethic. Moreover, we should not allow any single vocabulary to monopolize such conversations. We must not fall into the trap of believing that any particular vocabulary would necessarily possesses universal appeal and applicability, or that it could be equally legitimate or justifiable across all religious, cultural, or geographic boundaries. While my approach provides one way to locate potential points of engagement between different traditions, we should allow for a considerable degree of cross-cultural learning and theoretical hybridity. The environmental challenges facing human communities are so massive and complex that it is unreasonable to believe any single tradition or conceptual framework could supply a panacea. Here I agree with Melissa Lane that we must be willing to use our individual and collective imaginations to reconceive and provide inertia to act upon "new frameworks for judging harm and value," and rethinking the meaning of rule could help push us to "imagine a different relationship between the individual and the polity, and instantiate this in a new set of habitual responses and motivations in everyday life as well as in engaging with specific political institutions" (2012, 12, 15). Like Lane, my vision of rule is intended more to illustrate and stimulate rather than to provide strict prescriptions and policies, although I have tried to outline a few concrete connections to practices and institutions in this Conclusion.

Expressions of panocratic thought and practice may look different across time and space, involving a plurality of practices based on local conditions and varying historical (religious, political, social, and economic) backgrounds. Employing a historical-comparative approach to examine the meaning of rule in the earliest traditions of Greek and Indian thought, and then using this examination as a platform for increasing intercultural intelligibility and garnering new conceptual resources for theory building, the four-dimensional cosmology sketched here leaves significant room for a variety of theoretical approaches. In undertaking a comparative examination of two ancient traditions, I have sought to clarify how a cosmological approach to rule can open new space for cross-cultural dialogue and need not privilege any specific tradition. Scholars should remain skeptical of cultural or normative essentialism because various non-Western traditions may offer novel perspectives on pressing contemporary debates. One of the central aims of this book has been to identify traditions and vocabularies that can provide broader historical and cultural perspective, and thus leverage, for critical dialogue on issues of shared concern across national boundaries. I am sympathetic to the claim that a diversity of moral sources exist within a wide variety of traditions around the globe, and that we must engage them and reflect critically on which ideas and practices are worthy of our allegiance. This means that the theory and language of universal rights, for example, must also be an object of critical reflection and not automatically accepted as equally valid or plausible to the same extent or degree in all places and at all times. Liberal, democratic, or republican vocabularies and practices are not the only ones available for thinking more sensitively about the political dimensions and stakes of human–nonhuman relations.

An overarching lesson here is that we must view human livelihood and our capacity to rule in a more cosmological fashion, which then allows us to better appreciate and reflect on our duty as rulers to serve as stewards of the needs and interests of various nonhuman beings in deeply relational and contextual ways. This involves thinking more systematically about how we engage in ruling-over, ruling-with, ruling-for, and ruling-in a broader network of human beings, on the one hand, and nonhuman nature, on the other. In turn, we should look more closely at how our capacity to rule involves us in an ongoing, dynamic process of building the world around us on a daily basis. We are more than mere citizens with rights that need protection. We are fellow rulers whose decisions, activities, habits, and rituals demand recognition of stewardship and participation in processes of world-building. So the question is: What kind of world do we want to help build?

NOTES

PREFACE

1. While rule indicates a particular modality of power, for the purposes of this project I maintain a distinction between rule and power for the following reason. In the time period that I examine, the early Greek and Indian traditions focus specifically on the concept of rule and not "power" or "political power." Put another way, the theoretical vocabulary of power in contemporary scholarship is not a vocabulary that either tradition uses in conceiving the particular historical stakes or dilemmas surrounding rule. On a theoretical level, I do not wish to deny that power relations and differentials underpin many aspects of ruling relations, some of which are reflected in the particular dimensions of rule that I outline below. For example, Michel Foucault explains how power can be broadly understood as a force-field of unequal relations between bodies and that "power is everywhere; not because it embraces everything, but because it comes from everywhere" (1990, 92–93).
2. I thank an anonymous reviewer for helping me clarify and articulate these points.
3. While Arendt's idealization of action is inspired in important ways by Greek thought, Dean Hammer (2002b, 124–49) clarifies how Arendt was also strongly influenced by Roman political thought. I thank an anonymous reviewer for pointing out how scholars often idealize or overemphasize the Greek strain of her thought that I discuss in the Preface.
4. For example, see Sheldon Wolin's discussion of Plato, which is indebted to Arendt's reading of Platonic political philosophy and, as he explains, "the task of philosophy and of ruling was to rid the community of politics" (2004, 39).
5. This is not to say that Arendt's phenomenological accounts of action, distinction, and politics utterly fail, but merely to suggest that these phenomena may always rely upon, and thus be connected to, hierarchies in some significant way. This would then suggest that her horizontal vision of politics may not be thoroughly horizontal insofar as it relies on an underlying vertical or hierarchical set of relationships.
6. I thank an anonymous reviewer for helping me clarify this point.

7. See Aristotle's *Politics*, book 3, chapter 16 and books 4–7. It is worth noting, however, that the role of rational rules and durable constitutions develop predominantly after about 400 BCE. For example, see Rhodes (2015, 132–45) and Cohen (2015, 167–78).
8. Here Geuss unpacks Lenin's classic, albeit dense, formulation of politics as centered on a recurring question in political life, namely, "Who whom?"
9. In this and subsequent chapters I define "interest" as an advantage or benefit of something, especially the benefit something gains not only in continuing its existence in its current state but also in flourishing. What constitutes "flourishing," including questions of whether or not something might be damaging to other beings, must be considered on a case-by-case basis. This conception of interests need not assume subjectivity or human-like selfhood, which may hold for many sentient beings but remains too limited or narrow from a broader cosmological perspective. Because many entities and phenomena do not necessarily have a "self" akin to a human self, this does not mean that they do not possess varying degrees of agency and interests.
10. While Friskics (2001, 396) also uses the term "response-ability," he uses it primarily in an ethical and not in a political sense.
11. Here I do not want to suggest that the reverse is impossible—namely, that nonhuman beings and phenomena do not rule over human beings and aspects of human life in various ways. My intent is merely to focus on the human capacity to rule in order to clarify how our understanding of ruling relations, as human beings, can be improved upon.
12. My intent in applying the ability to rule in this second sense to nonhuman beings and forces, while metaphorical in some respects, is to heighten our awareness that we are not in complete, instrumental control of the world and that nonhuman nature retains some power, and perhaps even agency, over human life that remains politically relevant. Put another way, there is a way in which nonhuman nature rules insofar as it dictates to human beings some things that are possible or reasonable, and some that are not. From this vantage point, nonhuman nature assists in structuring and thus influencing our political choices and institutions.
13. I thank an anonymous reviewer for drawing my attention to this point.
14. Studies that appeal to Greek political thought frequently begin with or focus on Plato. For example, see Lane (2012), Ophuls (2011), and Plumwood (1993, ch. 3). While I also find Greek political thought a fruitful resource for addressing environmental concerns, my focus on Homer and Hesiod contrasts with existing approaches by suggesting that we examine pre-Classical thinkers to locate some of the more problematic beliefs inherited and developed by Classical figures.
15. Without passing judgment one way or another on the topic, I would also point out that Democritus's position on harm would place very stringent demands on human beings in terms of food or diet; that is, it would commit almost everyone to some form of vegetarianism or veganism.

INTRODUCTION

1. Notable exceptions to this trend in the history of political thought include: Ames (1983); Black (2001, 2009b); Crone (2004); El Amine (2015); Lewis (1988); Oakley (2006). While the categorical distinction between "Western" and "non-Western" traditions can be problematic for a variety of reasons, it is useful for the purposes of my project because it serves as a practical acknowledgment that major traditions of political thought in some regions of the world have been systematically neglected in the Anglo-European academic study of political theory, philosophy, and history of ideas. I fully acknowledge that this is a very broad distinction, as the category "non-Western" includes a tremendous diversity of traditions and voices.
2. Here I borrow the language outlined by Mark Bevir (1999) in his defense of a particular logic of the history of ideas. I will explain the relationship between my analytic position and Bevir's later in the Introduction.
3. For the importance of acknowledging shared questions across cultures in comparative political theory, see also Euben (1997, 32; 1999, 10) and Salkever and Nylan (1994).
4. See Richter (1990) for a helpful comparative exposition of alternative approaches to conceptual analysis. In his article he lays out German *Begriffsgeschichte* (history of concepts) as practiced in the lexicon *Geschichtliche Grundbegriffe* and the "Cambridge School" approaches of Quentin Skinner and J. G. A. Pocock. For a parallel defense of historical-comparative studies to the one I employ in this project, see also Jordan and Nederman (2012).
5. While the most precise levels of methodological individualism that Bevir defends are not applicable to the texts examined in this project, this does not mean that these texts cannot be treated historically or that one cannot examine historical meaning in them (see Bevir 1999, 54–55). As long as one can situate the individual viewpoints expressed in works on a reliable chronological spectrum and assign them to a specifiable group of individuals (e.g., the Homeric poet(s) and brahmanical composers of the Veda), even if that spectrum is based upon relative chronology, one can justifiably argue about historical meaning. Even though biographical knowledge of the specific authors of the works examined in this comparative study is lacking in some respects, one can confidently situate the relative chronology of the basic unit of analysis, namely, the expressed beliefs about rule.
6. "First, it can give us the sort of critical distance that supports reflective judgment within our own societies (knowing ourselves through knowing the other). Second, to the extent that it renders their thought intelligible to us in a form that is recognizably valid for them, the practice of comparative political theory contributes to the social conditions of possibility for the emergence of intercultural collective subjects of practical reason—that is, intercultural public" (Williams and Warren 2014, 36).
7. On the present generation's responsibility for helping build a better world, see also Vogel (2016, 149–58).

8. On resilience and vulnerability in particular, see Barry (2012).
9. See also Loubna el Amine (2016, 112), citing Taylor on the value of "'elaborating a common language' and 'common set of practices,'" which may provide a basis for engaging in meaningful cross-cultural normative judgments on issues of shared concern (Taylor 1984, 30).
10. For studies of early linguistic and mythological similarities in Greece and India, see also Baldick (1994); Doshi (1985); Puhvel (1970).
11. On various conceptions of poetry as recall, construction, weaving, and carpentry, see West (2007, 33–40).
12. On this relationship, see also Kantorowicz (1957).
13. Archaic Greek ruling should not be understood as firmly institutionalized, and it would be incorrect to assume a clearly delineated and institutionalized class system (Raaflaub 1997, 635). Archaic *basileus*-rule entailed a loose combination of leadership during wartime, speaking and distinguishing oneself in the assembly, and adjudicating disputes between citizens and households. Raaflaub argues that kings were not "monarchs," strictly speaking, but rather an "aristocracy-in-formation" (634). Seaford mentions how Homeric kingship, from a comparative anthropological perspective, should be considered a "low-level chiefdom" in which the "power of the political leader (*basileus*) was based not on centralized institutions, stratification, or a formal apparatus of repression, but on wealth, prestige, military prowess, an informal authority over the other like-named chiefs (*basileis*), and on his ability to act as redistributor" (1994, 22; see also Donlan 1997, 39). This type of kingship, or chiefdom, stands in opposition to "more complex, centralized redistributive [and] political integrated societies such as the Mycenaean 'palace' economy" (Seaford 1994, 22).
14. However, contra those such as Drews, I focus on the concept and meaning of ruling and not the nuanced historical characteristics of figures designated as *basileis*. That is, I am not primarily interested in the particular historical conditions under which a *basileus* should alternatively be called a leader, head, chief, noble, or king. Regardless of the word chosen to translate the Greek term, a *basileus* is a ruler.
15. As Raaflaub points out, there could be many *basileis* in a given community, and of various types (1997, 634).
16. As Drews (1983, 104) has pointed out, the term *basileus* is not applied to deities in the *Iliad* and *Odyssey*, including Zeus. Nevertheless, Zeus is called an *anax*. This contrasts with the Vedic case, wherein gods were the first beings given the distinct epithets for rulers and kings.

CHAPTER 1

1. Greek citations will refer to the following: *Iliad* (ed. Monro and Allen, 1920); *Odyssey* (ed. Allen, 1917); *Theogony* (ed. West, 1966); *Works and Days* (West, 1978). Translations are my own unless otherwise noted. For useful overviews and

commentaries on the "Homeric question," as well as the composition of the epics within historical context, see Foley (1997); Nagy (2010); Turner (1997); West (2011). For an excellent overview of scholarship on Homer and political thought, see also Hammer (2009). Because my textual analytic approach focuses on historical meaning as expressed beliefs and not on identifying particular authors or audiences, the Homeric question and debates about whether the texts are either formulaic and lack poetic originality, or are the sophisticated aesthetic expression of a single author, are not directly pertinent to my approach and argument in this chapter. In terms of dating the material of Homeric texts, I agree with John Wallach in "understand[ing] the Homeric poems as epic poetry written down in the eighth century BC that seamlessly combine accounts of contemporaneous Greek life with those of a sometimes mythical, Mycenaean past that preceded it by at least four hundred years" (2011, 185).

2. For an example of such an alternative approach to Homeric political thought, see Seaford (1994, 2004, 2012).
3. This is not to say, however, that some sort of communal good is never a consideration for *basileis* (see Hammer 2005, 116; e.g., see *Il.* 1.117; *Od.* 3.126–29).
4. Hence, one constantly hears about objects, figures, or events described in the following ways: marvelous, shining, splendid, blazing, or gleaming (*dios, aglaos, glaukē, lampros, phaidimos*); fearful or cowardly (*deilos, kakos*); beautiful or lovely (*kalos*); dreadful, frightful, terrible, or harsh (*ainos, deinos, stugeros, chalepos*); quick or swift (*thoos, tachus*); mighty or stout (*iphthimos, karteros, megas*).
5. On the relationship between *kleos* and poetic recall, see Nagy (2013, 48–73).
6. For a similar interpretation, see Halliwell (1990, 38–39), contra Adkins (1970, 26–27) and Dodds (1951, 16).
7. On the nature and meaning of *thumos*, see also Onians (1951, 50) and Bolton (1973, 9).
8. On the nature and meaning of *psuchē*, see also Onians (1951, 94).
9. Contra later thinkers such as Plato, however, Homer does not outline any consistent or necessary normative-hierarchical structure between the various parts of one's self-possessed individuality. Sometimes the *thumos* rules, but at other times the *noos* plays a more decisive and justifiable role in one's actions.
10. Competition and contestation arise in varying ways between gods and humans in the *Iliad* and *Odyssey*. These varieties can be generally categorized as: god vs. god (e.g., *Il.*, book 20), human being vs. human being (e.g., *Il.*, book 23), and god vs. human being (e.g., Diomedes versus Aphrodite and Ares in *Il.*, book 5).
11. In book 9 Nestor states: "Most glorious son of Atreus, lord of men Agamemnon . . . with you I will end, with you I will begin, because you are the lord [*anax*] of many troops, and Zeus has placed in your hands both the scepter and protection of rightful customs [*themis*], so you will advise them" (9.96–99). See also *Il.* 2.46 and *Odyssey* (*Od.*) 4.691 for a reference to divine appointment.
12. See also *Il.* 9.160–61: "how much more of a king [*basileuteros*] I am."

13. See also Haubold (2000, 83–95) on the dependent relationship between Hector and the city.
14. An example of this favor-seeking in the *Odyssey* arises when Helios (sun god) appeals to Zeus after Odysseus's men ate Helios's beloved cattle (*Od.* 12.366–76). Athena also addresses Zeus as "our father, highest of rulers" in the *Odyssey* (e.g., 1.45 and 1.81).
15. "Then the Earth-shaker Poseidon replied to him: 'At once I would have done, O god of the dark cloud, as you publicly state [i.e., and avenge himself however he sees fit]; but always I regard your *thumos* with awe and dread, and shrink away'" (*Od.* 13.146–48 [125–58]).
16. In fact, Odysseus views Zeus as his "controller" throughout his travels in the *Odyssey* (14. 235–310).
17. Nestor explains how a cosmic hierarchy exists and that human beings need the gods, including Zeus's kingly rule (*Od.* 3.48 [36–61]).
18. In this passage Zeus is the "spinner" of fates (verb: *epi-klōthō*). Perhaps because he decides or dictates human beings' fates he also *knows* everything (see *Od.* 20.75–76).
19. According to the Homeric concordances (Marzullo 1962, 1971), *dikē* only appears five times in the *Iliad* (see also Lloyd-Jones [1983, 186], who counts seven) and fifteen times in the *Odyssey*. While this term and the attendant conception of justice are not completely absent in Homeric works, I disagree with both Balot (2006) and Lloyd-Jones (1983) that justice is of central importance in Homeric political thought.
20. For arguments that Thersites is a "proto-democratic" figure, see Balot (2001, 66–67); Ferguson (1975, 11); Stuurman (2004, 181).
21. Contra arguments that Telemachus was the rightful hereditary successor to Odysseus, see Finkelberg (2005, 70–71). She argues that dynastic succession was most likely transmitted through the female line, which would give the power of choosing the next king to Penelope and exclude Telemachus for incestuous reasons (70). This argument, while persuasive in some respects, does not completely mitigate the ruling tensions introduced when suitors are acting arrogantly toward Telemachus as a prince and son of Odysseus. Since Telemachus seems to share ownership of the household and its wealth, I side with Finley's (1979) assessment that matriarchy may not provide an ultimately coherent solution to this succession issue.
22. Because omens indicate the gods' will and inform the suitors that Odysseus is returning, the omens can be seen as a divine support system for Odysseus's rule. The suitors' challenges display a blatant disregard for these divine messages, and as a result they pay a gruesome price (see *Od.*, book 22).
23. For an excellent overview of gender and the Homeric epics, including Penelope's political role in the *Odyssey*, see Felson and Slatkin (2004).
24. Elmer's argument highlights the instrumental role and value of consensus but not necessarily the more personal, long-term goals and interests that explain why agents aim or arrive at consensus, such as individual distinction.

25. See also *Il.* 6.486–89, when Hector tells his beloved wife Andromache: "Assuredly, do not grieve for me at all in your heart; for no man will send me forth to Hades against my fate. No man, I say, can flee Fate [Moira], neither the coward nor the brave man, when he is first born."
26. See also *Il.* 5.888–90, 15.14–33, 119–41, where other gods fear Zeus's rage.
27. In *Il.* 8.438–83, both Hera and Athena compete with Zeus for decision-making power during the war.
28. See also *Il.* 23.373–883, where the gods compete in the funeral games for Patroclus.
29. "These two mighty sons of Kronos, divided in their considerations, wrought miserable pains for mortal heroes. On the one hand, Zeus was willing victory for the Trojans and Hector . . . while Poseidon secretly emerged from the gray sea and roused the Argives" (*Il.* 13.345–47, 351–52).
30. If Zeus really was a just ruler then Odysseus's suffering would be just and Poseidon's behavior fully justified, since Zeus is presumably responsible for everything as the supreme ruler. The presumption that Zeus is responsible can be seen in Athena's question: "Now why do you hate him [i.e., Odysseus] so much?" (*Od.* 1.62). Segal (1994) claims that Zeus "at once imposes a moral structure on the tale: he recognizes Odysseus' piety and gives assurance of his safe return (1.63–7)" (225). Here the question could be asked: Why now? Surely Zeus was aware of Odysseus's suffering, since he sees and knows everything, so why does he decide to step in and help at this particular moment? Contra Segal, I do not believe this move is about establishing any "moral structure" or justice. Rather, Zeus's move is better interpreted as a strategic attempt to gain the favor of the other gods and establish supremacy over his brother.
31. On the role of cosmology in early Greek political thought from Homer to Aeschylus, see Seaford (2012).
32. For example, Agamemnon refuses to accept bribes or gifts on the battlefield when his victims offer them in book 11 (*Il.* 11.126–42).
33. See also *Il.* 1.148–271, 188–205, 223–44, 292–303, 488–89, and 22.345–48.
34. It is interesting to note that Polyphemus is in fact "unruly" insofar as he is neither ruled over by any of his fellow Cyclops nor, he claims, by Zeus (*Od.* 9.272–80).
35. Hector responds to this concern by stating: "And truly all these things are a concern for me, woman; but I would feel intense shame before the Trojan men and the long-robed Trojan women if ever I sought to escape from battle like a coward; and my *thumos* does not urge me to do so, since I have learned to be brave, always, and to fight among the first ranks of the Trojans, earning great glory (*kleos*) for both my father and myself" (*Il.* 6.441–46).
36. Throughout the *Iliad*, Hector fights for honor and glory in competitive struggles with various heroes and the mass. See also *Il.* 6.354–58, 8.175–76/489–91, 10.104–5, 15.64–67, 16.844–45, 17.566, and 22.342–43.
37. For an alternative approach to the political significance of hospitality, see Seaford (1994).

38. Other words that can be used to gloss *timē*, depending on context, are esteem, dignity, and worship. Liddell and Scott (1945) explain *timē* as "that which is paid in token of worth or value."
39. My support for this claim is Menelaus's own statement about how he remembered and cherished the good hospitality he was shown. I do not believe there is a good reason to suspect that Telemachus and Pisistratus will not remember and cherish good hospitality in the same manner, or that *basileis* in general would not remember the exceptional hospitality shown by past hosts. This is one reason I believe this point can extend to most kings in the *Odyssey*, including Odysseus.
40. I thank an anonymous reviewer for drawing my attention to this point.

CHAPTER 2

1. A comprehensive introduction and analysis of Hesiodic poetry is outside the scope of this project, but interested readers should consult the following: Hamilton (1989); Thalmann (1984); Walcot (1966); West (1966).
2. To contemporary readers any inherent connection between the nonhuman and femininity is clearly problematic. However, it should also be noted that numerous masculine, nonhuman forces also appear in Hesiod's *Theogony*, so the gender connection runs both ways.
3. This association of justice with distributing what is most fitting or appropriate should remind the reader of Plato's account of justice in the *Republic*. In this and other respects, Hesiod helps lay some of the conceptual groundwork for Plato's political thought.
4. Bartlett astutely highlights how Hesiod differs from Homer when Hesiod contends that the heroes and demigods were just and interested in the well-being of their communities, which is precisely the normative account of rule that Hesiod pushes in his works. However, I believe the evidence for the defectiveness of Zeus's rule is a bit overstated. One might contend that these celebrated characters of the fourth race live apart from Zeus's rule simply because they can—that is, because they are just and so do not require Zeus's enforcement of justice as the currently corrupt race of human beings does.
5. While Kronos could presumably have the same defense, it would not have a just stabilizing effect because Hesiod calls Kronos, in contrast to Zeus, a "crooked" ruler.
6. One could claim that Hesiod is indirectly referring to his brother and how the *basileis*, being complicit in Perses's deeds, are responsible for the resulting "famine" and "pestilence" (*WD* 242–43).
7. One might ask how this interpretation squares with Hesiod's claim that human beings once lived like gods (*WD* 112) and came into being from the same source (*WD* 106–8). I would contend that these passages primarily explain how the living conditions for human beings have changed due to various events and Prometheus's deceptive actions. In addition, the ontological distinction concerning immortality

versus mortality does not negate the more basic distinction concerning self-possessed individuality, which continues to characterize the contours of both gods' and human beings' individuality. In fact, the term *homothen* suggests something like this: namely, that gods and men "started on the same terms." See West's "Commentary" (1978) and Verdenius (1985, vv. 1–382).

8. I owe this observation to an anonymous reviewer.
9. See also Bryant (1996, 19); Donlan (1980, 28–30); Raaflaub (2004, 36); Robinson (1997, 69). On the historical significance of Hesiod's comments regarding justice for early Greek political thought, see Havelock (1978, ch. 11); Martin (1984, 29–48); Voegelin (1957, 126–64).
10. I provide a rather general definition because in Homer *dikē* is not consistently laid out as an independent principle or concept with a single, clear definition. Havelock (1978) provides a more detailed definition of justice in the *Iliad* as: "a procedure . . . arrived at by a process of negotiation between contending parties carried out rhetorically" (137), or more generally across both epics, "contextual . . . rule[s] of propriety" (181).
11. See also Balot (2006, 20–21), who points out that Hesiod understands justice as a "distinctive marker of humanity." Hesiod (*WD* 276–85) explains that justice exists for human beings but not for animals, and this belief will display an important difference between Greek and brahmanical ruling ideas.
12. Gagarin (1986, 47–50) argues that this is an early form of procedural justice.
13. Here I disagree slightly with Bartlett, who argues that this allegory is intended specifically to address the "conflict between political power and the wisdom specific to poetry . . . a conflict between king and poet" (2006, 192). I believe Hesiod employs this allegory, in part, to teach *basileis* that they have the power, and hence responsibility, to protect the community's well-being. The allegory thus serves a dual function. First, as Bartlett (2006, 192) points out, it applies to the conflict between king, poet, and the corresponding "status of justice" as it pertains to the singer's knowledge of the truth. Second, it aims to teach *basileis* a more general lesson regarding their responsibility for the community's well-being, since they are superior (*areiōn, WD* 207) members of society. I advance this interpretation by focusing on the issue of strength and a corresponding responsibility to make straight judgments, whereas Bartlett focuses on the issue of the nightingale being a singer and representing Hesiod's own claims to truth-telling.
14. In book 1 of the *Iliad*, the seer Calchas explains why Apollo is angry and what the Achaeans must do to propitiate the god. While Agamemnon becomes offended and understands this reading as a personal challenge, it is important to note that Calchas is not directly and personally critiquing Agamemnon. Rather, Calchas is simply serving as a divine intermediary. Therefore, this Homeric scenario is different than the one found in Hesiod's *Works and Days* where Hesiod serves both as intermediary and personal critic.

15. Some ambiguity exists as to whether "crooked" (*skolion*) refers to specific judgments of reckless or arrogant (*atasthalos*) kings, or whether Hesiod is simply referring to the general concept or condition of crookedness. Because Hesiod generally refers to arrogant *basileis* as the source of crooked judgments, I believe the reference here is to *basileis* and their judgments. Contextual support for this interpretation can also be found in Raaflaub and Wallace (2007, 33) and Morris (1996, 28–29).
16. Again, this scene differs from what takes place in a similar Homeric scenario, for example, when Chryses appeals to Apollo to punish Agamemnon in book 1 of the *Iliad*. In this passage, Chryses does not appeal to a king—Zeus—but rather to his personal god whom he believes will avenge the wrongs Chryses suffered at Agamemnon's hands. In addition, Chryses's issue is personal and not communal or political in nature. Chryses does not critique Agamemnon based on a notion of justice and communal well-being under any assumption that a *basileus* is responsible for preserving such things.
17. On the innovative connection between a critical, individualist mode of inspiration and knowledge of the truth, see also Bartlett (2006, 196).
18. For example, in Plato's *Apology*, Socrates partly defends himself through appeals to the god/oracle of Delphi and his *daimonion* (divine power). Alternatively, in the *Euthyphro*, Plato references an external standard for piety and justice that is separate from the will of a god.
19. This is not to say, however, that Hesiod does not understand the seasons to have their "attendant pleasures" (Bartlett 2006, 202; see *WD* 493–95, 585).

CHAPTER 3

1. This layering is largely consistent with the more specific stratigraphy of early Vedic literature offered by Witzel (1997a, 1997b). For particular geographic and historical information about various layers of Vedic texts, see also the aforementioned works of Witzel.
2. For existing analyses of political thought and institutions in the Saṃhitās and Brāhmaṇas that are organized chronologically as opposed to topically, see Bandyopadhyaya (1980, 25–97); Ghoshal (1966, 19–35); Jayaswal (1967, 183–213); Prasad (1968, 11–19); J. P. Sharma (1968); Sinha (1938, 1–76).
3. Drekmeier's (1962) study extends to the early Hindu period, Ghoshal's (1966) study extends to the Medieval Hindu period (ca. 1200 CE), and Bandyopadhyaya's (1980) study extends all the way to the Muslim period (see also Prasad 1968; Sinha 1938).
4. See also Bhandarkar ([1925] 1988); Law ([1921] 1960); Mabbett (1972); Scharfe (1989); R. S. Sharma (1968); G. P. Singh (1993); Spellman (1964); Varma (1974).
5. For example, see Altekar (1958); Bandyopadhyaya (1980); Ghoshal (1966); Jayaswal (1967); Law ([1921] 1960); Mabbett (1972); Prasad (1968); Saletore (1963); R. S. Sharma (1968); Sinha (1938); Spellman (1964); Varma (1974).

6. See Drekmeier (1962), who focuses on kingship, authority, and community from the Vedic period to the first few centuries of the common era.
7. See Boesche (2002), who focuses specifically on Kauṭilya's *Arthaśāstra*.
8. For example, see Bhandarkar ([1925] 1988) on Kauṭilya and the concept of state; Gonda (1966) on kingship from a religious point of view, and Dumont (1970, 62–88) on kingship in ancient India; Scharfe (1989) on the state in general; and Singh (1993) on the saptāṅga ("seven-limb") theory of the state. See also Sinha's (1938) examination of sovereignty, which surveys many texts and genres stretching from the early Vedic period to the fifth century CE.
9. One reason may be that many of these studies are published collections of lectures, synopses of lectures, or were intended as general textbook-style introductions aiming to familiarize students with the broad contours of ancient Indian (usually Hindu) political thought. For example, Bandyopadhyaya's (1980) and Bhandarkar's ([1925] 1988) studies were originally a series of lectures. This critique is not meant to detract from the tremendous scope and learning required to undertake such surveys. I have learned much from these studies and appreciate the time and skill required to collect so much information and examine it in an organized manner. Rather, I raise this issue to explain why the thesis I defend regarding the meaning of kingly rule in the Saṃhitās and Brāhmaṇas does not frequently confront clearly delineated positions in the existing scholarship.
10. For example, Law states: "It appears that the council of the Vedic period was more or less of a democratic character" ([1921] 1960, 37). For arguments that deliberative ruling assemblies and some form of "public debate" existed, see Altekar (1958, 116, 143–44); Bandyopadhyaya (1980, 60–64); Jayaswal (1967, 12–20); Law ([1921] 1960, 10–11, 37); Prasad (1968, 17); R. S. Sharma (1968, 99, 105–106); Singh (1993, 44); Sinha (1938, v); Spellman (1964, 93–94); Varma (1974, 19–20). Contra, see Mabbett (1972, 22–23) and Varma (1974, 21).
11. For arguments that kings were elected or that there was an element of popular choice and control in early assemblies, at least on occasion, see Altekar (1958, 80–81, 116–17); Bandyopadhyaya (1980, 48–51); Drekmeier (1962, 19–20, 22); Jayaswal (1967, 12, 186–87, 211); Law ([1921] 1960, 10–11); Prasad (1968, 17); R. S. Sharma (1968, 104); Singh (1993, 43–44); Sinha (1938, v); Spellman (1964, 51); Varma (1974, 11, 19–20). For statements questioning or qualifying these claims, see Drekmeier (1962, 24; 83); Mabbett (1972, 23–24); Scharfe (1989, 58); Spellman (1964, 19); Varma (1974, 21).
12. For arguments that the king's power was independent and sometimes superior to the brahmin's, see Altekar (1958, 54), Drekmeier (1962, 32), and Jayaswal (1967, 210). For arguments that his power was more or less independent, but not necessarily superior, see Drekmeier (1962, 32), Ghoshal (1966, 34–35), and Varma (1974, 48–49). For arguments that the two groups and their powers were fundamentally connected and interdependent—for example, that the brahmin's authority was superior and subsumed the *kṣatriya*'s, or that the *kṣatriya*'s power depended upon

or derived from the brahmin's: Drekmeier (1962, 33); Dumont (1970, 64–65); Gonda (1966, 40–41, 62–66, 74–75); Prasad (1968, 13–14); Scharfe (1989, 113–14); Spellman (1964, 72–79).

13. *Śruti* refers to the traditional brahmanical understanding that these texts were directly discerned—both "seen" and "heard"—by *ṛṣis* (inspired sages or seers) at the beginning of each cycle of creation. The term *mantra* will refer to the verse portions of the Saṃhitās. In this and the following chapter, I focus solely on early and middle Vedic works, the Saṃhitās and Brāhmaṇas.
14. The term *deva*, or god, can also be translated as "luminescent one." This latter translation helps evoke the sense of the underlying verb root (*div*, to shine or be brilliant). For discussion of the role of light in early Vedic metaphysics, see Mahony (1998, 17–25).
15. On the historical significance of this point, see Witzel (2003, 70).
16. For a more recent explication of this tripartite social organization, see Dumézil (1988).
17. Nonetheless, it is important to clarify that Dumont is concerned first and foremost with *jāti*s, or castes, and not with the idealized *varṇa*s. While *varṇa* is a Vedic category, the *jāti* system is post-Vedic.
18. However, this is a debatable point in the literature, and I will spend more time discussing it in the next chapter.
19. While it is more frequently used in later texts, in this early layer the term *kṣatriya* only occurs seven times: ṚV 4.12.3, 4.42.1, 5.69.1, 7.64.2, 7.104.13, 8.25.8, 8.67.1. However, the term is not used for human kings in this early layer as it is so used in later layers.
20. All Sanskrit translations are my own unless otherwise noted.
21. For example, see ṚV 5.73.4, 7.67.9, 7.72.2, and 8.73.12.
22. Early references to *ṛta* in the Ṛg-Veda include: 3.4.7, 3.7.8, 4.1.13, 4.2.14, 5.12.2, 7.21.5, 7.23.4, 8.25.4, and 8.27.19. See also Mahony (1998, 48).
23. These four orders are the natural order (*adhibhūta*), divine order (*adhidaiva*), human order (*adhyātma*), and sacrificial order (*adhiyajña*). Holdrege explains how these four orders constitute an important aspect of Vedic metaphysics.
24. The term *dharman*, as a neuter noun, is derived from the verb root *dhṛ*, meaning "to uphold, sustain, or support." In the early sacrificial ritual context, *dharman* literally means, "that which supports or sustains," referring to the power of sacrificial ritual and its ability to sustain *ṛta* and the existing cosmic order.
25. For example, see Ṛg-Veda 5.15.2, 5.51.2, 5.63.1, 5.63.7, 9.7.1, and 9.110.4.
26. The term *varṇa* literally means "color," and originally refers to the distinction between the *dāsa* or *dāsyu* (foreign foes, or enemies of the Āryans) and the Ārya *varṇa* (members of the original three "upper classes" mentioned in the Ṛg-Veda: Brāhmaṇ, Kṣatriya or Rājanya, and Vaiśya) (see Ṛg-Veda 1.104.2, 2.12.4, and 3.34.9). Some scholars speculate that the *dāsa* color (*varṇa*) originally alluded to

the black or darker skin of the native population encountered by the Āryan invaders (Macdonell and Keith 1967, 1:356).

27. Enemies such as the Dānavas engage in a continual cosmic battle with the *devas*. The Dānavas embody darkness, death, disorder, and untruth, while the *devas* embody light, life, order, and truth. According to brahmanical thought, without *soma* the *devas* such as Indra, Mitra, and Varuṇa would not possess the necessary strength to defeat the Dānavas. Here *yajña* is conceived as providing a fundamental connection between human beings and divinities, with each group of beings depending on the other for its well-being.
28. These cosmogonic hymns include ṚV 10.81, 10.82, 10.90, 10.121, 10.129, and 10.130.
29. The creative principles include: (1) the un-manifest Absolute (Tad Ekam, That One, or Aja, Unborn); (2) the personal creator god (e.g., Prajāpati and Viśvakarman); (3) the waters (*ap, ambhas*, or *salila*), which are sometimes associated with Vāc, the goddess of speech; (4) the cosmic embryo or egg (*garbha*); (5) Puruṣa, the cosmic Man. The creative means include: (1) desire; (2) *tapas* (meditative heat); (3) procreation; (4) sacrifice (*yajña*); (5) speech (*vāc*) (see Holdrege 1996, 35).
30. For statements regarding the destructive aspects of and fear surrounding *nirṛti*, see Ṛg-Veda 1.38.6, 5.41.17, 7.37.7, 7.104.9, 10.10.11, 10.36.2; Yajur-Veda 12.65; Atharva-Veda 2.10.5, 3.6.5, 4.36.10, 6.63.1, 6.84.1, 7.73.1; Śatapatha Brāhmaṇa 7.2.1.1–20, 9.1.2.9, 10.4.3.22–23.
31. Smith's reading pertains mostly to elements that I would place in the second, manifest tier. My interpretation of Vedic reality on this tier will be slightly more comprehensive than the one Smith offers, as my reading does not revolve predominantly around the role of ritual.
32. Only males were capable of being "born again," and this is why much of my discussion about ontology—especially when referring to rituals such as the *upanayana*—centers on the masculine gender. Smith (1989, 92–93) further explains that while the Ṛg-Veda does not specifically mention the *upanayana*, it appears to be a fixed ritual in the Atharva-Veda Saṃhitā (11.5) and Śatapatha Brāhmaṇa (11.3.3, 11.5.4). One must also note that the term *dvija* does not refer generically to members of the three higher *varṇa*s until the mid- to late-Vedic period in the *dharmasūtra*s (Lubin 2013, 18).
33. *Upanayana* is a nominal derivation from the verb root *nī* and prefix *upa*, which together literally mean "carrying or leading toward."
34. The term *samiti* is a noun derived from the root *i* (to go) and prefix *sam* (together). Hence, the term literally means a place or occasion of coming together.
35. For agreement on this general point, see Spellman (1964, 93) and Varma (1974, 11). For examples of scholars who have not made this observation and tend to analyze the texts as if they described actual historical circumstances, see Altekar (1958, 139–41), Jayaswal (1967, 12–20), and Prasad (1968, 17).

CHAPTER 4

1. Examples of references to these various *devas* as *rājans*, or some term for ruler (e.g., *samrāj*), in Ṛg-Veda Saṃhitā 1, include (Indra) 3.46.2, 3.53.11, 4.17.5, 6.22.9, 8.15.3, 8.37.3; (Varuṇa) 2.27.1, 2.28.9–11, 4.42, 7.34.11, 7.87.5; (Mitra) 2.27.1, 3.59.4; (Agni) 3.1.18, 6.7.1, 7.6.1; (Soma) 9.7.5, 9.96.10.
2. ṚV 2.28.5/10, 4.42.1, 5.62–72, 6.51.3, 6.67, 7.64.1–2, 8.25.
3. See ṚV 2.11.9–10, 3.32.6, 3.43.8, 4.16.7, 5.31.4, 6.17.2–3/9, 6.36.1–2, 7.19.5, 8.1.7. Adjectives used to describe Indra's warrior characteristics include *nṛtama* (strong), *śākina* (mighty), and *ugra* (mighty, fierce, terrible). Another important term generally associated with divine *rājans* is *śrī*, which can denote beauty, radiance, or the goddess Śrī. As Scharfe points out, scholars have interpreted *śrī* as meaning various things, including beauty, prosperity, and well-being (1989, 36).
4. These enemies are usually *dāsas*, *dāsyus*, or in later texts, *asuras* (celestial demons). Specific enemies such as Vṛtra threaten and constrain something vital for human life. An exception to this general tendency in the Greek case would be Zeus's coordinated leadership of the other gods when they defeat the Titans, as portrayed in Hesiod's *Theogony*.
5. See also ṚV 5.73.4, 7.67.9, 8.73.12, 9.97.17.
6. See ṚV 3.38.5 (Indra), 4.17.1 (Indra), 4.21.1 (Indra), 5.27.6 (Agni, Indra), and 5.34.9 (Indra).
7. ṚV 2.28.4, 2.30.1, 3.4.7, 3.7.8, 3.54.3, 5.63.1, 8.60.5.
8. For an example of analysis that makes claims about actual historical events and developments, see Bandyopadhyaya (1980, 1–97).
9. For example, see ṚV 7.7.4, where the term refers to the master of a house. See also ṚV 7.55.5, 8.23.13, 8.25.16, and 9.108.10.
10. On the meaning of the term *kratu*, see Gonda (1963, 111).
11. See ṚV 1.24.7/12/14 (Varuṇa), 1.63.7 (Indra), 1.91.4 (Soma), and 1.122.11 (Viśvadevas).
12. According to *A Grammatical Word-Index to the Four Vedas* (Shastri 1960–63) the term *rājanya* appears a total of fourteen times in the following texts: Atharva-Veda 5.17.9, 5.18.1/2/3, 6.38.4, 10.10.18, 12.4.32/33, 15.8.1, 19.6.6; Ṛg-Veda 10.90.12; Yajur-Veda 22.22, 30.5, 39.11. In fact, I do not find a term employing the verb root or nominal stem *rāj-* that is consistently applied to human rulers prior to Ṛg-Veda Saṃhitā 2. For example, the terms *rāj*, king or chief (ṚV 5.46.8, 6.12.1), and *saṃrāj*, king of all (e.g., ṚV 3.54.10, 6.7.1, 7.6.1, 8.27.22), predominantly refer to divine kings. The term *pati* (lord) and nominal compounds including the term *pati* designate human lords, leaders or "kings" in the earlier layer, for example, *nṛ-pati* (lord of men; e.g., ṚV 4.38.2) and *go-pati* (lord of cattle; e.g., ṚV 6.28.3).
13. Interestingly, a passage in the Śatapatha Brāhmaṇa (13.4.2.17) retains the term *rājan* for a human king and distinguishes it from *rājanya*. This passage is found in

the context of the horse sacrifice, or *aśvamedha*, where only the sacrificial patron—presumably a *rājanya*—who completes the sacrifice can earn the title *rājan*.

14. The Brāhmaṇas also explain how divine kings such as Varuṇa (KB 7.10, 12.8; ŚB 4.1.4.1) and Indra (KB 12.8; TB 3.9.16.3; ŚB 2.5.2/7) are identified with *kṣatra*, just as the earthly king is so identified (AB 8.6; ŚB 5.1.5.3; 13.1.5.3). A member of the ruling class is also connected to and equated with *ojas* (might, force, power) and *vīrya* (virility, manly strength) (AB 8.2).
15. This contrasts with the brahmin's divine correspondence within the tripartite cosmology. Brahmins are associated with Agni, a deity connected to priestly functions and sacrificial ritual.
16. The closest connection, I argued, was the ontological similarity between human beings and gods concerning self-possessed individuality. However, this similarity has the effect of disconnecting rather than connecting gods and humans, and not only from each other but also from nonhuman beings that do not share this bond.
17. For Indra, see TB 1.5.9.1, 2.2.7.2 and 3.1.3; for Varuṇa, see JB 3.152.
18. However, as Smith (1994, 30, 51) notes, *kṣatriya* rulers and warriors are also characterized by other essential attributes, including: *bala* (physical strength), *vīrya* (virility), *vayas* (youthful vigor), *ojas* (power, force, or might), *sahas* (force, might), and *indriya* (command of the body).
19. The *kṣatriya*'s likeness to a Nyagrodha tree is interesting because the word can be parsed in the following way: *ni-* is a prefix meaning "down, into, or in," while—*añc* is a locational suffix meaning "-ward." Combined, they mean "downward." The verb root *ruh* or *rudh* meaning "climb, reach to, or grow." Therefore, the Nyagrodha—and by cosmological and metaphysical association, the *kṣatriya*—is something that stretches outward into its source of nourishment, becoming firmly rooted in this source. Here we observe a theme I will discuss in more detail below: that of a king being rooted in the *viś* (his people, or subjects) and depending upon them for nourishment in the same way a tree is rooted in and depends upon the soil.
20. For example, a passage in the Śatapatha Brāhmaṇa (10.4.2.2–3, Smith 1989, 60, trans. slightly modified) states: "Having emitted all the beings, Prajāpati felt empty, and being afraid of death he thought to himself: 'How might I insert all these beings into my self (*ātman*) again, how might I place them in my self again? How might I again be the self of all these beings?'"
21. The *upanayana* appears to be a fixed ritual by the time of the Atharva-Veda Saṃhitā and Śatapatha Brāhmaṇa (Smith 1989, 93). For example, see AV 11.5; ŚB 11.3.3, 11.5.4.
22. For details about the ritual, see ŚB 5.2.3 and PB 18.8–11.
23. See TS 7.5.18.1 and TB 3.8.13.1. See also AB 7.19; VS 22.22; ŚB 13.1.9.1–2; MS 3.12.6. In these passages the various combinations of weapons and attributes are listed.
24. For a study of agonistic elements in Vedic thought, especially as they concern the topic of masculinity, see Whitaker (2011).

25. Smith explains how the brahmin is conceived as "first among humans in both a temporal and hierarchical sense and are thus the 'lord of the classes'" (1994, 32). He cites a passage from the Śatapatha Brāhmaṇa (8.4.1.3) where *brahman* is regarded as a deity and declared to be the "highest among the gods" (1994, 53). The brahmin's superior and encompassing role can also be seen in the following areas: the *brahman* power and brahmin social group are regarded as the mouth or head (*mukha*) of everything (ŚB 3.9.1.14); *brahman* as chief among the powers (AV 19.22.21); *brahman* as the "first born" (VS 13.13; ŚB 7.4.1.14, 14.1.3.3); the *brahman* power creates everything else (TB 2.8.8.9–10); the *brahman* power is most excellent (ŚB 10.3.5.10–11); the brahmin literally is everything and encompasses everything, including the other social groups (JB 1.86; ŚB 11.5.3.12, 13.6.2.19) (Smith 1994, 32, 53).
26. Interestingly, Smith (1994, 31, 53) also points out that the *śūdra* is associated with *anṛta* (disorder, untruth) (ŚB 14.1.1.31).
27. Even the term "public" can be deceptive here, because it can imply that these assemblies were essentially secular places or that purely secular activities took place in them. Importantly, none of the hymns that include these terms exclude theological and cosmological claims. Expressed beliefs contradict a purely secular reading of the *sabhā* and *samiti*. For example, brahmanical thought consistently invokes these two assemblies as the two daughters of Prajāpati, giving them a distinct theological and cosmological meaning.
28. He further explains how the *sabhā* does not always refer to a communal space, occasionally meaning "house" or "parlor" (1898, 18).
29. These passages relating to Agni are ṚV 3.1.18 and 3.27.7.
30. J. P. Sharma and H. W. Bailey (1965) have also argued against the *vidatha* being interpreted as a political institution.
31. Most scholars' analyses of these assemblies extend from the Ṛg-Veda to the Atharva-Veda. A list of these scholars would be quite long, but examples include: Altekar (1958, 140–44); Bandyopadhyaya (1980, 58–65); Drekmeier (1962, 19–20, 24); Gonda (1966, 8, 49, 53); Prasad (1968, 17); G. P. Singh (1993, 43–45); Spellman (1964, 92–97); Varma (1974, 17–22).
32. Jayaswal cites ṚV 2.1.4, 3.26.6, and 3.38.5 as evidence for these distinctions.
33. It is possible to read the regions and cardinal directions as metaphors for surrounding peoples, such as tribes and clans. However, this reading downplays the fact that the cardinal directions in Vedic thought had their own distinct, ontological existence as entities within the broader cosmology. It is the latter emphasis on a cosmological interpretation, I have argued, that is needed in the political theory literature.
34. The "oppressor" (*brahmajya*) is likely the *rājan* mentioned in an earlier verse of the same hymn (AV 5.19.6). The relationship referred to here is that between the *rājan* and brahmin, not the people (*viś*) and the king (*rājan*), as Jayaswal seems to suggest.

35. Jayaswal claims a "free right of discussion" existed in the *samiti*, without first explaining how a system or understanding of "rights" existed in the first place (1967, 14). He is more restrained in his interpretation of the *sabhā*, about which he states: "It was certainly related to the *samiti*, but its exact relationship is not deducible from the data available" (1967, 18). However, he does not refrain from claiming that, like the *samiti*, the *sabhā* included "free discussion" (1967, 18).
36. Jayaswal (1967, 12–16) also claims *samitis* display popular representation (AV 3.4.2, 6.87.1, 6.88.3), deliberation (AV 2.27, 7.12.1, 12.1.56), and discussion of "state" matters (AV 6.64).
37. While the specific subject matter of deliberation may not be discernible in textual evidence, it is fairly clear, as Sharma explains, that a variety of activities are associated with the *sabhā*, including what we might consider today to be religious, military, gambling, administrative, and pastoral affairs.
38. For example, see AV 3.3.1–6 (restoring an exiled king); 3.4.1–7 (prayer at the acceptance of a king); 3.5.1–8 (praise of an amulet derived from the *parṇa* tree, designed to strengthen royal/kingly power); 4.8.1–7 (prayer at consecration of king); 4.22.1–7 (charm to secure the superiority of a king); 6.38.1–4 (prayer for kingly brilliance and power).
39. For example, see AV 2.27.1–7 (charm against opponents in debate, undertaken with the *pāṭā* plant); 3.30.1–7 (charm to secure harmony); 6.64.1–3, 6.73.1–3, 6.74.1–3 (charms to alleviate discord); 7.52.1–2 (charm against disagreement and violence).
40. For example, see AV 5.18.1–15, 5.19.1–15 (imprecations against oppressors of brahmins); 11.1.1–37, 12.3.1–60 (the preparation of the *brahmaudana*, the porridge given as a fee to brahmins).
41. To be sure, this point is not intended to be an apology for a rank-order society and caste system, or a complete dismissal of the value of individualism and agonistic plurality.

CHAPTER 5

1. For example, see Bremmer (1994, 2008); Burkert (1985); Easterling and Muir (1985); Hughes (1991); Parker (1983); Price (1999).
2. Especially in Classical Athens, religion was not neatly severed from politics (e.g., see Price 1999, 76, 78).
3. However, as Dolgert (2012) argues, this "humanistic" conception was accompanied by a hierarchical sacrificial economy involving the subordination of the nonhuman, whose suffering was understood as necessary to secure order in human communities.
4. One notable exception that is not directly expressed in the Homeric and Hesiodic works examined here is Agamemnon's sacrifice of Iphigenia. For example, see Euripedes's *Iphigenia at Aulis*.

5. This is not to suggest, of course, that sacrifices and rituals were not also conducted for personalized purposes in Vedic thought.
6. In later Hindu texts such as the Dharma-Sūtras and Dharma-Śāstras, the term *dharma* perhaps shows the greatest similarity to Hesiod's *dikē*.
7. While I argued that Dikē appeals to Zeus and he is influenced by her complaints, Dikē does not possess the moral or cosmic force that *ṛta* holds in brahmanical thought.
8. For a detailed analysis of Sanskrit concepts revolving around the metaphor of light, splendor, and distinction, including their relation to political sovereignty, see Proferes (2007, ch. 2).
9. Along these lines, see Whitaker (2011). My approach to Vedic thought, following from my pointed attempt to locate a Vedic political theory, differs from Whitaker's in focusing on the concept of rule and its role within a broader cosmological, metaphysical, and ontological context. Whitaker, on the other hand, focuses specifically on male identity, masculinity, and militarism in the Ṛg-Veda.

CONCLUSION

1. For an explanation of the importance of ecological stewardship and how it can be compatible with multiple cultural worldviews, including both religious and secular ethical commitments, see also Barry (2002, 133–52).
2. This is not to suggest that various traditions or indigenous cultures do not conceive of relations of reciprocity as flowing porously across human and nonhuman spheres, or that we have nothing to learn from such traditions. I thank Anatoli Ignatov for bringing this point to my attention.
3. For example, see Dobson (2003, 119–21), who argues for equal rights to livable and sustainable environmental space within which one can choose among wide options for a good life; Donaldson and Kymlicka (2011), who look to extend a liberal, rights-based conception of sovereignty to animals; Stephens (2016, 68), whose green liberalism holds that nonhuman nature must be protected because liberalism's core value of liberty is protected through nature experience.
4. For rights-based approaches to environmental justice, see Caney (2010) and Vanderheiden (2008). See also Schlosberg (2007, 2012), who extends Nussbaum's (2000, 2006) and Sen's (1999a, b) capabilities approach to debates about environmental justice.
5. On population, environmental discourse, and sustainability, see Coole (2016).
6. See also McKibben (1998) on how smaller family sizes, particularly in the global North, could contribute to global environmental well-being.
7. For a discussion of "peaks" and de-growth, see Heinberg (2007) and Latouche (2009). On the importance of the concept of sacrifice for environmental politics, see Maniates and Meyer (2012).
8. I thank an anonymous reviewer for helping me sharpen this point.

9. Here I agree with Vogel (2015) that making claims about a unique human ability or status, especially the ability for dialogic speech, "is not to say that nonhuman entities do not . . . deserve human care or protection, or that they are mere means for human ends. . . . [or] to assert a metaphysically based anthropocentrism" (194–95).
10. See http://www.fooddemocracynow.org/about.
11. For an example of such a position, see Donaldson and Kymlicka (2011).
12. For additional philosophical arguments about how we contribute to constructing or building nature, which work from positions in postmodern and critical theory, see Biro (2005) and Vogel (2015). For a green republican stance on constructed landscapes, see Cannavò (2007, 2016).

REFERENCES

PRIMARY SOURCES

Greek

Allen, Thomas W. 1917. *Homeri Opera*, Volumes 3 and 4. London: Oxford Classical Texts.

Aristotle. 1995. *Politics*. Translated by Ernest Barker. New York: Oxford University Press.

Hesiod. 2006. *Theogony, Works and Days, Testimonia*. Edited and translated by Glenn Most. Cambridge, MA: Harvard University Press.

Homer. 1961. *The Iliad of Homer*. Translated by Richmond Lattimore. Chicago: University of Chicago Press.

Monro, David B., and Thomas W. Allen, eds. 1920. *Homeri Opera*, Volumes 1 and 2. Oxford: Oxford Classical Texts.

West, M. L., ed. 1966. *Hesiod. Theogony*. Critical Edition. Oxford: Oxford University Press.

West, M. L., ed. 1978. *Hesiod. Works and Days*. Critical Edition. Oxford: Oxford University Press.

Sanskrit

Aitareya Brāhmaṇa. 1895–1906. Edited by Satyavrata Sāmaśramī. 4 vols. Bibliotheca Indica, no. 134. Calcutta: Asiatic Society of Bengal.

Atharva-Veda Saṃitā. 1960–1964. Edited by Vishva Bandhu et al. 5 vols. Vishveshvaranand Indological Series, 13–17. Hoshiarpur: Vishveshvaranand Vedic Research Institute.

Gopatha Brāhmaṇa. [1872] 1972. Edited by R. Mitra and H. Vidyabhusana. Calcutta: Bibliotheca Indica; reprint, Delhi: Indological Book House.

Jaiminīya Brāhmaṇa. 1954. Edited by Raghu Vira and Lokesh Chandra. Sarasvati-Vihara Series. Vol. 31. Nagpur: International Academy of Indian Culture.

Kāṭhaka Saṃhitā. 1943. Edited by V. Santavelekar. Bombay: Bhāratamudraṇālayam.

Kauṣītakī Brāhmaṇa (Śāṅkhāyana Brāhmaṇa). 1970. Edited by Harinarayan Bhattacharya. Calcutta Sanskrit College Research Series, no. 73. Calcutta: Sanskrit College.

Maitrāyaṇī Saṃhitā. 1941. Edited by Śrīpāda Dāmodara Sāṃtavalekara. Aundharājadhānī Svādhyāyamaṇḍala.

Maitrāyaṇī Upaniṣad. 1958. Edited by V. P. Limaye and R. D. Vadekar. In *Eighteen Principal Upaniṣads*. Poona: Vaidika Saṃśodhana Maṇḍala.

Pañcaviṃśa Brāhmaṇa (Tāṇḍya Brāhmaṇa). 1870–1874. Edited by Ānandachandra Vedāntagīśa. 2 vols. Bibliotheca Indica, no. 62. Calcutta: Asiatic Society of Bengal.

Pañcaviṃśa Brāhmaṇa (Tāṇḍya Brāhmaṇa). [1931] 1982. *Pañcaviṃśa-Brāhmaṇa: The Brāhmaṇa of Twenty Five Chapters*. Translated by W. Caland. Bibliotheca India, no. 255. Calcutta: Asiatic Society of Bengal.

Ṛg-Veda Saṃhitā. 1890–1892. Edited by Max F. Müller. 2d ed. 4 vols. London: Oxford University Press.

The Rigveda: The Earliest Religious Poetry of India. 2014. Translated by Stephanie W. Jamison and Joel P. Brereton. New York: Oxford University Press.

Śatapatha Brāhmaṇa. 1855. Edited by Albrecht Weber. 2nd ed. (reprint). Chowkhamba Sanskrit Series, no. 96. Varanasi: Chowkhamba Sanskrit Series Office, 1964.

Taittirīya Brāhmaṇa. 1911. Edited by A. Mahadeva Sastri. Delhi: Motilal Banarsidass.

Taittirīya Saṃhitā. 1860–1899. Edited by E. Röer (vol. 1), E. B. Cowell (vols. 1–2), Maheśachandra Nyāyaratna (vols. 3–5), and Satyavrata Sāmaśramī (vol. 6). 6 vols. Bibliotheca Indica, no. 26. Calcutta: Asiatic Society of Bengal.

Vājasaneyi Saṃhitā. 1852. Edited by Albrecht Weber. Berlin: Ferd. Dümmler; London: Williams and Norgate.

SECONDARY SOURCES

Adkins, A. W. H. 1970. *From the Many to the One: A Study of Personality and Views of Human Nature in the Context of Ancient Greek Society, Values, and Beliefs*. Ithaca, NY: Cornell University Press.

Ahrensdorf, Peter J. 2014. *Homer on the Gods and Human Virtue*. New York: Cambridge University Press.

Altekar, A. S. 1958. *State and Government in Ancient India*. Delhi: Motilal Banarsidass.

Alter, Joseph S. 2000. *Gandhi's Body: Sex, Diet, and the Politics of Nationalism*. Philadelphia: University of Pennsylvania Press.

Ames, Roger T. 1983. *The Art of Rulership: A Study in Ancient Chinese Political Thought*. Honolulu: University of Hawaii Press.

Arendt, Hannah. 1998. *The Human Condition*. Chicago: University of Chicago Press.

Baldick, Julian. 1994. *Homer and the Indo-Europeans: Comparing Mythologies*. London: I. B. Tauris.

Balot, Ryan K. 2001. *Greed and Injustice in Classical Athens*. Princeton, NJ: Princeton University Press.

Balot, Ryan K. 2006. *Greek Political Thought*. Malden, MA: Blackwell.

Bandyopadhyaya, N. C. 1980. *Development of Hindu Polity and Political Theories*. New Delhi: Munshiram Manoharlal Publishers.

Barry, John. 2002. "Vulnerability and Virtue: Democracy, Dependency, and Ecological Stewardship." In *Democracy and the Claims of Nature: Critical Perspectives for a New Century*, edited by Ben A. Minteer and Bob Pepperman Taylor, 133–52. Lanham, MD: Rowman and Littlefield.

Barry, John. 2012. *The Politics of Actually Existing Unsustainability: Human Flourishing in a Climate-Changed World*. New York: Oxford University Press.

Bartlett, Robert C. 2006. "An Introduction to Hesiod's *Works and Days*." *Review of Politics* 68 (2): 177–205.

Bennett, Jane. 2010. *Vibrant Matter: A Political Ecology of Things*. Durham, NC: Duke University Press.

Bevir, Mark. 1999. *The Logic of the History of Ideas*. Cambridge: Cambridge University Press.

Bhandarkar, D. R. [1925] 1988. *Some Aspects of Ancient Hindu Polity*, The Manindra Chandra Nandy Lectures, 1925. Patna: Eastern Book House.

Bhargava, Rajeev. 2006. "Indian Secularism: An Alternative, Trans-Cultural Ideal." In *Political Ideas in Modern India: Thematic Explorations*, edited by V. R. Mehta and Thomas Pantham, 285–306. New Delhi: Sage Publications.

Bhargava, Rajeev. 2010. *The Promise of India's Secular Democracy*. Oxford: Oxford University Press.

Biro, Andrew. 2005. *Denaturalizing Ecological Politics: Alienation from Nature from Rousseau to the Frankfurt School and Beyond*. Toronto: University of Toronto Press.

Black, Antony. 2001. *The History of Islamic Political Thought: From the Prophet to the Present*. London: Routledge.

Black, Antony. 2009a. "Toward a Global History of Political Thought." In *Western Political Thought in Dialogue with Asia*, edited by Takashi Shogimen and Cary J. Nederman, 25–42. Lanham, MD: Lexington Books.

Black, Antony. 2009b. *A World History of Ancient Political Thought*. Oxford: Oxford University Press.

Bloom, Irene. 2002. "Biology and Culture in the Mencian View of Human Nature." In *Mencius: Contexts and Interpretations*, edited by Alan Kam-leung Chan, 91–102. Honolulu: University of Hawaii Press.

Bloomfield, Maurice. 1898. "The Meaning and Etymology of the Vedic Word *Vidátha*." *Journal of the American Oriental Society* 19:12–18.

Boesche, Roger. 2002. *The First Great Political Realist: Kautilya and his Arthashastra*. Lanham, MD: Lexington Books.

Bolton, James David Pennington. 1973. *Glory, Jest and Riddle*. London: Duckworth.

Bremmer, Jan N. 1994. *Greek Religion*. Oxford: Oxford University Press.

Bremmer, Jan N. 2008. *Greek Religion and Culture, the Bible and the Ancient Near East*. Leiden: E. J. Brill.

Bryant, Joseph M. 1996. *Moral Codes and Social Structure in Ancient Greece*. Albany: State University of New York Press.

Burkert, Walter. 1985. *Greek Religion*. Trans. John Raffan. Cambridge, MA: Harvard University Press.

Caney, Simon. 2010. "Climate Change, Human Rights, and Moral Thresholds." In *Human Rights and Climate Change*, edited by Stephen Humphreys, 69–90. Cambridge: Cambridge University Press.

Cannavò, Peter F. 2007. *The Working Landscape: Founding, Preservation, and the Politics of Place*. Cambridge, MA: MIT Press.

Cannavò, Peter F. 2016. "Environmental Political Theory and Republicanism." In Gabrielson et al., eds., 72–88.

Cohen, David. 2015. "Tyranny of the Rule of Law? Democratic Participation in Legal Institutions in Athens." In *A Companion to Greek Democracy and the Roman Republic*, edited by Dean Hammer, 167–78. Malden, MA: Wiley Blackwell.

Connolly, William. 2011. *A World of Becoming*. Durham, NC: Duke University Press.

Coole, Diana. 2013. "Too Many Bodies? The Return and Disavowal of the Population Question." *Environmental Politics* 22 (2): 196–215.

Coole, Diana. 2016. "Population, Environmental Discourse, and Sustainability." In Gabrielson et al., eds., 274–88.

Coole, Diana, and Samantha Frost, eds. 2010. *New Materialisms*. Durham, NC: Duke University Press.

Crone, Patricia. 2004. *Medieval Islamic Political Thought*. Edinburgh: Edinburgh University Press.

Dallmayr, Fred. 1996. *Beyond Orientalism: Essays on Cross-Cultural Encounter*. Albany: State University of New York Press.

Dallmayr, Fred. 2002. *Dialogue among Civilizations: Some Exemplary Voices*. New York: Palgrave Macmillan.

Dallmayr, Fred. 2004. "Beyond Monologue: For a Comparative Political Theory." *Perspectives on Politics* 2 (2): 249–58.

Davis Acampora, Christa. 2013. *Contesting Nietzsche*. Chicago: University of Chicago Press.

Detienne, Marcel. 1989. "Culinary Practices and the Spirit of Sacrifice." In *The Cuisine of Sacrifice among the Greeks*, edited by Marcel Detienne and Jean-Pierre Vernant, 1–20. Chicago: University of Chicago Press.

Dobson, Andrew. 2003. *Citizenship and the Environment*. New York: Oxford University Press.

Dobson, Andrew. 2016. "Are There Limits to Limits?" In Gabrielson et al., eds., 289–303.

Dodds, E. R. 1951. *The Greeks and the Irrational*. Berkeley: University of California Press.

Dolgert, Stefan. 2012. "Sacrificing Justice: Suffering Animals, the Oresteia, and the Masks of Consent." *Political Theory* 40 (3): 263–89.

Dolgert, Stefan. 2015. "Animal Republics: Plato, Representation, and the Politics of Nature." *Politics and Animals* 1 (1): 75–88.

Donaldson, Sue, and Will Kymlicka. 2011. *Zoopolis: A Political Theory of Animal Rights*. New York: Oxford University Press.

Donlan, Walter. 1980. *The Aristocratic Ideal in Ancient Greece: Attitudes of Superiority from Homer to the End of the Fifth Century* B.C. Lawrence, KS: Coronado Press.

Donlan, Walter. 1993. "Duelling with Gifts in the *Iliad*: As the Audience Saw It." *Colby Quarterly* 29 (3): 155–72.

Donlan, Walter. 1997. "The Relations of Power in the Pre-State and Early-State Polities." In *The Development of the* Polis *in Archaic Greece*, edited by Lynette G. Mitchell and P. J. Rhodes, 39–48. London: Routledge.

Doshi, Saryu, ed. 1985. *India and Greece, Connections and Parallels*. Mumbai: Marg Publications.

Drekmeier, Charles. 1962. *Kingship and Community in Early India*. Stanford, CA: Stanford University Press.

Drews, Robert. 1983. *Basileus: The Evidence for Kingship in Geometric Greece*. New Haven, CT: Yale University Press.

Dreyfus, Hubert, and Sean Dorrance Kelly. 2011. *All Things Shining: Reading the Western Classics to Find Meaning in a Secular Age*. New York: Free Press.

Dumézil, Georges. 1988. *Mitra-Varuṇa: An Essay on Two Indo-European Representations of Sovereignty*. Trans. Derek Coltman. New York: Zone Books.

Dumont, Louis. 1970. *Homo Hierarchicus: An Essay on the Caste System*. Chicago: University of Chicago Press.

Easterling, P. E., and J. V. Muir, eds. 1985. *Greek Religion and Society*. Cambridge: Cambridge University Press.

Eckersley, Robyn. 2004. *The Green State: Rethinking Democracy and Sovereignty*. Cambridge, MA: MIT Press.

El Amine, Loubna. 2015. *Classical Confucian Political Thought: A New Interpretation*. Princeton, NJ: Princeton University Press.

El Amine, Loubna. 2016. "Beyond East and West: Reorienting Political Theory through the Prism of Modernity." *Perspectives on Politics* 14 (1): 102–20.

Elmer, David. 2013. *The Poetics of Consent: Collective Decision Making and the* Iliad. Baltimore, MD: Johns Hopkins University Press.

Euben, Roxanne L. 1997. "Comparative Political Theory: An Islamic Fundamentalist Critique of Rationalism." *Journal of Politics* 59 (1): 28–55.

Euben, Roxanne L. 1999. *Enemy in the Mirror: Islamic Fundamentalism and the Limits of Modern Rationalism—A Work of Comparative Political Theory*. Princeton, NJ: Princeton University Press.

Euben, Roxanne L. 2006. *Journeys to the Other Shore: Muslim and Western Travelers in Search of Knowledge*. Princeton, NJ: Princeton University Press.

Farrar, Cynthia. 1988. *The Origins of Democratic Thinking: The Invention of Politics in Classical Athens*. Cambridge: Cambridge University Press.

Felson, Nancy, and Laura M. Slatkin. 2004. "Gender and Homeric Epic." In *The Cambridge Companion to Homer*, edited by Robert Fowler, 91–116. Cambridge: Cambridge University Press.

Ferguson, John. 1975. *Utopias of the Classical World*. London: Thames and Hudson.

Finkelberg, Margalit. 2005. *Greeks and Pre-Greeks*. Cambridge: Cambridge University Press.

Finley, Moses. 1979. *The World of Odysseus*. New York: New York Review of Books.

Foley, John Miles. 1997. "Oral Tradition and Its Implications." In *A New Companion to Homer*, edited by Ian Morris and Barry Powell, 146–74. Leiden: Brill.

Foucault, Michel. 1990. *The History of Sexuality*, Volume 1: *An Introduction*. New York: Vintage Books.

Freeden, Michael, and Andrew Vincent. 2013. *Comparative Political Thought: Theorizing Practices*. New York: Routledge.

Friskics, Scott. 2001. "Dialogical Relations with Nature." *Environmental Ethics* 23 (4): 391–410.

Frost, Samantha. 2016. "Challenging the Human X Environment." In Gabrielson et al., eds., 178–92.

Gabrielson, Teena, Cheryl Hall, John M. Meyer, and David Schlosberg, eds. 2016. *The Oxford Handbook of Environmental Political Theory*. New York: Oxford University Press.

Gadamer, Hans-Georges. 2004. *Truth and Method*. New York: Continuum.

Gagarin, Michael. 1986. *Early Greek Law*. Berkeley: University of California Press.

Geuss, Raymond. 2001. *History and Illusion in Politics*. Cambridge: University of Cambridge Press.

Geuss, Raymond. 2005. *Outside Ethics*. Princeton, NJ: Princeton University Press.

Geuss, Raymond. 2008. *Philosophy and Real Politics*. Princeton, NJ: Princeton University Press.

Geuss, Raymond. 2014. *A World without Why*. Princeton, NJ: Princeton University Press.

Ghosal, Pranati. 2006. *Lifestyle of the Vedic People*. New Delhi: D. K. Printworld.

Ghoshal, U. N. 1966. *A History of Indian Political Ideas: The Ancient Period and the Period of Transition to the Middle Ages*. Oxford: Oxford University Press.

Godrej, Farah. 2006. "Nonviolence and Gandhi's Truth: A Method for Moral and Political Arbitration." *Review of Politics* 68 (2): 287–317.

Godrej, Farah. 2009. "Towards a Cosmopolitan Political Thought: The Hermeneutics of Interpreting the Other." *Polity* 41 (2): 135–65.

Godrej, Farah. 2011. *Cosmopolitan Political Thought: Method, Practice, Discipline*. Oxford: Oxford University Press.

Godrej, Farah. 2012. "Ascetics, Warriors, and a Gandhian Ecological Citizenship." *Political Theory* 40 (4): 437–65.

Godrej, Farah. 2016. "Culture and Difference: Non-Western Approaches to Defining Environmental Issues." In Gabrielson et al., eds., 39–56.

Gonda, Jan. 1963. *The Vision of the Vedic Poets*. The Hague, Netherlands: Mouton.

Gonda, Jan. 1965. *Change and Continuity in Indian Religion*. The Hague, Netherlands: Mouton.

Gonda, Jan. 1966. *Ancient Indian Kingship from the Religious Point of View*. Leiden: E. J. Brill.

Gray, Stuart. 2010. "A Historical-Comparative Approach to Indian Political Thought: Locating and Examining Domesticated Differences." *History of Political Thought* 31 (3): 383–406.

Gray, Stuart. 2016. "Cross-Cultural Intelligibility and the Use of History: From Democracy and Liberalism to Indian Rajanical Thought." *Review of Politics* 78 (2): 251–83.

Gray, Stuart, and Thomas Hughes. 2015. "Gandhi's Devotional Political Thought." *Philosophy East and West* 65 (2): 375–400.

Griffin, Jasper. 1980. *Homer on Life and Death*. Oxford: Clarendon.

Halbfass, Willhelm. 1988. *India and Europe: An Essay in Understanding*. New York: State University of New York Press.

Halliwell, Stephen. 1990. "Traditional Greek Conceptions of Character." In *Characterization and Individuality in Greek Literature*, edited by Christopher Pelling, 32–59. Oxford: Clarendon.

Hamilton, Richard. 1989. *The Architecture of Hesiodic Poetry*. Baltimore, MD: Johns Hopkins University Press.

Hammer, Dean. 2002a. *The* Iliad *as Politics: The Performance of Political Thought*. Norman: University of Oklahoma Press.

Hammer, Dean. 2002b. "Hannah Arendt and Roman Political Thought." *Political Theory* 30 (1): 124–49.

Hammer, Dean. 2005. "Plebiscitary Politics in Archaic Greece." *Historia* 54 (2): 107–31.

Hammer, Dean. 2009. "Homer and Political Thought." In *The Cambridge Companion to Ancient Political Thought*, edited by Stephen Salkever, 15–41. New York: Cambridge University Press.

Haubold, Johannes. 2000. *Homer's People: Epic Poetry and Social Formation*. Cambridge: Cambridge University Press.

Havelock, Eric A. 1978. *The Greek Concept of Justice: From Its Shadow in Homer to Its Substance in Plato*. Cambridge, MA: Harvard University Press.

Heath, John. 2005. *The Talking Greeks: Speech, Animals, and the Other in Homer, Aeschylus, and Plato*. Cambridge: Cambridge University Press.

Heesterman, J. C. 1957. *The Ancient Indian Royal Consecration: The Rājasūya According to the Yajus Texts and Annotated*. Gravenhage: Mouton.

Heesterman, J. C. 1993. *The Broken World of Sacrifice: An Essay in Ancient Indian Ritual*. Chicago: University of Chicago Press.

Heinberg, Richard. 2007. *Peak Everything: Waking Up to the Century of Decline in Earth's Resources*. Forest Row: Clairview Books.

Held, David. 2006. *Models of Democracy*. 3d ed. Cambridge: Polity Press.

Held, David, Anthony McGrew, David Goldblatt, and Jonathan Perraton, eds. 1999. *Global Transformations: Politics, Economics and Culture*. Stanford, CA: Stanford University Press.

Holdrege, Barbara. 1996. *Veda and Torah: Transcending the Textuality of Scripture*. Albany: State University of New York Press.

Holdrege, Barbara. 2004. "Dharma." In *The Hindu World*, edited by Sushil Mittal and Gene Thursby, 213–48. New York: Routledge.

Hughes, Dennis D. 1991. *Human Sacrifice in Ancient Greece*. London: Routledge.

Jayaswal, K. P. 1967. *Hindu Polity: A Constitutional History of India in Hindu Times*. Bangalore: Bangalore Printing and Publishing.

Jenco, Leigh. 2007. "'What Does Heaven Ever Say?' A Methods-Centered Approach to Cross-Cultural Engagement." *American Political Science Review* 101 (4): 741–55.

Jenco, Leigh. 2010. *Making the Political: Founding and Action in the Political Theory of Zhang Shizhao*. Cambridge: Cambridge University Press.

Jenco, Leigh. 2014. "Histories of Thought and Comparative Political Theory: The Curious Thesis of 'Chinese Origins for Western Knowledge', 1860–1895." *Political Theory* 42 (6): 658–81.

Jenco, Leigh. 2015. *Changing Referents: Learning across Space and Time in China and the West*. New York: Oxford University Press.

Jordan, Sara R., and Cary J. Nederman. 2012. "*The Logic of the History of Ideas* and the Study of Comparative Political Theory." *Journal of the History of Ideas* 73 (4): 627–41.

Kantorowicz, Ernst. 1957. *The King's Two Bodies: A Study in Medieval Political Theology*. Princeton, NJ: Princeton University Press.

Kateb, George. 2011. *Human Dignity*. Cambridge, MA: Belknap Press.

King, Richard. 1999. *Indian Philosophy: An Introduction to Hindu and Buddhist Thought*. Washington, DC: Georgetown University Press.

Klausen, Jimmy. 2014. "Economies of Violence: The *Bhagavadgītā* and the Fostering of Life in Gandhi's and Ghose's Anticolonial Theories." *American Political Science Review* 108 (1): 182–95.

Lane, Melissa. 2012. *Eco-Republic: What the Ancients Can Teach Us about Ethics, Virtue, and Sustainable Living*. Princeton, NJ: Princeton University Press.

Latouche, Serge. 2009. *Farewell to Growth*. Cambridge: Polity Press.

Law, N. N. [1921] 1960. *Aspects of Ancient Indian Polity*. Bombay: Orient Longmans.

Lewis, Bernard. 1988. *The Political Language of Islam*. Chicago: University of Chicago Press.

Liddell, H. G. and R. Scott. 1945. *Liddell and Scott's Greek–English Lexicon*. 7th ed. Oxford: Clarendon.

Littleton, C. Scott. 1982. *The New Comparative Mythology: An Anthropological Assessment of the Theories of Georges Dumézil*. Berkeley: University of California Press.

Lloyd-Jones, Hugh. 1983. *The Justice of Zeus*. Berkeley: University of California Press.

Lubin, Timothy. Forthcoming. "The Householder Ascetic and the Uses of Self-Discipline." In *Asceticism and Power in South and Southeast Asia*, edited by Peter Flügel and Gustaaf Houtman. London: Routledge.

Mabbett, Ian W. 1972. *Truth, Myth and Politics in Ancient India*. New Delhi: Thomson Press.

Macdonell, Arthur Anthony. 1897. *Vedic Mythology*. Strassburg: Verlag Von Karl J. Trübner.

Macdonell, Arthur Anthony. [1916] 2005. *A Vedic Grammar for Students*. New Delhi: D. K. Printworld.

Macdonell, Arthur Anthony. [1917] 2010. *A Vedic Reader for Students*. LaVergne, TN: Kessinger.

Macdonell, Arthur Anthony, and Arthur Berriedale Keith. 1967. *Vedic Index of Names and Subjects*. Volumes 1 and 2. Delhi: Motilal Banarsidass.

MacIntyre, Alasdair. 1988. *Whose Justice? Which Rationality?* Notre Dame, IN: University of Notre Dame Press.

Mahony, William K. 1998. *The Artful Universe: An Introduction to the Vedic Religious Imagination*. Albany: State University of New York Press.

Maniates, Michael, and John Meyer, eds. 2012. *The Environmental Politics of Sacrifice*. Cambridge, MA: MIT Press.

Mantena, Karuna. 2012. "Another Realism: The Politics of Gandhian Nonviolence." *American Political Science Review* 106 (2): 455–70.

March, Andrew. 2009. "What is Comparative Political Theory?" *Review of Politics* 71 (4): 531–65.

March, Andrew. 2010. "Taking People As They Are: Islam as a 'Realistic Utopia' in the Political Theory of Sayyid Qutb." *American Political Science Review* 104 (1): 189–207.

Martin, Richard P. 1984. "Hesiod, Odysseus, and the Instruction of Princes." *Transactions of the American Philological Association* 114:29–48.

Martin, Richard P. 1989. *The Language of Heroes: Speech and Performance in the* Iliad. Ithaca, NY: Cornell University Press.

Marzullo, Benedetto. 1962. *A Complete Concordance to the Iliad of Homer*. Hildesheim: Georg Olms Verlagsbuchhandlung.

Marzullo, Benedetto. 1971. *A Complete Concordance to the Odyssey of Homer*. Hildesheim: Georg Olms Verlag.

McKibben, Bill. 1998. *Maybe One: A Personal and Environmental Argument for Single-Child Families*. New York: Simon and Schuster.

Morris, Ian. 1996. "The Strong Principle of Equality and the Archaic Origins of Greek Democracy." In *Dēmokratia: A Conversation on Democracies, Ancient and Modern*, edited by Josiah Ober and Charles W. Hendrick, 19–48. Princeton, NJ: Princeton University Press.

Morris, Ian. 2000. *Archaeology as Cultural History: Words and Things in Iron Age Greece*. Malden, MA: Blackwell.

Nagy, Gregory. 2010. *Homer the Classic*. Cambridge: Center for Hellenic Studies.

Nagy, Gregory. 2013. *The Greek Hero in 24 Hours*. Cambridge, MA: Belknap Press.

Nicolson, Adam. 2014. *Why Homer Matters*. New York: Henry Holt.

Nilsson, Martin P. 1968. *Homer and Mycenae*. New York: Cooper Square Publishers.

Nussbaum, Martha. 2000. *Women and Human Development: The Capabilities Approach*. Oxford: Oxford University Press.

Nussbaum, Martha. 2006. *Frontiers of Justice: Disability, Nationality, Species Membership*. Cambridge: Cambridge University Press.

Oakley, Francis. 2006. *Kingship: The Politics of Enchantment*. Malden, MA: Blackwell.

Onians, Richard Broxton. 1951. *The Origins of European Thought: About the Body, the Mind, the Soul, the World, Time, and Fate*. Cambridge: Cambridge University Press.

Ophuls, Patrick. 2011. *Plato's Revenge: Politics in the Age of Ecology*. Cambridge, MA: MIT Press.

Parekh, Bhikhu. 1989. *Gandhi's Political Philosophy: A Critical Examination*. Notre Dame, IN: University of Notre Dame Press.

Parel, Anthony J. 2006. *Gandhi's Philosophy and the Quest for Harmony*. Cambridge: Cambridge University Press.

Parel, Anthony J. 2008. "Gandhi and the Emergence of the Modern Indian Political Canon." *Review of Politics* 70 (1): 40–63.

Parker, Robert. 1983. *Miasma: Pollution and Purification in Early Greek Religion*. Oxford: Clarendon.

Patton, Laurie. 2004. "Veda and Upaniṣad." In *The Hindu World*, edited by Sushil Mittal and Gene Thursby, 37–51. New York: Routledge.

Plumwood, Val. 1993. *Feminism and the Mastery of Nature*. New York: Routledge.

Prasad, Beni. 1968. *Theory of Government in Ancient India*. Allahabad: Indian Universities Press, Central Book Depot.

Price, Simon. 1999. *Religions of the Ancient Greeks*. Cambridge: Cambridge University Press.

Proferes, Theodore. 2007. *Vedic Ideals of Sovereignty and the Poetics of Power*. American Oriental Series, Volume 90. New Haven, CT: American Oriental Society.

Puhvel, Jaan, ed. 1970. *Myth and Law among the Indo-Europeans: Studies in Indo-European Comparative Mythology*. Berkeley: University of California Press.

Raaflaub, Kurt A. 1993. "Homer to Solon: The Rise of the Polis." In *The Ancient Greek City-State*, edited by Mogens Herman Hansen, 41–105. Copenhagen: Royal Danish Academy of Sciences and Letters.

Raaflaub, Kurt A. 1997. "Soldiers, Citizens, and the Evolution of the Greek Polis." In *The Development of the* Polis *in Archaic Greece*, edited by Lynette G. Mitchell and P. J. Rhodes, 49–59. London: Routledge.

Raaflaub, Kurt A. 2000. "Poets, Lawgivers, and the Beginnings of Political Reflection in Archaic Greece." In *The Cambridge History of Greek and Roman Political Thought*, Christopher Rowe and Malcolm Schofield, 23–59. Cambridge: Cambridge University Press.

Raaflaub, Kurt A. 2004. "Homer and the Beginning of Political Thought in Greece." In *Ancient Greek Democracy: Readings and Sources*, edited by Eric W. Robinson, 28–40. Malden, MA: Blackwell.

Raaflaub, Kurt A., and Robert W. Wallace. 2007. "'People's Power' and Egalitarian Trends in Archaic Greece." In *Origins of Greek Democracy in Ancient Greece*, edited by Kurt A. Raaflaub, Josiah Ober, and Robert W. Wallace, 22–48. Berkeley: University of California Press.

Rhodes, P. J. 2015. "The Congruence of Power: Ruling and Being Ruled in Greek Participatory Democracies." In *A Companion to Greek Democracy and the Roman Republic*, edited by Dean Hammer, 131–45. Malden, MA: Wiley Blackwell.

Richter, Melvin. 1990. "Reconstructing the History of Political Languages: Pocock, Skinner, and the *Geschichtliche Grundbegriffe*." *History and Theory* 29 (1): 38–70.

Robb, Kevin. 1994. *Literacy and Paideia in Ancient Greece*. Oxford: Oxford University Press.

Robinson, Eric W. 1997. *The First Democracies: Early Popular Government Outside Athens*. Historia 107. Stuttgart: F. Steiner.

Saletore, Bhasker Anand. 1963. *Ancient Indian Political Thought and Institutions*. Bombay: Asia Publishing House.

Salkever, Stephen, and Michael Nylan. 1994. "Comparative Political Philosophy and Liberal Education: Looking for Friends in History." *Political Science and Politics* 27 (2): 238–47.

Sandilands, Catriona. 2016. "Floral Sensations: Plant Biopolitics." In Gabrielson et al., eds., 226–37.

Scharfe, Hartmut. 1989. *The State in Indian Tradition*. Leiden: E. J. Brill.

Schlosberg, David. 2007. *Defining Environmental Justice: Theories, Movements, and Nature*. New York: Oxford University Press.

Schlosberg, David. 2012. "Climate Justice and Capabilities: A Framework for Adaptation Policy." *Ethics and International Affairs* 26 (4): 445–61.

Schlosberg, David. 2013. "Theorizing Environmental Justice: The Expanding Sphere of a Discourse." *Environmental Politics* 22 (1): 37–55.

Schlosberg, David. 2016. "Environmental Management in the Anthropocene." In Gabrielson et al., eds., 193–208.

Schlosberg, David, and Romand Coles. 2016. "The New Environmentalism of Everyday Life: Sustainability, Material Flows and Movements." *Contemporary Political Theory* 15 (2): 160–81.

Schofield, Malcolm. 1986. "*Euboulia* in the *Iliad*." *Classical Quarterly* 36 (1): 6–31.

Seaford, Richard. 1994. *Reciprocity and Ritual: Homer and Tragedy in the Developing City-State*. Oxford: Clarendon.

Seaford, Richard. 2004. *Money and the Early Greek Mind: Homer, Philosophy, Tragedy*. Cambridge: Cambridge University Press.

Seaford, Richard. 2012. *Cosmology and the Polis: The Social Construction of Space and Time in the Tragedies of Aeschylus*. Cambridge: Cambridge University Press.

Segal, Charles. 1994. *Singers, Heroes, and Gods in the* Odyssey. Ithaca, NY: Cornell University Press.

Sen, Amartya. 1999a. *Commodities and Capabilities*. Oxford: Oxford University Press.

Sen, Amartya. 1999b. *Development as Freedom*. New York: Anchor.

Sharma, J. P. 1968. *Republics in Ancient India, c. 1500 B.C.–500 b.c.* Leiden: E. J. Brill.

Sharma, J. P., and H. W. Bailey. 1965. "The Question of the Vidatha in Vedic India." *Journal of the Royal Asiatic Society of Great Britain and Ireland* 1/2 (April): 43–56.

Sharma, Ram Sharan. 1968. *Aspects of Political Ideas and Institutions in Ancient India*. Delhi: Motilal Banarsidass Press.

Shastri, Vishva Bandhu. 1960–63. *A Grammatical Word-Index to the Four Vedas*. Ann Arbor: University of Michigan Press.

Silvermintz, Daniel. 2004. "Unravelling the Shroud for Laertes and Weaving the Fabric of the City: Kingship and Politics in Homer's *Odyssey*." *Polis* 21 (1): 26–42.

Singh, G. P. 1993. *Political Thought in Ancient India: Emergence of the State, Evolution of Kingship, and Inter-State Relations Based on the Saptanga Theory of State*. New Delhi: D. K. Printworld.

Sinha, H. N. 1938. *Sovereignty in Ancient Indian Polity: A Study in the Evolution of Early Indian State*. London: Luzac & Co.

Sirriani, Carmen. 2009. *Investing in Democracy: Engaging Citizens in Collaborative Governance*. Washington, DC: Brookings.

Smith, Brian K. 1989. *Reflections on Resemblance, Ritual, and Religion*. Delhi: Motilal Banarsidass.

Smith, Brian K. 1994. *Classifying the Universe: The Ancient Indian* Varṇa *System and the Origins of Caste*. Oxford: Oxford University Press.

Snodgrass, Anthony. 1980. *Archaic Greece: The Age of Experiment*. Berkeley: University of California Press.

Söhnen, Renate. 1997. "Rise and Decline of the Indra Religion in the Veda." In *Inside the Texts, Beyond the Texts: New Approaches to the Study of the Vedas*, edited by Michael Witzel, 235–43. Cambridge, MA: Harvard University Dept. of Sanskrit and Indian Studies.

Spellman, John W. 1964. *Political Theory of Ancient India: A Study of Kingship from the Earliest Times to Circa a.d. 300*. Oxford: Clarendon Press.

Stephens, Piers H. 2016. "Environmental Political Theory and the Liberal Tradition." In Gabrielson et al., eds., 57–71.

Strauss Clay, Jenny. 2003. *Hesiod's Cosmos*. Cambridge: Cambridge University Press.

Stuurman, Siep. 2004. "The Voice of Thersites: Reflections on the Origins of the Idea of Equality." *Journal of the History of Ideas* 65 (2): 171–89.

Tarrant, Seaton Patrick, and Leslie Paul Thiele. 2016. "Environmental Political Theory's Contribution to Sustainability Studies." In Gabrielson et al., eds., 116–30.

Taylor, Charles. 1984. "Philosophy and Its History." In *Philosophy in History: Essays on the Historiography of Philosophy* (Ideas in Context), edited by Richard Rorty, J. B. Schneewind, and Quentin Skinner, 17–30. New York: Cambridge University Press.

Taylor, Charles. 1989. *Sources of the Self: The Making of the Modern Identity*. Cambridge, MA: Harvard University Press.

Thalmann, William G. 1984. *Conventions of Form and Thought in Early Greek Epic Poetry*. Baltimore, MD: Johns Hopkins University Press.

Thiele, Leslie Paul. 2013. *Sustainability*. Cambridge: Polity.

Turner, Frank M. 1997. "The Homeric Question." In *A New Companion to Homer*, edited by Ian Morris and Barry Powell, 123–45. Leiden: Brill.

Vanderheiden, Steve. 2008. *Atmospheric Justice: A Political Theory of Climate Change*. Oxford: Oxford University Press.

Varma, Vishwanath Prasad. 1974. *Studies in Hindu Political Thought and Its Metaphysical Foundations*. Delhi: Motilal Banarsidass.

Verdenius, W. J. 1985. *A Commentary on Hesiod: Works and Days*. Leiden: E. J. Brill.

Vernant, Jean-Pierre. 1989. "At Man's Table: Hesiod's Foundation Myth of Sacrifice." In *The Cuisine of Sacrifice among the Greeks*, edited by Marcel Detienne and Jean-Pierre Vernant, 21–86. Chicago: University of Chicago Press.

Vlastos, Gregory. 1947. "Equality and Justice in Early Greek Cosmologies." *Classical Philology* 42 (3): 156–78.

Voegelin, Eric. 1957. *Order and History*, Volume 2: *The World of the Polis*. Baton Rouge: Louisiana State University Press.

Vogel, Steven. 2015. *Thinking like a Mall: Environmental Philosophy after the End of Nature*. Cambridge, MA: MIT Press.

Vogel, Steven. 2016. "'Nature' and the (Built) Environment." In Gabrielson et al., eds., 149–59.

Walcot, P. 1966. *Hesiod and the Near East*. Cardiff: Wales University Press.

Wallach, John R. 2011. "*Demokratia* and *Arete* in Ancient Greek Political Thought." *Polis* 28 (2): 181–215.

Walzer, Michael. 2012. *In God's Shadow: Politics in the Hebrew Bible*. New Haven, CT: Yale University Press.

Wapner, Paul. 2010. *Living through the End of Nature: The Future of American Environmentalism*. Cambridge, MA: MIT Press.

Weber, Max. 1973. *The Vocation Lectures*. Edited by D. Owen and T. Strong. Translated by R. Livingston. Indianapolis, IN: Hackett Publishing.

Wees, Hans van. 1997. "Homeric Warfare." In *A New Companion to Homer*, edited by Ian Morris and Barry Powell, 668–93. Leiden: Brill.

West, M. L. 2007. *Indo-European Poetry and Myth*. New York: Oxford University Press.

West, M. L. 2011. *The Making of the* Iliad. New York: Oxford University Press.

Whitaker, Jarrod. 2011. *Strong Arms and Drinking Strength: Masculinity, Violence, and the Body in Ancient India*. New York: Oxford University Press.

Williams, Bernard. 1993. *Shame and Necessity*. Berkeley: University of California Press.

Williams, Melissa S., and Mark E. Warren. 2014. "A Democratic Case for Comparative Political Theory." *Political Theory* 42 (1): 26–57.

Witzel, Michael. 1997a. "The Development of the Vedic Canon and its Schools: The Social and Political Milieu." In *Inside the Texts, Beyond the Texts: New Approaches to the Study of The Vedas*, HOS Opera Minora 2, edited by Michael Witzel, 257–345. Cambridge, MA: Harvard University Department of Sanskrit and Indian Studies.

Witzel, Michael. 1997b. "Early Sanskritization: Origins and Development of the Kuru State." In *The State, Law, and Administration in Classical India*, edited by Bernhard Kölver and Elisabeth Müller-Luckner, 29–52. Munich: R. Oldenbourg Verlag.

Witzel, Michael. 2003. "Vedas and Upaniṣads." In *The Blackwell Companion to Hinduism*, edited by Gavin Flood, 68–101. Oxford: Blackwell.

Wolin, Sheldon. 2004. *Politics and Vision: Continuity and Innovation in Western Political Thought*. Expanded Edition. Princeton, NJ: Princeton University Press.

INDEX

Acampora, Christa Davis, 24, 37
Achilles, 22
  Agamemnon and, disagreements, 47, 49, 51, 52
  Agamemnon and, relationship with, 29, 37, 47
  as Agamemnon's equal, 49
  on Agamemnon's kingly rule, 36–38, 74, 97
  basileus as, 36
  bribes or gifts, 49
  character, 44
  equality among rulers, 62
  fate of death, 43
  glory, 27, 51–52, 102
  headstrong, 55
  Hector and, 52, 56, 57
  honor, 36–37, 50–53
  individualist ontology, 177
  on Odysseus, 53
  rage, 27, 48–53
  as responsible for own being, 178
  ruling-for and ruling-with, 50–53
  self-possessed individuality, 62
  shield, trial scene on, 93
  status, *vs.* Agamemnon, 29, 32–33, 49, 50–51
  struggles, 24
Agamemnon, 22
  Achilles and, disagreements, 47, 49, 51
  Achilles and, ordering to battle, 52
  Achilles and, relationship, 29, 37, 47
  Achilles' criticisms, kingly rule, 36–38, 74, 97
  Achilles' status *vs.*, 29, 32–33, 49, 50–51
  anaktes, 92
  basileus as, 36–38, 92, 184
  bribes and gifts, 49, 229n32
  equality among rulers, 62
  glory, 49
  honor, 47–49
  individualist ontology, 177–178
  kingship and hierarchical rule, 31–32, 34, 36–40, 51, 227nn11–12
  Odysseus on, 37, 39, 97
  rage, 48–50, 229n32
  as responsible for own being, 178
  ruling-over, mortal, 48–50, 229n32
  self-possessed individuality, 62
  Thersites on, 38–40, 62, 100, 228n20
Agni, 120, 136–138, 141
Agonism, 24, 37–38, 67, 75, 82, 101–102, 204
Ahrensdorf, Peter, 53
Alētheia, 27
Altekar, A. S., 110, 166, 235n35

Anax, 18–19, 19n16, 81
Andromache
on Hector as city's guardian, 33
on Hector's family commitments, 57–58
on Hector's heroic courage, 57
Hector to, on his Fate, 42, 229n25
Hector *vs.*, 56
Anger. *See also* Rage
Homer on, 23, 30
kingly distinction, 44
of Odysseus, 61
of Zeus, 45
Anṛta, 125, 238n26
Anti-hierarchical beliefs and disconnectedness of rule, 35–44, 88, 228nn22–24
Agamemnon, 36–40
consensus, 42, 228n24
Eurymachus *vs.* Halitherses, 40–41
gender and rule, 41–42, 228n23
justice *(dikē)*, 36–37, 228n19
laoi and battle success, 36, 38–40, 228n20
Odysseus and omens, 40, 228nn21–22
self-possessed individuality *vs.* communal obligation/ well-being, 36
Zeus, fate and, 42–44
Approval, 42, 77
Aretē, 23, 227n3
Aristotle, *Politics*, 64, 95–96, 224n7
Arthaśāstra, 107
Arya Samaj, 18
Asura, 147, 150, 236n4
Atharvan, 113, 131, 133, 170
Atharva-Veda Saṃhitā, 106, 112, 164–171, 237n21
assemblies, democratic deliberation and election of rulers, 131–133, 235nn34–35
assemblies, stewardship, 164–171, 238–239nn27–40
brahmanical understanding, 171, 239n40
Athena
child of Zeus, 79
Odysseus and, 41–42, 47, 48, 55, 61
Zeus and, 30, 34, 62–63, 68, 228n14, 229n27
Ātman, 153–154, 179
Atropos, 26, 42–43, 75

Balot, Ryan, 36, 228nn19–20, 231n11
Bandhu, 195, 202, 214
binding, 173
connections, 115
divine–human ruler connection, 115, 117–118, 125, 137, 234n21
kṣatra, 138
ritual, 153
varṇa, 125, 146, 164
and Vedic justice, 186–187, 240n8
and hierarchical categories, 125
Bandyopadhyaya, N. C., 110, 170, 233n9
Banyan (Nyagrodha) tree, *kṣatriya* and, 152, 155, 180–181, 186, 190–191, 200, 201, 205, 237n19
Barry, John, 205, 208, 212, 216–217, 226n8, 240n1
Bartlett, Robert, 21, 80–83, 91–92, 230n4, 231n13, 232nn17, 19
Basileus (pl., *basileis)*, 18–19, 226nn13–16. *See also specific individuals*
Achilles, 36
Agamemnon, 36–38, 92, 184
challenges, 35–44, 228nn19–25 (*see also* Anti-hierarchical beliefs and disconnectedness of rule)
distinction, 65, 92
glory, 65 (*see also* Glory)
Hector, 36, 57–58
Hesiod's critique, 92–93, 231n9

honor, 65 (*see also* Honor)
hospitality, 58–61, 84–85, 229–230nn37–39
justice, 88–100, 231–232nn8–18
vs. kṣatriya, 179–180
Zeus, 32, 227n11
Zeus, Hesiod's, 65, 83–100, 179, 186
Zeus, Homer's, 65, 179
Bennett, Jane, 201
Bevir, Mark, 4–5, 9, 225nn2, 5
Bhagavad Gītā, Gandhi and, 108
Bhandarkar, D. R., 233n8, 233n9
Black, Antony, 1, 17–18, 17n12, 225n1
Bloomfield, Maurice, 164–165, 238n28
Brahman, 125, 127, 153–154, 177
kṣatra and, 159–160
Brāhmaṇas, 106–107, 112–117, 123–131
cosmogony and cosmology, 124–126
metaphysics, 126–127
ontology, 127–131
political thought, 112–116
Brahmin, 119, 234–235n26
kṣatriya stewardship, 157–162, 237–238nn23–25
twice born, 128, 235n32
Bremmer, Jan, 182, 239n1
Bribe-eating kings, 66, 85–88
Burkert, Walter, 182–183

Cannavò, Peter, 195
Caste, 114, 234n17
Chaos, 25, 40, 45, 73, 87
Cholos, 44
Citizen-rulers, 207, 215, 219
Citizenship, language, 11
Civic virtues, 12
Clay, Jenny Strauss, 82
Co-building, 220
Coles, Romand, 209
Collaborative governance, 208
Commanding, 23
Common good, 12–13, 35, 51, 213
Common mass *(laoi),* 23, 31
battle success, 36, 38–40, 228n20
Communities of shared fate, 7
Comparative political theory and history, 6-9
Connectedness of rule, 12, 194, 197, 215, 219. *See also* Panocracy
human–god, 12, 13, 85 (*see also Bandhu*)
Consensus, 42, 228n24
Coole, Diana, 201, 240n5
Cosmic agonism, 24
Cosmic interconnectedness, human–god, 13, 85. *See also Bandhu*
Cosmogony
Greek, Hesiod, 65–66, 73–75, 80, 87–88
Ṛg-Veda Saṃhitā, human kingship, 140–145, 236nn11–13
Saṃhitās and Brāhmaṇas, 125–126, 235n30
Saṃhitās and Brāhmaṇas, rule as stewardship, 145–152, 237nn14–17
Cosmology
Brahmanical political thought, 112–116, 234nn13–17
definition, 22
Saṃhitās and Brāhmaṇas, 125–126, 235n30
Cosmology and metaphysics, Homeric, 22, 24–31
agonism and competitive engagement, 24
fate, 25–26
Gods, fate, and temporality, 25–26
immediate experience and individualist ontology, 26–31, 227nn4–10
metaphysics, 24
rulers' distinction, 24
Cosmopolitan approach, 6, 7
Cosmos *(kosmos),* Homeric, 25

Dalit, 109
Dallmayr, Fred, 1, 6
Dānava, 144, 235n27
De-growth, 200, 207, 240n7
Democracy, 7, 211–212, 215
Democratic assemblies, 111, 131–133, 165
Destinies *(moirai),* 75
Detienne, Marcel, 183
Deva-gopṛ, 141
Devas, 113, 234n14. *See also specific gods*
  kings, 116, 117 (*see also Rājan*)
Dharman, 118, 202, 234nn24–25
  rājan, 138
Dikē (justice). *See* Justice
Disconnectedness of rule, 35–44, 88, 228nn19–25. *See also* Anti-hierarchical beliefs and disconnectedness of rule
Distinction
  basileus, 65, 92 (*see also Basileus*)
  Homer on, 23
  Indra, 189
  justice, 92–93, 231nn9–11
  kingly, 44–61 (*see also* Kingly distinction)
  Mitra-Varuṇa and, 189
  in peacetime, 58–61, 229–230nn37–39
  pursuit, 23
  ruling as, Thersites on, 41
  ruling-for, 37
  ruling-over, 46–47
  ruling-with, 37
  Zeus, Homer's, 45–48 (*see also* Zeus, Homer's)
Divine command, 67–68
Divine rule. *See* Indra; Zeus
Dobson, Andrew, 196, 199, 240n3
Dolgert, Stefan, 195, 239n3
Donaldson, Sue, 199, 240n3
Donlan, Walter, 49, 83, 231n8
Drekmeier, Charles, 110, 233n6
Drews, Robert, 18–19, 226nn14, 16
Dreyfus, Hubert, 30
Dumézil, Georges, 114, 234n16
Dumont, Louis, 114–115, 122, 233n8, 234n17
Duty
  green republicanism, 12, 226n8
  varṇa-duty, 149

Eckersley, Robyn, 208–209
Eirēnē (peace), 79
Elmer, David, 38–40, 42, 229n25
Engaged political theory, 6
Environmental justice, 215–217
Environmental political theory, 9–14, 226nn8–9
Epainos, 42, 77
Equality, 11
Eris, 69–71, 81
Euben, Roxanne, 6, 225n3
Eunomia, 79
Excellence, 23, 227n3

Fame
  kīrti, 188
  kleos, 23, 30–31, 44, 187–188, 229n35
  śravas, 187–188
Fate *(moira, kēr),* 75
  Hector, 42–43, 229n25
  Hesiod on, 75–76
  Homer on, 25–26, 41–44, 55
  Zeus, 42–44, 92, 178
Fates *(kēres)*
  Hesiod on, 75–76
  Zeus, 42–44, 92, 178
Female/earth figures, 15–16
Foresight
  Hesiod on, 70–71, 190, 202
  Prometheus on, 80–81
Forethought, 79–82. *See also* Prometheus
Forgetfulness, 15, 27, 71–72

Freeden, Michael, 5, 6, 9
Frost, Samantha, 201

Gadamer, Hans-George, 8–9
Gaia, 15–16, 71, 73–75, 194, 202
Gandhi, 7, 108
Gender
  cosmo-political gendering, 16
  Homer, rule and, 41–42, 228n23
Gēras, 69
Geuss, Raymond, 213, 224n8
Ghoshal, U. N., 110, 146
Gift-devouring kings, 85–87, 94, 97
Glory
  Achilles, 27, 51–52, 102
  Agamemnon, 49
  basileus, 65
  Hector, 57–58
  Hesiod on, 62, 65, 75, 87, 92
  Homeric rulers, 23, 30–31, 44, 45, 58, 62, 85, 87, 98, 100, 189, 229n35
  hospitality, 60
  Indra, 189
  Muses granting, 67, 72
  Odysseus, 55, 56, 61
  Vedas, 187–188
  Vedic *vs.* Greek, 187–188
  Zeus, 45–47, 65, 87, 98, 188
Godrej, Farah, 1, 6, 7, 13–14, 108
Gonda, Jan, 110, 130, 137, 140, 233n8, 236n10
Gray, Stuart, 108, 111, 115
Green republicanism, 12, 207–208, 212, 241n12
Green states, 208–209
Griffin, Jasper, 29–30
Guardianship. *See also* Stewardship
  rājan, divine, 136–137
  Ṛg-Veda Saṃhitā, 136–140, 236nn1–10

Halbfass, Wilhelm, 8–9
Halliwell, Stephen, 29, 227n6
Hamilton, Richard, 81–82, 99, 230n1, 230n5
Hammer, Dean, 53, 223n3, 227n1
Haubold, Johannes, 36, 228n13
Haviryajña, 113
Heath, John, 190
Hector
  Achilles and, 52, 56, 57
  Andromache and, 33, 56, 57–58, 229n25
  basileus as, 36, 57–58
  in battlefield, 52
  Fate and, 42–43, 229n25
  glory and honor, 57–58
  hierarchical rule, 33, 228n13
  Iliad, 57–58, 229nn35–36
  kingly distinction and ruling-for oneself *vs.* others, 57–58, 229nn35–36
  moira, 42, 229n25
  self-possessed individuality, 58
  Trojan palace, 32–33
Heesterman, J. C., 156–157, 161–162
Heinberg, Richard, 240n7
Hera
  divinity and immortality, 29
  on hierarchical rule, 42
  Zeus and, 29, 33, 34, 42, 45, 46, 229n27
Hermeneutic-dialogic approach, 6
Hesiod, 64–104, 224n14. *See also* *Theogony; Works and Days; specific topics*
  bribe-eating kings and interconnected well-being, 66, 85–88, 230–231n7
  Chaos, 73, 87
  cosmogony, theogony, and hierarchical rule challenges, 65, 73–76
  cosmo-political vision, 66
  destinies, 75
  fate and Fates, 75–76
  foresight, 70–71

Hesiod (*Cont.*)
Gaia, 71, 73–75
gift-devouring kings, 85–87, 94, 97
on glory, 62, 65, 75, 87, 92
on honor, 69, 75, 84–86, 88, 92–95, 177
hospitality, 84–85
individualism, anthropocentrism, and disconnectedness, 100–104, 232n19
justice, 65, 83–100, 230–232nn7–18 (*see also* Justice *(dikē)*)
justice, anti-hierarchical, 92–94, 231nn9–13
justice, Zeus, 66, 79, 82, 88–92
Kalliopē, 68–69
on Kronos, 65, 74–75, 81, 82, 230n5
labor, necessary, 71
Muses and memory, 66, 67–72, 230n2
nonhuman, feminine knowledge sources, 68–69, 230n2
Ouranos, 65, 73–74
overview, 64–67, 230n1
Pandora, 80–81, 82
polis politics, transition, 66
political synchronicity, 66
Prometheus, 68, 79–82, 183
Rhea, 74–75
ruling-in and ruling-for, 86
ruling-over *vs.* ruling-for, 65
speech, 86
Strife (Eris), 69–71
synchronic and diachronic analysis, 21
Titans, 74
Typhoeus, 77–78
voice, 69–70
Zeus (*See* Zeus, Hesiod's)
Hierarchical rule, Homeric, 31–35
Agamemnon, 31–32, 34, 36–40, 227nn11–12
Hector, 33, 228n13
in interconnected world, 218–222, 241n12
Odysseus, on Zeus's power, 34, 46, 228n16
Poseidon, 33, 228n15
as stewardship (*see* Saṃhitās and Brāhmaṇas)
Trojan royal family, 32–33
Zeus, 32–35, 46–47, 227nn11–12, 228nn14–18 (*see also* Zeus, Homer's)
Hierarchy, 4, 16–17. *See also Varṇa; specific topics and individuals*
Brahmanical political thought, 112–116, 234nn13–17
Historical-comparative political theory, 1–20. *See also specific topics*
analytic challenges, 2–6, 225nn2–5
approach, 1–2
categories and concepts, 4
cross-cultural comparisons, 3–5, 225nn3–5
cross-cultural vantage points, 2
environmental political theory, 9–14, 226nn8–9
Greece and India, 14–20, 226nn10–16
historical meaning, 8
individuality, 4
multiple-method *vs.* single-method, 5–6
non-Western traditions, 1–2, 225n1
premodernity, 6–9, 225nn6–7
Procrustean logistics, 3–4, 113
rule, 4
sources, historical, 2–3, 225n2
terminology, 4
Historical meaning, 8
Holdrege, Barbara, 113, 118, 120, 123, 126, 234n23, 235n29
Homer, 21–63, 224n14. *See also specific topics*
anti-hierarchical beliefs and disconnectedness of rule, 35–44, 228nn19–25

commanding, 23
competition and contestation, 23, 30, 227n10
cosmology and metaphysics, 22, 24–31, 227nn4–10
distinction, 23
excellence and reputation, 23, 30–31, 229n35
gender and rule, 41–42, 228n23
on glory, 23, 30–31, 44, 45, 58, 62, 85, 87, 98, 100, 189, 229n35
vs. Hesiod, 65
hierarchical rule, early challenges, 31–35, 227–228nn11–18
on honor, 23, 30–31, 39–40, 58, 65, 103, 185, 189, 200, 229n35
justice, 46–47, 228n19, 231n10
kingly distinction, 44–61, 229–230nn26–39
neglect, 21
overview, 21–24
poetry, 22 (*see also Iliad; Odyssey*)
rage and anger, 23, 30
ruling tensions and transitions, 61–63
self-possessed individuality, 28–30, 36, 227n6
synchronic and diachronic analysis, 21
Zeus (*see* Zeus, Homer's)

Homo Hierarchicus, 114

Honor
Achilles, 36–37, 50–53
Agamemnon, 47–49
basileus, 65
Hector, 57–58
Hesiod on, 69, 75, 84–86, 88, 92–95, 177
Homer on, 23, 30–31, 39–40, 58, 65, 103, 185, 189, 200, 229n35
hospitality, 59
kingly, 23, 44, 75, 230n38
Odysseus, 53–56, 59–61
Poseidon, 47
ruling-for, 37
suitors, 41
yajña, 120
Zeus, 32, 34, 42, 45–47, 52, 72, 76–77, 81, 85, 90–91, 96, 99, 188

Hospitality
distinction in peacetime, 58–61, 229–230nn37–39
glory, 60
honor, 59
kingly rule and, 85
xenia, 84–85
Zeus and, 84

Hughes, Thomas, 108
Human-centrism, 219
Human–nonhuman scale, 172–174, 239n41
Humility, rulers, 68
Hundred Handers, 76–77

Identity, 10–12
human–nonhuman, 12
kṣatra, 179

Iliad, 21. *See also specific individuals and topics*
basileus-rule, Agamemnon's critics, 36–38
battle, brutality, 27–28
context, 44
gods and men, 29
gods' individual interests, 25
Hector, 57–58, 229nn35–36
honor, 38
laoi and battle success, 23, 31, 36, 38–40, 228n20
Odysseus, 53–57, 229n34 (*See also* Odysseus)
remembrance, 27
ruling tensions and transitions, 61–63
thumos, 29–30
Zeus, 45–48, 229nn26–31

Immediate experience, 26–28, 227nn4–5
Individualism
  Hesiod, 100–104, 232n19
  agonistic, 44, 62, 75, 100–101, 172, 177, 183
Individualist ontology, 28–30, 227nn6–9
Individuality, 4
  definition, 22–23
  self-possessed, 28–30, 36, 58, 227n6
Individuality, comparative ideas, 176–182
  Greek, 176–178
  kṣatriya, brahmanical and, 177–179
  kṣatriya, Nyagrodha tree and, 152, 155, 180–181, 237n19
  kṣatriya vs. basileus, 179–180
Indra
  birth of, 189
  chief–clan ruling relations, 15–16
  cosmic role, 135, 189
  divine *rājan*, 136–137, 140, 141, 163, 170, 186
  divine rule and human rule, 147–148
  glorious deeds, 188–189
  glory, 189
  human king and, 170
  kīrti and greatness, 188
  *kṣatriya*s and, 125, 126, 138, 146–147, 149–151, 156–157, 162, 186
  ṛta, 185
  sacrifices to, 183
  soma, 139
  strength lost, 156
  thunderbolt, 157–158
  warrior god, 16, 136, 146, 149–150, 157, 236n3
  vs. Zeus, 188–189
Industrialization, 207
Interconnected well-being, 13, 87–88, 230–231n7. *See also Bandhu*
Interconnected world, ruling in, 218–222, 241n12
Jāti, 114, 234n17
Jayaswal, K. P., 110, 164, 165–167, 169, 235n35, 238–239nn32–36
Jenco, Leigh, 7–9
Justice
  kingly rule, 90, 98
  Plato on, 97
  Zeus, 65–66, 73, 77, 79, 82, 84–85, 88–92, 101, 230nn3–4, 231n8
Justice *(dikē),* 36, 184–186, 228n19, 240nn6–7
  bribery *vs.,* 95–96
  communal, 94–95, 231nn12–13
  cosmological, comparative, 184–191, 240nn6–9
  distinction, 92–93, 231nn9–11
  divine inspiration, 96, 231nn14–17
  fairness, 95–96
  Hesiod, 65, 83–100, 231–232nn7–18 (*see also* Zeus, Hesiod's)
  Hesiod, anti-hierarchical, 92–94, 231nn9–13
  Vedic *(ṛta* and *bandhu),* 185–187, 240n8
  Zeus, Hesiod's, 66, 79, 82, 88–92, 185–186
  Zeus, Homer's, 46–47, 231n10

Kalliopē, 68–69
Kateb, George, 210
Kauṭilya, 107, 233n8
Keith, Arthur Berriedale, 19, 117, 118, 131, 234n18
Kelly, Sean Dorrance, 30
Kēres (Fates), 42–44, 75–76, 228n5
King, Richard, 8
Kingly distinction, 44–61
  Achilles, ruling-with and ruling-for, 50–53
  Agamemnon and mortal ruling over, 48–50, 229n32
  glory or fame, 23, 30–31, 44, 187–188, 229n35

Hector, ruling-for oneself *vs.* others, 57–58, 229nn35–36
hospitality, 58–61, 229–230nn37–39
Iliad, 44
Odysseus, ruling-in and unruly cosmos, 53–57, 229n34
Odyssey, 44
rage or anger, 44, 50–53
Zeus, distinction and ruling-over, 32–34, 45–48, 229nn26–31
Kingly honor, 23, 44, 75, 230n38. *See also* Honor
Kingly rule, 16–18. *See also* Hierarchical rule; *Rājan;* Saṃhitās and Brāhmaṇas; *specific qualities; specific rulers*
Agamemnon's, Achilles on, 36–38, 74, 97
Agamemnon's, Odysseus on, 37, 39, 97
anax, 18–19, 19n16
basileus, 18–19, 226nn13–16
flawed, 99
guardianship, 136
Hesiod's skepticism, 99
hospitality, 85
justice, 90, 98, 101
Odysseus, 40
origin, 142–143
patis, 19–20
rājan, rājanya, and *kṣatriya,* 18, 19
Ṛg-Veda Saṃhitā cosmogony, 140–145, 236nn11–13
terminology, 18–19
Zeus, Hesiod's, 83–84, 88, 90 (*see also* Zeus)
Kingly rule, Vedic divine. *See also specific rulers*
beliefs contextualizing, 111
divine–human ruler connection, 117–118
meaning, changes, 116–117
rājan, 117 (*See also Rājan*)
secular, 112
textual layers, 106
Kīrti, 188
Kleos, 23, 30–31, 44, 187–188, 229n35
Klōthō, 25–26
Kronos
fall of, 194
Hesiod on, 65, 74–75, 81, 82, 230n5
Zeus and, 74, 75
Kṣatra
bandhu, 138
Brahman, 159–160
identity, 179
meaning and role, 118, 130, 137–138, 236n6
metaphysics and stewardship, 149
rulers, 137–138, 236n6
Saṃhitās and Brāhmaṇas, liturgical, 146–147
Kṣatriya, 18, 19, 234–235n26
ātman and *brahman,* 153–154
Brāhmaṇas, 124, 125
brahmin's superiority, 121, 233–234n12
classification, 125
cosmologies and divine connections, 149–152, 177, 203
hierarchy, 121–122
individuality, 155
Indra and, 125, 126, 138, 146–147, 149–151, 156–157, 162, 186
king and warrior, 117, 234n19
metaphysics, 118–119
metaphysics, stewardship and, 149–152
natural order, 126
Nyagrodha tree, 152, 155, 180–181, 186, 190–191, 200, 201, 205, 237n19
power, 111, 121–122
protectors, 137
from *rājanya,* 111, 117

Kṣatriya (*Cont.*)
rājasūya ritual, 156–157, 237n22
sacrificial ritual role, 153
Saṃhitās and Brāhmaṇas, liturgical, 145–148
stewardship, with *brahmin*, 157–162, 237–238nn23–25
stewardship, with *vaiśya* and *śūdra*, 162–164, 238n26
twice born, 128–130, 235nn32–33
upanayana, 128–130, 155–156, 235nn32–33, 237n21
varṇa-duty, 149
Kudos, 23, 30–31, 44, 187–188, 229n35
Kymlicka, Will, 199, 240n3

Labor
Hesiod on, 71
Works and Days, 81
Lachesis, 26
Lane, Melissa, 12, 221, 224n14
Laoi, 23, 31
battle success, 36, 38–40, 228n20
Lattimore, Richmond, 27–28, 101–102
Lawfulness, 79
Lēthē, 71–72
Littleton, C. Scott, 114
Lloyd-Jones, Hugh, 93, 228n19
Lyric poetry, 22. See also *Iliad; Odyssey*

Mabbett, Ian, 132
Macdonell, Arthur Anthony, 19, 117, 118, 131, 136, 141, 165, 234n18
Machiavelli, 5
MacIntyre, Alasdair, 30
Mahābhārata, 135
Mahābhiṣeka, 146–147
Mahony, William K., 139, 141
Male/sky figures, 15–16
Mantras, 113, 123, 234n13
March, Andrew, 6, 7, 176
Martin, Richard, 51, 231n8
Memory *(mnēmosunē),* 27, 69, 227n5
Muses born from, 69, 71–72
Menelaus, 59–60, 230n39
Mēnis, 44
Metaphysics. *See also specific topics*
Brāhmaṇas, 126–127, 235n31
definition, 22
Homeric, 22, 24–31 (*see also* Cosmology and metaphysics, Homeric)
kṣatra, 149
kṣatriya, 118–119, 149–152
Ṛg-Veda Saṃhitā, 116–122 (*see also* Ṛg-Veda Saṃhitā)
Saṃhitās and Brāhmaṇas, 125–127, 235nn30–31
Saṃhitās and Brāhmaṇas, stewardship, 152–155, 237nn18–20
Methods, historical analytic, 4–6, 225n5
Mētis, 79, 82, 230n5
Micro-metaphysics
immediate experience, 26–28, 227nn4–5
individualist ontology, 28–30, 227nn6–9
Mitra-Varuṇa, 117, 135–138, 189
purohita/ruler relationship, 159
rain and, 166
as *ṛta* guardians and overseers, 141
Mnēmosunē (memory), 27, 69, 227n5
Moira
Hector, 42, 229n25
Hesiod, 25–26
Zeus, 42–43, 92, 231n8
Moirai, 75
Monarchy, 17
Mortality, 15, 25
Multiple-methods approaches, 5–6
Muses, 15, 66
cosmo-political agents, 67–69
divine command, 67–68
glory granting, 67, 72
from Zeus and Memory, 69, 71–72

Nagy, Gregory, 44, 51, 53, 227nn1, 5
Nestor, 32, 38–39, 50, 227n11, 228n17
  on cosmic hierarchy, 228n17
Nicolson, Adam, 31, 33
Nirṛti, 125, 235n30
Non-instrumental approaches, 12–13
Noos, 28, 227n9
Not forgetting, 27
Nyagrodha tree, *kṣatriya* and, 152, 155, 180–181, 186, 190–191, 200, 201, 205, 237n19

Oakley, Francis, 17–18, 225n1
Odysseus
  Achilles on, 53
  on Agamemnon, 37, 39, 97
  anger, 61
  Athena and, 41–42, 47, 48, 55, 61
  character, 44
  Eurymachus' challenge, 40–41
  fate *(moira)*, 26
  female weavers, 41
  glory, 55, 56, 61
  as guest in others' homes, 60–61
  as hero, versatile, 44
  homecoming, 25, 27, 40, 102
  honor, 53–56, 59–61
  as just ruler, 37
  kingly rule and distinction, 40, 44
  omens, 228n22
  Poseidon, 46, 102
  roles, multiplicity, 30
  ruling-in and unruly cosmos, 53–57, 229n34
  sacrifices, 183–184
  Telemachus' challenge, 40, 228n21
  Thersites' silencing, 39, 40
  Zeus and, 34, 46, 228n16
Odyssey, 21. *See also specific individuals and topics*
  context, 44
  gods and men, 29
  gods' individual interests, 25
  hospitality, 58–61, 229–230nn37–39
  Menelaus, 59–60
  Penelope and weaving, 41
  remembrance, worthy of, 27
  ruling tensions and transitions, 61–63
  Zeus (*See* Zeus, Homer's)
Olympus, 29
  divine, 25
  kingly rule, challenges, 42
  Muses on gods of, 72
  Prometheus' theft of fire from, 81
  ruler of (*See* Zeus)
Ontology
  definition, 22
  Saṃhitās and Brāhmaṇas, 126–131, 235n31
  Saṃhitās and Brāhmaṇas, stewardship, 155–157, 237nn21–22
Ouranos (Sky), 15–16, 65, 73–74, 194

Pandora, 80–82
Panocracy, 11, 12, 193–222. *See also* Connectedness of rule
  definition, 12
  environmental justice, 215–217
  etymology, 212
  non-reciprocal and non-contractual, 198–199
  polycentrism, 10, 196–198, 200, 202, 212
  poly-temporality, 10, 198, 217
  representation, 217–218
  ruling-for, 211–214
  ruling-in, 214–218
  ruling in interconnected world, 218–222, 241n12
  ruling-over, 194–204, 240nn1–7
  ruling-with, 204–211, 241–242nn8–11
Parekh, Bhikhu, 109
Parel, Anthony, 107–108
Pati, 19–20, 116–117

Patton, Laurie, 113
Peace, 79
Penelope, 41, 56, 73, 228n21
Perses, 71–72, 83–84, 95–96, 230n6
Personal agonism, 24
Phōnē, 69–70, 190
Phrēn, 28
Plato
  on justice, 97
  on Lachesis, 26
  political philosophy, 223n4, 224n14
  Republic, 28, 64, 126
  theory of the forms, 126
Poetry. *See also specific works*
  Indo-European, 15, 226n11
  protest, 65, 88–100, 231–232nn8–18 (*see also* Justice)
Political agents, nonhuman, 68
Politics of sight, 216
Polycentrism, 10–11, 196–198, 200, 202, 212
Poly-temporality, 10–11, 198, 217
Polytropism
  definition, 53
  Odysseus, 53–57, 229n34
Poseidon
  honor, 47
  ocean for, 102
  Odysseus and, 46, 102
  Zeus and, 33, 45–49, 228n15, 229n30
Praise, 42, 77
Prajāpati, 127, 148–149, 153–155, 202
Pramā, 126, 149, 153, 164
Pratimā, 126–127, 149, 153, 164
Premodernity, 6–9, 225nn6–7
Procrustean logistics, 3, 4, 113
Prometheus
  as forethought, 79–82
  Zeus and, 68, 79–82, 183
Pṛthivī, 15–16
Psuchē, 28–29, 178, 227n8
Public agonism, 24
Purohita, 158–159
Puruṣa, 119–122, 126, 143, 145–146, 179, 198, 200, 202, 203, 235n29
Puruṣa-Sūkta, 117, 119, 143, 145–146, 163, 197, 200

Qutb, Sayyid, 7

Raaflaub, Kurt A., 19, 21, 23, 36, 38–39, 83, 85, 226nn13, 15, 231n8, 232n15
Rage. *See also* Anger
  of Achilles, 27, 48–53, 57
  of Agamemnon, 48–50, 229n32
  Homer on, 23, 30
  kingly distinction, 44
  mēnis, 44
  Zeus', 229n26
Rājakṛts, 166
Rājan, 18, 19. *See also specific deities*
  Atharva-Veda Saṃhitā, 132–133
  bandhus, 137
  chief and tribal king, Ṛg-Veda Saṃhitā, 116–117
  dharman, 138
  divine rulers, Indra, 136–137, 140, 141, 163, 170, 186
  divine rulers, Ṛg-Veda Saṃhitā, 116–117, 136–140, 236nn1–7
  guardians, 136–137, 236n4
  hierarchy, 138–139
  kṣatra, 138
  power, 111
  Śatapatha Brāhmaṇa, 236–237n13
Rājanya, 19, 111, 116–117, 119, 121–122
  Śatapatha Brāhmaṇa, 236–237n13
  Vedic texts, 236n12
Rājasūya, 150, 156–158, 187, 237n22
Religion–politics connection, 17–18
Representation, 217–218
Republic (Plato), 28, 64, 126
Reputation, 23, 44, 227n3

Resilience, 12, 226n8
  environmental, 13
Response-ability, 12, 204, 206, 210, 212–214, 224n10
Responsibility, green republicanism, 12, 226n8
Ṛg-Veda Saṃhitā, 19, 112
  cosmogony and human kingship, 140–145, 236nn11–13
  human rulership, 139–140, 236n8
  kṣatriya, 140, 143–145
  rājan as chief and tribal king, 116–117
  rājan as divine ruler and guardian, 136–140, 236nn1–10
  rājanya, 140–143
  ṛṣi, 15, 120, 121, 139
Rhea, 74–76
Ritual. *See also specific types*
  bandhus, 153
  human–nonhuman connection, 182–184, 239–240nn1–5
  kṣatriya, 153
  rājasūya, 156–157, 237n22
  Saṃhitās and Brāhmaṇas, stewardship, 155–157, 237nn21–22
  yajña, 113, 120, 131, 165, 202, 235n27
Ṛṣi (seer), 15, 120, 121, 139
Ṛta (truth, order), 118, 128, 136–139, 185–186, 195
  justice, 185–186, 240n7
  rājan, 136–139
  dikē vs., 240n7
Rule (ruling), 4. *See also specific topics and types*
  comparative, 175–192
  cosmological justice and connectedness, 184–191, 240nn6–9
  dangers and limitations, 175–176
  Homeric hierarchical, 31–35, 227–228nn11–18 (*see also* Hierarchical rule, Homeric)
  human ability or capacity, 224n11–12
  human–nonhuman connection, 182–184, 239–240nn1–5
  nonhuman ability, 224n11
  openness and complexity, 176–182 (*see also* Individuality, comparative ideas)
  power, 223n1
  as stewardship (*see* Saṃhitās and Brāhmaṇas)
Rulers. *See also specific rulers*
  Greek terms, 18–19
  human, like divine ruler, 142 (*see also* *Rājans; Rājanya*)
  as patrons for poets, 15, 226n11
  Sanskrit terms, 18–20
Ruling-for, 31, 36, 40, 68, 84, 170, 211–214
  Achilles, 50–53
  distinction, 37
  Hesiod, 65, 86
  honor, 37
  kṣatriya stewardship, with *vaiśya* and *śūdra*, 162–164, 238n26
  oneself *vs.* others, Hector, 57–58, 229nn35–36
  vs. ruling-over, Hesiod, 65
  stewardship in Saṃhitās and Brāhmaṇas, human rule as, 157–164, 237–238nn23–26
  Zeus, 84
Ruling-in, 31, 40, 53, 55, 68, 84, 152, 170, 214–218
  Hesiod, 84, 86
  Odysseus, 53–57, 229n34
  Vedic, 106, 115, 124, 145, 152, 170
  Zeus, 84
Ruling-over, 194–204
  Agamemnon, 48–50, 229n32
  distinction, 46–47
  kṣatriya stewardship, with *brahmin*, 157–162, 237–238nn23–25

Ruling-over (*Cont.*)
kṣatriya stewardship, with *vaiśya* and *śūdra*, 162–164, 238n26
Penelope and art of weaving, 41, 228n23
vs. ruling-for, Hesiod, 65
ruling-in and, 68
ruling-with and, 39, 68
stewardship, Saṃhitās and Brāhmaṇas, 157–164, 237–238nn23–26
surreptitious, domineering form, 68
Zeus, 32–34, 45–48, 77, 84, 229nn26–31
Ruling-with, 31, 68, 204–211, 241–242nn8–11
Achilles, 50–53
distinction, 37
ruling-over and, 39
Vedic, 147, 181

Sabhā, 131–133, 164–165, 168, 170–171
Sacrifice
human–nonhuman connection, 182–184, 239–240nn1–5
yajña, 113, 120, 131, 165, 202, 235n27
Sādhya, 121
Saletore, B. A., 110
Sāma-Veda Saṃhitā, 112, 123
Saṃhitās, 106–107, 112–113. *See also specific types*
cosmogony and cosmology, 125–126, 235n30
metaphysics, 126–127, 235n31
ontology, 127–131
Saṃhitās and Brāhmaṇas, 135–174. *See also specific* Saṃhitās *and topics*
Atharva-Veda Saṃhitā, 131–133, 164–171, 238–239nn27–40
cosmology and human–nonhuman scale, 172–174, 239n41
liturgical, 202
liturgical, human rule as stewardship, 145–164, 202 (*See also* Stewardship, Saṃhitās and Brāhmaṇas, human rule as)
liturgical, Vedic political thought, 123–131, 235nn30–33
Ṛg-Veda Saṃhitā 1, *rājans* and guardianship, 136–140, 236nn1–10
Ṛg-Veda Saṃhitā 2, cosmogony and human kingship, 140–145, 236nn11–13
Vedic political thought, 123–131, 235nn30–33
Samiti, 131–133, 164–165, 168, 170–171, 235n34
Samrāṭ, 140
Sandilands, Catriona, 201
Scharfe, Hartmut, 116, 233n8
Schlosberg, David, 209, 215–217
Seaford, Richard, 182, 226n13, 227n2, 229nn31, 37
Seers, Vedic, 15, 120, 121, 139
Segal, Charles, 93–94, 229n30
Self. *See also Noos*; *Thumos*
agency and interests, 224n9
comparative ideas, 176–182 (*see also* Individuality, comparative ideas)
Self-possessed individuality, 28–30, 36, 45, 58, 62, 78, 103, 153–154, 177–178, 227n6
Achilles and Agamemnon, 62
Hector, 58
Zeus, 45, 62, 154
Sharma, J. P., 112
Sharma, R. S., 146, 164, 168–169, 239n37
Shizhao, Zhang, 7
Silvermintz, Daniel, 41, 56
Single-method approaches, 5–6
Sinha, H. N., 112, 233n8
Sirriani, Carmen, 208
Smith, Brian K., 115–116, 120, 124–130, 145–146, 149–150, 153–156, 162, 235nn31–32
Soma, 120, 136, 139, 141, 235n27

Soul
  psuchē, 28–29, 178, 227n8
  thumos, 28–29, 76–77, 179, 227nn7, 9, 228n15, 229n35
Spellman, John W., 136, 143, 144, 235n35
Śravas, 187–188
Stewardship, 11, 218–222
  Atharva-Veda Saṃhitā, 164–171, 238–239nn27–40
Stewardship, Saṃhitās and Brāhmaṇas, human rule as, 145–164
  cosmogony and cosmology, 145–152, 237nn14–17
  metaphysics, 152–155, 237nn18–20
  ontology and ritual, 155–157, 237nn21–22
  ruling-over and ruling-for others, 157–164, 237–238nn23–26
Strife, 69–71, 81
Śūdra, 119, 121, 234–235n26
  classification, 125
  kṣatriya stewardship with, 162–164, 238n26
Suitors, honor, 41
Sustainability, ecological, 12, 13, 208
Sustainable material flow, 209

Tarrant, Seaton Patrick, 13
Telemachus, 40–41, 59–60, 228n21, 230n39
Temporality, 10–11, 25–26, 43–44
Tensions, ruling, 61–63. *See also specific individuals*
Terminology, analysis, 4, 18–19
Themis, 79, 185
Theogony, 64–66
  Chaos, 73, 87
  destinies, 75
  fate and Fates, 75–76
  Gaia, 71, 73–75
  Kalliopē, 69
  kingly honor, 75
  Kronos, 65, 74–75
  lēthē, 72
  Mētis, 79, 82, 230n5
  Muses, 67
  Prometheus, 79–82
  Titans, 74
  Typhoeus, 77–78
  Zeus, 76–83, 230nn3–6
Thersites, 36
  Achilles and, 62
  Agamemnon and, 38–40, 62, 100
  Odysseus' silencing, 39, 40
  ruling as distinction, 41
Thiele, Leslie Paul, 13
Thumos, 28–30, 196, 227nn7, 9
  Agamemnon, 37
  ātman, 179
  Hector, 33
  Hesiod on, 69
  Muses, 72
  Zeus', 32, 46, 48, 76–77
Timē, 23, 44, 230n38
Titans, 74, 76–77
Tolerance, 11
Transition movement, 208
Transitions, ruling, 61–63
Trojan royal family, 32–33
Truth, 27, 231n13, 232n17
  Vedic (*ṛta*), 117–118, 128, 136–138
Twice born, 128–130, 235nn32–33
Typhoeus, 77–78, 98

Upanayana, 128–130, 200, 235nn32–33

Vaiśya, 121
  kṣatriya stewardship with, 162–164, 238n26
  twice born, 128, 235n32
Varṇa, 109
  bandhus and, 125, 146, 164
  cosmogony, 124, 125, 128
  differentiation, 114, 235n17
  meaning, 119, 234–235n26
  twice born, 128–129, 235n32

Varuṇa, 117, 135–138, 141, 148, 189
as *ṛta* guardian and overseer, 141
Vedic political thought, 105–134. *See also specific topics*
adhibhūta, adhidaiva, adhiyajña, and *adhyātma*, 126, 234n23
analytical organization, 106
ancient Indian, 107–112, 232–234nn1–12
atharvans, 113, 131, 133, 170
Atharva-Veda Saṃhitā, 106, 112–113, 131–133, 235nn34–35
bandhu, 115, 117–118, 125, 137, 234n21
Brahman, 125, 127
Brāhmaṇas, 107, 113, 123
Brahmanical political thought, 112–116, 234nn13–17
brahmin, 119, 234–235n26
deva, 113, 116–117, 234n14
dharman, 118, 234nn24–25
existing scholarship, 111–112, 233nn9–10
Gandhi and Bhagavad Gītā, 108
hierarchy, social and political, 130–131 (*See also specific topics*)
jāti, 114, 234n17
kṣatra, 118, 130, 137–138, 146–147, 152, 159, 179–180
kṣatriya, 18–19, 111, 117–119, 121–122, 124–126, 128–130, 233–235nn12, 19, 26, 32–33 (*see also Kṣatriya*)
mantras, 113, 123, 234n13
pati, 19–20, 116–117
pramā, 126, 149, 153, 164
pratimā, 126–127, 149, 153, 164
Puruṣa, 119–122, 126, 143, 146, 179, 198, 200, 202, 203, 235n29
Puruṣa-Sūkta, 117, 119, 143, 146, 163, 197, 200
rājan, 18, 19, 111, 116–117, 132–133
rājanya, 19, 111, 116–117, 119, 121–122 (*see also Kṣatriya*)
Ṛg-Veda Saṃhitā, 112
Ṛg-Veda Saṃhitā, cosmogony, metaphysics, and hierarchical rule, 119–122, 234–235nn26–29
Ṛg-Veda Saṃhitā, *rājans*, early cosmology, and metaphysics, 116–118, 234nn18–25
ṛṣis, 15, 120, 121
ṛta, 118, 128, 136–139, 185–186, 195
sabhā, 131–133, 164–165, 168, 170–171
Sāma-Veda Saṃhitā, 112
samiti, 131–133, 164–165, 168, 170–171, 235n34
śūdra, 119, 121, 125, 234–235n26
synthetic interdisciplinary approach, 106
twice born, 128, 235n32
upanayana, 128–130, 235nn32–33
vaiśya, 121, 128, 235n32
varṇa, 109, 114, 119, 125, 128–129, 234–235nn17, 26, 32 (*see also Varṇa*)
viśpati, 19, 117
Yajur-Veda Saṃhitā, 112, 123
Vedic Saṃhitās and Brāhmaṇas, 135–174. *See also* Saṃhitās and Brāhmaṇas
Vernant, Jean-Pierre, 183
Vidatha, 164–165, 167–168
Vincent, Andrew, 5, 6, 9
Viśpati, 19, 117, 139, 140, 236n9
Viśvadevas, 141
Vogel, Steven, 220, 225n7, 241nn9, 12
Voice (*phōnē*), 69–70, 190
Vrata, 139
Vṛtra, 136–137, 144, 156–157, 236n4
Vulnerability, 12, 226n8

Wallace, Robert, 38–39, 232n15
Walzer, Michael, 18
Wapner, Paul, 206
Warren, Mark, 7–8, 225n6

Welfare, human–nonhuman, 12
West, M. L., 15–16, 226n11, 227n1, 230–231nn1, 7
Williams, Melissa, 7–8, 225n6
Works and Days, 64, 66
  corrupt rulers, 66
  gift-devouring kings, 85–87, 94, 97
  kingly rule, 99
  labor, 81
  Muses, 67
  Perses, 72
  Prometheus, 79–80
  Strife, 69–70, 81
  voice, 69–70
  Zeus, 79–84, 88–89, 230nn4–6
World-building, 11, 130, 218, 220–222

Xenia, 84–85

Yajamāna, 180
Yajña, 113, 120, 131, 165, 202, 235n27
Yajur-Veda Saṃhitā, 112, 123

Zeus
  chief–clan ruling relations, 15–16
  glory, 45–47, 65, 87, 98, 188
  Hera and, 29, 33, 34, 42, 45, 46, 229n27
  honor, 32, 34, 42, 45–47, 52, 72, 76–77, 81, 85, 90–91, 96, 99, 188
  Poseidon and, 228n15
  Prometheus and, 68, 79–82, 183
Zeus, Hesiod's, 66, 72, 76–100
  ascendance of, 74, 76–83, 230nn3–6
  Athena and, 68, 228n14, 229nn27, 30
  basileis, 65, 83–100, 179, 186, 230–232nn7–18
  birth, 189
  bribe-eating kings and interconnected well-being, 85–88
  capricious and cruel, 83, 230n6
  cosmic interconnectedness, 85
  cosmic monarch, sole, 68
  dikē (justice), 66, 79, 82, 88–92, 185–186
  Eirēnē, 79
  Eunomia, 79
  fate, 92, 231n8
  vs. Homer's, 64–65
  hospitality, 84
  Hundred Handers, 76–77
  just ruler and justice, 65–66, 73, 77, 79, 82, 84–85, 88–92, 101, 230nn3–4, 231n8
  kingly rule, 83–84, 88, 90
  Kronos, 74–75
  Muses from Memory and, 69
  Pandora, 80–81, 82
  poetic protest and standard of justice, 88–100
  Prometheus, 79–82, 183
  ruling-for, 84
  ruling-in, 84
  ruling-over, 77, 84
  speech, 72, 77–78
  strength, physical, 77–78
  Typhoeus, 77–78, 98
  voice, 70
  wife, Mētis, 79, 82, 230n5
  wife, Themis, 79
Zeus, Homer's
  anger, 45
  Athena and, 34, 62–63, 228n14, 229nn27, 30
  basileis, 65, 179
  challenge to rule, 46
  defender of suppliants, 35
  distinction and ruling-over, 32–34, 45–48, 229nn26–31
  distinguishing characteristics, 53
  divine rule, 34–35
  divinity and immortality, 27, 29
  egalitarianism, 47
  equality among rulers, 62

Zeus, Homer's (*Cont.*)
fate (Fates) and, 42–44, 228n18, 229n25
gender, female figures and, 42–43, 228n23
glory-seeking, 45–47, 188
hierarchical (kingly) rule, 32–35, 46–47, 227nn11–12, 228nn14–18
hierarchical (kingly) rule, limitations, 42–44
honor-seeking, 42, 45–47, 52, 99, 188
vs. Indra, 188–189
justice, 46–47
masculine, warrior-god traits, 16
Odysseus and, 34, 46, 228n16
Odyssey finale, 62–63
peace-loving, 62–63
Poseidon and, 33, 45, 46–49, 229nn30–31
power, 34, 228n16
rage, Gods' fearing, 229n26
reputation, 45–46
self-possessed individuality, 45, 62, 154
supreme ruler, 229n30